CAREER
OPPORTUNITIES
IN THE VISUAL ARTS

CAREER OPPORTUNITIES IN THE VISUAL ARTS

Rɪᴄʜᴀʀᴅ P. Cʟᴀʀᴋ and Pᴀᴍᴇʟᴀ Fᴇʜʟ

Checkmark Books®
An imprint of Infobase Publishing

Career Opportunities in the Visual Arts

Checkmark Books
An imprint of Infobase Publishing
132 West 31st Street
New York NY 10001

Library of Congress Cataloging-in-Publication Data
Clark, Richard P.
  Career opportunities in the visual arts/Richard P. Clark and Pamela Fehl.
     p. cm.
  Includes bibliographical references and index.
  ISBN 0-8160-5927-6 (hc: alk.paper)–ISBN 0-8160-5928-4 (pb: alk. paper)
  1. Art—Vocational guidance—Juvenile literature. I. Fehl, Pamela. II. Title.
  N8350.C53 2006
  702′.3′73—dc22   2005018077

Checkmark Books are available at special discounts when purchased in bulk quantities for businesses, associations, institutions, or sales promotions. Please call our Special Sales Department in New York at (212) 967-8800 or (800) 322-8755.

You can find Facts On File on the World Wide Web at http://www.factsonfile.com

Cover design by Cathy Rincon

Printed in the United States of America

VB Hermitage   10   9   8   7   6   5   4   3   2   1

This book is printed on acid-free paper.

CONTENTS

THEATRICAL

APPENDIXES

FOREWORD

While most businesses are defined by the laws of supply and demand, the art business is defined by desire. There are more people who want to be artists than there is room for, and this makes competition inevitable, messy, and sometimes unfair. It also gives the art business the character of Noah's ark. Between the big-shot designer trying to surf the latest trend and the aging hippie cartoonist still inking his graphic novel after 30 years, there is a world of freelance artists, staff artists, short-order artists, and nine-to-fivers. There are dedicated craftspeople and self-promoters, hustlers and bottom-feeders, innovators and copycats, straight shooters and chiselers. There are oddballs, goofballs, dreamers, and day-dreamers. The art business is made up of all sorts, and if you have picked up this book, you are probably one of them.

So welcome to the ark.

It has been a long time since I committed myself to a life of drawing pictures for a living, but it is a commitment I have never regretted. The thrill of taking a blank piece of paper and turning it into something that did not exist before is so palpable that I sometimes wonder how other people get through life without experiencing it. As a kid, I was so eager to be an artist that—knowing I would have to start at the bottom—I wanted to get to the bottom as fast as possible.

I began working at a small studio in Chicago, pasting up catalogs of tractor parts and drawing cartoons for electric blanket and hospital newsletters. A few years later I was lucky enough to be doing regular work for *Playboy* and the *New York Times*. Ten years out of high school, I saw a banner bearing one of my drawings unfurled outside the Musée des Beaux-Arts in Bordeaux, France, and another drawing on the cover of the exhibition catalog *The Art of the Times*. Someone who did not know me then (and thought I should be older) asked me how I had managed to "climb the ladder of success so quickly." I thought this was a silly question, for which I had only a meaningless answer. I never knew there *was* a ladder of success, I told him; I just stumbled upstairs in the dark, and when the lights came on, there I was.

In the small town near Lake Erie where I grew up, there were no artists as far as anyone knew. . . so, no role models, as people like to say these days. There *was* a guy who lived out by the stone quarry at the edge of town who worked at the local seat-cover factory. On his days off, he painted landscapes using sponges and was listed in the Yellow Pages as an artist. But in Fremont, Ohio, a Yellow Page artist was a guy who could paint lawyers' names on the doors of their offices, not someone who could produce pictures to make you laugh or touch your heart. The sponge painter came to our high school once and did a demonstration. But watching him putter around with his sponges, getting paint up to his elbows and producing some sloppy landscapes when it was all over, made it clear to me that art was never going to save his soul—nor would he ever expect it to. For him, art was a hobby, in the same way doodling funny faces on the margins of schoolbooks was one for me. If he could have afforded golf clubs, he would have been just as happy spending his Saturdays on the links. He had never taken the big leap of believing that your art supplies can be the extension of your hand, and your hand an extension of your being.

Just as there were no artists in town, the advice I got from others—"It's OK to have a *hobby*, but what are you going to do for a *living*?"—was not the kind of advice I was looking for or the kind I needed. So, in desperation, I imagined a fictional guru for myself, who, in time, I came to call Thirty-Year-Old Brad.

Thirty-Year-Old Brad was no mere imaginary kid's playmate. He was a tough critic who was determined that I would not become Fremont's next sponge painter. He judged everything I did according to how much it would matter to me when I was 30: "That blue ribbon you won for drawing in 7th grade, will you care about it when you are 30? Ignore it. The *Boys Life* illustration contest you lost, will it matter when you're 30? Keep plugging." When the neighbor-lady told me I could "draw good," Thirty-Year-Old Brad suggested it might not be good enough to work for Walt Disney, so I worked harder. And when my 10th-grade art teacher said to forget drawing and just "express yourself," Thirty-Year-Old Brad said, "learn to draw anyway." Thirty-Year-Old Brad kept his eye on the horizon while I navigated the bumps on the road. Then when I was 17, Thirty-Year-Old Brad bought me a Greyhound bus ticket, and we both left home for Chicago. Over the next few years, I gradually became him, although he learned a lot from me along the way.

It is always helpful to have a Jiminy Cricket to sit on your shoulder and tell you the facts of life. Many people start their careers in art under the illusion that it is a field for the sensitive individual. It is; but it helps if the sensitive individual develops the hide of a rhino. Setbacks and disappointments are inevitable. In addition, young people tend to overrate the importance of talent and handicap their own prospects based on how others judge their skill. But an artist needs talent the way a racehorse needs legs: it is the minimum, not the decisive, equipment. In the long run, enthusiasm, vision, integrity, resourcefulness, and stamina count for more. It also helps to be able to think for yourself; and the ability to think for the long run counts most of all. In a business where people are easily exploited, it is not hard to let yourself be used and discarded. Finding the skills to survive, thrive, and endure is as much a creative act as developing an individual style—and it is one you will have to cultivate as a separate set of skills.

As with any profession, there are no exact rules to follow to become a graphic artist. No advice trumps common sense, which is the best sense, and the secret of liking what you do for a living is first to find out what it is you like to do, then to do it for a living. That is easier to say than do, of course, but it can be done, and the art business is full of people who are living examples.

As you make your way into the art business, you will find yourself receiving advice of all kinds from colleagues and peers. Much of that advice will be contradictory, because wherever you find five artists, you will find six opinions. Take all the advice you get or take none of it—but take whatever you take with a grain of salt. I have found it useful to count all advice as information and use it only as I need it, in whatever combinations I feel appropriate. Be creative. It is better to be influenced by a lot of different people than by any one person, because you can find bits and pieces of yourself in everyone else but never all of yourself in anyone.

A lot of the decisions you will have to make along the way will be simply matters of preference: to draw, to paint, to animate, to art direct or design. Other decisions will be temperamental: to work from dark to light or light to dark. Other decisions will reflect your basic character. The ancient Greek poet Archilochus said that everybody can be defined as either a hedgehog with one big idea or a fox with many little ones. The art business is full of hedgehogs and foxes that have made entirely different decisions yet done great work by doing what they were meant to do. How your own decisions add up for you will be part accident and part design. You will have as much control of your fate as you can wrest from circumstance, but in my experience, the smallest choices often turn out to be the most consequential. A whole career may be decided, for example, by a summer job, and it pays to be alert to the potential in seemingly unlikely opportunities. I have never considered any assignment too low to try making the most of—although not every professional would agree with me about that.

When I first left the Midwest and came to New York, I showed my work to a famous designer, who shuffled through my samples and said, "You're very clever, you'll get lots of work." But then he added that I should be careful, whenever I accepted an assignment, never to give my clients more value for the buck than they were paying for. It was a rule of thumb that apparently worked for him, but I always found the advice shortsighted, and I never took it. The logic of business may dictate that price governs quality. But the illogic of art is that most of us want each picture we do to be our best. When I started working, I would work for anybody, and I put as much of myself into a cheesy line drawing as I did a cover painting.

When students ask me for advice, I advise not to ask for advice from middle-aged artists. When I was in high school, you could consult an out-of-date book about the art business and know that it would still reflect the business you would find when you left school. But now such a book can become obsolete very quickly. Over the last 20 years, computers have given us new means of making pictures but shortened the time in which clients expect them. The Internet has challenged the viability of print and created a culture of entitlement in which re-mix artists now assume the right to exploit the work of others; "copy leftists" attack the principle of copyright; and "free culture" advocates promote legislation that would undermine centuries of law written to protect your work. All these forces have created a defining moment in the history of popular art, and everybody from the veteran to the art school grad will have to fight new battles and learn new rules to adapt. In most cases, this will mean stumbling upstairs in the dark until the lights come on, improvising your way through assignments, and learning from your mistakes. It is a world in flux, but in flux there is often opportunity.

I suppose that by now, some of you may think that I have made the art world sound like a sort of reality show where graphic artists survive on bugs and vote each other off the island. It is not like that, of course, but the satisfaction of being a professional will always be inseparable from the challenges that go with it. For most people, the field of graphic art will be like any other, and the test of a pro will simply be how well you can do what you once did for fun on those days when it is not fun any longer. But for those of you with a passion to create, *fun* will never be the defining word. No matter how much fun your work provides you, it will pale beside the satisfaction of being engaged. Try to imagine Michelangelo climbing down from the Sistine Chapel scaffolding, covered with plaster and paint after two years of standing on his head to cover the ceiling with God and saints and prophets and sinners, craning up to peer into the ghostly vault with a crick in his neck that would never go away, and saying "Boy was that fun!" Or picture Van Gogh painting doggedly into the night by the light of candles tied to his hat, thinking "Gee, this is really satisfying," and you will see how irrelevant the concept of fun can be. For the person who wants to be more than a sponge painter, satisfaction is the result of getting up in the morning and going to bed at night knowing that in-between you have been completely engaged with your own life.

That kind of satisfaction is hard to come by, but it is there to be had. This book is unlikely to provide you with any shortcuts to it. No book can do that. But let us hope it gives you some insights you can use and provides a resource you can keep coming back to.

—Brad Holland

Called "an undisputed star of American Illustration" by the *Washington Post* and nominated for a Pulitzer Prize in 1976 by the *New York Times*, Brad Holland has been a professional artist since the age of 17. His work has been exhibited around the world, including retrospectives of his paintings at the Musée des Beaux-Arts, Clermont-Ferrand, France, 1999, and the Museum of American Illustration, New York City, 1999. His illustrations and paintings have appeared in nearly every major U.S. magazine, including the *New Yorker*, *Time*, *Newsweek*, the *Atlantic Monthly*, the *New York Times Magazine*, *Graphis*, and *U.S. News & World Report*. He has painted CD covers for Billy Joel and Stevie Ray Vaughn and is represented in the permanent collection of the National Portrait Galley, Washington, D.C.; the U.S. Library of Congress; and many corporate collections. A recipient of 27 gold medals from various organizations, he was inducted into the Society of Illustrators Hall of Fame in 2005. In 1999, Holland cofounded the American Illustrator's Conference in Santa Fe, New Mexico (now called ICON), and in 2002 represented the rights of artists at The American Assembly's Art, Technology and Intellectual Property forum, sponsored by Columbia University.

INDUSTRY OUTLOOK

In order to provide a clear understanding of the visual art industry, we'll begin by taking a look at what visual art is, discuss its applications—including a brief look at the history of visual art in the United States to give context to the current professional markets—and discuss how these facets of visual art apply to the working world.

This Industry Outlook will introduce in broad strokes how professional artists work in the United States and the qualities required in order to be a professional. Finally, we'll take a look at the employment prospects for visual artists in the contemporary working world by looking at current trends and peek ahead at some indicators for the market in years to come.

So, what *is* visual art? Anything printed, photographed, sculpted, painted, drawn, or designed. It's everything from the images found in an instruction manual to the grandest mural executed for public display. The applications for visual art are therefore myriad: illustration; cartooning; interior design; graphic design; set and costume design for film, television and theater; and everything else you'll find in the Table of Contents.

Visual arts boil down to two distinct applications, fine and applied arts. While it's not the intent of this volume to weigh in on the merits of these distinctions or make value judgments on either brand of art, a brief overview of the division bears noting here to give context to the working world of the professional visual artist.

All early examples of visual art in the United States have some direct practical application—from sign-making to portrait painting for record-keeping's sake—and are therefore considered applied arts. It wasn't until the late 19th and early 20th centuries, when the nation started to emerge as a world economic and military power, that more time became available for leisurely pursuits. Wealthy people began to collect European fine art, and the 1913 Armory show in New York City introduced the nation to wildly new ideas about art. Design became a key component of American visual art around this time, and the notion of art for art's sake crossed the Atlantic, bringing with it new ideas about high-culture art and popular art. In the strictest terms, any art executed for public consumption is some form of popular—or applied—art, while art for art's sake is considered high-culture—or fine—art. (This division has been painted in very broad strokes solely to act as an introduction to the concept; for further reading material on the topic, please see the Bibliography.)

This division has become a very important facet in visual arts and still influences decision making in the 21st century.

Everything from choosing a career to what manner of expression one employs in one's chosen field has some bearing on this division. (Some artists contend that they don't think about the difference and simply execute their work while leaving the cataloging to others; even this more passive participation in the debate acknowledges its existence.)

Another key component of the professional art world, whether high culture or popular culture, reflects a facet of professional American life in nearly every other industry—white-hot competition. Professional artists work extremely hard at improving their craftsmanship and improving their business acumen to protect their jobs and markets, especially since a great many of them are self-employed.

According the U.S. Department of Labor's (DOL) Bureau of Labor Statistics (BLS), 53.8 percent of artists were self-employed in 2002 (the most recent year available for statistical purposes as of this writing). According to the BLS's *Occupational Outlook Handbook* (2004–05 edition), this number represents nearly eight times the average percentage of self-employed workers seen in other professions. This statistic is very important; it cannot be understated. It speaks to a number of factors weighing on the professional visual artist's working life.

This circumstance dictates that a professional artist exhibit a good deal of business savvy. Weighing cost analyses, managing cash flow, structuring one's debt advantageously, budgeting for equipment upkeep and supply reserves, and allocating funds for medical insurance, retirement expenses, and income taxes all may seem very counterintuitive to the artistically inclined, but they become a reality to face when trying to earn a living. Education on how to run a small business has become a key component to continued success for the professional artist.

Of the professional artists employed in staff positions, designers and art directors hold the vast majority of positions. More than two-thirds of workers in design and art direction are employed as staff. (This statistic is still high, though; with one-third of designers and art directors self-employed, it's nearly five times the average of all other occupations.) Of significant note: While this certainly applies to designers and art directors, it's also true of professional artists working on staff in other fields—income earned from freelance assignments completed during off-hours can greatly augment one's annual earnings.

A high number of professional artists are college educated; the U.S. DOL reports an increase of more than 30,000 bachelor's degrees held by those employed in professional art jobs from 1989–90 to 2001–02. Part of this circumstance owes to the increasing levels of competition for available positions and a need to keep mechanical skills very sharp. Another part has to do with the aforementioned business acumen required of self-employed artists, as business courses are offered at most institutes of higher learning, and yet another is a consideration primary to the long-term health of a creative professional's earnings—learning about managing one's copyrights.

Since the Copyright Act of 1976 went into effect, anyone who creates any work of art, visual, literary, or musical, is considered the owner of the copyright by default, unless the work is made on a work-for-hire basis. That means, unless otherwise stated in writing, once a person has made something, he or she owns it and can license that intellectual property however he or she sees fit. There are, however, many considerations to be made in order to protect one's copyrights. How to register one's copyrights and how best to go about managing them are just the beginning of what one can learn about this topic in college.

One also typically learns to keep a wary eye out for contracts that take advantage of inexperienced visual artists. Several corporations—among them Conde Nast, the New York Times, Marvel Comics, and DC Comics, to name just four—require that contributors sign over all copyrights to works commissioned by the company in order to get paid. This is especially onerous in a digital age when licensing one's work for limited edition prints or reprints for other publications proves to be a large component of one's income possibilities. (Anyone who doubts the veracity of these possibilities need only look at the ubiquity of Getty and Corbis images in print and on the Web; these are very large, extremely well-funded companies that exist solely by generating revenue from licensing images for reproduction.)

While managing one's personal copyrights may not seem important to a professional artist seeking a staff position, awareness of the basic tenets of copyright affords him or her a better understanding of contract negotiation with outside vendors. In addition, he or she may be able to use this knowledge to wrangle a better deal when seeking such a position.

In addition to self-employment and copyright issues, a very large component of a professional artist's working life involves working with digital media. Whether you are an analog artist executing imaging in traditional media or a designer dependent upon the desktop publishing capabilities of computer hardware and software, the advent of personal computing has affected every working artist to a greater or lesser degree. Addressing this key component of today's working world requires yet another skill set for the professional artist, much like the business acumen required in many ways. (After all, to a purely analog artist, meaning one who's not digital, many of the workings of a computer may also seem counterintuitive.) The most obviously affected artists are those whose jobs have become defined by the digital tools they employ—graphic designers (including art directors for any manner of print); animators, whose final products are almost entirely finished in a virtual environment; and special effects artists, whose jobs continue to move away from traditional painting and sculpting.

What may not be as apparent is how dramatically traditional artists have been affected. Photographers have had to invest millions of dollars in computer hardware and software that scan and transmit their images to clients, even when these images have been shot on traditional film. Painters find themselves in need of high-end digital imaging equipment to prepare catalogs and promotional materials to generate interest in their work. Moreover, advances in printing technology have paved a way to new avenues of income by making affordable archival editions of their images. Illustrators rely more and more on digital imaging equipment to deliver their jobs to clients and in some cases to compose their images. Art teachers at all levels make more and more use of computer equipment in order to prepare and present lesson plans, develop syllabi, and project presentations to classes. Interior designers have come to use 2-D and 3-D rendering applications to present their concepts to clients. The list goes on, especially when factoring in the communication aspect of the digital age—more and more people communicate via e-mail and promote themselves on the Internet, and that trend shows no sign of abating. Several different sources expect broadband Internet access to be in half the homes in the United States by 2020, which will bring unprecedented opportunities for professional artists to directly reach their prospective customers.

Based on that, one would expect that this industry has very great growth potential. Indeed, the U.S. DOL projects a 12 percent growth rate over the next 10 years. One gets the sense, though, that this number exists as a measure in keeping with the projected job growth in other industries as an average, especially when interviewing working professionals extensively. (When making growth predictions, the U.S. DOL weighs many factors, among them population statistics, particularly in age brackets from 18- to 24-year-olds; past trend markers for individual industries as well as the overall job market in the United States; and the number of retirement-age people holding jobs in a particular industry.) Without exception, professional artists polled and interviewed for this volume expect many current fields to continue their shrinking trends and that the greatest expectation of growth are in areas related to new media (Internet, interactive gaming, etc.), television, and film.

Imaging specialists who craft the dazzling environments in computer-generated imagery (CGI) films such as *The Matrix* trilogy, *The Lord of the Rings* trilogy, and *Sky Captain and the World of Tomorrow* are and will be in high demand. Similarly, CGI animation films such as *Shrek* and

The Incredibles have gained enormous popularity and will require a steady flow of professional artists to satisfy this demand. These projects—and several other, less obvious ones that employ digital imaging specialists for color-correction, small effects shots, and the like—all require large teams of artists to execute. Everything from conceptual images drafted by hand to final images created by scores of computer whizzes has to be crafted in order to bring these products to market, and all trends point to a continued growth in this particular field.

Entering into the visual arts industry is not for the faint of heart. Given that more than half of all professional artists employ themselves and have to work within a constantly evolving digital age—therefore requiring the investment of extra hours in the classroom and office to succeed in these areas—it's a difficult way to earn a living, whatever the field. It's so difficult, in fact, that according to the U.S. DOL, only 1.2 percent of the entire U.S. working population hold jobs in this industry, even factoring in the related sports, entertainment, and media professionals categorized as professional artists.

Professional artists invest large sums of money and many years of time pursuing higher education in order to satisfy the skill requirements of their chosen fields. They must be able to work on demand, independent of "feeling it," in order to meet deadlines and satisfy clients' needs. They must also contend with market influences too numerous to recount for the purposes of this book. (As a brief overview, big business exerts a powerful influence over the working lives of professional artists. Corporate media mergers continue to shrink markets, worsen intellectual property rights, and fix prices in a number of fields. Additionally, several imaging resources have gobbled up market shares once heavily populated by independent contractors.)

Despite these cautionary warnings, some key points about the finer aspects of pursuing a career as a visual artist bear note. These are jobs most people seek out of a love for the vocation. A component exists beyond the rational consideration of the facts-and-figures of choosing a profession when one seeks employment in the visual arts industry. Surely, one can indeed earn a living in this industry—depending upon the field, the median incomes for salaried employees range from $35,000 to $62,000 a year—but that's not always the primary driver for prospective professional artists.

They do it for the joy of the work. "And if you can do it for joy, you can do it forever," says Stephen King in *On Writing, A Memoir of the Craft*. Stephen King knows a thing or two about being a professional popular artist, and while he may be literary instead of visual, the fundamental things still apply. Loving the work you do makes it far easier to deal with the extraneous matters surrounding it. In fact, in the best circumstances, the extraneous matters typically become the "work" aspect of one's job, and the rest of the time is spent doing what one loves to do.

ACKNOWLEDGMENTS

Business associates, friends, family, and people we have never even met in person took time out to help tremendously with this project by providing references, resources, research materials, interviews, and inspiration. We could not have written this book without this supportive community, and we thank them from the bottom of our hearts.

William Anderson, president, Magic by Design; Paul d'Auriac, president, Metroart, Inc; Cletus and Barbara Anderson, art professors and production designers; Cathy Angiel, owner/jewelry designer, Gallery Eclectic; David Atlas, art director, The Pere Partnership; Mary Blackstock, screenprinter/ceramist; Rachel Blackwell, artist/store manager, Soho Art Material; Tim Bower, independent illustrator; John Brown, sculptor; Terry Brown, director, Society of Illustrators; Nick Buccalo, principal, The Drawing Studio; Amy Cappell, art teacher, Stuyvesant High School; Nina Carlson, director of education, The Aldrich Museum; Dr. James M. Cervino, marine biology professor, Pace University; Kathryn Winiarski-Cervino, associate communications director, The New York Academy of Medicine; Sara Chun, graphic designer, CNN; Peter Comitini, Web designer; Oscar Consedo, owner/framer, Gallery Frames; Randi Coran, general manager, shoot digital; Theresa Cirnigliaro, lead retoucher, shoot digital; Drew Dailinger, photographer's assistant; Dennis Drummond, department chair of drawing and printmaking, Columbus College of Art and Design; Kelly Evans, director of operations & technology, Creative Time; Bradley Fehl, handheld camera operator, CNN; Debra Fehl, teacher, Rutgers Preparatory School; Eunice Feller, vice president, marketing, The Art Store, Inc.; Laura Ferrera, editorial stylist; Anne Fizzard, artist/actress; James Fogle, storyboard artist/illustrator; Keith Gardner, animation designer, 4 Kids Productions; Carin Goldberg, principal, Carin Goldberg Design; Richard Grefé, executive director, American Institute of Graphic Arts; Richard Gress, president, ADI Printing; Aaron B. Harper, scenic manager, CNN New York Bureau; Fred Harper, independent illustrator; Allison Hemming, principal, The Hired Guns; Amy Grabowski, public relations manager, The Aldrich Museum; Edward C. Greenberg, attorney, Greenberg & Reicher, LLP; Kathleen Hansson, financial manager, Society of Illustrators; Dean Haspiel, sequential artist; Walter King, visual communications professor; Richard Klein, curator, The Aldrich Museum; Ken Krug, textile designer; Yungo Lee, jewelry designer; Rusty Levinson, conservator; Brayner Martinez, owner, BWarrior Martial Arts; Tanya Mastrogiovanni, makeup artist; Stuart McKissick, visual communications professor; Abby Messitte, gallery director, Clementine Gallery; Beverly Miller, business representative, United Scenic Artists; James Mokarry, package designer; Tom Mordasky, production artist; Vicki Morgan, illustration representative, Morgan & Gaynin Associates; Anne Murphy, graphic designer/Web designer; Myko, photographer/owner, Mykophoto.com; Regina Ortenzi, surface designer; Martin Pakledinaz, costume designer; Anne Pasternak, president and artistic director, Creative Time; Glen Pere, president, The Pere Partnership; George Pratt, sequential artist, art professor; Mike Quon, graphic dsigner/Web designer, Mike Quon Designation; Lauren Rabinowitz, cartoonist/teacher; Yael Reinharz, assistant director, Creative Time; Fred Rosen, ceramist/owner, Chelsea Ceramic Guild; Ron Rowley, Professional Framers Association; Kristine Scheuler, photo preservationist; John Seigel, store owner, Soho Art Material; James Shaw, general manager, Integrated Display Company; Abby Siegel, director of college office, Stuyvesant High School; Daniel Smith, deputy art director, the *Wall Street Journal;* Victor Sotenberg, technical writer, North American Airlines; Mark Texiera, sequential artist; Wayne Theobold, creative director, Art Merchandising, Inc.; Lowell Tolstedt, dean of fine arts, Columbus College of Art and Design; Emily Tsangarakis, textile designer; Ann Tuite, art buyer; Cynthia Turner, medical illustrator; Rick Uhler, owner/operator, Vivid Image Editions; Chad Vaughan, graphic designer; Eric Vaughn-Flam, attorney, Rubin Bailin Ortoli Mayer & Baker, LLP; Lee Wade, creative director, Simon & Schuster; Steve Worthington, storyboard artist; Matthew Yokobosky, exhibition designer, Brooklyn Museum of Art.

Above-and-beyond thanks go to
Brad Holland, for both inspiration and education beyond telling; Susan Clark, for inspiration and patience beyond measure; Michael Winiarski, for excellent ideas, productive brainstorming sessions, and sheer humorous relief; and James Chambers, for patience, guidance, and belief.

HOW TO USE THIS BOOK

The job descriptions in this book, 69 in all, provide readers with basic information about the industry and specific information about various positions in the visual arts field. As you read this book, it's important to be aware that unlike employees in other industries, artists do not necessarily follow clear career paths, and employers of artists don't necessarily promote in structured, hierarchical manners. Skills and techniques acquired and honed in one particular discipline can often be transferred to other areas of art, and employers are often interested in hiring versatile, multidisciplined artists. Additionally, artists are frequently self-determining workers, with more than 50 percent self-employed. For these independent workers, career ladders can be as creative as they want them to be.

The position descriptions are a starting point in conducting your career research. The writers gathered information for these positions by interviewing working professionals and industry experts, gleaning information available through the U.S. Department of Labor (DOL; specifically, the Bureau of Labor Statistics and the *Occupational Outlook Handbook*), various associations, and colleges, and researching trade magazines, books, and Web sites, as referenced in the Appendixes and Bibliography. The positions are divided into eight categories: Advertising, Business, Art Organizations, Education, Independent, Museums/Galleries, and Theatrical. Please note that some of the independent positions span several fields in the industry, with many having the option of being freelance or staff. Job titles are listed in order by level of experience, starting with the entry-level or more junior position.

The structure of each profile is as follows:

Career Profile

The Career Profile section provides a brief summary of the job duties, any alternate title or titles that may exist, the salary range, employment and advancement opportunities, prerequisites (which include education, training, work experience, and special skills and personality traits), and, if they apply, licensing or certification requirements.

Career Ladder

The Career Ladder indicates the job that can lead to the title profiled, and the next job up. The top job listed is usually the senior-level position, the middle job is frequently the job profiled, and the bottom job is the entry-level position, forming a "career sandwich," if you will. In some instances,

the job profiled is a senior-level position and may be listed at the top. Senior artists often advance by growing their businesses and branching out into other disciplines, as well as teaching and writing.

Position Description

This section provides a more in-depth look at the job. You will learn what a typical working day and work environment is like for a Web designer, set designer, animator, ceramist, museum curator, high school art teacher, and many others.

Salaries

Salary ranges are provided as best as could be ascertained from working professionals, trade associations and organizations, and the DOL. Some jobs profiled are too specialized for inclusion in the DOL reports. In those instances, information was extrapolated from the more general job titles and industry outlooks covered by the DOL and then corroborated by industry experts. Salary ranges reflect either annual wages, flat day or project rates, or hourly rates. Factors that can impact salaries are also mentioned, such as years of experience, educational background, technical expertise, type of clientele, type of product, how the work will be used, the medium in which the work is used, geographical location, size of budget, overtime, rush jobs, and more. Tips about how certain artists enhance their incomes are also included.

Employment Prospects

We identify which jobs and fields are more or less competitive in this section. Employment prospects are rated poor, fair, good, or excellent based upon discussions with professionals who are currently working in the jobs profiled and those who have experience in the field. The DOL's *Occupational Outlook Handbook (OOH)* provided predictions through the year 2012 for employment opportunities in various visual arts jobs. The reasons for the predictions, both by the *OOH* and working professionals and experts, are explained. Factors that can impact employment prospects include the economy, technological advances, whether the job is in an exciting and/or glamorous environment (i.e., animator, scenic artist , set designer for television or theater, Web designer, etc.) and, therefore, highly competitive, as well as the prospective employee's background and initiative.

Advancement Prospects

As previously mentioned, visual artists do not necessarily follow straight career paths. A sculptor may have been a hair stylist at one point in his or her life. A textile designer may have been a ceramist before moving into the discipline. Graphic designers and Web designers often cross paths. What is suggested in this section should be taken as advancement *possibilities,* and not the rule of thumb in the industry. Keep in mind that this is in print, but it is not in stone. The information is, again, based on discussions with professional artists and industry experts and research gathered from various organizations and publications. Even administrative and business positions in the visual arts are susceptible to the creative career ladder. While most employees need some management expertise, what is equally important is appreciation for the artwork and a deep understanding of artists.

Education and Training

Four-year college degrees with specializations are often recommended for the jobs listed in this book. A bachelor's degree provides an overall, well-rounded education that serves as a solid basis for working in any field, visual arts or otherwise. For some fields, advanced degrees are required. The types of courses individuals should take as well as any additional training, such as computer design software, are mentioned in this section, also.

Experience, Skills, and Personality Traits

Work backgrounds, special skills, and personality traits that are important to being successful, comfortable, and happy in this particular field are spelled out. Freelance employees share two common traits overall: independence of mind and an entrepreneurial spirit. Staff employees will, perhaps, prefer more structured environments. This section will help you determine where you best fit in.

Unions and Associations

Membership in trade associations and other professional organizations can enhance artists' careers by offering them workshops, conferences, and other educational opportunities targeted to their specific niche. Special events and networking opportunities help them meet other artists and gain valuable contacts. Membership often entitles artists to discounts on various services and products, also. Some industries in the arts, such as the entertainment field, require artists to belong to unions. For instance, scenic artists belong to the union United Scenic Artists. Union membership assures members of better wages and fair working conditions. The associations discussed in this section are suggestions based on recommendations from working professionals and research. This is not an exhaustive list, as there are a myriad of professional associations throughout the country. To learn more and find organizations that may be based near you, use an Internet search engine (e.g., Google) and read Web sites to see what's right for you.

Tips for Entry

Each position profile ends with three to five tips that shed light on important steps a prospective employee can take to get a foot in the door. Professional artists shared this advice based on their personal experiences as well as what they know to be the protocol for entry, whether it is an apprenticeship or internship, networking, creating a stellar portfolio, or a combination of all.

OTHER RESOURCES
IN THIS BOOK

Appendixes

The appendixes provide further information about schools and associations that specialize in the visual arts, as well as trade associations and unions. The colleges/schools appendix is divided into two parts: postsecondary schools and degree-granting schools. The postsecondary schools section features schools requiring diplomas or GEDs for entry. These nondegree institutions are vocation-specific; they offer specialized study and help students learn and hone particular skills. The degree-granting section includes schools that offer two-year degrees, four-year degrees, and master's programs. The trade associations and unions in the final appendix are associations and unions that, for the most part, cater to specific disciplines.

Bibliography

This contains the books, magazines, and Web sites that were referenced in composing this book. Reading sources are based upon special interests, such as design, illustration, painting, and so on.

Glossary

Terminology commonly used in the industry and mentioned in the book is included here, with meanings clearly defined. Learn what *speculation* and *work-for-hire* mean, the difference between *copyright* and *trademark,* and more. Before you begin any work, you need to understand the specifics of the assignment and what you have agreed to in the contract. Knowing the terminology is critical.

The pursuit of visual arts dates back to the origin of our species—it's both a noble and practical quest. We hope you find within this volume a career track that will interest you, fulfill your artistic aims, and provide a meaningful way to earn a living for many years to come.

ADVERTISING

PRODUCTION ARTIST (ADVERTISING)

CAREER PROFILE

Duties: Works closely with art directors, graphic designers, print production managers, printers and print vendors, and others to create advertisements for print; uses design software to create comps and mechanicals; resizes advertisements; maintains documents, graphics, and image files; maintains production calendar

Alternate Title(s): None

Salary Range: $60 to $250 per hour

Employment Prospects: Good

Advancement Prospects: Good

Best Geographical Location(s): Major urban areas

Prerequisites:

Education or Training—Bachelor's degree in art, with coursework in graphic design, typography, design software, and print production

Experience—Two to five years of advertising agency or design studio experience preferred

Special Skills and Personality Traits—Strong graphic design and technical skills; solid knowledge of design software; drawing ability helpful; detail and deadline oriented; patient; able to work with various staff and consultants to accomplish goals; strong written and verbal communication skills

CAREER LADDER

```
┌─────────────────────────────────────┐
│   Art Director or Studio Manager     │
└─────────────────────────────────────┘

┌─────────────────────────────────────┐
│             Retoucher                │
└─────────────────────────────────────┘

┌─────────────────────────────────────┐
│          Production Artist           │
└─────────────────────────────────────┘
```

Position Description

Production Artists work closely with graphic designers and art directors to create display advertisements in magazines and newspapers, billboards, posters, CD cases, postcards, brochures, and more. Production Artists are responsible for taking graphic designs and preparing them for print.

Production Artists create mechanicals (or prepress files) and assemble mock-ups (or comps) for advertising agency presentations to clients, as well as for scanning, trimming, and mounting. Production Artists may also serve as production managers, liaising with various staff and consultants to make sure work is on schedule. They may call printers or clients to confirm that jobs will be delivered and to discuss the specifications for and any changes to current and upcoming jobs. They will keep detailed notes of these telephone exchanges, as well as printouts of e-mail exchanges, for inclusion in the project files. Based on conversations with clients, printers, designers, art directors, and others, Production Artists will create production schedules, making sure that the dates are realistic based on availability.

Production Artists create design templates from graphics files by using such software programs as Adobe Photoshop, Adobe Illustrator, Adobe InDesign, QuarkXPress among many others. They also frequently use Acrobat and font management software in their work. Production Artists are responsible for revising and modifying documents for alterations and proofing (often in PDF). They may also retouch designs using Photoshop. They often use such file verification processes as Flight Check to collect and process documents for release to vendors. They have a quality-control aspect to their role as well, in that they make sure the final designs accurately match the requirements of the assignment. They handle color matching as well as provide instructions to printers. Production Artists also maintain all documents and graphics and image files related to the project.

Salaries

Freelance Production Artists can earn anywhere from $66 to $200 per hour for layout comp work; $65 to $250 per hour for tight layout work; and $60 to $150 per hour for electronic preflight/prepress work, according to the Graphic Artists Guild *Handbook of Pricing & Ethical Guidelines* (11th edition). These rates are based on surveys conducted in the field, with practitioners reviewing the summaries prior to publication. Production Artists can earn slightly higher rates if clients request rush jobs or order work over weekends or holidays. It is industry standard to charge slightly higher rates, such as a 10 to 20 percent increase, to accommodate these circumstances.

Employment Prospects

The Production Artist is often considered an entry-level position by agencies and studios. Production Artists who have two or more years of production experience will have greater chances of finding work. The picture brightens even further because, according to the Bureau of Labor Statistics *Career Guide to Industries,* employment in the advertising industry is expected to grow 19 percent through 2012. One reason for the predicted growth is the Internet and all the opportunities it brings with it. Additionally, as more services and products are introduced to the marketplace, more advertisement campaigns will be needed. Competition for jobs in advertising, as with all "glamour" industries, will be keen, however. Production Artists with solid design software skills will be more employable. Production Artists will also be able to find work with design studios that have advertising clients. Studios usually prefer to hire Production Artists with two to five years of production experience.

One caveat: Production Artists who work in advertising agencies should always have backup plans ready. Employment in the advertising world can be a roller-coaster ride, exciting at times, but it's wise to have a safety net. Agencies hire employees when accounts are landed, but when clients take their accounts to other agencies or experience budget cuts, typically the first thing advertising agencies slash is jobs. Wise Production Artists have a "Plan B," and they continue to network, maintain their contacts, and stay tuned in to industry news while they're working on projects.

Advancement Prospects

With years of experience, and depending on their specific strengths and interests, Production Artists can advance to become retouchers, working specifically in advertising agencies or design studios. They can also advance to become art directors or design studio managers.

Education and Training

A four-year degree in art is preferred, with coursework in graphic design, advertising, publishing, typography, and design software. Some training in, or exposure to, the printing process is extremely helpful, as Production Artists work closely with printers and print vendors. They must understand the specifics so that they can accurately convey printing instructions for designs. Production Artists must have a solid working knowledge of flight checking, font management, scanning, and archiving software.

Experience, Skills, and Personality Traits

Most advertising agencies prefer to hire Production Artists with at least two to five years of experience in a design studio or advertising agency. Production Artists must have solid design and layout skills and be fluent in typography. They need to be comfortable and flexible working with design software programs such as QuarkXPress, Adobe Illustrator, Photoshop, and others. Their job requires them to coordinate with diverse staff, so strong interpersonal and communication skills are critical. It also helps if Production Artists are well-versed team players with upbeat attitudes. The work is often pressured; those who can keep their wits about them while working quickly and accurately to successfully meet deadlines will thrive in this position.

Unions and Associations

Production Artists can join organizations such as the American Institute of Graphic Arts, Association of Graphic Communications, and Graphic Artists Guild for networking opportunities, educational resources, professional support, and group discounts from various service providers. Production Artists can also access job listings, discounted educational classes and training, and more through the Graphic Arts Information Network (http://www.gain.net), an organization affiliated with the Printing Industries of America.

Tips for Entry

1. There are plenty of employment agencies that focus on placing artists in advertising agencies. Find listings of the ones in your area and register with them. The jobs will usually be on a freelance, temporary basis and will give you the chance to experience firsthand the advertising agency's culture and structure, as well as allow you a foot in the door.
2. Many advertising agencies and design studios post Production Artist job openings on such Web sites as Monster, Hotjobs, Craigslist, Mediabistro, the *New York Times,* and others. Registration is free, and with some you can sign up for specific jobs to be e-mailed to you as they're posted. This way, if you don't have time to visit the Web site, you at least won't miss the job advertisement.
3. Keep abreast of what's going on in the field by regularly reading industry magazines such as *Advertising Age.*
4. When you are freelancing, be sure to add to your portfolio samples of work you created for projects. And before you go to your interview, do your homework. Make sure the pieces in your portfolio pertain to the style and type of work the company is seeking.

GRAPHIC DESIGNER (ADVERTISING)

CAREER PROFILE

Duties: Composes design and typographic elements of advertising campaigns

Alternate Title(s): Designer

Salary Range: $35,000 to $50,000+, including performance bonuses

Employment Prospects: Fair to Good

Advancement Prospects: Good

Best Geographical Location(s): Major urban areas with large businesses that support advertising agencies

Prerequisites:

Education or Training—Facility with two-dimensional design and typography; while no degree requirements per se, best candidates have at least a bachelor of arts and sciences or fine arts (B.A.S., B.F.A.)

Experience—College internships; some professional design/layout experience.

Special Skills and Personality Traits—Quick-thinking, creative mind; ability to marry text and imaging elements; ability to take direction gracefully

CAREER LADDER

```
┌─────────────────────────────┐
│     Creative Director       │
└─────────────────────────────┘

┌─────────────────────────────┐
│        Art Director         │
└─────────────────────────────┘

┌─────────────────────────────┐
│ Assistant Art Director or   │
│     Graphic Designer        │
└─────────────────────────────┘
```

Position Description

Graphic Designer is an entry-level position that revolves chiefly around the day-to-day nuts and bolts of assembling and drafting the typographic and shape design elements present in advertising campaigns. Seldom do Graphic Designers play large roles in determining the direction these campaigns will take, but they are the skilled hands and sharp minds that contribute a great deal to the overall look of the final advertisements.

While most of the high-concept ideas supporting an advertising campaign are drafted at the creative director level, a Graphic Designer often contributes several key ideas to the finished product based upon his or her grasp of primary shape and type design principals. As an advertisement takes shape under the Graphic Designer's hand, he or she typically has call to insert subtle tweaks about leading and kerning in type design, juxtaposition of shape elements, and the relationship of imaging to text. The keener one's eye is for these small but important details, the greater the oppor-

tunity will be for contributing to final advertisements and the greater the designer's chances for advancement.

Graphic Designers must have an excellent command of the tools used in crafting the typographic and imaging aspects of advertisements—the Macintosh platform and the primary software packages used in these areas, including Adobe Photoshop, Adobe Illustrator, Adobe InDesign, and QuarkXPress. These tools are used not only to create and optimize the artistic elements of the advertisements, but also to draft the final mechanical files delivered for print. That being the case, a good Graphic Designer knows as much as possible about this mechanical aspect, including reading and speaking the language of production and how to deliver files that are ready for film and plate output.

The best Graphic Designers also have a bit of a jack-of-all-trades mentality when it comes to composing these advertisements. In the most common scenarios, imaging culled from stock agencies or delivered by independent contractors must undergo some optimization to ensure the best possible reproduction. Additionally, typographic elements integrating tightly with imaging components requires that a Graphic Designer have the ability to work with the imaging flawlessly, be it photographic or illustrative. While not necessarily expected to have the full range of imaging capabilities of an independent illustrator, Graphic Designers usually find themselves called upon to have a high level of imaging ability.

In the contemporary world of tight deadlines and constantly changing client needs, a Graphic Designer also maintains a widely varied and shifting workload. Direction will come from a superior (in a perfect work world, the chain of command would be very clear-cut, but often a Graphic Designer has input from everyone from creative directors to art directors to account representatives), and a project may have to be shelved for interruption by a high-priority project. Graphic Designers who can cut on a dime, make alterations quickly, and still manage to keep deadlines are valued employees and stand a very good chance at success and advancement.

Salaries

Location serves as a primary driver in salary expectations for advertising Graphic Designers. In large metropolitan areas, such as New York City, Atlanta, Chicago, and Los Angeles, large advertising agencies have grown around many major corporations that employ ad agency services. These larger agencies generate far greater revenues than do their counterparts in smaller markets around the country and thereby can afford higher payrolls. However, the cost of living usually reflects the higher salary expectations in these areas as well, so careful attention must be paid to weighing the cost of living against salary expectations.

Entry-level Graphic Designers can expect to earn around $35,000, plus benefits. (Median earnings for Graphic Designers in advertising were $39,510 in 2002, according to the Bureau of Labor Statistics.) As one approaches assistant art director status by taking part in managerial responsibilities, salaries begin to approach $50,000.

Employment Prospects

Entry-level positions are very common in advertising. While the U.S. Department of Labor does not have a specific listing for this entry-level position in advertising, its Bureau of Labor Statistics reported 212,000 Graphic Designer jobs for 2002. In major urban areas where large numbers of advertising agencies are clustered, getting a foot in the door with a strong portfolio, good education, and positive attitude remains a strong likelihood.

One must consider another variable in this aim, however. A great many people compete for any opening at this level. Several ad agencies polled for this volume reported a minimum of 400 resume submissions for every job opening posted.

Advancement Prospects

Graphic Designers hold entry-level positions in the advertising field. While there are some professional artists who make a career of holding this position as they wish to have no part in managerial duties and want to focus solely on the creation of the typographic and design elements of advertising campaigns, it's more common to expect to use this position as a stepping stone toward a position of higher management, from Graphic Designer to assistant art director to art director to creative director.

Being an entry-level position, the prospects of rising up the career ladder from this position are good. While turnover remains high in the advertising field, it's quite reasonable to expect to cut one's teeth at a particular agency for a period of three or more years and begin moving up the ladder. Often, positions opening at rival agencies at higher levels present the opportunity for upward movement.

Education and Training

Though no specific certification exists for Graphic Designers that requires earning a degree, it's extremely rare to earn this position without a bachelor's degree in arts and sciences or fine art. In some cases, it's possible to secure employment while finishing one's education through the completion of an internship.

Completing these degrees forces the potential candidate to manage his or her time well and familiarizes him or her with the other aspects of creative endeavor present in the making of a finished advertisement (chiefly, photography and illustration). These courses also familiarize the potential candidate with current trends in design and how to incorporate them into his or her own creative ideas.

Earning a master's degree in visual art, typically design, also provides added benefit. In most cases, however, M.F.A.'s tend to start their employment at a more senior-level position, such as assistant art director.

Experience, Skills, and Personality Traits

The key component to successful advertising remains generating instant attention. While Graphic Designers seldom have large roles in determining the overall direction taken by an advertising campaign, knowing how type, shape, and imaging work together to generate this immediate impact serves to streamline workflow, make one more autonomous, and prepare one for upward movement.

Additionally, an advertising assistant art director must have a sharp eye for what's current in popular culture. Style trends in mass media play a large role in determining how text and imaging work together. Much of this is determined early on in the campaign drafting stage, where a Graphic Designer has less input, but knowing how the work one is doing fits in with current popular culture helps keep focus.

He or she must also have the ability to juggle several projects at once, as the workload usually includes serving many different clients' needs in any given day. This facet, coupled with the intense deadline pressure, dictates that a successful Graphic Designer have the ability to manage stress very well. The best Graphic Designers are good team players, ones who take direction and accept criticism well.

Unions and Associations

While there are no specific national unions to which Graphic Designers must belong in order to seek employment, they benefit greatly from membership in the American Institute for Graphic Arts (AIGA). This organization leads the pack for design professionals in the United States, with 47 local chapters nationwide in addition to its headquarters in New York City. It offers a variety of special events and seminars as well as a comprehensive members-only section on its Web site (which includes resources such as a library of essays published by members dealing with design and a member directory). The AIGA presents many opportunities for any design professional to stay in touch with what's current and offers significant networking opportunities.

Tips for Entry

1. Apply for internships at advertising agencies while in college.
2. Keep an eye out for what's current in popular culture.
3. Keep in touch with like-minded creative professionals as they make their way in the professional world. In many cases, friends from college will work with agencies that have openings at the graphic design or assistant art direction level, and these can grow into creative director positions over time.
4. Pay attention to what's current in popular culture imaging.

trends in mass media play a large role in determining how text and imaging work together. Much of this is determined early on in the campaign drafting stage where an Assistant Art Director may have less input, but knowing how the work fits in with current popular culture helps keep focus and prepares one for upward movement.

He or she must also have the ability to juggle several projects at once, as the workload usually includes serving many different clients' needs in any given day. This facet coupled with the intense deadline pressure dictates that a successful Assistant Art Director have the ability to manage stress very well. The best Assistant Art Directors are good team players, ones who take direction and accept criticism well.

Unions and Associations

While there are no specific unions to which Assistant Art Directors must belong, they benefit greatly from membership in the American Institute for Graphic Arts (AIGA). This organization leads the pack for design professionals in the United States, with 47 local chapters nationwide in addition to its headquarters in New York City. It offers a variety of special events and seminars as well as a comprehensive members-only section on its Web site (which includes resources such as a library of essays published by members dealing with design and a member directory). AIGA presents many opportunities for any design professional to stay in touch with what's current and offers significant networking opportunities.

Tips for Entry

1. Accept positions early in one's career in advertising agencies.
2. While in college, seek out internships with agencies in your surrounding areas.
3. Keep in touch with like-minded creative professionals as they make their way in the professional world. In many cases, friends from college will work with agencies that have openings at the graphic design or assistant art direction level, and these can grow into creative director positions over time.
4. Pay attention to what's current in popular culture imaging.

ART DIRECTOR (ADVERTISING)

CAREER PROFILE

Duties: Offers input into creative direction for advertising campaigns; oversees type, shape, and imaging conception; manages junior-level Art Directors, assistant art directors, graphic designers, and imaging specialists

Alternate Title(s): Designer

Salary Range: $40,000 to $100,000+, including performance bonuses

Employment Prospects: Fair to Good

Advancement Prospects: Fair

Best Geographical Location(s): Major urban areas with large businesses that support advertising agencies

Prerequisites:

Education or Training—Facility with two-dimensional design and typography; while no degree requirements per se, best candidates have at least a bachelor of arts and sciences or fine arts (B.A.S., B.F.A.)

Experience—Minimum five years in advertising business as a creative professional

Special Skills and Personality Traits—Quick-thinking, creative mind; ability to translate advertising concepts across different media; diplomacy and management skill

CAREER LADDER

```
┌─────────────────────────────┐
│      Creative Director      │
└─────────────────────────────┘

┌─────────────────────────────┐
│        Art Director         │
└─────────────────────────────┘

┌─────────────────────────────┐
│  Assistant Art Director or  │
│      Graphic Designer       │
└─────────────────────────────┘
```

Position Description

Art Directors in advertising hold very important positions. Being a single step below creative directors on the management and creative ladders, they bear a great deal of responsibility for both management and visual content.

As befits a position of this type, one must possess great facility with two-dimensional shape design and typography. Typically, Art Directors play the part of gathering all the visual elements together for an advertisement and putting them together in an eye-catching manner that fulfills the campaign identity drafted by the creative director. (The visual elements usually consist of headline text, logos, subheadlines, body copy, and imaging.) Whether all these elements are created in-house by employees of the advertising agency or supplied by outside vendors—most often, imaging comes from either independent contractors or stock image sources—it falls to the Art Director to see that they all relate to one another and form a cohesive unit once compiled.

In order to accomplish this feat, an Art Director has to know several key tenets about the voice of type, how type relates to imaging (either photographic or illustrative), and hierarchy of shape. He or she must also have the ability to switch from one style of application to another, as in many agency environments there will be several different types of clients to satisfy on a continual basis. (For instance, in some smaller, regional advertising agencies, an Art Director may work on campaigns for clients in luxury cosmetic sales and video rentals at the same time. Each of these clients will have need of a specific visual voice, and the Art Director has to be able to keep appropriate design principals in mind when composing the advertisements.) An Art Director employs all these skills daily and comes to make decisions on the fly to keep up with the breakneck pace of the advertising industry.

The exact amount of hands-on design executed by an Art Director will vary from agency to agency. However, it's almost unheard of for someone to hold the position of Art

Director without having a great deal of skill in manipulating the tools used to create finished advertising designs. In today's climate of quickly advancing computer technology, this means a great deal of knowledge about the workings of the Macintosh platform and the various industry standard design and imaging applications, namely Adobe Photoshop, Adobe Illustrator, Adobe InDesign, and QuarkXPress. The most successful candidates applying for Art Director positions in the advertising arena keep very current with the constant updates these programs undergo and can seamlessly fit these into their daily workflow.

Since imaging plays such a large role in any finished advertisement (be it print, television, or Internet), a good Art Director has to be familiar with and able to direct the efforts of outside vendors supplying imaging. While it's common to have illustrators working on-staff at advertising agencies, these professionals seldom produce finished work for print. An Art Director works with staff illustrators chiefly in generating comps, or quick mock-ups, which are shown to a client at preliminary stages of the campaign. It has become more common to employ the resources of stock agencies such as Corbis and Getty Images, as the time constraints are very tight in the advertising industry, but the most successful Art Directors have the ability to manage the production of custom imaging. After all, images culled from stock agencies are preexisting images and often have been used for other purposes; most clients prefer to know the imaging for which they're paying a high premium is tailored specifically for their use.

Given that this position has several different permutations depending upon the specific environment in which the advertising Art Director works, there are several variables to consider about this position. In many cases, this job is a mid- to high-level management position and comes with expectations of managing the efforts of one or more subordinates, typically assistant art directors or designers. Additionally, in the higher echelons, an Art Director, along with an account representative, may meet directly with clients. He or she may also be charged with taking a role in directing photo shoots or being on set for film shoots.

Salaries

Location remains a primary driver in determining salary expectations for advertising Art Directors. Agencies in larger metropolitan areas such as New York City and Los Angeles serve clients whose revenues are far greater than are those in smaller, middle American markets. Since revenues generated by clients determine advertising budgets, larger amounts of money coming in equals larger amounts of money spent on advertising. As an example, two large advertising agencies in North Carolina had revenues between $10 million and $20 million in 2002 (the most recent figures available for the market), while the country's sixth-largest agency in New York City had billings of $3.4 billion in 2003.

According to the U.S. Department of Labor (DOL)'s Bureau of Labor Statistics, in 2002 the median annual earnings of salaried Art Directors in advertising were just over $64,000, and the middle 50 percent of those earned between $44,000 and $85,000. The highest 10 percent of salaried Art Directors, however, earned in excess of $115,000.

Employment Prospects

Advertising budgets have plummeted in many industries over the past several years, in large part due to the emergence of the public relations industry, but this field remains a multi-billion dollar per year industry—the top 10 agencies for 2003 billed more than $3 billion each. Given that this much money still changes hands in this industry, there are a great many positions to be had, especially at this mid- to senior level. (The DOL's Bureau of Labor Statistics listed more than 51,000 Art Director jobs in 2002.)

One thing to keep in mind—the higher up one aims (bigger agency, larger salary, higher-profile clients, etc.), the stiffer the competition. Advertising remains a highly competitive field overall, but the competition ratchets up a notch the higher one goes.

Advancement Prospects

Turnover remains high in the advertising field. Factors as diverse as a creative director leaving to a client being lost to a competing agency can herald the repositioning or release of entire creative teams. Given this, opportunity is rife for lateral movement or advancement by changing agencies.

Education and Training

While there's no hard and fast rule that an Art Director have any specific degree, most advertising agencies require at least a bachelor's degree (B.F.A. or B.A.S.) in graphic or advertising design. Earning a master's degree in visual art, typically design, also provides added benefit. Completing these degrees forces the potential candidate to manage time well and familiarizes one with the other aspects of creative endeavor present in the making of a finished advertisement (chiefly, photography and illustration). These courses also familiarize the potential candidate with current trends in design and how to incorporate them into creative ideas.

Experience, Skills, and Personality Traits

The vast majority of an Art Director's responsibility boils down to creating immediate visual interest, whether concocting a single advertisement or directing a large multimedia advertising campaign. Be it a subtle visual statement or a high-impact design, advertising has to garner the consumer's instant attention.

An advertising Art Director must also have a keen eye for what's current in popular culture. Style trends in mass media play a large role in determining how an Art Director gets text and imaging to work together. Much of this is determined early on in the campaign drafting stage, in which an Art Director will work with the creative director to determine how the interactions will play, but the Art Director keeps tabs on how the advertisements shape up during their construction.

As stated above, the Art Director bears quite a lot of management responsibility in many agency environments. He or she has to manage staffs who report directly to him or her as well as those outside vendors who supply imaging. Given the diverse personalities of those reporting to the Art Director, he or she must exhibit diplomacy when addressing them.

He or she must also have the ability to juggle several projects at once, as the workload usually includes serving many different clients' needs in any given day. This facet, coupled with the intense deadline pressure, dictates that a successful Art Director have the ability to manage stress very well. The best Art Directors are good leaders, ones who lead by example.

Unions and Associations

While there are a great many components to any advertising campaign, shape and type design remain the primary facets.

To that end, an advertising Art Director can benefit greatly from membership in the American Institute of Graphic Arts (AIGA). The AIGA is the leading organization for design professionals in the United States and has 47 chapters nationwide in addition to its headquarters in New York City. Offering a wide variety of special events and seminars as well as a robust members-only section on its Web site (which includes resources such as its library and member directory, among others), the AIGA presents many opportunities for an advertising Art Director to stay in touch with what's current. It also offers a great deal of networking opportunities.

Tips for Entry

1. Accept positions early in your career in advertising agencies.
2. While in college, seek out internships with agencies in your surrounding areas.
3. Keep in touch with like-minded creative professionals as they make their way in the professional world. In many cases, friends from college will work with agencies that have openings at the graphic design or art direction level, and these can grow into creative director positions over time.
4. Pay attention to what's current in popular culture imaging.

CREATIVE DIRECTOR (ADVERTISING)

CAREER PROFILE

Duties: Conceives and oversees production of advertisements for print, television, and Internet; manages creative department of advertising agency

Alternate Title(s): None

Salary Range: $60,000 to $200,000+, including performance bonuses

Employment Prospects: Fair

Advancement Prospects: Almost none

Best Geographical Location(s): Major urban areas with businesses that support advertising agencies

Prerequisites:

Education or Training—Facility with design and the written word; while no degree requirements per se, best candidates have at least a bachelor of arts and sciences or fine arts (B.A.S., B.F.A.)

Experience—Minimum 10 years in advertising business as a creative professional

Special Skills and Personality Traits—Quick-thinking, creative mind; ability to translate advertising concepts across different media; diplomacy and management skill

CAREER LADDER

```
┌─────────────────────────────┐
│     Creative Director        │
└─────────────────────────────┘

┌─────────────────────────────┐
│        Art Director          │
└─────────────────────────────┘

┌─────────────────────────────┐
│    Assistant Art Director    │
└─────────────────────────────┘
```

Position Description

Creative Directors have extremely powerful positions in the advertising field. Be it a small agency dealing mostly with local clients advertising to their immediate communities or large multinational agencies generating multimedia campaigns, Creative Directors sign off on all final decisions concerning the creative aspects of the end product.

Creative Directors manage all aspects of the final advertising product. This involves juggling many different types of creative endeavor, everything from the written word to the visual product. While not ultimately responsible for generating every aspect of the final advertising product (except in rare cases in small, boutique agencies), a Creative Director coaches the best possible work out of the different creative professionals he or she works with, whether they're salaried staff employees of the same agency, independent contractors, or subcontracting firms. For instance, a single advertising campaign that ties together print advertising in national magazines and newspapers with television commercials selling the same client's wares will require the skills of writers for both print and television, art directors for the same, illustration or photography for the print aspect of the campaign, and entire crews of filmmakers with all the attendant professionals involved in film projects (storyboard artists, stylists, film directors, and production designers). All of this management takes place at the same time the Creative Director works with an account representative who sells the agency's services to the client paying for the final advertising product, often even dealing directly with the client. Creative Directors often find themselves providing several different types of services for clients. One client, a start-up company, might require a corporate identity campaign from the advertising agency. Existing clients may require updates or modifications to multimedia campaigns already run by the agency in previous months or years, consisting of print, television, and Internet media. Existing clients have steady relationships with the agency, may have the agency on a retainer, and have proven worth many millions of dollars in billings over a period of years or decades. Yet another long-standing client, responsible for millions of dollars in billings over the years, may decide that it's time for a complete overhaul of its current advertising identity. Landing a new client for the agency means creating a proposal and pitching for the new business, vying against several different advertising agencies. Winning the pitch could lead to millions of dollars for the agency.

All these clients sell different goods and services to different audiences, ranging from teen-targeted to the ultra-conservative mature audiences. All have high priority for different reasons, and all have delivery dates within weeks of one another. A trafficker may be employed in some agencies to help manage the workflow into the Creative Director's office.

Once faced with a set of parameters for a client's campaign, the creative work begins. A Creative Director begins the work of drafting conceptual material for each client. A Creative Director takes this very quick, preliminary material and begins working with art directors, graphic designers, and copy writers in brainstorming sessions. In most cases, these teams work on several concepts for a single client's needs, as it's rare that a single concept gets presented to any given client. In these brainstorming sessions, the participants discuss possible solutions to deliver the required results, including potential outside resources to bring in on the projects. Then it's off to the races, with the Creative Director overseeing the individual parts as they come together to flesh out the conceptual material drafted at the project's inception. It's during this management phase of a given set of projects that a Creative Director must assign priority to clients (quite often with input from agency ownership in smaller agency environments) and to individual concepts within a client's eventual presentation. During the days or weeks the presentations are being fleshed out in this management phase, a Creative Director continues to refine and zero in on the initial intent of the conceptual material, never turning off the creative impulses driving the material. This back-and-forth is as much a juggling act as is managing workflow, since the Creative Director must weigh the time required to shift gears in mid-concept against the looming deadline.

After several concepts have been developed thoroughly enough for presentation, the Creative Director oversees the building of presentations for delivery to the client. In most cases, this consists of mounting printed sheets containing all aspects of the eventual campaign to blackboards. Each medium has its own board—one for television, one for print, one for the Internet, and, possibly, one for prospective product placement concepts. These individual boards are grouped together in several series of boards, some Creative Directors electing to bind them together for a clearer depiction of the different media relating to one another. Each presentation is tailored to the individual clients's preferences.

Delivery of presentations differs, too, depending upon agencies and circumstances. For instance, an account representative may request the company of the Creative Director when pitching a new or existing client, even when interstate travel is involved. Some existing clients may not be local and require only delivery of the boards and a conference call. Others may be willing to view the presentation at the agency, in which case a conference room may be equipped with audiovisual (AV) equipment to incorporate some movement and sound when pitching campaigns to clients. These AV presentations require the Creative Director to oversee their completion, as do the printed versions, and also require the skills of a different creative professional, one adept at authoring AV presentations.

Salaries

Like many other positions available in the visual art field, a great deal depends upon the market in which you seek employment. Small adverting firms that deal with local businesses placing ads in small, independent publications or running television advertisements on local channels don't generate nearly as much revenue as do the big firms with presences in several large markets (such as BBDO and Grey Worldwide, to name just two, which have offices in many large cities in the United States). Small agencies may generate $1 million in billings in a good year, whereas several of the largest agencies bill in the billions.

Accordingly, salaries at large agencies buying media on a national level are higher than at small agencies placing advertisements in local media. In addition, the larger the recompense, the higher the stress level and bigger the responsibility, not to mention the fewer the opportunities.

Employment Prospects

While advertising budgets have taken a pounding over the last several years with the American economy lagging, advertising is still a multibillion-dollar-a-year industry with positions available at many levels, from large agency to small. Many people achieve Creative Director positions by working their way up from graphic designer and art director positions within the same agency, but in some cases this vertical leap takes place by positions opening with different agencies.

Advancement Prospects

With few exceptions (some Creative Directors can be offered officer positions at some agencies with equity in the business, but that's extremely rare), attaining the level of Creative Director means the climb up the ladder has ended. This position is at the top of the food chain.

Education and Training

While there's no hard and fast rule that a Creative Director have any specific degree, completing a course of study at an accredited art college or university in graphic design gives a leg up. Completing a master's degree in visual art—an M.F.A. in design, painting, or illustration—also provides added benefit. Completing these degrees forces the potential candidate to manage time well and become familiar with the written word, a decided advantage to the Creative Director position, as so much of the job involves the written word. These courses also familiarize the potential candidate with current trends in design and how to incorporate them into his or her own creative ideas.

Experience, Skills, and Personality Traits

The vast majority of a Creative Director's responsibility boils down to creating visual interest, whether concocting a single advertisement or directing a large multimedia advertising campaign. Thus, it stands to reason that a Creative Director has experience in a visual medium, typically graphic design. The job also requires a facility with the written word, as part of the Creative Director's management deals with the text element of an advertisement or advertising campaign. Everything from headlines to body copy gets funneled past the Creative Director's desk, and while he or she may not be actively writing this copy (in some cases it does fall to the Creative Director to generate copy), he or she must make sure the text written for an advertisement or advertising campaign has a voice that fits with the overall message being delivered visually. That said, it's not necessary to be a literary scholar to aspire to this position, but one certainly needs to be comfortable with the written word.

Market awareness also plays a role in dictating creative direction. At the largest agencies, separate marketing departments with marketing specialists, trend analysts, and even pollsters support the creative and account management departments. At smaller agencies, however, a Creative Director has to exhibit market awareness. Account representatives often have much to say on this point—as does the client, most certainly, as he or she will no doubt have very definitive ideas concerning to whom his or her wares are being sold—yet it behooves a Creative Director on any level to be aware of what's "hot" or what's subtle and to use an approach for the appropriate audience.

The buck ultimately stops, creatively speaking, with the Creative Director. This job requires the ability to manage an enormous workload and keep a great many balls in the air at any given time. It requires taking input from account representatives who deal directly with a client, managing staff artists and writers, overseeing independent contractors—illustrators, photographers, stylists, and writers among them—and bearing the ultimate responsibility for meeting what are often crushing deadlines.

In addition to management skills, a Creative Director must have the ability to think quickly and act decisively. A Creative Director solves problems and creates consumer interest in the client's wares with an advertisement or advertising campaign. It bears repeating that a tremendous amount of pressure accompanies this position. Deadlines are tight, and clients invest very large portions of their annual budgets in the product a Creative Director delivers. Additionally, juggling what may seem at times an army of creative professionals and the various personalities that coincide with those creative professionals can be daunting. A good Creative Director needs to be a good leader, a good visual thinker, and have the ability to manage high-pressure, stressful situations well.

Unions and Associations

While there are a great many facets to any advertising campaign, design remains a primary factor. To that end, an advertising Creative Director can benefit greatly from membership in the American Institute of Graphic Arts (AIGA). The AIGA is the leading organization for design professionals in the United States and has 47 chapters nationwide in addition to its headquarters in New York City. Offering a wide variety of special events and seminars as well as a robust members-only section on its Web site (which includes resources such as its library and member directory, among others), the AIGA presents many opportunities for an advertising Creative Director to stay in touch with what's current. It also allows for a great deal of networking opportunities.

Tips for Entry

1. Accept positions early in your career in advertising agencies.
2. While in college, seek out internships with agencies in your surrounding areas.
3. Keep in touch with like-minded creative professionals as they make their way in the professional world. In many cases, friends from college will work with agencies that have openings at the graphic design or art direction level, and these can grow into Creative Director positions over time.

ART BUYER (ADVERTISING)

CAREER PROFILE

Duties: Researches and secures artists for advertising projects; works closely with art directors, photographers, photographers' representatives, and others; reviews portfolios; negotiates fees and work terms; creates cost estimates for client approval; coordinates and oversees photography shoots; ensures contract terms are adhered to; coordinates retouching work; handles billing; manages staff

Alternate Title(s): Art Producer, Art Manager

Salary Range: $40,000 to $80,000+

Employment Prospects: Fair

Advancement Prospects: Fair

Best Geographical Location: Major urban areas

Prerequisites:

Education or Training—B.A. recommended; coursework in art history, photography, and computer design software helpful

Experience—Two to three years of experience in production or creative department of advertising agency

Special Skills and Personality Traits—Creative; strong knowledge of artists and art styles; excellent communication and interpersonal skills; extremely organized; able to juggle projects and meet deadlines; well versed in basic office software (MS Word, Excel, etc.); working knowledge of Adobe Photoshop and Illustrator helpful

CAREER LADDER

```
┌─────────────────────────────────┐
│   Managing Art Buyer or         │
│   Senior Art Buyer              │
└─────────────────────────────────┘

┌─────────────────────────────────┐
│   Art Buyer                     │
└─────────────────────────────────┘

┌─────────────────────────────────┐
│   Junior Art Buyer,             │
│   Administrative Assistant, or Artist │
└─────────────────────────────────┘
```

Position Description

Art Buyers play a key role in the selection of artwork used in advertisements. While it is the art director's role to come up with advertising concepts, it is the Art Buyer who solicits artwork directly from artists as well as from artists' representatives. Once the art director's idea is approved by the client, the art director tells the Art Buyer the type of artwork that is needed (e.g., sketch, stock image, photographic image) and the style (e.g., cubist, modern art, strong black-and-white images).

The Art Buyer is given the budget within which to work and seeks out the talent that will fit the budget and the project. He or she may solicit illustrations, stock photographs, or even combinations of the two. Art Buyers with years of experience have a pool of familiar people they can draw from. They call in portfolios of people they know or research new talent. After reviewing portfolios, they narrow down the selections and present their choices to the art director. The art director decides on the artist based on the Art Buyer's recommendations.

The chain of command within agencies varies slightly, but the client usually has the final approval once the costs are established. Art Buyers are responsible for securing estimates for photography shoots, which can include such items as photographers' assistants, location scouting, stylists, animal handlers, and more. Art Buyers work closely with photographers or photographers' representatives to solidify all the numbers to make sure there are no surprises later on in the project. Art Buyers also commit a great deal of time negotiating the terms of usage for images, which, because of the various media outlets available and the new ones being created each year, is a critical issue for advertising agencies as well as for creators. The Art Buyer's job is not only to protect the agency and the client, but artists as well. The Art Buyer field is small; word travels fast about a person's character. Art Buyers who are professional, ethical, and treat artists fairly will be able to maintain healthy relationships.

Art Buyers coordinate and oversee photography shoots. They make sure that everyone shows up who is supposed to show up. They make sure that what is being photographed is what was agreed to in the contract. Their level of involvement in shoots will vary, depending on the art director's years of experience. More experienced art directors will not rely as much on Art Buyers during shoots as those who have less experience in the field. After the shoot, Art Buyers handle billing and follow through on remaining paperwork. The photographs are usually sent as chromes or contact sheets to either in-house retouchers for corrections, or, more commonly these days, to outside vendors. By this stage, the Art Buyer's job is usually done. He or she will usually stay involved, though, if the photographer chooses to do the retouching him- or herself.

Salaries

Art Buyers can earn salaries ranging from $40,000 to $80,000 or more, depending upon the agency, the client base, and the project. With years of experience, Art Buyers can command higher salaries because of their expertise and their connections in the industry.

Employment Prospects

Employment in the advertising industry, overall, is expected to grow 19 percent through 2012, according to the U.S. Department of Labor's *Occupational Outlook Handbook (OOH)*. Advertising agencies usually hire very few Art Buyers for projects, so competition for work should be fierce. Advertising is directly linked to the economy, and as new products and services are introduced, new jobs will open up to accommodate the needs for advertising. Also, the *OOH* predicts that demand for advertising in new and different media outlets will create new job opportunities for Art Buyers.

Advancement Prospects

Art Buyers can advance to more senior positions either in creative or production departments of advertising firms. If they have been on staff, they can move on to freelance, open their own art buying firms, network in areas of art that are new to them, and explore unique and interesting advertising projects.

Education and Training

A four-year degree in art is preferred. Art Buyers should be familiar with artists and art styles as well as photography techniques. Thus, coursework in art history, contemporary art, and photography is helpful. Solid knowledge of office software such as MS Word and Excel is required. Art Buyers also need to be comfortable using the Internet and have some ability with Adobe Photoshop and Illustrator, particularly if fast changes need to be made (e.g., formatting) to digital art files.

Experience, Skills, and Personality Traits

Advertising firms usually look for Art Buyers with at least several years of experience either in creative or production departments. Many also look favorably upon Art Buyers with diverse backgrounds, as advertising projects often feature unusual messages and art styles. Those Art Buyers who have connections to the offbeat will be able to secure artists to fit those types of projects and may be more marketable to some agencies. Art Buyers travel through different worlds each day, from communicating with art directors and clients to artists' representatives and artists themselves. To succeed, they must be excellent communicators, capable of adjusting their language and lingo to each individual and each situation. Organization skills are also critical in this field. Art Buyers are responsible for all of the paperwork involved in the shoots and transactions. While legal departments often create the contracts, Art Buyers make sure that each of the terms is honored throughout the project, from start to finish. Strong negotiation skills and attention to detail are critical in this job.

Unions and Associations

There are no specific unions for Art Buyers in the advertising industry. For general networking and educational resources, Art Buyers can join the American Advertising Federation (AAF). Art Buyers can also become associate members of the American Society of Media Photographers (ASMP), the Graphic Artists Guild, the Society of Illustrators, and more to network with artists and participate in conferences and workshops.

Tips for Entry

1. Do your homework before job hunting. Make sure you have the right person at the agency to send your letter and resume to by calling the main reception desk. It's simple, and yet so many people don't do it. Being a good Art Buyer means being a good researcher. Sending your materials to the wrong person wastes his or her time and yours. Getting the name, title, and spelling right sends the message that you pay attention to details and scores you valuable points.

2. Be absolutely sure you want to be an Art Buyer. Work as an intern so that you can experience the environment firsthand.

3. Networking is critical. People in the advertising business are more interconnected than you might imagine, and the Art Buyer field is an especially small niche. It's important to stay in touch with and share resources with others, when appropriate, because you never know when you might need suggestions or help with a project. Having a network you can call upon is a great boon. Don't ever burn your bridges, either!

STYLIST (ADVERTISING/EDITORIAL)

CAREER PROFILE

Duties: Sets style directions for advertisements and magazines; works closely with art directors, photographers, assistants, and possibly models; often chooses photographers for projects; recommends colors, clothing, objects, and more; researches trends in all areas of fashion, art, music, furnishings, etc.; attends photo shoots; may travel; may manage staff

Alternate Title(s): Style Consultant

Salary Range: $200 to $6,500 or more per day

Employment Prospects: Fair

Advancement Prospects: Good

Best Geographical Location(s): Major cities

Prerequisites:

Education or Training—Four-year degree in art; specification in fashion design helpful

Experience—Two to three years of experience assisting or interning at fashion magazine or agency recommended

Special Skills and Personality Traits—Creative; problem-solver; able to work well and quickly under deadline pressure; patient; excellent communication and interpersonal skills; knowledgeable about variety of trends, styles, designs, designers, and materials; professional with strong work ethic

CAREER LADDER

```
+-----------------------------+
|     Lead Stylist or         |
|  Designer Line Consultant   |
+-----------------------------+

+-----------------------------+
|         Stylist             |
+-----------------------------+

+-----------------------------+
|      Assistant Stylist      |
+-----------------------------+
```

Position Description

Stylists who specialize in advertising and editorial are responsible for choosing the styles of clothing, accessories, furnishings, decorations, colors, and overall themes for photographs used in print advertisements, magazine covers, and magazine articles. Advertising Stylists are hired by agencies to help sell products by appealing to specific audiences. For instance, Stylists who work on the Gap print advertisements are aware that the Gap has a specific image that appeals to a specific customer base. With many designer labels, it's not so much about the clothing, but more about the image. Good Stylists know this. They are familiar with fashion and brand history as well as advertising and marketing tactics and choose photographers and photography styles that match the product's image and the client's expectations.

To successfully accomplish their jobs, Stylists need to be aware of trends. They need to know what people are buying now and what is on the horizon. They stay abreast by immersing themselves in fashion and style magazines, attending fashion shows, and networking with other stylists, art directors, photographers, and designers. Many Stylists go beyond the fashion world, though, because they are often responsible for helping to set the whole photographed scene. They attend music concerts and art shows. They also read up on furniture design, interior design, furnishings, and accessories as well as color and themes. Stylists choose the photographers whose work best matches the needs of the project. For instance, if the theme of a print ad is "bohemian," Stylists will not choose photographers who have stark styles. Photographers also will hire Stylists to work on projects. Stylists have varying degrees of input depending on the photographers and art directors they work with.

Stylists meet with clients before shoots to discuss all aspects of the projects. They learn who the target audience is, the models and objects that will be included in the images, where the images will appear, and the overall themes, moods, and styles. They also find out the specific sizes of clothing, shoes, and accessories that will be required. Their detailed notes help them in the next phase of their work: research and shopping. Stylists take their lists and seek out the clothes, accessories, and objects that match the clients' specifications. They know where to find period pieces, where the best vintage clothing is, and how to locate all the various nook-and-cranny stores that can provide them with what they need. They negotiate prices, purchase items, and keep track of all expenses to ensure accurate invoices once the project is completed. Stylists are usually on hand during shoots to make sure all the styles and clothing work. If something needs to be replaced, they make sure it happens. Their level of input with photographers will also depend upon their years of experience in the field. Veteran stylists will be better equipped to contribute their insights and fast solutions to problems when and if they arise.

Most Stylists work as freelance consultants and set up and manage their own offices. They are responsible for all aspects of their business, from creating a brand image and Web site, to planning direct mail and advertising campaigns to secure more clients, to maintaining office equipment and overseeing accounts receivables and payables.

Salaries

Freelance Stylists usually charge clients flat day rates, which can vary depending on their years of experience and the types of projects. While new Stylists can earn upwards of $200 per day, those with many years of experience and solid reputations in the business can earn as much as $6,500 or more per day. Stylists who are able to secure big-name photographers for projects are also able to secure significantly higher rates.

Employment Prospects

Stylists who seek work in advertising and editorial will face fierce competition. While the U.S. Department of Labor's *Occupational Outlook Handbook* foresees employment growth in both industries through 2012, because only a handful of Stylists are typically needed for projects, there are far more job seekers than available jobs. Stylists with excellent reputations and the right connections (e.g., to famous and respected photographers) will fare better in the marketplace. Many burgeoning Stylists get their feet in the door by assisting or apprenticing for free. Naturally, this is not the ideal employment situation, but it is frequently the

best way to get firsthand experience when people are just starting out. Working for free in the beginning, at least for one or two projects, also enables new Stylists to get tear sheets of their work to show to magazines and advertising agencies. With at least 10 years of experience, Stylists can hire representatives to help them secure more work.

Advancement Prospects

With years of experience, Stylists can advance to become lead or senior stylists. They can work on larger, more complicated projects, working with more photographers and art directors and managing larger staffs. They can work as consultants, also, advising on designer lines and suggesting design changes based on trends. Stylists can move into other areas of the media, such as film, television, or theater. Stylists can also share their expertise and help the next generation entering the business by teaching college-level students. They can shed light on trends as well as educate the general public by writing articles and columns for fashion and style magazines and Web sites.

Education and Training

A four-year degree in fashion design with coursework in fashion history is preferred. Companies look favorably upon Stylists who have at least two to three years of on-the-job training as an apprentice or assistant stylist at a fashion magazine, advertising agency, or fashion house, with experience working at photo shoots and coordinating with art directors, photographers, models, and other staff.

Experience, Skills, and Personality Traits

Stylists need to be creative and aware of trends not only in fashion, but also in music, art, furnishings, color, architecture, and more. The advertising and magazine industries are highly pressured environments. Stylists need to be able to work well under pressure. They must be able to stay creative and focused, always aware of the goals. Naturally, Stylists need to be savvy about clothing and designs, but they must also have strong business skills to thrive in this field. They must also have excellent communication skills. Patience, diplomacy, and a great deal of tolerance are tremendously beneficial, particularly if working with renowned art directors and photographers. Egos can come into play and challenge even the calmest individuals. Stylists who are able to maintain professionalism and rationale throughout the rough spots will earn respect and be hired back for future projects.

Unions and Associations

Fashion Group International (FGI) and the Association of Stylists and Coordinators (ASC) provide Stylists with educational resources, opportunities to network with industry professionals, access to employment listings, and more. Stylists can also benefit by becoming associate members of such groups as the American Society of Media Professionals (ASMP).

Tips for Entry

1. Find an assistant job or internship at a fashion house or fashion magazine, even if you have to work for free. In this industry, apprenticeships are the key to getting a foot in the door, but people are not often willing to pay salaries *and* teach simultaneously. Networking is critical, and an apprenticeship will give you the opportunity to meet people. You'll have the chance to attend photo shoots and meet art directors, photographers, models, and other staff members.

2. Be prepared to work hard, swallow your pride, and grow a thick skin if you don't have one already. Many people enter this field thinking it's completely glamorous and one big party. It can be glamorous, but keep in mind it is, after all, a business. And like many jobs, in the beginning you may be handling the less-than-glamorous tasks, such as taking stock of shoes and shoe sizes for upcoming fashion shoots. Remember that everything you do contributes to the project. Complete each task professionally and efficiently, and you will soon be known for your work ethic and performance. This will make a difference in your career and in your attitude toward your job.

3. With years of experience and consistent work performance, you will develop a reputation in the business for being a professional with whom people want to work. Until that point in your career, dress the part. Once you are a known name, you can wear whatever you please and it won't impact your business. For now, make sure that *your* image matches the image you want colleagues, clients, and prospective clients to remember you by. Choose your brands, designs, and colors carefully.

ADVERTISING ILLUSTRATOR

CAREER PROFILE

Duties: Draws a wide variety of subjects on demand with varying levels of finish, from quick sketch to presentation level

Alternate Title(s): None

Salary Range: $25,000 to $100,000+

Employment Prospects: Fair

Advancement Prospects: Good

Best Geographical Location(s): Major urban areas with advertising agencies

Prerequisites:

Education or Training—Expert-level draftsmanship in a wide range of subjects

Experience—Many hours of observational drawing and a portfolio that reflects an ability to draw people, places, and things in believable space

Special Skills and Personality Traits—Ability to accept criticism and work with others

CAREER LADDER

```
┌─────────────────────────────┐
│   Advertising Illustrator   │
└─────────────────────────────┘

┌─────────────────────────────┐
│   Independent Illustrator   │
└─────────────────────────────┘

┌─────────────────────────────┐
│ Student / Intern / Artist Assistant │
└─────────────────────────────┘
```

Position Description

In the extremely fast-paced world of advertising, a great many artists collaborate to meet increasingly more rigid client demands. Advertising Illustrators play a key role in presenting ideas for advertising campaigns to clients, as their work solidifies concepts drafted by creative directors and art directors. Advertising Illustrators do this by translating advertising concepts into quick images.

Any advertisement, be it a multimedia campaign involving television, print, and Internet or a single print advertisement, begins by having a client's needs brought to an advertising agency by an account representative. The specifics of the job are relayed by the account representative to the agency's creative team, composed of a creative director, one or more art directors, graphic designers, and Advertising Illustrators, and that team collectively brainstorms to draft rough concepts that will suit the client's particular needs. Most typically, a creative director takes the lead in cooking up the original material, then involves the rest of the creative team in refining these ideas into final concepts. Once crafted, the final concepts must be presented to the client in a rough form as printed sheets mounted to blackboards for selection of the final advertising product. An Advertising Illustrator's role in this process is drafting clean, clear, presentable images that will later become final art once a direction is selected by the client. Final art can take the form of motion picture, photography, or illustration.

The demands placed on an Advertising Illustrator vary by agency and the specific list of clients handled. In certain cases, an advertising agency may specialize in handling one specific type of client, such as automotive advertising. It is almost universally true, however, that an Advertising Illustrator will face the need to work on a multitude of differing subjects, including but not limited to automotive advertising, food and beverage, clothing and apparel, appliances, environmental products, pharmaceuticals, gaming, and consumer electronics. An Advertising Illustrator will face this need because most advertising agencies cater to a large number of clients who sell a wide range of goods and services to the consumer.

This means that an Advertising Illustrator must have a very well-rounded visual vocabulary. An ability to compose images for presentation containing multiple figures in a believable environment quickly for conceptual purposes is only one of many possible requirements faced by the artist. On any given day, an Advertising Illustrator's duties may include composing three different images, all incorporating the same consumer appliances in an interior space, followed by six images containing multiple figures surrounding automobiles in an outdoor environment, followed by two rough images of fashion models sporting high-end hair styles. In many cases, an Advertising Illustrator is expected to craft these images on the fly, often without specific reference. In any case involving a specific consumer product, detailed imagery of the product will be supplied to the Advertising Illustrator, but he or she will be charged with placing the item believably in a visual space to suit different perspectives while maintaining fidelity to the proportions of the product.

The manner in which an Advertising Illustrator executes visual art will also vary, depending upon the environment and the clients being served. Many artists still apply traditional methods when composing their art, those being pencil roughs over which ink lines and permanent markers are applied. In certain circumstances, just the pencil roughs will suffice. Typically, this occurs when deadlines are even tighter than usual and a high level of familiarity exists between agency and client. These traditional marker renderings are often quick, deft indications of form with little specific detail, as the images are meant to emphasize placement of product on the page or screen within the context of the final advertisement.

In more upscale environments—or when trying to impress a new or prospective client—an agency may require a high level of finish and detail to the Advertising Illustrator's imagery. With modern computers, the ability to apply texture and polish to rough advertising illustration quickly has become more common, so much so that in some circumstances presentation illustration can be used for final print. When composing images electronically, the Advertising Illustrator scans a rough sketch and employs digital painting applications to render the image. The rough sketches imported into the digital environment range from roughest pencil sketch to partially rendered marker drawings, depending upon the needs of a specific assignment and an individual artist's preferences and abilities.

When drafting imagery, an Advertising Illustrator must always keep in mind the end goal—a final advertisement purchased by a client and presented to the public. As such, several additional elements play a part in the final product: headline text and body copy in printed ads, movable text and sound when drafting images used in television or Internet advertisements, graphic elements working with or superimposed over the image, and the client's branding identity. The illustrator's work is only part of a larger whole comprised of these other parts, and he or she must keep in mind how the image will be used (e.g., leave room for type to lay over parts of the image).

While not typical, as stated above, an Advertising Illustrator working on staff for an agency may be called upon to craft an image for final print. In most advertising circumstances, a staff illustrator's time is better served by moving on to the next series of projects in which preliminary imaging is needed. This scheduling requirement creates the need for an independent illustrator to draft images for final art when an advertiser chooses illustration, in most cases. When called upon to deliver imaging for final art, however, an Advertising Illustrator working on staff must keep something in mind: Any art created while working as an employee belongs to the agency. Unlike independent illustrators, staff illustrators work as employees of the agency, thereby making the agency the rightful owner of copyright and original art. In rare instances, an Advertising Illustrator with years of experience and a large body of work on which to draw can work out an individualized contract with an agency governing the use of any art he or she creates on-staff. Without a separate written agreement, however, an Advertising Illustrator owns no claim to the art created as an employee.

Salaries

Entry-level Advertising Illustrators typically don't command huge salaries in any region of the United States, though it's reasonable to expect to start at a higher salary range when living and working in larger metropolitan areas. For instance, the U.S. Department of Labor's Bureau of Labor Statistics lists New York state as having the third-largest concentration of workers per capita in the field including illustrators and the highest average wage in the field for 2003. Advertising agencies catering mostly to local or regional clients don't generate the same types of billing as those who serve large Fortune 500 companies and thus don't have the same resources to pay salaries. In the larger agencies, one can expect to start at a higher salary range but also to face much stiffer competition for available openings. Advertising Illustrators with years of experience and a large body of work either as an independent illustrator or as an Advertising Illustrator with another agency can expect higher compensation commensurate with experience.

Employment Prospects

Professional art colleges, private and public universities, and non–degree granting art schools send thousands of graduates into the general field of illustration every year. Add to that a workforce of nearly 10,000 already employed nationwide and one can easily divine that there are more applicants than positions available. The specific field of advertising illustration tends to burn many artists out, though, and turnover takes place at a high rate.

Advancement Prospects

Once proven in this specific field and adept at handling the pressures of the position, an Advertising Illustrator can expect performance-based bonuses and salary increases proportionate to his or her abilities.

Education and Training

A strong portfolio showcasing a broad range of subjects and a high degree of skill as a draftsman is the only rigid requirement for entry into this field. While one can develop these skills by combining postsecondary night courses at colleges or art schools with a concerted personal effort to expand one's visual vocabulary on one's own, the best training for this position takes place at professional art colleges. Curricula in these institutions have been specifically designed to train students for entry into this field. Additionally, relationships with fellow-minded students from these institutions often turn into job opportunities in the advertising field.

Familiarity with the workings of personal computers, especially the Macintosh platform and the graphics applications suited to it (Adobe Photoshop, Adobe Illustrator, Adobe InDesign, and QuarkXPress), also gives a prospective candidate a leg up in seeking employment. Listing experience with these applications puts an agency at ease when considering an applicant, as the work crafted by an Advertising Illustrator will invariably be subject to scanning and manipulation in a digital environment.

Experience, Skills, and Personality Traits

As the position requires an ability to draw consistently and on demand, the primary experience requirement for the prospective Advertising Illustrator is drawing. The ideal Advertising Illustrator is someone who draws as naturally as he or she breathes, and for most Advertising Illustrator hopefuls, that means uncountable hours spent working in sketchbooks to develop skills.

He or she must also have a highly developed ability to draw objects, people, and environments in proper proportion and in believable perspective. A sense of color relationships, two-dimensional design, and a working knowledge of typography all come in handy as well, since the work cre-ated by an Advertising Illustrator is merely a single piece of a puzzle using all these elements to create a final product.

An illustrator working on-staff for an advertising agency experiences unusually tight deadlines and quick turnaround times. As such, an Advertising Illustrator must possess an ability to manage stressful situations and juggle a large and often diverse workload. He or she must also have the ability to work with others in a team environment and accept criticism well, as there's absolutely no shortage of it in the advertising field. Everyone from coworkers to superiors to clients will from time to time have a word or two to say about how an Advertising Illustrator depicts an object.

Unions and Associations

There are several trade associations to which an Advertising Illustrator can belong and from which a great deal of education and networking opportunity can be had. Primary among them are the Illustrators' Partnership of America (IPA) and the Society of Illustrators (New York). These two organizations exist solely to benefit the professional practice of illustration, and while the primary focus of these two organizations is the independent illustrator, Advertising Illustrators share many of the same concerns facing the full-time freelancer. The country's leading professionals discuss and write at length about fees, contracts, and copyrights, and while this may not apply to life at an advertising agency, it's not unusual for a full-time staff Advertising Illustrator to bolster his or her income by taking freelance assignments. Additionally, the Graphic Artists Guild has chapters around the country that offer a very fine opportunity to network with like-minded professionals and those working in other disciplines.

Tips for Entry

1. Sharpen your ability to draw and be as all-inclusive as you can in your visual investigations into life.
2. Forge relationships with other people interested in or already working in the advertising field.
3. Apply for internships at advertising agencies while a student and learn as much as you can about the day-to-day working environment.

POINT-OF-PURCHASE DISPLAY DESIGNER

CAREER PROFILE

Duties: Designs and mocks up point-of-purchase (POP) displays for use in retail environments

Alternate Title(s): Designer

Salary Range: $25,000 to $100,000+

Employment Prospects: Fair

Advancement Prospects: Good

Best Geographical Location(s): Major urban areas with agencies specializing in point of purchase display design and production

Prerequisites:

Education or Training—Facility with three-dimensional design and two-dimensional design, both hand-drawn and computer-aided; knowledge of materials and processes employed in manufacture of POP displays

Experience—Entry-level, none; senior-level, minimum five years of experience in agencies specializing in production of POP displays

Special Skills and Personality Traits—Ability to juggle variety of projects at once; knowledge of perspective and ability to draw designs to proper scale; management skill

CAREER LADDER

```
┌─────────────────────────────────┐
│  Senior-level Point-of-Purchase │
│       Display Designer          │
└─────────────────────────────────┘

┌─────────────────────────────────┐
│  Junior-level Point-of-Purchase │
│       Display Designer          │
└─────────────────────────────────┘

┌─────────────────────────────────┐
│  Entry-level Point-of-Purchase  │
│       Display Designer          │
└─────────────────────────────────┘
```

Position Description

Almost everyone has seen the work of a Point-of-Purchase (POP) Display Designer, probably without being aware of it. At supermarket checkout lanes, in beverage cold-cases, hanging from ceilings in all manner of retail environments, and at movie theaters, the work of Point-of-Purchase Display Designers performs a myriad of functions.

Point-of-Purchase Display Designers create physical structures for advertising and merchandising purposes. Nearly every industry that sells its wares in a retail environment to consumers has need of point-of-purchase displays. These needs are different in some cases, but in most the chief function of a point-of-purchase display is to create a visual interest in the products being sold, much as it is in any advertising field. This need gets satisfied in differing ways. In many cases, Point-of-Purchase Display Designers create physical structures to hold merchandise or marketing materials (shelving units, counter display units, free-standing merchandise racks, etc.). In others, their job consists of designing items that affix to shelving or display units already in place, such as clip-ons or stick-ons. (The many types of clip-on and stick-on items are far too varied to list comprehensively, but some examples are wobbling displays that affix to the interior of cold cases selling bottled beverages with suction cups, shelf-talkers that affix with adhesives or clips or are held in place by gravity on shelving units in stores, and even static clings that affix directly to window glass or flooring to generate excitement about a product.) In any case, a Point-of-Purchase Display Designer must have the ability to design a physical product to meet the client's need.

Most Point-of-Purchase Display Designers work in agencies that cater to this specialization, and the structure within these agencies bears a striking resemblance to traditional advertising agencies. There are account representatives who drum up business by selling the agency's services to potential clients; senior-level Point-of-Purchase Display Designers who mirror a traditional agency's creative directors, mid-level positions resembling art director jobs, and entry-level Point-of-Purchase Display Designers who act similarly to graphic designers. There may even be on-staff illustrators and graphic designers to meet clients' needs in those regards. (For more information about those positions, see their descriptions elsewhere in this section.)

When a new project enters the workflow, an account representative presents the client's needs to the creative department and has initial discussions with the senior-level Point-of-Purchase Display Designer about how to best serve these needs. When going over these project parameters, one of the chief concerns discussed is permanent vs. temporary display design. Some examples of permanent display design are cabinetry built to house retail items, wire rack displays to hold lighter items such as eye glasses or makeup, mobile carts used to set up temporary store locations in malls and larger retail stores, and permanent shelving displays. Temporary displays break into two subcategories, semipermanent and throw-away. Semipermanent displays often incorporate materials similar to those used in crafting permanent displays, but the client's display needs dictate that the end product be removable from a retail environment quickly and fairly easily. A short list of semipermanent displays includes plastic racks or shelves manufactured for seasonal items, such as holiday decorations; wire shelving units that retrofit onto existing, permanent shelving units; wood pedestals to showcase the high-end product in a line of clothing or shoes; and plastic brochure dispensers for placement on counters. Throw-away displays are exactly what they sound like—items crafted out of impermanent materials such as corrugated cardboard, paper, or light plastics for use within a limited time frame. Examples of these are corrugated beverage holders for specialized merchandising opportunities, such as tie-ins to movies; light plastic containers for specialized seasonal products such as suntan lotions; the corrugated movie displays that adorn theater lobbies to attract attention to a soon-to-be-released motion picture (these often incorporate the use of lights or motion produced by battery-operated mechanisms affixed to the cardboard structure); and shelf-talkers printed on light cardboard called oak tag that affix to retail shelves in an impermanent way. These lists by no means include every type of display material and display usage, as such a list would require a great deal of space.

Once the large picture describing the needs of the project at hand has been established, the team of Point-of-Purchase Display Designers have brainstorming sessions similar to those in traditional advertising agencies. In these sessions, the designers cook up conceptual material about how best to solve the problem posed. Senior-level Point-of-Purchase Display Designers take the lead in these sessions, as they've accumulated more experience in the field. Knowing which materials will best suit a specific need, how best to affix a particular type of display to existing structures, and what processes can be employed to manufacture the displays in

the optimal materials are just a few of the areas in which Point-of-Purchase Display Designers can gain experience on the job.

Once a series of concepts has been drafted in rough form, the Point-of-Purchase Display Designers at all levels work to execute two-dimensional representations of the proposed physical structures. These two-dimensional representations are executed in different manners, depending upon the skill sets of the Point-of-Purchase Display Designers employed by a given agency. In some agencies, these artists create traditional ink and marker renderings, though this has become increasingly rare with the ubiquity of digital technology. In other circumstances, rough design sketches are scanned and turned into digital illustrations representing the proposed structural designs. This is the most common method of presenting display designs. Some Point-of-Purchase Display Designers also use three-dimensional rendering applications and build virtual models in a digital environment. Whatever the method, once the two-dimensional representations of the display designs have been executed, they are printed and most typically affixed to blackboards for presentation to the client.

After arriving at a final design, a Point-of-Purchase Display Designer provides detailed instructions for the creation of a model. The details include accurate measurements, suggestions of materials, and engineering guidelines. Once constructed, the account representative presents this scale model to the client for final sign-off. This scale model becomes the template used by manufacturers to mass-produce the physical structures seen by the buying public in retail environments.

Salaries

Entry-level Point-of-Purchase Display Designers typically don't command huge salaries in any region of the United States. At the highest end, however, region can play a much bigger part in determining salary. In any region with a high concentration of agencies specializing in point-of-purchase display design, such as the New York metropolitan area, competition between agencies for experienced, highly skilled Point-of-Purchase Display Designers will drive salary expectations up.

Employment Prospects

As stated above, a great demand exists for this specialty, even in a soft economy. For a prospective candidate in this field with knowledge of industrial design and the materials common to this industry, the chances increase to good if located in a region with a cluster of agencies specializing in point-of-purchase displays.

Advancement Prospects

Once given a start in an agency specializing in point-of-purchase display design, an ambitious and knowledgeable Point-of-Purchase Display Designer can work his or her

way up the ladder to more senior positions with hard work and dedication. This field remains very specialized, and those with a particular interest in it can find stable, career-advancing prospects.

Education and Training

Completing an undergraduate degree in industrial design prepares a candidate for most of the design challenges presented to an agency based upon clients' needs. A minor in graphic design, advertising, or marketing increases one's prospects greatly and gives candidates a leg up on seeking employment.

Experience, Skills, and Personality Traits

A good Point-of-Purchase Display Designer must have a working knowledge of several types of display material—plastics, wood, metal, cardboard, and paper—and how to design physical structures that will fulfill the requirements of any given assignment's requirements. This means the prospective candidate must know how to design an object that will support weight and stand upright and what materials will be required to manufacture the item in a cost-effective way. Education in these materials and design principals can be had at many professional art colleges and universities offering industrial design programs.

One also needs the ability to draw proposed structural designs to proper proportions in different perspectives, ideally both digitally and by hand. Additionally, the ideal candidate will possess the ability to work with the several types of physical materials listed herein and wield the necessary tools to mold these materials into scale models of the displays. While not necessarily a requirement, such a skill set added to those required increases one's bargaining position when seeking employment.

As anyone seeking employment in an agency environment would, the prospective Point-of-Purchase Display Designer needs to demonstrate the ability to work with others to arrive at the best possible design suited to the client's needs. In most agencies there exists a near-constant pressure to perform one's duties at optimal levels. In order to do this, a good Point-of-Purchase Display Designer should have the ability to manage stressful situations and work long days as he or she climbs the corporate ladder.

Unions and Associations

While there is no union protecting the labor interests of Point-of-Purchase Display Designers, POPAI (Point of Purchase Advertising International) is an excellent resource for anyone employed in the point-of-purchase display industry. It holds an annual show that exhibits the best work done every year in the POP industry, gives awards, publishes a Web site with a wealth of information and resources, and keeps track of trends in the industry.

Tips for Entry

1. Read industry-specific publications such as *POP Design* and *Point of Purchase Magazine* to become aware of trends and agencies in your area.
2. Hone your skills, both manual and digital, to their sharpest.
3. Apply your knowledge and skill to self-generated projects and present them in a clean, clearly organized portfolio.

BUSINESS

ART STORE MANAGER

CAREER PROFILE

Duties: Selects and purchases art supplies based on sales reports and inventory; establishes relationship with manufacturers and distributors; negotiates contracts; manages finances; schedules staff; handles payroll and rent; may help create and manage marketing and advertising campaigns; creates and maintains relationships with customers, artist community, and schools; may handle phones; may conduct demonstrations of materials and techniques

Alternate Title(s): None

Salary Range: $18,025 to $29,000+

Employment Prospects: Fair

Advancement Prospects: Good

Best Geographical Location(s): Major urban cities, but can manage a small store anywhere

Prerequisites:

   Education or Training—Four-year college degree (preferably a bachelor's of fine arts, or B.F.A.) preferred but may not be required if knowledgeable about art materials

   Experience—Creative background is helpful and strong interest in art materials and techniques most beneficial; one to three years of experience as cashier or stock clerk in art supply store

   Special Skills and Personality Traits—Organized; flexible; strong interpersonal skills; diplomatic; reliable and responsible; some agility with numbers; comfortable handling sales transactions; knowledgeable about art

CAREER LADDER

```
┌─────────────────────────────┐
│   Distribution Manager      │
└─────────────────────────────┘


┌─────────────────────────────┐
│      Store Manager          │
└─────────────────────────────┘


┌─────────────────────────────┐
│   Cashier or Stock Clerk    │
└─────────────────────────────┘
```

Position Description

An Art Store Manager needs to have a balance of business and communication skills. Managers of small stores have a more diverse job than those of larger chains as there are fewer, if any, staff members and therefore more responsibilities. Depending on staff size, managers may be responsible for managing and overseeing staff as well as customer service. Small store managers handle incoming telephone inquiries as well as on-site customers. Art Store Managers also maintain and/or oversee art supply inventories, checking regularly on the status of the stock. They need to be organized and on top of order and delivery schedules, keeping a list of what is running low. They need to be aware of the products that are in regular or high demand and when and how much to order to keep the shelves stocked and the product moving. The Art Store Manager may be required to receive and sign for stock deliveries as well as literally unpack the boxes and stock the shelves. It is important for the Art Store Manager to pay attention to details, making sure that what is delivered is exactly what was requested at the price it was quoted at. Art Store Managers may also need to be technologically comfortable if the store is computerized. They need to be comfortable handling cash and charge sales and may be responsible for banking for a small store.

Many art stores promote products and materials by scheduling demonstrations. Art Store Managers may be asked to set up and actually do the demonstrations. They develop relationships and maintain contact with factories and distributors. Art Store Managers are also responsible for customer service and must approach customers directly to make sure they are

finding what they need. Managers need to know the products, how they work, what materials they work best with, and more in order to intelligently field questions and make appropriate sales. The position is not necessarily one of intense sales; most artists who walk into an art supply store are there to buy something specific that they need to accomplish their work. But Art Store Managers with firm knowledge of the inventory will be able to reassure customers that they're educated and that the store is worth returning to.

Managers may also be responsible for invoicing and handling money, as well as some light bookkeeping and, if it's a small store, opening up in the morning and locking up at night. They might have the opportunity to work with the store owner on direct marketing, advertising, and promotional campaigns.

Salaries

Salaries for Art Store Managers can range from $18,025 to more than $29,000, depending on experience and the location and size of the art store. Large art store chains do not necessarily pay higher salaries to their staff. Some stores provide benefits to their managers to compensate for lower salaries, such as paid vacation time, employee discounts, and, in some instances, health insurance and employer-sponsored retirement plans.

Employment Prospects

Art Store Managers have more opportunities in major urban cities where artists flock. They also have opportunities in those areas where art schools are located and therefore art stores are needed. Because art supply stores are few and far between overall, however, competition is fierce, and employment prospects are only fair. While the Department of Labor's *Occupational Outlook Handbook* does not cite information specifically for Art Store Managers, employment for retail store managers overall is expected to grow more slowly than average, with an increase of only 3 to 9 percent through 2012. A decline in self-employed sales worker supervisors is also anticipated.

Advancement Prospects

Art Store Managers can move on to become buyers, distribution managers, or even, if working for a small store and the timing is right, the owner of the art store itself. Advancement is slower for Art Store Managers in small stores, something to bear in mind when considering where to work. In larger stores, Art Store Managers have more career options and can advance more quickly either at the same location or at another store within the chain.

Education and Training

Art stores may prefer a four-year college degree (preferably a B.F.A.), but it may not be necessary if an individual is interested in and knowledgeable about art materials. Many Art Store Managers gain ground-level experience by working for at least one to three years as cashiers, inventory clerks, or sales associates. Larger art stores will typically have formal training programs for managers, where they will learn all functions of the business, from budgeting, marketing, and management to purchasing and product preparation.

Experience, Skills, and Personality Traits

Because the Art Store Manager will be immersed in art supplies and speaking daily with artists about the products and their work, a creative background is helpful as well as a strong interest in and knowledge of art materials and techniques. Customer service is a key aspect of this job, and patience and diplomacy are essential, particularly when facing a difficult client. The Art Store Manager must not only have strong people skills but a good head for business. He or she must be organized, self-disciplined, and have some agility with numbers. The Art Store Manager must also be able to motivate staff and communicate clearly with customers.

Unions and Associations

Art Store Managers may join local community associations such as their chamber of commerce for networking purposes and to increase visibility of their stores.

Tips for Entry

1. Take time to figure out the environment you like. There are many different kinds of art stores you can work in, from crafts to painting supplies. There are chains and then there are the mom-and-pops. Which suits you best? If there's a store you like and frequent, see if you can work there.
2. Research and identify the stores, and then contact them to see if they are hiring.
3. Check classified listings on the Internet (e.g., http://www.craigslist.org) as well as local newspapers and art publications.
4. Once you get the job, learn as much as you can about the products. Read everything.
5. Talk to customers and ask them what products they're using and why. You need to understand the reasoning for their purchases so that the next time they come in, you can point them in the right direction. This information is also useful to the store owner when deciding what to stock the shelves with next.

ART STORE OWNER

CAREER PROFILE

Duties: Determines store location, design, and set-up; creates business plans and budgets; hires and manages staff; oversees inventory; may order supplies; develops and maintains relationships with distributors and manufacturers; builds relationships with customers; oversees payroll, billing, and tax payments; sets retail prices; may network and create relationships with local community businesses and schools; may create advertising and marketing campaigns

Alternate Title(s): None

Salary Range: $30,000 to $80,000+

Employment Prospects: Fair

Advancement Prospects: Poor

Best Geographical Location(s): Major urban cities

Prerequisites:

    Education or Training—A four-year college degree; business management courses or background helpful

    Experience—Two to five years of prior experience as an art store manager

    Special Skills and Personality Traits—Entrepreneurial; flexible; knowledgeable about art supplies; professional; able to handle stress; diplomatic; strong communication skills; business savvy; solid management skills

CAREER LADDER

```
┌─────────────────────────────────────┐
│          Art Store Owner            │
└─────────────────────────────────────┘


┌─────────────────────────────────────┐
│         Art Store Manager           │
└─────────────────────────────────────┘


┌─────────────────────────────────────┐
│ Cashier, Sales Clerk, or Fine Artist│
└─────────────────────────────────────┘
```

Position Description

Art Store Owners deal with and oversee all aspects of the store, from hiring and managing staff and pricing items to promoting the store and dealing with challenging customers. They create business plans and budgets for the company and consult regularly with a bookkeeper or accounting department to follow profits and losses and ensure the company is in tax compliance. They analyze financial reports to determine which products sell best. Depending on staff structure, they may work closely with a store manager to set prices, order inventory, and stock shelves. They decide on the look of the store itself to help make it an inviting place to shop. The lighting, shelves, wall, and floor colors and textures, lengths and widths of aisles, how and where products are stocked and displayed, cash register location(s), sig-

nage, and more are important factors in customer satisfaction and strong sales.

Store owners create store policy and make sure that policy is enforced. They are the final authority store staff will approach when faced with a difficult customer or issue, and they will therefore spend some time mediating situations.

Research and marketing are other key aspects of the Art Store Owner's job. Owners need to understand their clientele in order to best serve them and generate a profit. Owners research and establish the services the store offers. Depending on what they learn, they may choose to focus solely on the sales of art supplies, or they may want to offer other services. They size up their clientele and the market and decide on the services that will fill a niche and attract more customers. If they choose to offer canvas stretching

and priming and framing, they research and secure a canvas supplier and a framer.

Store owners develop and maintain relationships with a wide variety of people: staff, customers, manufacturers, distributors, local business owners, schools, and more. They may network at various events to help promote the store. They may also work closely with the store manager and other staff to create advertising and direct marketing campaigns to further business.

Salaries

Salaries for Art Store Owners can range between $30,000 to more than $80,000. They greatly depends on the geographical location of the store and number of years in business. Owners of new, small stores don't usually start making a net profit for at least one year. The first one to three years of any business are generally considered the break-even, if that, phase, which is why small store owners need to budget a salary for themselves. They must be sure to give themselves a paycheck but invest the rest of the money back into the business.

Employment Prospects

Art Store Owners are self-employed, and therefore employment prospects are driven by the economy and the need for art supplies. The U.S. Department of Labor's *Occupational Outlook Handbook* predicts that from now until 2012, the employment of artists is expected to grow as fast as the average (10 to 20 percent), and with that employment comes wages to purchase supplies. If the Art Store Owner chooses the store location wisely and knows how to effectively promote, he or she may be able to work successfully for many years. Be aware, however, that owners of small art stores still face the daunting challenge of competing with larger chains.

Advancement Prospects

Art Store Owners are at the top of the staff ladder. Owners of large chains can retire and hold an active seat on the board of directors. Small store owners who have a successful store can branch out and open stores in other locations.

Education and Training

A four-year college degree is helpful, with courses in business management and small business ownership. A strong

knowledge of art supplies, materials, and techniques is critical. Art Store Owners must continually learn about the business by reading books, magazines, and Internet articles on these subjects.

Experience, Skills, and Personality Traits

Art Store Owners have a diverse, challenging job and must have flexible, entrepreneurial spirits to thrive. They must be open to learning, always reading about new products to stay on top of the market and know where and how to get these products at the most feasible cost. Owners must also be outgoing, able to develop rapport with their customers to understand their work and their needs. The job can be stressful because they're managing a store and a staff and dealing with customers; patience, diplomacy, and professionalism will be their strong suit. They also need to be fair, effective leaders to create a loyal, hardworking staff. Strong business skills and a head for numbers are also extremely important.

Unions and Associations

Art Store Owners may want to join their local chamber of commerce, as well as other associations prospective clients may belong to, for networking and educational purposes.

Tips for Entry

1. Check out other art stores. See what kind of store you want yours to be.
2. Location, location, location. Identify where your store should be located and why. If you can't afford a main street, opt for the closest side street. Don't be afraid to open near the competition. You'll already have a built-in market.
3. Find schools in the area you can approach to advertise your store. Decide whether you'll offer students a discount.
4. Diversify your services (e.g., offer canvas stretching and primed canvases). That extra income will be important. Learn how to stretch the canvas yourself, and if you can't do it, hire people who can. Find a wholesaler for the linens.
5. Set up a budget. If you need to renovate a store, do as much as possible yourself. Keep it simple. People want visual ease and access. Smaller stores should stock everything within the line of sight.

FRAMER

CAREER PROFILE

Duties: Meets with clients and reviews and discusses artwork to be framed; recommends framing materials and designs to best preserve and present the artwork; commissions and/or oversees creation of frame; has glass or acrylic sized; may cut mats and mount artwork; hires and manages staff; oversees finances and payroll

Alternate Title(s): Preservationist

Salary Range: $20,000 to $100,000+

Employment Prospects: Fair

Advancement Prospects: Fair

Best Geographical Location(s): Major urban cities, but a store can be set up in any community anywhere

Prerequisites:

Education or Training—Four-year college degree in art or liberal arts helpful; classes or on-site training in framing important

Experience—One to three years of experience working as an artist, e.g., printmaker, painter, illustrator, or visual artist; one to two years of experience training in a frame shop

Special Skills and Personality Traits—Artistic; strong aesthetic eye and awareness; deep knowledge of framing materials and techniques; solid understanding of various art media; keen communication and customer service skills; sound business management abilities; diplomatic; patient

CAREER LADDER

```
┌─────────────────────────────┐
│    Frame Business Owner      │
└─────────────────────────────┘

┌─────────────────────────────┐
│           Framer            │
└─────────────────────────────┘

┌─────────────────────────────┐
│       Assistant Framer      │
└─────────────────────────────┘
```

Position Description

The Framer's primary responsibility is to help enhance artwork, whether it is a painting, illustration, photograph, or collage, and to preserve it for future enjoyment and presentation. The Framer approaches the artwork with two aims:

- Conservation—The mission is not to decorate the art so that it matches the couch and living room, but rather to preserve the artwork and protect it from dirt, dust, and environmental hazards that can wear away at it.
- Enhancement—The Framer makes an effort not to distort the artwork and stays close to its original intention.

Framers have strong knowledge of all of the materials needed to effectively protect the artwork and of how to determine what to use. They work with a variety of acid-free papers and ultraviolet glass or acrylic. The best Framers are those who respect the artwork. They review the artwork with clients and evaluate the framing materials that will work best. They recommend materials for framing to their clients not based on expense, but rather on the best modes of conservation. Framers look at artwork from a historical perspective, approaching decisions about materials and designs by always asking the question, *how will this be seen 50 years from now?* They aim to put the art into the best and most appropriate light, regardless of what it is.

Framers' duties are diversified, and depending on the way the business is set up, the duties can be divided among staff. They or one of their staff members or outside contractors are responsible for:

- Creating the physical frame for the artwork. This might be done by a woodworker either on premises at the frame shop or offsite.
- Fitting the glass and closing the frame, making sure to keep it dust- and dirt-free. ("Fitters" often handle this aspect of the job.)
- Handling and mounting the artwork. Framers may have "artwork mounters" or "art handlers" on staff to take care of this critical part of the job. They are usually the most trained as to aesthetics. They put the hinges in the back and put in the mat. These tasks are interchangeable and usually handled by one or several people.
- Customer service and sales. Typically, Framers who own small businesses work up front, meeting and greeting clients. They are responsible for clearly communicating the full spectrum of the job, quoting and negotiating prices, and in many instances educating the client about framing materials and techniques.

Salaries

Framer salaries can range from $20,000 to $100,000 or more, depending on business size and customer base. Framers for high-end galleries, museums, or wealthy collectors can earn upwards of $100,000. Those who have a more diversified clientele or operate a small mom-and-pop shop may realize lower salaries. Location, overhead, staff size, clientele, and materials used are all factors in determining a Framer's salary.

Employment Prospects

Employment of Framers is driven by the economy. Framers perform an aesthetic service, and therefore when the economy takes a downturn, people tend to scale back on the things that entertain and bring pleasure and focus instead on sheer necessity. Framers who work with museums, galleries, and well-heeled customers fare best. As framing becomes more specialized, however, there may be greater opportunities for Framers with backgrounds in conservation and preservation.

Advancement Prospects

Framers who own small businesses are at the pinnacle of their careers. They can further their careers by securing an advanced degree in art conservation and restoration and securing work as conservators or restorers with museums. Staff Framers with several years of experience can always start their own businesses.

Education and Training

A four-year college degree is recommended, though not critical. Artists can learn framing in art school and also by working with a Framer for one to three years before joining the staff of a framing business. Framers who have a B.F.A. or M.F.A., however, and have studied art conservation and restoration will be able to serve either a wider clientele or a more specific niche, depending on their area of study. Framers can receive certification from various associations, but the certification may not cover areas of conservation and restoration, nor will it necessarily teach the aesthetics of framing. Framers can stay abreast of framing industry trends and new and improved materials and techniques by researching the Internet and reading books and magazines such as *Décor, Photo Marketing,* and *Picture Framing.*

Experience, Skills, and Personality Traits

Framers enjoy artwork and are aesthetically aware. They must be able to respect all types of art. They must be flexible and patient, as they may need to educate clients about framing materials and techniques. If working with a diverse clientele, they must be able to treat a five-year-old girl's crayon drawing on construction paper as seriously as the professional artist's oil painting on canvas.

Clients generate work for Framers, so it is key that a Framer either have strong communication and people skills, or be sure to surround himself or herself with employees who can handle this end of the job. Clients often need guidance, information, and an explanation of the materials and the fees for framing their art. Diplomacy and patience are key, as well as an ability to gauge where your client is coming from. Some clients will be well educated and know what they want; others will need to understand more before deciding which direction to take. The business is based on trust and word of mouth; a good reputation for professional, quality work will lead to repeat business.

Unions and Associations

Framers can join the Professional Picture Framers Association (PPFA) for networking, education, and industry reports.

Tips for Entry

1. Call local frame shops and ask them if you can come in for an informational meeting. Tell them you are interested in framing. See if you can watch a Framer in action.
2. Check the classified advertisements in your local newspapers for "Art Framers." Call art galleries to find out who handles their framing. Contact those Framers for an informational interview. Networking is always helpful. The more people you meet, the greater your odds of finding work.

ARTISTS' REPRESENTATIVE

CAREER PROFILE

Duties: Solicits work for artists; provides art and talent for clients; provides project business management for artists, that is, negotiates and reviews contracts, handles accounts payable and receivable, designs or helps design portfolios, coordinates and implements promotions

Alternate Title(s): Agent

Salary Range: $30,000 to $100,000+

Employment Prospects: Fair

Advancement Prospects: Fair (Artists' Representatives are generally sole proprietors. Advancement prospects may not apply.)

Best Geographical Location(s): Major cities, urban centers

Prerequisites:

Education or Training—Four-year degree in art preferable, but can have business background provided there is a strong knowledge of the art industry and art business

Experience—Two- to five-year apprenticeship with art buyer or representative

Special Skills and Personality Traits—Excellent communication, organization, and business management skills; excellent sales savvy; good interpersonal skills; entrepreneurial spirit; solid knowledge of art media and types of artists chosen to represent; thorough awareness and understanding of art industry practices and ethical standards

CAREER LADDER

```
┌─────────────────────────────────────────┐
│  Owner, Artists' Representative Firm     │
└─────────────────────────────────────────┘

┌─────────────────────────────────────────┐
│       Artists' Representative            │
└─────────────────────────────────────────┘

┌─────────────────────────────────────────┐
│       Assistant Art Buyer or             │
│    Assistant Artists' Representative     │
└─────────────────────────────────────────┘
```

Position Description

Artists' Representatives help artists secure work. Artists' Representatives usually represent a group of artists who work in certain disciplines and/or have a certain slant or message in the content of their work. They usually choose artists based on their own personal tastes and either the potential or proven marketability of the artwork. Illustrators and photographers are the types of artists who often choose representation. Typically, each Artists' Representative tends to represent an average of eight to 13 artists.

Many Artists' Representatives have either trained or have worked professionally as artists. They understand the creative spirit and appreciate how important it is for artists to focus solely on their artwork. Artists' Representatives handle the business side of things so that artists can stay creatively productive. They promote artists by:

- coordinating promotional mailings, such as postcards and brochures
- selecting and placing artwork in industry directories (e.g., *American Showcase, The Black Book, Graphic Artists Guild Directory of Illustration,* etc.)
- helping to create a Web presence
- networking with prospective clients

Technology has changed the scope of the business. Years ago, only local talent was represented to a local clientele. With the advent of e-mail, the Internet, and express mail services, Artists' Representatives can now, if they choose, match international talent with an international client base without ever leaving their office.

Artists' Representatives usually own their own businesses or partner with other representatives who specialize in different media and fields. An Artists' Representative is often the first and only impression a client has of the artist, which is why it is crucial that the representative have a solid and visually appealing brand identity. They must have their own logo, Web site, stationery, advertising, and promotions in place so that both the artist and client recognize their company in the marketplace.

Artists' Representatives review their artists' portfolios and help them arrange their work, or design their portfolios so that their talent is represented in the best and most marketable light. They offer an objective, keen eye that helps the artist gain recognition. Alternatively, clients can now have more of their work done in-house, thanks to advanced technology. Artists' Representatives have to be sharp marketers to succeed in this business.

In addition to creating promotions for their artists, Artists' Representatives spend time contacting and meeting prospective clients to present their artists' portfolios. When the client offers a project, the Artists' Representative shares the proposed contract first with the artist, recommending any changes to terms if needed, and then negotiates the final terms with the client. Artists' Representatives also handle billing clients and collecting payments. They stay abreast of business issues by joining associations and attending industry-related workshops and programs. If you are self-motivated, have a strong entrepreneurial spirit, and can work with independent creative souls, this type of work may be for you.

Salaries

Artists' Representatives' salaries depend on the number of artists they represent, the popularity of the artist(s), and the number of assignments garnered each year. Artists' Representatives charge typically between 25 to 30 percent per commissioned project fee. Based upon these variables, earnings will vary depending upon which artists are represented, how many artists are represented, and the markets to which the representative sells. For instance, an Artists' Representative selling the work of a dozen or fewer small- to mid-market artists would expect to earn $30,000 to $50,000 a year, while another Artists' Representative selling the work in a major market such as New York City with a similar number of artists could earn more than $100,000.

Employment Prospects

Prospects for employment in this field are only fair because computers have changed the way artists get work and the way clients themselves work. While it is still possible for Artists' Representatives to break into the field, secure their own group of artists, and make inroads to steady projects, it takes an extraordinary combination of skills these days to make a living.

Advancement Prospects

A two- to five-year apprenticeship with an art buyer or representative, coupled with a degree in art or related work experience, is usually sufficient to advance to Artists' Representative. As in many jobs, advancement depends on one's drive, persistence, and reputation. In some cases, an apprentice or sales associate at an Artists' Representative agency will leave the fold to form his or her own agency. In others, sales associates with many years at the same agency will be invited to buy into the partnership.

Education and Training

While it is most beneficial to have a four-year degree in art, it is by no means a critical requirement. What is most essential is a thorough understanding of the art business—knowing the medium of art itself, the artists, the buyers, and the market, as well as a strong knowledge of what it takes to run a business. Artists' Representatives can learn about art business issues by attending professional education workshops run by associations such as the Graphic Artists Guild, the American Institute for Graphic Arts (AIGA), Volunteer Lawyers for the Arts, and other such groups. In the day-to-day maintenance of their own business, they can learn by participating in their local chamber of commerce and other such associations with the mission to support and educate small business owners.

Experience, Skills, and Personality Traits

The type of person who is happiest working as an Artists' Representative has a strong desire to own his or her own business, is truly sensitive to artists and appreciates their independent spirits, is a good listener, and has an innate ability to juggle projects and people. This is a multilayered job because you are creating and running your *own* business while you are helping to create and run certain aspects of your *artists'* business. Simultaneous to those two missions, you are also listening to what the client wants and needs, sizing up the projects, and determining whether your artist and your client can work together. In a sense, you are a matchmaker. Patience, excellent negotiating skills, diplomacy, and strong ethical standards are just some of the traits that make for a good Artists' Representative.

Unions and Associations

Artists' Representatives can participate in activities of membership organizations such as the Graphic Artists Guild, the Society of Illustrators, The Society of Photographers and Artists Representatives (SPAR), the Illustrators' Partnership of America (IPA), and the American Society of Magazine Photographers (ASMP).

Tips for Entry

1. The best way to enter this field is to apprentice. Research and identify the Artists' Representatives whose body of work represented visually appeals to you. Make a list of the people you would like to work with and write down your reasons for each choice. Call or e-mail the Artists' Representative, briefly introduce yourself, and tell him or her you're interested in this career and in working for him or her in an entry-level capacity.

2. Join associations that Artists' Representatives belong to and network.

3. Join associations that artists belong to and network with them also. You have to learn several sides of the business, and you especially must know your artists.

4. Take continuing education classes that will teach you tips and tactics for starting and running your own business.

LAWYER

Duties: Reviews and negotiates contracts; meets with clients to review cases; strategizes approaches to cases; helps protect artists' rights; defends artists in legal disputes; writes letters; may litigate cases in the courtroom; may write and lecture on artists' legal issues

Alternate Title(s): Attorney; in some instances may be known as Business Manager

Salary Range: $45,000 to $150,000+

Employment Prospects: Good

Advancement Prospects: Good

Best Geographical Location(s): Major urban cities

Prerequisites:

Education or Training—Four-year college degree; three years of law school; must pass bar examination; advanced degree may be required for specialized fields of practice

Experience—Law clerk experience; two to three years of full-time experience with a firm or agency

Special Skills and Personality Traits—Strong verbal, written, and analytical skills; sharp, creative thinker; logical; personable and outgoing; well versed in copyright, trademark, intellectual property, and other arts-related issues; entrepreneurial; risk-taker; flexible; excellent multitasker

```
Partner or Owner of Firm
```

```
Lawyer
```

```
Law Clerk or Law Intern
```

Position Description

Lawyers who represent artists provide a variety of services to help secure and protect their rights. The scope of their work depends on their field of specialization. Lawyers who specialize in intellectual property may review contracts presented to artists by corporations, agencies, artists' representatives, and so on to ensure that the terms are legal and in accordance with industry standards, that the artists' copyrights are appropriately protected, and that the agreement is in the artists' best interests. The Lawyer will make changes to the contract if needed and either forward it to the artist or send it directly to the artist's client for review. Lawyers may draft contracts on behalf of artists for various professional and personal projects. Some Lawyers may focus solely on administration, handling forms for Social Security, benefits, pensions, and more. Tax Lawyers help artists with their state sales taxes. Artists who take their clients to court hire litigation or trial Lawyers to represent them. Litigation Lawyers

analyze, research, and prepare artists' cases, secure expert witnesses if needed, select juries, and speak on the behalf of artists in courtrooms.

Artists need the most help and protection in the intellectual property arena, meaning predominantly copyright and trademarks. The work they create is, by all rights, theirs. According to the 1989 U.S. copyright law, as soon as an artist creates a piece of artwork, he or she is the owner of this artwork unless ownership has been transferred in writing. Despite this law, with the development and evolution of the Internet and other technologies, it has been easier than ever before for people to take artwork, use it for multiple purposes, and distribute it throughout the world in any number of ways, all without securing the artist's approval and without paying the artist. Intellectual property Lawyers help artists protect their work by making sure the contracts are fair and that the terms cover all of the bases. They cross off the work-for-hire and buyout clauses if the artist is not interested in selling the rights to his or her work. They advise clients about registering artwork with the copyright or trademark offices and help them complete appropriate registration forms.

Lawyers are advocates and educators. Artists fully commit themselves to creating art and often don't have the time to search through dense contracts to decipher the language. They rely on their Lawyers to unearth the loopholes and fix them. Lawyers have a great deal of responsibility and authority in the arts industry. They maintain this authority and secure respect by speaking at association conferences, teaching workshops, and regularly reading and participating in online forums that focus on artists' issues. They develop a dialogue and rapport with their clientele by always asking questions and sharing information and news. They read voraciously to keep abreast of industry practices and abuses and past and current court cases and rulings.

Salaries

Depending on their clientele, specialization, and location, Lawyers can expect to earn salaries ranging anywhere from $45,000 to more than $150,000. Lawyers (who may be referred to as "Business Managers" in this instance) with famous artist clients will command salaries closer to $150,000 and more. Litigation Lawyers who specialize in intellectual property may also earn higher salaries. Some Lawyers may also volunteer time to advise or represent artists or arts organizations on certain issues and cases.

Employment Prospects

Overall, employment of Lawyers is expected to increase by only 10 to 20 percent, which is about as fast as average according to the U.S. Department of Labor's *Occupational Outlook Handbook (OOH)*. Competition will be fierce, but the need for artists' Lawyers will parallel the growth of artists' businesses. As more of the population uses the Web and infringes on artists' rights, Lawyers will be called upon to defend those rights.

Advancement Prospects

Independent Lawyers do not advance within their own law firms. They can, however, expand their area of expertise by getting advanced degrees. They can also branch out into other areas by teaching students, speaking on panels at conferences and educational programs, and writing articles and columns.

Education and Training

Lawyers must be licensed to practice law. A four-year college degree, three years at law school, and passing the bar examination are what it takes to be admitted to the bar. Lawyers must attend a law school accredited by the American Bar Association (ABA) to qualify for most state bar examinations. Some states may include a multistate essay examination (MEE) in their bar examination. Many are now requiring the inclusion of the multistate bar examination (MBE), which covers broad issues of interest, according to the *OOH*. Law students often acquire practical experience by participating in legal aid clinics or clerking for judges, law firms, government agencies, or legal departments of arts organizations. Lawyers who start their own businesses typically have at least three to five years of prior experience as staff lawyers. Lawyers must continue to learn; they must constantly read about issues and practices in the business. This is so important that many states and jurisdictions are now mandating Lawyers have continuing legal education (CLE) credits by taking additional courses.

Experience, Skills, and Personality Traits

Effective, successful Lawyers appreciate and respect their clients. Artists' Lawyers need to understand their clients and be patient, clear communicators to help educate them about their rights. Lawyers must be personable and able to convince their clients of their skills to secure their trust. Every day is different, and Lawyers must be able to handle the chaos, juggle projects, intelligently apprise clients over the phone and in person of their cases, write letters on their behalf, and, if litigation is their specialty, represent clients in court. It's a whirlwind of activity, and to maintain a good reputation and attract more business, Lawyers must stay sharp and focused.

Unions and Associations

Once they pass the bar examination, Lawyers are admitted to the ABA. Many join their local chamber of commerce for networking and speaking opportunities. They can also become associate members of such organizations as the American Institute of Graphic Arts (AIGA), the American Society of Media Photographers (ASMP), the Society of Photographers and Artists Representatives (SPAR), and other organizations. They may also participate in and contribute to online artists' forums such as The Ispot.

Tip for Entry

1. Work in the business! If you plan to work with artists, you need not only the legal knowledge of art but also first-hand appreciation of it to truly be passionate about it. Know the business inside out; it's the only way you will be able to effectively and intelligently represent your clientele.
2. Find work as a gallery assistant or an artist's assistant. Get a job in a design firm while you're in school or your first year out. Get in there so you will learn the nuts and bolts of the business from the inside.
3. Find a niche and become a guru of that niche. Make sure it's an area that the marketplace demands.

ART ORGANIZATIONS

ADMINISTRATIVE ASSISTANT

CAREER PROFILE

Duties: Arranges conference calls and meetings; may handle travel arrangements; may field phone calls; organizes and maintains e-mail and paper files; manages databases; conducts research; may train and orient new staff members; handles correspondence; provides administrative support to staff as needed

Alternate Title(s): Assistant, Coordinator, Office Manager, Secretary

Salary Range: $20,000 to $50,000+

Employment Prospects: Good

Advancement Prospects: Excellent

Best Geographical Location(s): Major urban cities

Prerequisites:

    Education or Training—High school education and strong communication skills for entry-level jobs. Four-year college degree and/or administrative business classes at vocational school for more advanced jobs

    Experience—Entry-level positions require solid interpersonal and computer skills. More advanced positions that command higher salaries require at least one to five years of prior office experience and strong project management skills

    Special Skills and Personality Traits—Extremely organized; able to juggle projects and meet deadlines; flexible and outgoing; team-player skilled at dealing with people; strong communicator; strong computer skills; good research skills; interest in and awareness of the arts helps

CAREER LADDER

The career ladder for Administrative Assistant can vary, depending on the area of arts administration that interests you most. One ladder might be:

```
┌─────────────────────────────────────┐
│       Director of Fund-raising        │
└─────────────────────────────────────┘


┌─────────────────────────────────────┐
│  Assistant Director of Fund-raising   │
└─────────────────────────────────────┘


┌─────────────────────────────────────┐
│       Administrative Assistant,       │
│         Fund-raising Department        │
└─────────────────────────────────────┘
```

Position Description

The Administrative Assistant plays a key role in helping to maintain the daily functions of an arts organization. As the title suggests, the work is administrative by nature, entailing maintaining files (both online and hard copy), databases, correspondence, and other paperwork. Administrative Assistants are also responsible for fielding phone calls, in some instances directly handling inquiries from the general public. The Administrative Assistant must have a strong working knowledge of the organization—its mission, publications, calendar of events, departments, and staff.

Administrative Assistants work and communicate with a wide range of people, including the immediate department that they support, human resources, accounting, computer support, outside vendors, the organizations' members, and/or the general public. Excellent verbal and written skills are therefore essential, as are organizational skills. In some organizations, the Administrative Assistant may also be the office manager and therefore responsible for maintaining and ordering office supplies, as well as speaking with vendors and service bureaus (for things such as telephone and voice mail, printers, credit card, water cooler, office equipment, and office cleaners).

In one working day, an Administrative Assistant's to-do list might include:

- set up conference call for director and five off-site individuals
- schedule staff meeting
- make travel and hotel arrangements for department to attend arts management conference

- research schools offering internship programs for arts organizations
- draft intern job description
- type and submit director's expense report to accounting
- draft thank-you letter to recent interviewee for associate position
- enter prospects' information into database

The job is varied, and the Administrative Assistant must be able to accomplish all tasks and know the status of each and every project. The successful Administrative Assistant knows how to keep all of the plates spinning and off the floor!

Salaries

An Administrative Assistant's salary depends upon the art organization's budget and staff size. Without previous office experience, entry-level Administrative Assistants can expect salaries that range anywhere from $20,000 to $30,000 per year. Individuals with office skills and previous work background may see salaries ranging from $30,000 to $50,000 or more. Administrative Assistants who train to keep current on software programs, as well as those who are certified, command higher salaries.

Employment Prospects

Administrative Assistant positions are expected to grow more slowly than other jobs until 2012, with a projected 3 to 9 percent increase over the next few years, according to the Bureau of Labor Statistics. In the past, many Administrative Assistants worked specifically for one person. Computers have revolutionized offices, enabling employees to easily handle much of the work that once was within their assistant's realm. The trend has been for Administrative Assistants to work for a department within the company, supporting several staffers rather than one individual. The Administrative Assistant's role is still critical, and there are opportunities to be had, but be aware that the job is evolving and continues to evolve as technology improves.

Advancement Prospects

Administrative Assistants have diverse opportunities to advance, depending upon their strengths, talents, and interests. Administrative Assistants can advance to the next level within the department they are working in, provided they demonstrate ease and confidence in their tasks and a strong knowledge of the company. For instance, an Administrative Assistant in the development department of an arts organization works closely with the associate and/or assistant development director. If the Administrative Assistant is able to accomplish the administrative tasks quickly and accurately, he or she will have time to focus on the larger development goals and help contribute to achieving them. Within one to three years, the Administrative Assistant might advance to one of these positions as they become vacant.

Education and Training

Entry-level Administrative Assistants may only need a high school degree, but the years of education will also dictate the salary. Those who have a four-year college degree often secure more money. Administrative Assistants can further their careers by getting certified. According to the U.S. Department of Labor's *Occupational Outlook Handbook,* associations such as the International Association of Administrative Professionals and Legal Secretaries, Inc., will test and certify for proficiency in entry-level office skills. After gaining experience by working a certain required number of years, Administrative Assistants can test for Certified Administrative Professional (CAP).

Experience, Skills, and Personality Traits

Most arts organizations are interested in hiring Administrative Assistants who have a combination of communication and technological skills and an interest in and appreciation for the arts. Because the job can vary widely, they look for people with flexible attitudes who can work independently and as part of a team. Administrative Assistants need to be self-initiating but also take direction well, characteristics that are not easily combined. Writing and editing skills will be important for print and online correspondence. An ability to work with database software and spreadsheet programs will also come in handy. Patient, adaptable, creative, and enthusiastic individuals who care about the mission of the organization do well in these positions.

Unions and Associations

For career support, networking opportunities, and continuing education, Administrative Assistants can join the National Association of Executive Secretaries and Administrative Assistants and the International Association of Administrative Professionals.

Tips for Entry

1. If you need to get your computer skills up to speed, check your local colleges for continuing education courses in MS Office and other computer programs. Some schools may offer certification programs in business administration that may be worth pursuing.
2. Check the classified advertisements, both online and in print publications, for administrative assistant positions in arts organizations. Surf the Web and make a list of arts organizations you would like to participate in.
3. Contact the heads of the departments that interest you to see if there is a need for administrative assistance. These departments might be communications, development and/or fund-raising, public relations, etc. You can also contact the human resources department, but be aware they are often barraged with resumes and you might get lost in the mix. It's always effective to contact the head of a specific department directly, as he or she will frequently have a clear idea of staffing challenges and needs.

ASSISTANT DIRECTOR

CAREER PROFILE

Duties: Assists director with administrative tasks, strategic plans, development, and special projects; organizes retreats; sets meetings and appointments, manages calendar; handles budget/expense report work; acts as liaison with board of directors, staff, volunteers, committees, consultants, constituents, media, and the general public; attends board meetings; keeps pulse on internal human resources; manages and trains interns

Alternate Title(s): Director's Assistant

Salary Range: $30,000 to $50,000+

Employment Prospects: Good

Advancement Prospects: Good

Best Geographical Location(s): Major urban cities

Prerequisites:

Education or Training—Four-year college degree, preferably in the arts; some positions may require a graduate degree

Experience—Prior work experience in an arts organization is important; two to four years of experience as intern and/or executive assistant in arts organization

Special Skills and Personality Traits—Strong background and interest in the arts; excellent communicator; extremely organized; self-motivated; team player; flexible; versatile; open to new challenges

CAREER LADDER

```
┌─────────────────────────────────────┐
│   Associate Development Director     │
└─────────────────────────────────────┘

┌─────────────────────────────────────┐
│         Assistant Director           │
└─────────────────────────────────────┘

┌─────────────────────────────────────┐
│   Intern / Gallery Assistant /       │
│      Executive Assistant             │
└─────────────────────────────────────┘
```

Position Description

The Assistant Director is the right-hand aide to the executive director and plays an important role in an organization. This is a high-profile job that requires great flexibility and solid communication skills. The Assistant Director supports the executive director in a wide variety of administrative tasks, which can include daily business correspondence (mail and e-mail), fielding telephone calls, maintaining the calendar, setting appointments, and handling database work. The Assistant Director also works with the executive director on his or her business cash management, organizing budgets and managing payables and receivables. In some cases, the Assistant Director may be required to create budgets, cash reports, and invoices. When the executive director is out of the office, the Assistant Director is often asked to handle e-mails, phone calls, mail, and inquiries in his or her absence. Reliability and consistency are important. What's most essential is the Assistant Director's ability to form a strong, trusting relationship with the executive director.

Assistant Directors attend staff meetings and participate to varying degrees in strategic as well as financial planning for the organization. In some organizations, Assistant Directors pitch in on fund-raising, outreach, public relations, and other mission-oriented drives. Depending on the size of the organization, executive directors' may also rely on their assistants for feedback regarding the overall morale and efficiency of the staff. The Assistant Director interacts frequently with all staff members, more so than the director, and therefore has a more accurate overview of how the staff is functioning, what is working well, what needs improvement, and where potential issues lurk. Arts organizations often hire interns to assist on short- and long-term projects, or to provide general staff support as needed. The Assistant Director may be asked to train and oversee the interns. The Assistant Director may be required to attend board meetings and may take the minutes. The Assistant Director participates in meetings with artists, donors, consultants, and various committees as directed by the executive director.

Salaries

Salaries for Assistant Directors range from $30,000 to $50,000 and more, depending on the organization's size and budget. Large museums may pay slightly more than the small nonprofit arts organization. Assistant Directors may also enjoy other perks to compensate for lower salaries, such as more vacation time and/or personal days or a flexible schedule.

Employment Prospects

Employment opportunities for Assistant Directors will exist as long as arts organizations continue to be funded and continue to thrive. Executive director jobs are expected to increase at the same rate as other jobs from now through 2012, according to the U.S. Department of Labor's *Occupational Outlook Handbook,* with 10 to 20 percent growth. As executive director jobs grow, so, too, will Assistant Director jobs.

Advancement Prospects

Assistant Directors face the possibility of working for an executive director who stays in his or her position for years. To round out their experience, Assistant Directors may need to seek other more self-directed positions within the company. After two to three years as Assistant Director, their experience and skills may be useful in such capacities as associate development director or associate membership manager.

Education and Training

A four-year degree is preferred for this position. Some organizations may require a graduate degree. The key to being successful in this position is having a strong knowledge and appreciation of the arts industry you work in as well as an understanding of the issues. It is also critical that you understand and have had at least some exposure to arts organization management. Many schools and organizations now offer management and business courses for the arts as well as certification programs. These programs can help boost Assistant Directors in their careers, and they look good on a résumé too.

Experience, Skills, and Personality Traits

Several years of prior experience working in the arts (a gallery, museum, or nonprofit arts organization) will help you understand the full scope of your job, your executive director's job, and the organization itself. Although the job has "assistant" in its title, don't believe that your work is entirely created and delegated by your director. Only the self-motivated and self-directed survive in these positions. Individuals cannot sit back and wait to be told what to do. A proactive team player is happiest in this job. The onus is on the Assistant Director to form solid, trusting relationships with the director, the entire staff, volunteers, consultants, constituents, prospects, and the general public. This is a big role that requires diplomacy, excellent verbal and written skills, strong presentation abilities (particularly for the times when you may have to fill in for the director), research abilities, and, most of all, an honest passion for your company's mission. Organization and time-management skills are especially critical. Assistant Director jobs are varied, but individuals must know how to prioritize, keep track of one's own paperwork (as well as the director's), maintain a calendar, and stay focused and tuned-in to the projects and issues at hand. Individuals must know how to type and use a computer. Agility with various word processing and Web software (e.g., MS Word, Excel, PowerPoint, Outlook, Adobe Photoshop) may be required.

Unions and Associations

Many Assistant Directors become members of the same professional associations as executive directors for networking and educational purposes. They participate in such groups as the American Society of Association Executives (ASAE), the Arts and Business Council, Inc., Art Table, and the Support Center for Non-Profit Management.

Tips for Entry

1. Work in an art gallery. It's a great place to get exposure and experience.
2. Internships are another excellent way to test different environments to see where you fit.
3. Volunteer! Arts organizations are always looking for volunteers. It's a perfect environment for you to show your skills, contribute, check out the environment, and get familiar with the staff. You will also have access to jobs posted internally and a greater chance of being hired.
4. Network! Stay in touch with the people you meet along the way. Always follow up with them, because if a job opportunity comes along, you'll be fresh in their minds.

FINANCIAL OFFICER

Duties: Oversees funds and cash management; directs financial goals; handles budgets; manages fund investments; may deal with mergers and acquisitions; creates or supervises preparation of financial reports; may create financial and accounting systems; helps raise capital

Alternate Title(s): Financial Manager

Salary Range: $36,050 to $100,000+

Employment Prospects: Fair

Advancement Prospects: Fair

Best Geographical Location(s): Major urban cities

Prerequisites:

Education or Training—Bachelor's degree in business or finance; accounting experience important but accountant certification not critical

Experience—Several years of experience in arts organization management

Special Skills and Personality Traits—Must be knowledgeable about tax and other issues specific to arts organizations; strong analytical and communication skills; computer savvy; business and financial management abilities; very organized; creative problem-solver

```
┌──────────────────────────────┐
│   Chief Financial Officer    │
└──────────────────────────────┘

┌──────────────────────────────┐
│      Financial Officer       │
└──────────────────────────────┘

┌──────────────────────────────┐
│     Financial Consultant     │
└──────────────────────────────┘
```

Position Description

Financial Officers are responsible for overseeing and/or personally handling all aspects of an arts organization's finances, depending on staff size and structure. In smaller arts organizations, Financial Officers may handle journal entries for income and expense, meaning they will take care of the bookkeeping in addition to a variety of other job tasks. They oversee payroll and in some instances may be responsible for the administration of medical, dental, life, and other employment benefits. This means they may participate in reviewing the organizations' benefits packages, comparing and analyzing for cost, and participating in the final decision-making process. They work closely with the human resources department in this arena. Financial Officers may also work in conjunction with outside payroll services and freelance payroll consultants to ensure payroll taxes are handled and reported appropriately and accurately.

Depending on the accounting system, Financial Officers may compile and reconcile month-end accounts receivable and payable and review bank statements to generate accurate financial reports. They extrapolate numbers and analyze them to make summaries about income and loss and suggest ideas to generate further income and stem cash flows if need be. The Financial Officer's core responsibility is to keep the organization's finances in check. Financial Officers report directly to the executive director as well as to the board members. They make sure that all who are given access to the organization's money are following proper channels for authorization in their spending habits. They are the gatekeepers for the money, and they must be adamant that it be invested and spent wisely and in ways that reflect well on the organization. Financial Officers must also always look to the future, researching creative avenues of investments that will ensure the organization's ability to continue its mission and thrive in the years to come.

Some Financial Officers may face the task of computerizing a financial and accounting system if a small arts organization has not yet done so. Financial Officers know current software and how to code the categories. They have a complete understanding of all aspects of the organization to appropriately allocate monies to specific line items. Financial Officers may also participate in board meetings and membership conferences. They are also responsible for hiring and managing the financial department staff, which may entail delegating work to and overseeing assistants, accountants, bookkeepers, and interns.

Salaries

Depending on the size and budget of the arts organization, Financial Officers can earn anywhere from $36,050 to $100,000 or more. Financial Officers who work for well-established and well-funded arts organizations, and those officers with more than 10 years of experience in the field, will earn salaries upwards of $100,000. While corporate Financial Officers can earn a median income of $67,020, according to the Bureau of Labor Statistics, arts organizations have smaller budgets and may pay their officers less.

Employment Prospects

Employment of Financial Officers in all industries is expected to grow about as fast as average, with an increase of 10 to 20 percent, according to the U.S. Department of Labor's *Occupational Outlook Handbook*. Financial Officers in small arts organizations tend to commit to their jobs for years, thus making it extremely competitive to secure work when the jobs finally open up. Large organizations may offer more opportunities for officers, as they might hire full-time or seek temporary or contract help to address a specific project or crisis. Officers in small organizations often secure their positions through networking and word of mouth.

Advancement Prospects

In many arts organizations, Financial Officers are at the top of the ladder. Advancement may be unrealistic. With years of experience under their belts, some officers choose to leave their staff positions and start or return to their own consulting firms. If further advancement is available within the company, it may be to chief financial officer, with delegation of daily accounting and reporting functions to more junior staff.

Education and Training

A four-year degree in business or finance is helpful. Some accounting experience is also beneficial. Some arts organizations will hire Financial Officers who have liberal arts degrees but have taken business, financial, and accounting classes and have prior financial management experience. It is recommended that officers have at minimum two to three years of experience at the company.

Experience, Skills, and Personality Traits

Financial Officers are key to the healthy, seamless daily functioning of arts organizations. Because they work with a staff, board of directors, and constituency that may not understand what Financial Officers do, they need to be thick-skinned and confident about their abilities. They also need patience and strong communication and interpersonal skills to clearly report and make sure everyone understands the organization's financial status. Financial Officers must also be persistent and persuasive if changes need to be made to improve the financial structure. Financial Officers need to have strong computer and research skills, always aware of the latest software that can ease accounting and financial reporting. Arts organizations each have their own unique systems, structures, and quirks. Creative Financial Officers who have a great deal of patience and flexibility, as well as a strong appreciation for the arts, do well in this environment.

Unions and Associations

Financial Officers may join the American Society of Association Executives and the American Finance Association to network and stay informed about issues in their industry. The Association for Financial Professionals and Financial Executives International serve a corporate Financial Officer constituency but can still be useful resources for arts officers.

Tips for Entry

1. Get familiar with the organization by working there for at least one to two years before becoming a Financial Officer.
2. Take financial analysis and accounting classes. You don't need to be an accountant, but you need to understand how budgets work.
3. Immerse yourself in the ledgers first to familiarize yourself with the setup. Study files and read correspondence to absorb the organization's history, programming, products, events, and names.

EXECUTIVE DIRECTOR

CAREER PROFILE

Duties: Creates and maintains beneficial relationships within the arts community; manages and directs staff; insures finances are managed appropriately and to organization's benefit; meets and brainstorms regularly with board of directors; public speaking and networking at various events and roundtable discussions; may fund-raise; creates and develops programs and events; speaks to and maintains relationship with press; oversees and participates in outreach; serves as steward of the membership

Alternate Title(s): Director, Manager

Salary Range: $60,0000 to $150,000+; small to mid-size arts organizations often allocate 10 percent of their annual budget to the Executive Director's salary

Employment Prospects: Fair

Advancement Prospects: Poor

Best Geographical Location(s): Major urban areas

Prerequisites:

Education or Training—At minimum, four-year college degree; graduate degree may be required in some cases

Experience—Prior nonprofit organization management or leadership experience is usually required

Special Skills and Personality Traits—Strong interpersonal and communication skills; excellent listener; leadership abilities; flexible; able to motivate and mobilize volunteers and staff; decisive; analytical; solid business acumen; able to analyze various data and input to make sound decisions and create a strategic vision that will benefit the organization; must have integrity and compassion

CAREER LADDER

```
┌─────────────────────────────┐
│   Owner, Art Organization   │
└─────────────────────────────┘

┌─────────────────────────────┐
│     Executive Director      │
└─────────────────────────────┘

┌─────────────────────────────┐
│    Development Director      │
└─────────────────────────────┘
```

Position Description

An Executive Director's work varies daily, which is why the position attracts individuals with a range of backgrounds, skills, and personalities. The Executive Director is responsible for all aspects of the organization: managing staff, fundraising, membership, programming, finance, legal, press, and outreach. The Executive Director works closely with the board of directors, meeting regularly to report on the daily functions, the projects, upcoming events, and finances. The Executive Director must be able to develop a strong rapport with board members. In addition to managing and overseeing staff employees, the Executive Director develops and maintains relationships in the arts community as well as in other industries that may prove mutually beneficial to members of the organization. Regular networking is an important part of the job. The Executive Director must have excellent presentation skills.

The Executive Director is often the "face" of the organization. He or she must have a passion for the organization's mission and a deep understanding of its members' needs in order to clearly communicate with the media and the general public. He or she is the public advocate for the organization and will be asked to speak at panels and contribute to articles in magazines, newspapers, and books. Public speaking and strong writing skills are essential.

The Executive Director must also have solid business skills. The days of arts organizations being "antistructure" are over. In fact, many schools now offer nonprofit management training programs. Often the most successful arts organizations are those with a strong mission statement and business plan. Executive Directors now need to know various software and database programs to effectively manage their work as well as accurately oversee staff. Some programs they may need to know include MS Office (Excel, PowerPoint, Word), Microsoft Outlook, and/or other Internet programs and Access or other database programs. They may also need to have a familiarity with Adobe Illustrator, Photoshop, and others. They must have an awareness of when computer equipment and software need upgrading for the organization to continue running smoothly and cost-effectively.

Executive Directors also need solid analytical skills to absorb the myriad of information that crosses their desks. They must stay diligent and focused. Regardless of how glamorous a product or service may seem, they must be able to see through the shiny stuff and ask the hard questions: What specifically is being offered? How will it improve and enhance our work, our services, etc.? How much will it cost? How much time will it take to implement? Overall, is it really justified? The Executive Director serves at the discretion of the board of directors but most importantly, he or she is representative of and accountable to the members.

Salaries
Executive Directors can expect to earn anywhere from $60,000 to $150,000 and more, depending on experience, the size of the organization, and its budget.

Employment Prospects
Because Executive Director positions are often as far up as you can go in many organizations, competition can be fierce. Many arts organizations have boards of directors at the helm, so there is often no place to advance to after achieving the position of Executive Director. Those who leave their positions often make parallel moves to the same jobs in other companies. Also, because the work is specialized, companies have more hiring options and can either promote from within or hire outside, further heightening the competition. Through 2012, jobs in this field are expected to increase at the same speed as other jobs, with a 10 to 20 percent growth, according to the U.S. Department of Labor's *Occupational Outlook Handbook.*

Advancement Prospects
The Executive Director position is usually the highest in an organization, and thus the pinnacle of an individual's career.

Some Executive Directors make lateral moves to other organizations. Because the work is diverse and challenging, most Executive Directors are satisfied to make long-term commitments to their positions at the same organization. Some may use their experience and start their own arts organization; others may expand their expertise by agreeing to more speaking and teaching engagements.

Education and Training
At minimum, Executive Directors have four-year degrees and have prior arts organization and/or nonprofit organization management experience. Many directors work their way up from the bottom, often starting as interns in museums, galleries, or arts associations. There is no specific course of study that will lead you to this job, but getting as much work experience as possible will help. A degree in nonprofit management is not necessarily key to holding this job successfully, but a blend of arts knowledge with strong business management skills is critical. Long gone are the days when art organizations were created and run in direct rebellion to the corporate, structured world. Many successful arts organizations now borrow their business models from thriving, well-known corporations.

Experience, Skills, and Personality Traits
Multitasking is a big part of this job. Executive Directors spend their days juggling projects and people. The work can range from reviewing the quarterly finance report and writing a summary for the next board meeting, to interviewing new staff, speaking to the press, and appearing at an evening event. You must have a thick skin and be able to face challenges square in the face and conquer them. This is a demanding job, and directors are not only interfacing with their hardworking (and often underpaid) staff, but with the board of directors and the membership. Patience, diplomacy, empathy, and strong management skills will help you thrive. Many arts organizations have dedicated staff who are not paid their worth but stay in the jobs because they are passionate about the organization. To be an effective leader and to maintain their loyalty, it's critical that you are supportive and accessible to them. You must have a clear vision for the organization and for yourself. And you must be passionate about the mission of your organization. You will be the face of the organization in the community; you will be the message-carrier. To incite interest, attract new constituents, and grow your organization, you must have a deep understanding of and enthusiasm for the mission. Be aware that even if you have a professional fund-raiser on staff, you are also responsible for fund-raising. You must know how to identify opportunities and know how to ask for what the organization needs.

Unions and Associations
Many Executive Directors join the American Society of Association Executives (ASAE), the Arts and Business

Council, Inc., Art Table, and the Support Center for Non-Profit Management.

Tips for Entry

1. Network! Word of mouth is often the best way to find work.
2. Find mentors. Learn from others who have held the job so that once you hold the position, you won't have to learn using the "trial by fire" method.
3. Learn to be open to your members' opinions and perspectives on problems. You are in the position of Executive Director as a steward to the membership, so always bear in mind that your members' input and how you handle it is critical to the success of your organization. Learn to create a broader policy that represents the organization's perspective.
4. Be consistent, fair, and equitable in your communications with all members.

EDUCATION

ART TEACHER (K–12)

CAREER PROFILE

Duties: Teaches art history, art techniques, and materials to students; assigns projects, reports, and homework; tracks students' progress and grades projects; takes attendance; depending on school structure, may have homeroom and study hall duties; oversees class trips; creates report cards; files paperwork with department heads and school administrators; works closely with assistant and/or student teachers; chooses books and articles for students to read; creates course outlines, curricula, and lesson plans; attends teacher meetings and conferences

Alternate Title(s): Art Instructor

Salary Range: $24,960 to $68,530

Employment Prospects: Good

Advancement Prospects: Fair

Best Geographical Location: Major urban areas may have more opportunities; suburban schools may offer higher salaries

Prerequisites:

Education or Training—Four-year degree required; coursework in teacher education program may be required; master's degree in art education may be required within five years of starting to teach

Experience—Three to five years of experience as a professional artist helpful

Special Skills and Personality Traits—Must like children and/or teenagers; excellent communication skills; public speaking and interpersonal abilities; creative; organized; able to meet deadlines; diligent; able to share ideas and thoughts in ways that engage others and generate enthusiasm; patient; tactful

Special Requirements—Public schools require a teaching license (requirements for the license vary by state); some schools may accept alternatives to certification for jobs that are hard to fill

CAREER LADDER

```
┌─────────────────────────────────────┐
│      Department Head or             │
│   Art Department Administrator      │
└─────────────────────────────────────┘

┌─────────────────────────────────────┐
│           Art Teacher               │
└─────────────────────────────────────┘

┌─────────────────────────────────────┐
│  Student, Assistant Art Teacher, or │
│        Professional Artist          │
└─────────────────────────────────────┘
```

Position Description

Art Teachers help students appreciate art and learn how art relates to everything around them by introducing them to art materials and techniques, discussing art history, showing films and slides, taking class trips to museums and galleries, having guest speakers and demonstrations, and assigning in-class art projects as well as homework. Depending on the topic of the class, Art Teachers introduce students to drawing, painting, graphic design, photography, ceramics, sculpture, and more. Students learn how to work with paintbrushes, carving tools, paints, clays, computer design and illustration software, cameras, charcoals, markers and pens, and other art tools and materials.

Art Teachers create their lesson plans and course curricula. They tailor their instructions and assignments so that they are appropriate for the age groups and skill levels. Art

Teachers observe and evaluate each student's performance and potential throughout the semester and work with students individually in the areas in which they most need help.

Art Teachers are responsible not only for guiding students in the physical creation of art projects but also in helping them think through their projects. They appreciate each student's individuality, distinct approach, and style and therefore do not impose their art style on, nor do they provide their own personal solutions to, art project challenges. They may shed light on options, but they give the student the breathing room to figure it out on his or her own. For older students, Art Teachers may provide a list of recommended books, relevant newspapers, and magazine articles for them to read. Art Teachers in the upper grade levels may become mentors to students, advising them about colleges and careers. They may also write reference letters for college applications.

Art Teachers are responsible for managing and controlling their classes. Keeping students engaged is the challenge. Art Teachers must be tuned in to students and watch for changes in attendance, behavior, performance, and physical appearance. Some students may at times be unruly and require disciplinary action. It is up to the Art Teacher to take steps that are appropriate to the school's policies.

Art Teachers, like all teachers, share in standard school tasks, such as overseeing homerooms and study halls and accompanying students on field trips. In addition to teaching, Art Teachers are responsible for completing a great deal of paperwork. They take attendance, complete progress reports and report cards, and fill out hall passes and various other school forms. They meet with school administrators and parents to discuss students' performance and progress, and they attend faculty meetings and teacher's conferences.

Art Teachers' work schedules are usually based on the school calendar. In most schools, teachers work for 10 months, then either have summers off or teach special summer classes.

Salaries

Salaries for Art Teachers vary depending on geographical location and years of experience. Public schools usually pay higher salaries than private schools, and schools located in the suburbs typically offer higher wages. The U.S. Department of Labor's *Occupational Outlook Handbook* states that in 2002 kindergarten through secondary school teachers in public schools earned salaries ranging from $24,960 to $68,530. According to the American Federation of Teachers (AFT), beginning teachers earned an average salary of $30,719 in the 2001–02 school year. Teachers with master's degrees and national certification usually earn higher salaries. Art Teachers who would rather teach smaller class sizes may do well to pursue private school employment, but they should be prepared to receive lower wages compared to those of public schools.

Employment Prospects

Employment opportunities for Art Teachers vary depending on geographical location. For teachers overall, the Bureau of Labor Statistics foresees excellent opportunities because many teachers (particularly at the secondary school level) will be retiring through 2012, and there is also high turnover of new teachers working in cities. In anticipation of teacher shortages and to speed the placement process, many states are offering incentives to encourage people to become teachers.

Advancement Prospects

Advancing in the school system is no easy task; there are few jobs to move up to, and the hunt for those jobs is extremely competitive. With years of experience and a master's degree in fine arts or administration, an Art Teacher may be able to advance to become a department head or an arts administrator in government or a foundation. Other avenues of advancement may include working at the board of education, United Federation of Teachers, or other organizations for teachers and art educators. Art Teachers can also expand their skills by working as art education consultants.

Education and Training

Art Teachers who work in public schools must have a four-year degree. They must also have completed an approved teacher education program and be licensed. Many states require teachers to pass the Praxis exams, a series of tests that prove an individual's ability to teach. Art Teachers also need to have supervised practice teaching experience. Frequently, teacher education programs offer what's known as a "pre-practicum" course, in which teaching students work closely with an Art Teacher in the classroom by observing and assisting. This offers students the opportunity to see how a class is conducted before actually teaching their own class. Throughout the course, students meet with their program advisers to discuss their observations and progress. Depending on the state, once they secure a teaching position, teachers may then be required to receive their master's degree in education within five years.

Special Requirements

Public schools throughout the United States require teachers to be licensed; private school teachers do not need a license. License requirements vary by state, and most teachers receive their license through the state board of education. Some states relax licensing requirements when school districts have been unable to fill certain teaching positions. If a prospective teacher qualifies based on his or her professional work experience but is not licensed, the school may require that individual to take education courses while teaching and to work closely with other experienced teachers. Licensed teachers can boost their marketability and enhance their teaching benefits by securing professional certification from the National Board for Professional Teaching Standards. By submitting a portfolio of their classroom work and passing a written test, Art Teachers may be able to secure higher salaries as well as teach in other states.

Experience, Skills, and Personality Traits

Art Teachers must be able to connect with and engage their students. Public school teachers work with larger class sizes (up to 30 or more students per class). To successfully educate and manage so many students, it is critical that Art Teachers have a vast supply of patience, empathy, diligence, and focus. With all of the distractions, they must always have an eye on the end goal and remember how to get there. They must also stay in touch with what interests their students in order to create excitement about art projects. Art Teachers work with diverse individuals with diverse needs. They are responsible not only for educating and guiding their students to hone and improve artistic skills but also for meeting administrative obligations and maintaining contact with parents. Art Teachers with strong communication and interpersonal skills who are able to maintain the required paperwork and meet deadlines will fare best.

Unions and Associations

While it is not mandatory, many elementary through secondary school teachers belong to the American Federation of Teachers (AFT) as well as the National Education Association. These unions negotiate on behalf of their members for better wages and working hours, fair treatment, and other benefits.

Tips for Entry

1. Substitute teach in a school that interests you. It's an excellent way for the school's administration to see you and your skills at work. Contact the board of education to find out about substitute teaching opportunities.
2. Make sure that you have fulfilled all of the requirements for your teaching license. Be diligent, and make sure you get everything in writing. If your phone calls to the board of education aren't providing you with the information you need, go there in person. You won't want to find out later on that you're short credits!
3. Find a mentor. When you assist in a classroom, keep a notebook handy to jot down your observations and questions, and be sure to ask those questions. This is your chance to learn from an experienced teacher, so take advantage while you can.

ART TEACHER (UNACCREDITED SCHOOLS)

CAREER PROFILE

Duties: Depending on background, teaches students art techniques, materials, tools, composition, balance, and color; may educate about current market opportunities and job hunting tactics; helps students hone their art skills by assigning and overseeing projects; works with various age groups, skill levels, and group sizes; may report to department chairperson, supervisor, or head of school; creates course syllabi and lesson plans; creates and submits progress reports and other forms that schools may require; may invoice schools

Alternate Title(s): Art Instructor

Salary Range: $8 to $30+ per hour

Employment Prospects: Good

Advancement Prospects: Fair

Best Geographical Location(s): Major urban areas

Prerequisites:

Education or Training—B.F.A. required, specialization in subject being taught recommended; some schools may require M.F.A.

Experience—Four to five years of professional experience in specific art discipline; some teaching or lecturing experience helpful

Special Skills and Personality Traits—Knowledge about subject being taught; excellent verbal and written communication skills; empathetic; good listener; able to inspire and motivate others; passionate about subject matter and about teaching; strong interpersonal skills; organized; creative; innovative; self-starter

CAREER LADDER

```
┌─────────────────────────────────┐
│        Assistant Chair          │
└─────────────────────────────────┘

┌─────────────────────────────────┐
│          Art Teacher            │
└─────────────────────────────────┘

┌─────────────────────────────────┐
│ Artist (in specific discipline),│
│  Guest Lecturer, or Teaching    │
│          Assistant              │
└─────────────────────────────────┘
```

Position Description

Art Teachers who work for unaccredited schools are responsible for teaching students various aspects of the art they specialize in. Some may focus their classes on art techniques and materials; others may choose to educate about the business of being an artist, such as negotiating contracts, promoting and marketing artwork, or even hiring and managing staff. Art Teachers choose subject matter for classes and pitch them to schools, or schools seek teachers out directly, with subjects the schools themselves have created. Art Teachers teach everything from graphic design, illustra-

tion, and cartooning to watercolor painting, pottery, and even right-brain/left-brain thinking.

Art Teachers usually report to a department chairperson, supervisor, or the head of the school. Most unaccredited schools, depending on structure and size, will require Art Teachers to create and submit a syllabus as well as progress reports for each student. Most schools also require Art Teachers to write their bios and course descriptions for promotional purposes (e.g., course brochures, flyers, e-mail announcements, and Web site content). Art Teachers typically create lesson plans, with outlines for each class. Once the schools send Art Teachers the list of registered students, some Art Teachers may also contact students in advance of the class to greet them and remind them of any specific materials they will need for the first class.

Art Teachers usually begin their classes by taking attendance. Teachers then structure their classes according to their own styles of communication. Some may do an art presentation, show a film or slide show, demonstrate a technique, have an open-class discussion, or combine any of these methods. They assign projects and homework at the end of class, and review work and discuss it with the students on scheduled deadline dates. Sometimes they assign work to be done during class, helping students learn to think and create quickly. Classes are usually two to three hours; class size can range anywhere from five to 25 or more students, depending on the school. Teachers can also be hired to teach one to four or more classes per week.

Salaries

Unaccredited schools usually hire part-time Art Teachers and pay them hourly rates. The rates can range from as low as $8 to $30 or more per hour. According to the U.S. Department of Labor's *Occupational Outlook Handbook,* Art Teachers at unaccredited schools, as well as other "self-enrichment" instructors, earned median hourly rates of $14.09 in 2002. Well-known, established schools typically pay higher rates. Teachers with years of experience who are stars in their industry are also able to secure higher salaries. Other options for better wages include negotiating to teach a package of classes, rather than just one or two, or suggesting a sliding-scale hourly rate that parallels enrollment—the higher the enrollment, the higher the hourly rate. Not all schools will agree to this, but offering to help spread word about the school and the class is usually a positive selling point.

Employment Prospects

The outlook for employment opportunities for self-enrichment teachers overall is bright. More people are seeking to enhance their skills or explore new ways to express their creative sides. They are seeking out unaccredited schools because the classes are more affordable than those offered at colleges and universities. The U.S. Department of Labor predicts employment in this field to grow faster than the average through 2012.

Advancement Prospects

Unaccredited schools are loosely structured, and as a result, advancement prospects for Art Teachers are only fair. With experience, Art Teachers can advance to become full-time (staff) teachers or department supervisors or chairpersons. Some may be able to start their own schools and/or market their educational programs to other schools and organizations. Others can take their experience and guest lecture around the country or write articles.

Education and Training

Unaccredited schools are not as stringent as colleges and universities in terms of administration, but most will still require Art Teachers to have a four-year degree, with a specialization in the art that is being taught a plus. Some schools may require an M.F.A. Depending on the art subject, some Art Teachers may need to apply for the job as they would an art position, by submitting their portfolio and art samples for review. Some training in public speaking or teaching will also be helpful.

Experience, Skills, and Personality Traits

Art Teachers must know the subject matter they are teaching. They should have at least four to five years of experience working professionally in the field so that they have firsthand knowledge of what they're sharing with others. They must be able to demonstrate techniques, intelligently and sensitively field questions, review work, and make constructive observations and recommendations. To create fulfilling educational experiences for students, Art Teachers need to know how to engage and speak to them in ways they will understand and appreciate. Successful Art Teachers are inspirational; they know how to motivate and excite. They must also have a great deal of patience and flexibility in dealing with students as individuals and in groups. To successfully instruct, clear verbal and written communication skills are critical. They also need to know how to tailor their lesson plans to skill levels and age groups.

Unions and Associations

There are no specific associations for Art Teachers at unaccredited schools. However, teachers can access valuable membership benefits, such as networking, educational resources, and job listings, by joining associations that focus on their specific art discipline (e.g., Society of Illustrators, American Institute of Graphic Arts, Textile Designer Association, etc.).

Tips for Entry

1. Be organized, and always plan your lessons ahead. Keep copies of your lesson plans in files, as well as reports you submit to schools.
2. Be firm and confident. You are in control of the classroom, not your students. Don't ever let them see you sweat.
3. Network as much as you possibly can. You never know who you will meet who will know of a job opening at a school. Word of mouth is always helpful. And visit the Web sites of the schools where you'd like to teach. Check for job postings frequently.
4. Join trade associations. They're always looking for classes to offer to their members.

ART PROFESSOR (ACCREDITED COLLEGE)

CAREER PROFILE

Duties: Educates undergraduate and graduate students about specific areas of art based on professional work experience (e.g. graphic design, illustration, animation, or ceramics) and academic acumen; teaches art techniques, methods, media, materials, tools, career options, and more; helps students understand how to approach and conceive projects, how to find subject matter, and how to solve problems; assigns projects and homework; provides book and magazine reading lists; creates class structure to effectively educate; works closely with class as a whole and with individuals; creates course curricula; takes attendance; creates student progress reports for school administration

Alternate Title(s): Art Instructor

Salary Range: $20,000 to $40,000 part time; $35,000 to $100,000+ full time

Employment Prospects: Fair to Good

Advancement Prospects: Good

Best Geographical Location(s): Major urban areas close to art colleges or universities

Prerequisites:

Education or Training—Master's degree in fine arts (in rare circumstances, accomplishments in visual arts field commensurate with completion of master's degree)

Experience—Teaching assistantships at the graduate level; several years of experience in the field being taught (in rare cases, professional experience commensurate with master's degree acceptable)

Special Skills and Personality Traits—Excellent communication skills; creative; strong interest in teaching; knowledgeable about topic of class; organized; reliable; able to guide without imposing; must enjoy working with students; able to meet deadlines; literary skill; ability to speak before large groups

CAREER LADDER

```
┌─────────────────────────────────────┐
│   Department Chairperson or Art      │
│     Education Consultant             │
└─────────────────────────────────────┘

┌─────────────────────────────────────┐
│          Art Professor               │
└─────────────────────────────────────┘

┌─────────────────────────────────────┐
│ Artist or Graduate Teaching Assistant│
└─────────────────────────────────────┘
```

Position Description

In teaching classes devoted to the pursuit of art, Art Professors share knowledge and help guide students in honing their skills and problem-solving abilities. They also help their students understand the realities of being an artist. Classes are typically grouped by skill levels, from beginner to advanced; Art Professors tailor their instructions to that specific level. Typically, an instructor begins his or her career by teaching freshmen foundation studies. In most colleges and universities, this means basic two-dimensional design, foundation-level drawing and painting, basic color theory, and, in many cases, basic three-dimensional design. These foundation studies are almost universally taught because they're the nuts and bolts of any applied art, ones on which nearly all professional artists draw, whatever their vocation.

After several years of teaching the introductory classes, many Art Professors move up the academic ladder and begin teaching mid- to high-level art courses that specialize in a particular discipline. Among these specialized courses are advertising design, painting, illustration, sculpture, and interior design, covering many of the job descriptions covered in this volume. (When making this leap into more profession-oriented instruction, it's usual to keep a few foundation-level courses as part of the workload.) In these more advanced courses, the Art Professor begins to impart the specific wisdom acquired in both the academic and professional art worlds, as he or she is now beginning to prepare students to enter the workforce. Art Professors often also teach some degree of art history to help students appreciate how the past influences the present and the future.

In colleges and universities that offer graduate programs, Art Professors who have had several years of teaching experience offer highly specialized courses of study in the master's program. Students in these programs expect to focus on one of two areas: the particular craft being studied (painting, illustration, design, etc.) or preparation for entering the workforce as an Art Professor.

Most art courses at colleges and universities are unique experiences and are structured in a way that best suits the material under examination. Art Professors articulate ideas in ways that help students understand how to think about things. For instance, in foundation studies, in which a great deal of information has to be disseminated, traditional lectures in front of the students begin the classes, but the material is immediately applied in studio sessions that follow. Often, the material discussed gets reinforced as the Art Professor works his or her way around the room and addresses students individually as they work. In more advanced courses the classes are structured to maximize studio time in active application of the discipline studied, freeing the Art Professor up to interact more in a one-on-one manner.

The best Art Professors give students a context in which to solve problems on their own. For example, if an Art Professor gives the class an assignment and a student comes back and is not successful in his or her work, the Art Professor still needs to find the germ of the student's idea and help the student work from there. The instructor must be careful not to impose his or her own style or solutions on the project. The Art Professor's role is to help students improve their work and make their work more sophisticated through guidance. They foster an environment that allows students to think independently and solve their own problems. Art Professors also set up the physical design of their classrooms to directly impact how students interact with each other, starting with something as simple as arranging chairs in a circle, rather than in rows.

Classroom and homework assignments are typically put up in front of the class upon completion for a general critique led by the Art Professor. These critiques offer students an opportunity to discuss each others' work and offer insights into the choices they've made while executing their own work. When grading these assignments—a task that often boils down to weighing subjective components as diverse as execution, ambition of a project's scope, and a piece's intent—these critiques help flesh out some of these less obvious components.

Additionally, the best Art Professors help students understand the different types of art careers they can pursue and what it takes to actually be in the "business" of being an artist beyond creating their work. Art Professors will often refer students to art associations for help in creating and negotiating contracts, pricing work, protecting artists' rights, cost estimates, and production schedules as well as self-promotion and job hunt tactics. Art Professors will bring in guest speakers who can speak about these and other topics and work especially closely with seniors on these and other career-related topics.

Art Professors are also responsible for a certain degree of administrative work; some of these administrative tasks include taking class attendance, creating and maintaining students' progress reports, grading assignments, and creating course curricula and lesson plans. Responsibilities vary depending on the school. Art Professors are usually required to submit course descriptions, bios, and the list of required supplies at the start of each semester to the students.

Salaries

Salary expectations vary greatly with this vocation, and the variable components of salary expectation are myriad. In very rare circumstances, accomplished professional artists with a very specialized brand of knowledge can be paid handsomely as Art Professors. Artists with household names within the industry can usually find highly compensated positions at professional art colleges or universities. It's not uncommon to see earnings in the low six figures for two to three days a week. However, these are extremely rare circumstances and occur only when the Art Professor in question has achieved lofty goals in other areas.

In more common circumstances, full-time Art Professors earn between $35,000 and $60,000 annually, depending on experience, specialty, and location. These positions come replete with medical and retirement benefits and often offer other perks as well, such as free schooling at the college or university for one's children.

Part-time Art Professors earn between $20,000 and $40,000 annually. Usually, professional artists working in another field supplement their income with these positions by teaching two to three days a week.

Employment Prospects

While the U.S. Department of Labor projects that job growth in college and university teaching positions will advance more rapidly than the average (based mostly upon a large number of 18- to 24-year-olds in the U.S. population), indicators for this specific branch of college education aren't as promising. While growth will continue as overall enrollment rises, downward trends in several key areas of the visual arts industry will seed the market with many qualified candidates. For instance, professional independent illustrators have labored through unprecedented market shrinkage over the past 10 years, and many of them have turned to college instruction to bolster their diminishing incomes.

Advancement Prospects

Once entrenched in the academic field, one can expect a good chance at climbing the job ladder. Motivated individuals who commit themselves to teaching and involve themselves with improving the quality of students' work are readily recognized by their peers and superiors. Tenure-track positions will continue to be highly sought-after. Competition will be stiff, but excellent instructors are a commodity colleges and universities cherish and reward.

An Art Professor who has been teaching for a decade or more can make his or her way up to the administrative level and become director of a program—visual communications, for example, which often means several commercially oriented disciplines—or dean of a school, college, or university. (In very rare circumstances, an exception can be made for the time requirement stated above.) In such positions, one typically maintains a teaching presence at the higher levels—undergraduate students at junior and senior level—while taking care of administrative duties, which include drafting syllabi; overseeing and grading individual Art Professors; charting particular areas of professional growth and assigning resources to the study of these areas; and recruiting/hiring Art Professors.

Typically, one starts out as an instructor, moves to assistant/associate professor, and finally becomes a full professor. (Part-time, or adjunct, positions often exist at all levels except full professor.) The most crucial components for one's advancement are often within one's own control: getting along well with administration, providing quality instruction to one's students, and proving one's commitment to teaching. Art Professors can also expand their reach by writing, participating in panel discussions, creating partnerships with organizations outside the school for interesting class and school projects, or possibly even starting their own schools.

Education and Training

In order to teach at the college level, one must have completed a master's degree in fine art or arts and sciences. (A master of fine arts is a terminal degree as, unlike other areas of study, there is no doctorate offered in fine arts.) In years past, those with a bachelor's degree held a great many of these positions at professional art colleges, but the trend is turning away from this practice.

Experience, Skills, and Personality Traits

As with any job that involves dealing with many different personalities and large groups of people, patience and diplomacy rank high on the necessary skills set. Both in the classroom and when taking direction and criticism from administration, employing a diplomatic approach to interpersonal relationships paves the way to advancement.

One must also have a highly developed ability to read and write. There are several different methods of teaching due to the differing ways in which people learn. For instance, one student may find it easier to learn by being shown how to perform a particular action, another might take to verbal instruction, and yet a third may find the path to learning easiest when reading. The most successful Art Professors—meaning primarily those whose students go on to good careers—have a facility with these several methods of imparting instruction and can recognize which students respond best to a particular method.

Additionally, an Art Professor must have an excellent command of the skills that he or she is teaching. If faced with a circumstance in which he or she has to apply the craft before an individual student or entire classroom as a demonstration, the professor must be able to perform. Familiarity with the various tools and methods of plying one's craft ranks high on the list of necessary skills.

Lastly, a proven track record in the professional world helps one immensely in gaining employment and advancing as an Art Professor, especially in the more commercially applicable courses of study. Not only does this solidify one's credibility both with administration and students, but it affords the opportunity to teach from personal experience. Having encountered the potential pitfalls of seeking a career aids one in preparing students. A cautionary note: Not all excellent artists are excellent teachers; again, the most successful Art Professors are measured by the success their students find in their careers.

Unions and Associations

While there is no nationwide union to which Art Professors must belong to gain employment, there are in rare circumstances unions specific to the college or university at which one teaches. Information about such matters can be found in job listings or at interviews.

Additionally, Art Professors usually belong to associations that pertain to their art specialty, among them the American Institute of Graphic Arts (AIGA), the Society of Illustrators, the Illustrators' Partnership of America (IPA), and the American Society of Media Photographers (ASMP).

Tips for Entry

1. In many art schools, the work you have created in your specific industry and the reputation you have achieved will often carry more weight than your degree. This does not negate the relevance of a

degree, but you need to have accomplished something in your work first in order to educate about the realities of the career for your students. Be sure you want to share what you have learned, and be prepared to be responsible for the impact you have when you step into the classroom.

2. Network. Meet other artists who you know are teachers. College-level Art Professor positions are often secured through word of mouth. Who you know can make a huge difference in your job hunt. Department heads usually first ask their teachers if they know anyone who can fill teaching slots when they open up, and usually they do. Even former students with a few years of work experience who are being recognized for their work can be recommended. Make sure you stay in touch with your teachers too!

3. Find your own voice and style; don't try to imitate someone else, and don't teach by rote. If you are enthusiastic, responsive, and thoughtful in how you speak with your students and conduct your class, the odds are good that you will succeed in engaging them and helping them learn.

4. Know your craft and never stop learning; accumulate as much skill in the particular discipline you propose to teach as possible. Keep an eye out for ways to improve your own facility, both as a craftsperson and as an instructor.

EDUCATION DIRECTOR (MUSEUM)

CAREER PROFILE

Duties: Identifies and sets educational goals for the museum and for the internal education department; designs educational programs; oversees all educational materials; teaches various groups in galleries; may write grant request letters; may train volunteers (or docents); may hire and manage staff; creates and manages education department budget

Alternate Title(s): Educational Chair

Salary Range: $25,000 to $65,000+

Employment Prospects: Fair

Advancement Prospects: Fair

Best Geographical Location(s): Major metropolitan areas

Prerequisites:

Education or Training—Bachelor's degree in art history, fine art, education, or related field; master's degree in museum education preferred by most museums

Experience—Several years of experience teaching in a museum or assisting a museum educator; some experience teaching children and/or adults

Special Skills and Personality Traits—Excellent communication and interpersonal skills; strong writing ability; patient and flexible; empathetic; able to set goals and direct staff; strong research skills; organized; passionate about the art and artists featured in the museum; leadership abilities

CAREER LADDER

```
┌─────────────────────────────────────────┐
│  Museum Director (larger museum or       │
│  cultural institution) or                │
│  Independent Educational Consultant      │
└─────────────────────────────────────────┘

┌─────────────────────────────────────────┐
│        Education Director                │
└─────────────────────────────────────────┘

┌─────────────────────────────────────────┐
│    Assistant Education Director          │
└─────────────────────────────────────────┘
```

Position Description

Education Directors are responsible for setting the educational goals of the museum itself, as well as the goals of the education department within the museum. In keeping with the mission of the institution, Education Directors create educational programs for various age groups, from young children to seniors. In larger museums, Education Directors may specialize in teaching or creating programs for specific age groups or for groups with specific educational needs. They are also responsible for overseeing and managing all educational materials that are published by and appear in the museum, such as wall labels that describe the art on exhibit and provide biographical information about the

artist, brochure text, event literature, Web site content, family guides, and even lectures and guides on tape.

Education Directors are involved in interpreting the art and translating it to the public in a way that educates and informs. They are responsible for the narrative. It is up to them to find a way to teach the aesthetics of the art and to help people understand the art in ways that are most meaningful to them. Education Directors may teach various groups, based on age or by organization, in the galleries. With their tailored education program for reference, they guide groups through exhibits, explaining the art, the artist, and the history related to each piece. They interact with teachers outside the museum and help them plan educational programs or create programs directly for them. Depending on the size of the museum and staff structure, some Education Directors may also train docents, or volunteers, so that they can take on the task of leading and teaching museum visitors and groups. While Education Directors must focus on educating the museum audience, they, too, must stay informed by regularly reading industry publications, visiting museum and arts Web sites, visiting other museums and arts institutions, as well as attending events and lectures within and beyond their workplace.

Education Directors delegate work to and guide their staff and create annual budgets for their department. They often partake in fund-raising for the museum. Because they work closely with the public and have a firsthand understanding of the museum's educational achievements and needs, they are often called upon to help with grant writing and create lists of potential sources of funding.

Salaries
Education Directors can expect to earn salaries ranging from $25,000 to $65,000 or more, depending on the size of the museum. Larger museums may offer higher salaries, although this does not preclude the possibility that smaller museums with large sources of funding may offer higher salaries, also. Education Directors with doctoral degrees may also command higher incomes.

Employment Prospects
According to the U.S. Department of Labor's *Occupational Outlook Handbook,* museum attendance has been increasing over the years, and thus more museum administrative employees will be needed. The museum education field is still extremely competitive, however, and there are more job seekers than there are available Education Director jobs. Education Directors with advanced degrees and prior museum education experience will have the advantage in the job hunt. Prospective Education Directors must also keep in mind that although museums have sparked public interest, museums remain dependent on the economy. If a recession looms, budget cuts follow, and staff is typically scaled back first. Some Education Directors freelance consult, teach, lecture, and/or write to supplement their incomes and create a safety net should the economy falter.

Advancement Prospects
Education Directors in smaller museums may find few avenues to advance within the institution. These directors can advance by leaving the museum to freelance consultant. They can also advance by becoming directors of other small museums, or division heads in larger museums (e.g., directors of public programs and education). Education Directors

in larger museums can move up to become museum directors or move on to freelance consult.

Education and Training
Most Education Directors have, at minimum, a bachelor's degree in art history, fine art, education, or a related field. Contemporary art museums, modern art museums, and all others that specialize in particular art styles favor Education Directors with backgrounds and interests that match. Most museums prefer to hire Education Directors with master's degrees in museum education and with some classroom experience.

Experience, Skills, and Personality Traits
Museum educators work directly with the general public, various educational groups and schools, as well as diverse staff and volunteers. To successfully teach and train others, they must have excellent interpersonal, communication, and public speaking skills, as well as vast supplies of patience and empathy. They must also be adept at juggling projects and meeting deadlines. It's critical that they appreciate the art and the artists, featured in the museum so that they can best express the meaning and the message in their educational programs. Education Directors must also be organized and have management and leadership skills.

Unions and Associations
Education Directors can join organizations such as the American Association of Museums (AAM) for networking opportunities, job listings, educational workshops and conferences, professional resources and support, and more.

Tips for Entry
1. Test out this type of work first by getting an internship. You have to make sure you love it to thrive and be happy. The salary may not be fantastic, but the rewards of doing work that you enjoy will make it worthwhile.
2. Get involved and stay involved in what goes on inside the museum. It's important for Education Directors to know what's happening on the museum floor. Visit the gallery regularly, even if you can only schedule it for small amounts of time.
3. Attend conferences. Network. Make yourself known. The best way to find work is often through word of mouth. The more people you meet, the greater your chances of connecting to an opportunity that's right for you.
4. Find job listings by subscribing to listservs, such as the American Association of Museums' "Aviso."

INDEPENDENT

ARTIST ASSISTANT

CAREER PROFILE

Duties: Facilitates employing artist's endeavors by performing a variety of tasks

Alternate Title(s): None

Salary Range: Zero to $10 per hour, typically; in more advanced, and rare, circumstances, $25,000 to $40,000 per year

Employment Prospects: Fair to Good

Advancement Prospects: Good

Best Geographical Location(s): Major urban areas that support a large number of independent creative professionals

Prerequisites:

Education or Training—High school or college curriculum focused on area of interest

Experience—Some craftsmanship skill relating to area of interest

Special Skills and Personality Traits—Some office-related organizational/secretarial skill; ability to take direction from and work with others

CAREER LADDER

```
┌─────────────────────────────────────┐
│ Professional Artist (Illustrator,    │
│  Painter, Cartoonist, Sequential     │
│           Artist)                    │
└─────────────────────────────────────┘

┌─────────────────────────────────────┐
│         Artist Assistant             │
└─────────────────────────────────────┘

┌─────────────────────────────────────┐
│            Student                   │
└─────────────────────────────────────┘
```

Position Description

Many different types of artists employ Artist Assistants to help them in their day-to-day working lives. These employing artists are independent contractors and in most cases have achieved a high level of success and can afford the financial burden of employing an Artist Assistant. Some unpaid internships also qualify as assistantships. Those who commonly employ Artist Assistants include painters, sculptors, ceramists, independent illustrators, sequential artists, cartoonists, and photographers. The working life of an Artist Assistant varies by occupation and the individual artist employing the Artist Assistant. In some cases, an Artist Assistant performs duties commonly attributed to secretarial positions. In others, an Artist Assistant actually aids in the execution of finished art pieces. A comprehensive listing of these individual occurrences would require more space than can be allotted for this entry, but some examples of duties and job expectations are common enough to provide a general overview.

For high-profile painters, an Artist Assistant is typically employed to perform a very specific set of duties. At the most basic level, an Artist Assistant keeps a painter's studio organized. In doing this, the assistant sees that brushes are kept clean, media are kept organized, palettes are kept clean and ordered by different types of paint, and the work area is kept clean. The assistant may make purchasing runs to art suppliers when stock runs low on particular items. Also at this most basic level, a painter may charge his assistant with keeping references ordered by project, be they photographs or physical objects. In more advanced yet still common circumstances, an Artist Assistant may prepare the painting surfaces on which a painter executes his or her imagery (e.g., stretching canvas, priming panels, stretching paper on boards or temporary supports, etc.).

At the most advanced level, when a relationship has developed to include a high degree of trust on the employing painter's part, an Artist Assistant keeps an office organized. Duties performed in this scenario can include a large number of sensitive tasks. For instance, a trusted assistant will answer correspondence, both professional and personal. He or she may also have a hand in keeping appointments and finances organized. In some atypical circumstances, a long-tenured and well-trusted Artist Assistant becomes an invaluable part of the painter's working and personal life. While it's rare that positions such as this occur, enough examples exist to warrant listing here.

Independent illustrators also employ Artist Assistants. Typically, only those who reach master illustrator status have the means and needs to hire an Artist Assistant, but some independent illustrators at the mid-level are forced to hire help as well. In the most common circumstance, an Artist Assistant working for an independent illustrator performs duties very similar to those fielded by a painter's Artist Assistant, keeping supplies and references organized, preparing surfaces for image execution, keeping the workspace free from clutter, and so on. There are some differences, though, given the nature of an independent illustrator's day-to-day working life. For instance, an independent illustrator typically has a greater need for assistance with billings. An independent illustrator deals with a great many clients and usually has at least a dozen or more active bills going out and coming in at a given time. An independent illustrator is far more likely to involve his or her Artist Assistant in this aspect of business than a painter would, and may seek to employ an Artist Assistant with experience in a professional office environment right from the start.

In the working life of a highly successful sequential artist, an Artist Assistant position takes on dramatically different permutations due to the eclectic nature of the vocation. For instance, a sequential artist specializing in the penciling phase of the process for a mainstream sequential narrative publisher may have need of an Artist Assistant for studio maintenance similar to the needs of a painter and independent illustrator, but will also require a specialized research assistant familiar with the specific needs of the sequential artist. This may include seeking out published sequential narrative materials executed by the employing artist and others, photographic references necessary to keep environments and characters consistent, and even modeling for the occasional tricky vantage point in a specific lighting. A highly skilled Artist Assistant working for this particular type of artist may also be charged with tightening up loose indications of background elements. In most Artist Assistant occupations, the chief benefit comes from learning the specialized tasks involved with becoming a professional in an art field in which the Artist Assistant is interested. With the noted few exceptions—in which the Artist Assistant becomes a trusted partner in the artist's business—an Artist Assistant hires on with both parties understanding that the position has time limitations built in. Consider this occupation a training ground, one that will provide a minimal income and further one's education in practical ways not available in any school.

The only caveat of which to be wary is the rare occasion when an Artist Assistant's artistic and professional growth gets stunted. In very, very rare circumstances, a professional artist may become dependent upon the Artist Assistant emotionally, professionally, or both. In these extremely rare cases, a professional artist can form an emotional bond with an Artist Assistant or become dependent upon the tasks an Artist Assistant performs. On these rare occasions, the Artist Assistant finds his or her own personal growth as an artist arrested as he or she becomes more and more involved in providing assistance to the professional for whom he or she works. The Artist Assistant finds less time available for individual exploration of his or her own craft and relies more and more on the income earned as an Artist Assistant.

Salaries

Some Artist Assistant positions exist as internships offered through postsecondary schools and universities. In these scenarios, school credit accrues while the Artist Assistant learns the hands-on, day-to-day working life lessons not available in academic environments. Often, these lead to low-paying positions once the Artist Assistant completes his or her studies should a good working relationship develop.

Occasionally, a professional artist will seek out a competent Artist Assistant by advertising available positions in the classified section of industry-specific publications or Web sites. In these circumstances, employment can range from minimum wage positions to fully involved advanced-level assistantships.

Employment Prospects

A great many professional artists work in the United States; the U.S. Department of Labor's Bureau of Labor Statistics puts the total number of arts professionals at just over 1.5 million in 2003. Many of these at the higher levels require time-saving help around the workplace.

Advancement Prospects

While working for an established professional artist, a motivated and sharp Artist Assistant learns a great deal about his or her area of professional interest and develops relationships with other professionals in the business. This includes prospective employers who use the services of professional artists.

Education and Training

The specifics of the particular vocation in which a candidate seeks employment as an Artist Assistant will dictate educational and training needs. For instance, a person seeking employment as an assistant to a professional painter needs to have a working knowledge of paint applications, surface preparations, studio organization, and material care. A prospective Artist Assistant candidate to an independent illustrator needs to have a working knowledge of the vagaries specific to the illustration industry.

Postsecondary education best prepares an individual for accepting these positions. In addition to familiarizing the prospective Artist Assistant with materials and methods employed by practitioners of the trades, postsecondary education also instills time-management skills and organizational abilities. These qualities will enhance a candidate's chances of landing lasting employment as an Artist Assistant.

Experience, Skills, and Personality Traits

Having a background in an office environment helps prepare an Artist Assistant for more advanced duties in working with a professional artist. This experience prepares the prospective Artist Assistant for the more specialized areas of handling the financial end of the job as well as the organizational aspect. Keeping a workspace neat and orderly often falls to the Artist Assistant, and observing such in an office environment provides a template.

The specific skill set required of an Artist Assistant varies by vocation. However, an ability to organize a workspace and artist materials specific to the profession is universal. Individual circumstances may require a greater facility with specific methods and media, and these are all handled on a case-by-case basis.

More than one professional artist used this exact phrase when interviewed for this entry: "Check your ego at the door." An Artist Assistant must remember the key word in the job title—"assistant." While personal growth as a professional artist is a natural by-product of one's employment as an Artist Assistant, one's key role in this position is to save the employing professional artist time and make his or her workflow more efficient. Hot-shots need not apply. Additionally, one must also exhibit a degree of patience about methods and materials application. An Artist Assistant more advanced in his or her studies may have arrived at some manners of working that are incongruous with the employing professional's. It's incumbent upon the Artist Assistant to bend his or her way of working to the employing professional artist's. This type of flexibility is a key ingredient to a successful working relationship.

Unions and Associations

In order to qualify for membership in unions and associations, individuals typically have to be professional artists. Therefore, there are no official unions or associations associated with Artist Assistants.

Tips for Entry

1. Read trade publications specific to your area of interest and scan the classified section. It may also be helpful to contact professionals who advertise their services in these publications and inquire about available positions.
2. Sharpen the skills inherent to the profession in which you're interested and prepare a clean, clear portfolio showcasing these skills.
3. Continually monitor job placement departments at your postsecondary institution for available openings.

PHOTOGRAPHER'S ASSISTANT

CAREER PROFILE

Duties: Assists photographer in wide variety of tasks: hauls equipment to and from shoots; helps set up lights; loads film; tracks shots; may run errands to lab and elsewhere; may paint sets; may drive the van to the shoot and back; may even make breakfast and coffee; may clean studio or location; may delegate work to more junior assistants or interns

Alternate Title(s): Assistant Photographer

Salary Range: $20,000 to $80,000+

Employment Prospects: Good

Advancement Prospects: Good

Best Geographical Location(s): Large metropolitan areas

Prerequisites:

Education or Training—Four-year college degree (B.A. or B.F.A.) may be useful but is not critical; photography and computer courses important

Experience—One- to three-year apprenticeship or internship with a professional photographer is critical.

Special Skills and Personality Traits—Flexible; organized; efficient; able to follow direction; creative; fast thinker; solid working knowledge of cameras, equipment, lighting, and computer software programs (e.g., Adobe Photoshop, Illustrator); discrete; professional; thick-skinned; in some cases must be physically strong enough to haul equipment

CAREER LADDER

```
┌─────────────────────────────────┐
│         Photographer            │
└─────────────────────────────────┘

┌─────────────────────────────────┐
│     Photographer's Assistant    │
└─────────────────────────────────┘

┌─────────────────────────────────┐
│       Apprentice or Intern      │
└─────────────────────────────────┘
```

Position Description

A Photographer's Assistant is the photographer's right hand and, as the title suggests, assists the photographer in all aspects of photography shoots. Photographers' Assistants work all varieties of hours, depending on the scope of the project and the clients' deadlines. On the day of the shoot, assistants arrive early at the studio to check on and lay out the equipment, discuss the project with the photographer, and map out the day's work. If the job is on location (off-site), assistants pack the bags, being careful to remember what's packed where for fast retrieval later on. For larger jobs with more freelance help, assistants receive more formal assignments from either staff assistants or producers and create written itineraries or job lists.

Assistants set up lighting equipment and may adjust other aspects of the set pertaining to the project. They might move furniture around, rig backgrounds into place, or use gels to modify lights. If a photographer is still scouting the location, assistants unpack the gear or help check logistics. If a photographer asks for a specific piece of equipment, such as a camera body and a favorite lens or a light meter, the assistant must know exactly where these things are and get them fast.

If it's a digital shoot, as many projects are fast becoming, assistants may set up computer equipment, and this is where assistants' true skills come through. They must work quickly and accurately to be ready when the photographer, the talent, and all of the other folks who might be there (e.g., makeup, wardrobe, producers, clients, art buyers, art directors, publicists, editors) are ready to work. During the shoot, assistants load and unload cameras, keeping careful track of film or memory cards and images. Assistants may have to keep a detailed shot log, marking down which shots are where and specifying whether they are on film or digital.

The Photographer's Assistant prepares film to be sent to the lab in stages. Either a messenger will pick up the film or the assistant will make the trek. Assistants process and upload digital films along the way. If it's a one-day shoot, at the end of the day assistants either take down the sets, pack up the gear and clean up, or pack up the gear and move it to the next location. If it's more than a one-day shoot at the same location, assistants may have to log all of the film, handle a final lab run, and make sure the location is secure.

Salaries

Photographers' Assistants can earn between $20,000 and $80,000 or more, depending upon their experience and their specialty. Salaries are higher in major cities. It is industry standard for Photographers' Assistants to charge a flat day rate, which can range from as little as $75 to as high as $500 per day. The amount will be based on all of these variables: the assistant's experience, the photographer's experience, whether the work is located in a major city, and the photography medium (e.g., editorial photography typically pays lower than digital photography). Assistants with three to five years of experience who have a good reputation in the industry command higher day rates.

Employment Prospects

Employment for Photographers' Assistants is directly connected to employment for photographers. The U.S. Department of Labor's *Occupational Outlook Handbook* predicts that through 2012, photographers will be employed about as fast as average for all occupations, meaning a 10 to 20 percent increase. Competition is fierce, and assistants who have a deep knowledge of the equipment and software and are quick on their feet will have better opportunities to find work.

Advancement Prospects

Advancement is self-determined. Most Photographers' Assistants hone their skills within five to six years of being on the job and are ready to move up to the photographer role. Assistant photographers need to be prepared for the challenge of transitioning from supporter to key player. The transition is not always easy. The industry is small, and many people will know your work only as an assistant; most won't know how many years you have worked or your readiness for the step up. To erase industry memory of their role, many assistants take one to two years off to focus on getting their portfolios together and create a plan to promote themselves as full-fledged photographers.

Education and Training

A B.FA. or B.A. can be helpful, but it is not critical. Many people work their way up, taking classes on the side at photography schools or training centers. It is critical now for assistants to know digital photography and software systems, such as Photoshop, for both PC and Macintosh platforms. You also increase your chances for being hired by knowing a range of specific brands of cameras and lighting equipment. The stronger your technical knowledge, the better odds you have for finding work.

Experience, Skills, and Personality Traits

Photographers' Assistants need to be flexible, because the job is extremely personality-driven. As a freelancer, you will be working with a whole host of personalities and management styles. One photographer may be very hands-on and micromanaging, while the next will give directions but want very little interaction. Each will have a different style and different preferences. It's up to you as the assistant to adapt to each situation and get the job done seamlessly. Discretion is another pivotal characteristic that can either make or break your reputation in the business. Some photographers may be stumped by a certain aspect of the project. They will either ask for your help or not. You must intuit when it is appropriate to offer your constructive insights and solutions and when it's better to keep quiet.

You must be open to learning and open to other people's ideas. The photographer will have a perspective on a job and may or may not discuss it with you to get your feedback. You must be willing and able to contribute. Even if you disagree and have a different vision, you must also be willing to go along with the photographer's direction.

Unions and Associations

Many assistants join or participate in the same organizations as photographers: Advertising Photographers of America (APA) and American Society of Media Photographers (ASMP).

Tips for Entry

1. First identify the medium you want to work in. Then identify the photographers who work in that medium and contact them to introduce yourself. Be sure to follow up. Competition is fierce right now; it's not abnormal for a phone call or e-mail to go unanswered. Allow a week or two to pass before calling to follow up.
2. Go to labs and put up flyers advertising your availability for work.
3. Volunteer internships are often the most valuable way to get into the business. Networking also helps tremendously. Look for good relationships in the business

with photographers, labs, rental houses, makeup people, and so on.

4. Set goals. Have an idea of what you want this job to do for you and how long you plan to do it. Think about where you want to go next and make sure that everything you learn and every experience you have will contribute to the education needed for that next step.

5. Learn the best and broadest sets of skills and techniques.

COMMERCIAL PHOTOGRAPHER

CAREER PROFILE

Duties: Takes photographs; may set up backgrounds and lighting to best capture the subject of the photograph; meets with clients to discuss projects; provides photographs to clients for a variety of uses; works with a lab; may hire and oversee staff; may handle studio management (everything from accounts payable and receivable to office management and maintenance)

Alternate Title(s): Fine Arts Photographer, Lifestyle Photographer, Magazine Photographer, Portrait Photographer, Sports Photographer, Wedding Photographer, or other title that reflects a specialty

Salary Range: $30,000 to $125,000+

Employment Prospects: Fair

Advancement Prospects: Fair

Best Geographical Location(s): Large metropolitan areas

Prerequisites:

Education or Training—A B.A. or B.F.A. may be useful when starting out, but it is not critical; computer and technical training recommended

Experience—Three to five years of prior experience as assistant photographer (or first assistant) and/or studio manager

Special Skills and Personality Traits—Self-starter; disciplined; organized; efficient; entrepreneurial; able to manage multiple projects and interact well with people; confident; creative; able to communicate creative thoughts both verbally and in photographs; must have an eye for capturing images; clear communicator; technologically comfortable (with cameras, lights, photo equipment, and computer equipment and software)

CAREER LADDER

```
┌─────────────────────────────┐
│        Studio Owner         │
└─────────────────────────────┘

┌─────────────────────────────┐
│        Photographer         │
└─────────────────────────────┘

┌─────────────────────────────┐
│  Assistant Photographer or  │
│       Studio Manager        │
└─────────────────────────────┘
```

Position Description

A good photographer understands all the pieces needed to create an effective picture. A lot of variables can make or break that image, and the photographer has to ask a lot of questions first before knowing how to best capture the product at hand. What is the product and what is it made of? Who is the target audience? What color scheme, if any, does the client have in mind? How is the picture going to be used? Where will it be published and what is the distribution? Successful photographers have a wide range of skills, from the natural creative eye to strong verbal and written communication abilities.

Commercial Photographers help "commercialize," or market, a product. The job begins when a client calls with new products that need to be photographed. The photographer asks specific questions to better understand the client's vision and needs. In order to establish a price, also, the photographer finds out how the photographs will be used, the background the client has in mind, whether the client wants the products glamorized or simply documented, and if they want black-and-white or color film.

After meeting with the client, if the product is small, the photographer takes it back to the studio and begins the process of setting up the shot(s). Based on the discussion with the client, the photographer picks the background, the surface area (table? floor?), the angle of view that best suits the object, and the perspective. The photographer chooses the camera, the lens, the lights, and the exposure. It is standard practice for the photographer to take Polaroid shots for testing before going to actual film. He or she will typically scan the Polaroid and e-mail it to the client for approval. Once the client gives the thumbs-up, the photographer shoots the film and sends it to the lab for processing. Once the lab sends the film back, the photographer examines the pictures using a lightbox, and if all looks fine, packs them up with the merchandise and messengers everything to the client.

Photographers hire assistants and staff as needed. Depending on the staff structure and size of the studio, photographers are also responsible for negotiating prices, creating contracts, invoicing clients, overseeing or directly handling accounts receivable and payable, bookkeeping and tax reporting, managing staff, and maintaining office supplies. They also make sure the studio is spotless and dust-free; this is critical in the business. Photographers often promote their businesses with promotion calls and direct mailings. Most have Web sites as well as traditional portfolios.

Salaries

Photographers can expect to earn anywhere from $30,000 to $125,000 and beyond, depending on their specialty and years of experience. Those with less experience command smaller salaries. Photographers based in major urban cities such as Boston, New York City, Chicago, and Los Angeles earn more money than those in the suburbs and smaller cities.

Employment Prospects

According to the Bureau of Labor Statistics (BLS), in 2002 photographers held about 130,000 jobs, with more than half self-employed. Be aware that this is a hard business to get started in, but once you are up and running and have a steady clientele, your business can in fact thrive. Photographers fill certain industry needs. For example, wedding photographers can either work independently or have a staff of photographers they can send out to cover the event. Catalog photographers can own their own studios and employ as many as 10 or more photographers to photograph various products. Some photographers also sell their work to stock photo agencies. Competition is keen because the work is interesting and appeals to many people. The BLS predicts

that employment of photographers is expected to increase about as fast as the average for all occupations through 2012. Portrait photographers will be more in demand as the population grows. While digital photographers will continue to be in need, they will be competing with the falling price of digital cameras. More people will be using the cameras on their own.

Advancement Prospects

Photographers who own their own studios are at the height of their careers, and the advances they make will be to stimulate or alter their careers. They may shake up the scope of their work, focusing on certain media or certain product lines and companies or branching out into a whole new area. Photographers who work for small studios may advance to become studio owners after three to five years.

Education and Training

A B.A. or B.F.A. may be useful when starting out but is not critical. Digital photography is more prevalent, and photographers will do well with computer and technical training under their belts. Many photographers gain their most valuable experience on the job, working their way up from apprentices to photographers' assistants. Photographers can learn from such magazines as *Photo District News, Print,* and *HOW.*

Experience, Skills, and Personality Traits

It is standard for photographers to have at minimum of five years of experience as a photographer's assistant and/or studio manager. Independent Commercial Photographers run their own businesses and must be disciplined self-starters. In addition to having strong business management skills, they must be creative and have an eye for design and composition to capture good photographs. They must be able to bring something special to the pictures to make them stand out. Photographers must be multitaskers, able to juggle various projects while interacting well with people (their assistants, other consultants, clients, and more). They must also be strong verbal communicators. They must be able to listen to their clients and know how to translate the clients' visions into photographs that work. Photographers must be technologically comfortable and open to learning about new things to stay current and to enhance and expand their business. They need to have strong knowledge of all of their camera equipment as well as computer equipment and software.

Unions and Associations

Photographers join Advertising Photographers of America (APA) and the American Society of Media Photographers (ASMP) to network and attend educational programs.

Tips for Entry

1. Explore all aspects of the business before deciding what you want to do. Work with fashion photographers, architecture photographers, and portrait photographers.
2. Don't be afraid to ask a lot of questions of people in the business. Find out how something was done. Get first-hand education while you're on the job; it's the best way to learn!
3. Be nice to everyone. Photography is a small world, and your reputation can follow you through the industry and through your career. Have integrity. Be professional and ethical.
4. Spend wisely. There are far too many things out there for photographers to buy, and you don't need all of them. Choose carefully.
5. Set goals for yourself while you work as a photographer's assistant. Have a plan for how long you plan to commit to the job, what you plan to learn while doing it, and the people you aim to work for.

CARTOONIST

CAREER PROFILE

Duties: Composes images and text, often in a sequence, to tell a humorous story

Alternate Title(s): Humorous Illustrator

Salary Range: Zero to $100,000+; in uncommon circumstances, $1,000,000+

Employment Prospects: Poor

Advancement Prospects: Poor

Best Geographical Location(s): Areas equipped with high-speed Internet access; major urban areas with local and national publications that feature cartoons and comic strips

Prerequisites:

Education or Training—None required

Experience—While none is necessarily required, an ability to draw consistent characters and environments that relate to one's stylizations is necessary

Special Skills and Personality Traits—The ability to tell a story or deliver a joke in pictures; a good sense of humor; a great deal of dedication and drive, including the ability to accept criticism and rejection

CAREER LADDER

```
┌─────────────────────────────────┐
│          Cartoonist             │
└─────────────────────────────────┘

┌─────────────────────────────────┐
│     Artist Assistant / Intern   │
└─────────────────────────────────┘

┌─────────────────────────────────┐
│            Student              │
└─────────────────────────────────┘
```

Position Description

Cartoonists fall into several modes and methods of drafting the final work. Despite these differences, several universal rules apply. First, the story or gag must be crafted. Next, the physical execution of the artwork takes place. Finally, the art gets delivered for print.

In order to begin, a Cartoonist must have a story or an idea to draw. In some circumstances, a strip writer works with the Cartoonist to craft the story lines and plot out a string of events. This is most typical in comic strips involving recurring characters. Other Cartoonists write their own material, most frequently single-frame gag strips involving changing characters and scenes. (While brilliant examples of recurring character strips written by Cartoonists exist—"Peanuts," "Calvin and Hobbes," "Doonesbury," and "Bloom County" among them—they are rarer than the Cartoonists described here.) In still other circumstances, a Cartoonist may employ the services of a ghost writer or gag writer to meet deadlines when stuck for an idea.

When a Cartoonist works side-by-side with a strip writer, the two begin by having conversations about the direction a story or series of stories will take. The amount of story and dialogue input a cartoonist has in these sessions also varies based upon the working relationship developed by the partners, as does the amount of visual suggestion made by the writer. In some circumstances, the amount of cooperation between writer and Cartoonist is minimal; in others, very great.

A Cartoonist who writes his or her own material will often be required to plot out story arcs and submit them to an editor. In the case of a political cartoonist, often this avenue doesn't exist, as the material generated by the Cartoonist relates directly to current events. The working relationship with the employer will of necessity be different, requiring a looser agreement about planned content. In addition, the material has to stay within certain parameters—for instance, in many Sunday comic strips, a three-tiered story with an introductory gag that stands alone must accompany the main story, told over two tiers (or strips of panels in a horizontal row). In other venues, a specific space for a single-column one-shot cartoon gets allocated, and the Cartoonist must make the art and story fit within these rigid boundaries. In all cases, the nature of the cartoon or comic strip will have its boundaries set from the very beginning, and these will need to be observed throughout the life of the strip.

Once the story has been written, the Cartoonist draws the cartoon or comic strip. The method employed can vary greatly, depending upon the specific requirements of the individual strip or cartoon as well as the working relationship with the employer/publisher. In almost all cases, the work begins as a rough pencil drawing. These roughs lay out the individual panels (or single panel, if a single-image cartoon), the characters, settings, and all action taking place. At this stage, the Cartoonist also sketches in the space required for lettering. Once completed, the Cartoonist moves from this preliminary stage to final art, which can be accomplished in a variety of ways. Some Cartoonists still execute final art by hand, everything from hand-drawn illustrations for each panel right down to hand-lettering all dialogue and captions. Cartoonists use everything from old-fashioned quill pens and brushes dipped in waterproof ink to disposable permanent markers to craft these hand-drawn strips and cartoons. Traditional methods still apply for some Cartoonists when it comes to executing color work as well, from transparent watercolor to water-based dyes and magic markers.

With the advent of digital technology, however, many Cartoonists find themselves relying on the use of personal computers to facilitate several steps in execution of final art. Among these many uses, a great many Cartoonists color and letter their art with the aid of a computer. Many artists even craft their entire strip or cartoon completely in a digital environment. Each individual Cartoonist arrives at a method of crafting final art based upon his or her experience and familiarity with the tools at hand, the only requirement being that an employer can count on receiving consistent results from the Cartoonist.

Once a strip or cartoon has been completed, the final work is delivered to an employer. Employers vary based upon the specific circumstances for each individual work, but two examples are an editor with a large syndicate, such as the King Features Syndicate, or an editor/art director if the strip or cartoon has been commissioned by a singular publication, be it a magazine or newspaper. Delivery methods vary depending upon the nature of the final art executed: A Cartoonist working in a traditional manner often delivers original art via insured courier or in person, while a Cartoonist using computer software in the workplace may transfer files electronically, uploading final art files over the Internet to a server from which the employer's production department can retrieve the data. Cartoonists working in digital environments also frequently save final art files to removable media, most typically writable CDs, and have these delivered with hard-copy proofs to the employer.

Salaries

Just breaking into the field, Cartoonists don't command much, if any, salary. Often, Cartoonists get their start working for a college newspaper that pays little, if at all. Similarly, small-town newspapers and periodicals offer space for printing one's comic strips or cartoons, but little if any recompense. Also at this entry level, artists' assistants working for established professionals can expect to make small hourly wages, anywhere from minimum wage to $25 per hour. Typically, this work is sporadic, based solely upon the requirements of the employing professional.

In the middle range, cartoonists with strips or cartoons syndicated to several newspapers can earn in the $40,000 to $100,000 range. In these circumstances, salary range depends upon how many publications carry the content and the popularity of it. Often, syndication requires sale of the intellectual property rights to the work to the syndicating organization, and individual contracts governing residuals and reprint rights vary too much to list here.

At the highest end, Cartoonists with a wildly popular strip or cartoon can command more than $1,000,000 per year. These extremely rare occasions have much to do with licensing characters for toys, apparel, food items, television, and film.

Employment Prospects

A great many people's introduction to the world of visual art comes by way of viewing the work of Cartoonists and animators. This usually instills warm feelings about the work that are often remembered fondly as an aspiring artist grows older. That nostalgia can drive the desire to investigate this career option while ignoring some of the real-world pitfalls involved with it. Pursuing a career as a Cartoonist is one of the most difficult aspirations and insecure vocations in the visual art field.

Starts can be had by generating one's own content, from characters and situations to character design and individual art style, and shopping it to local independent publications. One can also seek out professionals in the field to inquire about internships or assistantships available. Quite often, Cartoonists working in traditional methods employ artists who show promise and a high degree of technical skill to assist in the execution of final art. Examples include an artist assistant who applies ink to penciled background images; an artist skilled at hand-lettering to letter the dialogue, captions, and sound effects; and a research assistant to seek out reference materials for character costumes and settings.

Advancement Prospects

The number of available employment opportunities to those seeking employment weighs very heavily against the seeker.

Even factoring in the unpaid internships and local periodicals, cartooning remains a tough field to crack.

Education and Training

No official education or training is required of Cartoonists. However, Cartoonists with more education in traditional methods of drawing will have more visual tricks in the bag and a more well-rounded visual vocabulary. Any additional tool at a Cartoonist's command will help him or her figure out a solution to potentially sticky spots encountered when trying to solve a visual problem. Additionally, the more training and practice one has at the craft, the greater the ability to deliver consistent visual results, thereby increasing the likelihood of employment.

Experience, Skills, and Personality Traits

Being a Cartoonist requires no special experience per se, but one makes a mark more easily in the cartooning field when he or she has worked with another Cartoonist, be it as an intern, artist assistant, or office assistant. This experience helps define the parameters of the field for the aspiring Cartoonist.

The skill level of a Cartoonist's visual art varies from detail-rich realism ("Prince Valiant") to ultrastylized simplicity ("The Far Side"). Many Cartoonists execute their final art with the tried-and-true methods employed by the originators of the form—pencil, pen, brush, and ink—while many others use contemporary digital applications to make their art. The only absolute skill required of a cartoonist is the ability to deliver consistent visual results; if you desire to work in a detailed, observational style or a more primitive, expressive way or even somewhere in between, you must be able to draft a consistent look. Growth over a period of years is expected, but these changes must take place gradually and as a natural evolution of style.

A Cartoonist must be willing to work with others, have at least some flexibility, and possess a work ethic that makes meeting frequent deadlines possible. When working with another person in drafting stories and working with an editor for delivery of final art, a Cartoonist needs to be able to communicate verbally and accept criticism. It also helps quite a bit, especially for one who writes his or her own material, to have a well-honed sense of humor.

Unions and Associations

Several associations offer significant networking and educational opportunities for Cartoonists. (Current copyright law prohibits the formation of unions or collective bargaining agreements for independent contractors.) The longest-lived association devoted strictly to advancing the ideals and standards of professional cartooning in its various forms is the National Cartoonists Society (NCS). With 16 chapters around the United States, the NCS offers terrific opportunities for networking and a slate of events tailored to the concerns of Cartoonists. Additionally, the Graphic Artists Guild and the Society of Illustrators (New York) provide additional networking and educational opportunities.

Tips for Entry

1. Seek employment or internship with an established professional in the field and network with professional cartoonists.
2. Establish contact with employers who commission comic strips and cartoons.
3. Above all, though, sharpen your drawing skills and study the market widely to be aware of what's being done and has been done. This field has many vagaries—this is a pop culture medium, and the tastes of the day are often impossible to predict—and often requires a little bit of luck. (Why one strip takes off immediately and another languishes for years before becoming popular remains a mystery to many of the professionals who create them.) Hard work at one's craft will broaden one's skill set and help open more doors than a limited skill set will, and making acquaintances will increase the number of opportunities you encounter.

INDEPENDENT ILLUSTRATOR

CAREER PROFILE

Duties: Provides images for clients on demand; manages business of illustration

Alternate Title(s): Graphic Artist

Salary Range: $0 to $100,000+

Employment Prospects: Poor

Advancement Prospects: Fair

Best Geographical Location(s): New York City; major urban centers; areas equipped with broadband Internet service

Prerequisites:

Education or Training—Expert knowledge of basic drawing and/or painting, two-dimensional design, and color

Experience—None required

Special Skills and Personality Traits—Good business sense; ability to work with designers and take direction to formulate best course for final image; perseverance; visual versatility; flair for self-promotion

CAREER LADDER

```
┌─────────────────────────────┐
│      Master Illustrator     │
└─────────────────────────────┘

┌─────────────────────────────┐
│          Illustrator        │
└─────────────────────────────┘

┌─────────────────────────────┐
│            Student          │
└─────────────────────────────┘
```

Position Description

An assignment given to an Independent Illustrator typically goes through several stages, regardless of the client. Independent Illustrators create illustrations for everything from advertising to publishing to institutional bodies. The client supplies a write-up of the assignment. Once this material has been digested, the illustrator drafts thumbnail sketches, which are often small, minimally detailed drawings done to proportionate scale of the final piece. Once these have been discussed with the client and the client selects a direction in which to proceed, the illustrator drafts a final pencil drawing.

At this stage an illustrator gathers all the formal research he or she needs to execute the final image. Once the finished pencil drawing has been delivered, the client makes final comments about the composition, and the illustrator begins to make a color rough, which is a quick block-in of general color proposed for the piece. Usually, this means painting, either manually or digitally, a very broadly applied and non-specific representation of what the illustrator expects to deliver with the final image. This gives the client an eye for general color composition and is useful to the client most often when the illustrator's work is slated to appear within a larger body of work, be it a page on which text elements surround the image or with other works of visual art in a collected body of work. It's at this stage that all matters regarding the final image are resolved, and then work begins on the final image.

The ways in which Illustrators execute final art vary greatly and depend mostly upon the experiences and preferences of the individual artist. There are traditional illustrators who execute their imagery in tried-and-true methods of painting and drawing that date back to the Renaissance and include oil painting; watercolor, both transparent and opaque; egg tempera; encaustic (a wax-based method of painting); colored pencil; ink; charcoal; and graphite. The arrival of the desktop computer has given rise to the newest brand of illustrator, the digital illustrator. These artists employ a variety of techniques, using everything from vector-based drawing programs (such as Adobe Illustrator and Macromedia Freehand) to bitmap painting programs (Adobe

Photoshop) to three-dimensional rendering programs (Alias Maya). Digital illustrators typically work on the Macintosh platform, as most clients' work environments are Mac-based.

In unusual circumstances, changes may be requested by a client at this final stage. In most cases, the changes are small and amount to very little expenditure in time or effort on the illustrator's part. In the rare cases in which large changes are made, arrangements for such changes should be covered by the contract negotiated at the beginning of the commission. Additional compensation for changes made at this stage will be required of the client.

The time spent on each final image varies based upon several factors, among them amount of detail in the image, expectation of the client for delivery, and skill level of the illustrator. Once finished, the illustrator delivers the final image to the client in an agreed-upon method, one stipulated at the beginning of negotiating the assignment. Some illustrators deliver original painted art, some deliver high-resolution scans either on CD or removable media via courier, some deliver high-resolution scans electronically via Internet means, and some deliver digital content directly, in person.

Salaries

At the earliest stages, one cannot expect to make a tremendous living as an Independent Illustrator. By definition, anyone executing an image that gets printed is an illustrator, however humble the publication may be. Fledgling illustrators often accept low-paying assignments or even some small-press assignments that pay only with contributor copies. This is especially true of Independent Illustrators who wish to make a go of sequential narrative, be it graphic novels, comic books, or comic strips. School newspapers offer chances to get images in print but do not offer much, if anything, in the way of paid work.

Independent Illustrators working in larger markets at the highest end can expect to make more than $100,000. While these are not the average, with hard work and some fortunate breaks, Independent Illustrators (even those who live in more rural areas if they have access to digital delivery methods for their imaging) can fetch handsome incomes.

Employment Prospects

Due to the stiffening competition from inside the industry as well as outside, the likelihood of breaking in as an Independent Illustrator is poor. Within the industry, art colleges continue to enroll students into illustration programs at a very high rate, and unaccredited schools still thrive. Many of the students of these programs vie for illustration jobs on a freelance basis upon graduation, often while earning their primary income in other areas.

Outside the illustration industry, corporate stock houses offer millions of images at rates often far below what an Independent Illustrator would require in order to make a living. While there are still clients who balk at using these images, as they could have been used elsewhere, typically the bottom line rules when choosing a vendor to supply imagery. Offering extensive search engines available on the Web and delivering images in quick digital downloads, stock agencies have a significant advantage in speed over even the most speedy illustrator who works on demand.

Advancement Prospects

Once an illustrator has his or her foot in the door, managing to earn a living while growing his or her business by expanding the client list, the likelihood for advancement is fair to good. Providing professional quality in a timely fashion, building a reputation for doing so, and constantly sharpening one's skills can still lead to earning one's sole living as an Independent Illustrator.

As an illustrator builds a body of published work, adds to his or her client list, and sharpens skills, the beginning illustrator advances to a more intermediate level, a level that usually means beginning to earn his or her sole living as an independent freelance illustrator. At this stage, he or she begins promoting himself or herself to a larger audience, sending out mailings and doing the hard work of selling himself or herself to a national audience.

Beyond this level, the level where the illustrator has regular, repeat business from a broad client list and has begun to make a splash with some national publications, is the master illustrator. A master illustrator is someone who regularly works at the highest national—and international—levels. In addition, master illustrators become household names within the industry, often garnering awards at the highest level in the industry, such as gold and silver medals at the Society of Illustrators' annual exhibitions. The vast majority of illustrators who reach master illustrator level only do so after years of hard work, diligent self-promotion, reliably meeting deadlines with a few lucky breaks thrown in, though it's not unheard of for a very young person right out of college to ascend to this lofty perch quite quickly. (In these extremely rare circumstances, being a nationally recognized, award-winning student at a respected art college is the most common path to early advancement.)

As an illustrator progresses through his or her career, he or she often discovers the flip side of the stock house coin: As his body of work grows, the Independent Illustrator finds himself or herself in possession of a stock house of his or her own work. Resale of images to which an illustrator owns the copyright can bolster his or her income, oftentimes dramatically, with very little additional time invested. This type of licensing relates closely to the music industry, in which recordings can earn artists royalties long into the future.

Education and Training

While specialized training may not necessarily be *required,* the higher the level of expertise in executing visual art required of Independent Illustrators and the more versatile the individual's skill set, the better one will fare in the job market. Having the ability to execute different types of illustrations at a professional level increases the number of commissions one is able to accept, especially at the early stages of one's career. Those executing visual art of a single type (e.g., high-level realism, conceptual art, caricature, or cartooning) must be able to do so at the highest possible level. While there are specialists currently working in all parts of the United States, they are still rare in comparison to more jack-of-all-trades illustrators. As an illustrator progresses further into his or her career, he or she may narrow focus. Often, this owes to getting regular work of a specific type and repeat business from particular clients. It's better, however, to expose oneself to as many avenues of expression as possible, especially early on.

These visual art skills are often best honed by completing a course of study at a professional art college, university, or some independent institution. Additionally, one can often benefit from job referrals through these sources and take advantage of networking opportunities unavailable elsewhere.

Experience, Skills, and Personality Traits

It takes quite a thick skin and oftentimes a very strong-willed individual to make a living as an Independent Illustrator in the current job market. Competition is stiff not only among illustrators themselves; outside competition from corporate stock houses has further diluted opportunities for independent contractors in recent years. Opportunities to provide visual content still abound in the United States—everything from advertising campaigns and national magazines to small-market promotional mailers use imagery to drive their messages—but the ease of ordering stock photos online provides stiff competition to the slower process of commissioning an illustration. This creates a very high-pressure working environment for entry-level Independent Illustrators, and that pressure abates only slightly at even more accomplished levels.

In addition to the skill required to fulfill the imaging demands of one's clients, the Independent Illustrator must also have a very high working knowledge of the business surrounding his or her visual art efforts. The Independent Illustrator must know how to negotiate a contract, protect copyrights, and seek the best compensation possible for an assignment based upon the market value of the assignment offered. These business skills are the minimum. One must also know how to manage accounts receivable (moneys owed) and accounts payable (moneys spent) and to form a long-term small business

plan. These latter business skills can be acquired by taking small/home business courses at community colleges, night courses, and specialized courses offered by several of the trade organizations listed in Appendix I.

One cannot overstate the need for effective self-promotion, as well. While most business courses emphasize the need for self-promotion, this facet of business is particularly important to Independent Illustrators. There are several methods that have proven effective for different illustrators, from small, targeted mailings all the way up to large, national campaigns, and an Independent Illustrator must carefully consider his or her options in this regard and form a plan to execute this vital part of the business.

Unions and Associations

While there are several trade associations to which Independent Illustrators belong, there are no unions in the traditional labor union sense. This owes to a provision in the current labor relations laws that prohibits an individual who takes place in collective bargaining from retaining any individual copyrights to work executed under the collective bargaining arrangement.

The three primary trade associations that offer benefits specific to the illustration industry are the Graphic Artists Guild, the Illustrators Partnership of America (IPA), and the Society of Illustrators (New York). The Graphic Artists Guild has chapters in various regions of the country, and local chapter membership also enrolls you in national membership. While several satellites have opened in other parts of the country, the Society of Illustrators in New York City is the original and the one to which most illustrators belong.

Tips for Entry

1. Build your body of work by accepting opportunities to get your work in print, especially early in your career, and get these printed pieces circulating to art buyers, art directors, and creative directors who hire Independent Illustrators.
2. Promote your work and devise a long-term self-promotional plan—invest in your business.
3. Interview working illustrators while still a student and glean whatever you can about the day-to-day business of being a self-supporting Independent Illustrator.
4. Forge relationships with art directors, creative directors, and designers.
5. Objectively survey the markets and target those who use illustrations similar to the work you make.

ARCHITECTURAL ILLUSTRATOR

CAREER PROFILE

Duties: Illustrates building designs for architects, engineers, contractors, developers, and others; gives building designs visual reality by adding color, scenery, people, and other background elements; reads project descriptions, establishes budgets, and creates illustration production schedules; creates contracts; meets with clients to discuss projects and present illustrations; handles business administrative tasks; promotes and markets business

Alternate Title(s): Architectural Renderer

Salary Range: $35,000 to $100,000+

Employment Prospects: Good

Advancement Prospects: Fair

Best Geographical Location(s): Major urban areas

Prerequisites:

Education or Training—Bachelor's degree in illustration recommended; some firms may require either a bachelor's or master's degree in architecture, with illustration background; coursework in architecture, art history, graphic design, and design software recommended

Experience—Two to three years of experience as an artist with an architectural firm

Special Skills and Personality Traits—Excellent drawing, sketching, and painting skills; creative; self-starter; strong interpersonal skills; works well under pressure; professional with clear communication abilities; good listener who is able to follow detailed directions; understands composition, balance, and perspective

CAREER LADDER

```
┌─────────────────────────────────────┐
│ Owner, Architectural Illustration Firm │
└─────────────────────────────────────┘

┌─────────────────────────────────────┐
│      Architectural Illustrator       │
└─────────────────────────────────────┘

┌─────────────────────────────────────┐
│ Junior Architectural Artist or Designer │
└─────────────────────────────────────┘
```

Position Description

Architectural Illustrators illustrate building designs for a variety of clients, from architects, developers, engineers, and contractors to homeowners, interior and landscape designers, and more. Clients hire Architectural Illustrators to help them understand the projects they are working on or to express the project visually to others, such as the general public or other consultants. Clients often seek funding and support to help them realize their plans; illustrations help them pitch their ideas to people to achieve these goals. For example, contractors hire Architectural Illustrators to help them grasp the scope of projects by seeing the construction details laid out visually. Architectural Illustrators have the artistic and technical skills to create illustrations based on construction plans, as well as on elevations, sketch designs, and plans supplied by architects.

According to one industry expert, it is the Architectural Illustrator who makes the "visual leap between that which does not exist and reality. Architectural Illustrators are able to add light, texture, color, context (roads, trees, and other landmarks which help acknowledge the location of the project), people, and cars (for scale to help the observer understand how large the building will be) and other components to make the illustration convey a clear vision of what the project will feel like when it is built." Architectural Illustrators work in the medium they are comfortable with and in media that best suit the project. They draw using pens and inks, pencils, oils, pastels, prismacolor, markers, watercolors, paints, and computer design software, such as Adobe Photoshop and Illustrator.

Architectural Illustrators meet with clients to discuss projects. Upon reviewing the project details, Architectural Illustrators create budgets and set up production schedules, which detail dates of illustration submissions from drafts to final. Architectural Illustrators create contracts for client signature, making sure to include fees, terms of usage, credit lines, number of changes and revisions permitted before fees are charged, what those fees are, expenses for reimbursement, what is expected of the client, and what the Architectural Illustrator promises in return.

After the client signs the contract, Architectural Illustrators begin work usually by drawing and assembling the building, keeping in mind the preferred angle and view point. They assemble the building through line construction, digital modeling, or photographing an actual model. Before proceeding, they will set up a meeting to show the client the preview, discussing the perspective and style and ensuring that the illustration is in the right direction. Upon securing approval, Architectural Illustrators create the final rendering, adding the lively and colorful elements they imagine will exist once the building is constructed, such as shadows depending on time of day, cars, people, trees, and other foliage. Architectural Illustrators pay close attention throughout their work to the production schedule. Clients often have delivery dates based on meetings and presentations they've scheduled, so meeting their deadlines is a critical part of the job.

Salaries

Depending on the firm and the project, Architectural Illustrators can earn salaries ranging from $35,000 to $100,000 or more. Freelance Architectural Illustrators may be able to increase their salaries by offering a menu of services with various fees, including stepped-up rates for projects that are commissioned at the last minute and require fast turnarounds. These jobs are known as "rush jobs," and because they require Architectural Illustrators to change priorities, adjust their schedules, and deliver certain levels of service in less-than-ideal timeframes, it is accepted standard business practice to charge higher fees in these instances.

Employment Prospects

Whether a building comes to fruition or not, as long as it is being planned, Architectural Illustrators will find work. According to one industry expert, architects, engineers, interior designers, landscape designers, and other environmental planners are relying increasingly on the services of illustra-

tors to complete their projects. The U.S. Department of Labor's *Occupational Outlook Handbook* predicts that the employment of architects will grow about as fast as the average through 2012; logically, the need for Architectural Illustrators will parallel this growth. Institutional and residential construction, however, is expected to grow, so those involved in designing (and illustrating designs of) houses, schools, nursing homes, hospitals, government buildings, and so on should fare better. Architectural Illustrators can find freelance and staff work in architectural firms, architectural design offices, contract or commercial facilities planning, interior design firms, landscape and environmental planning organizations, industrial and graphic design firms, art studios, and government agencies.

Advancement Prospects

There is no career ladder, per se, for freelance Architectural Illustrators. With experience, Architectural Illustrators can advance by growing their businesses, hiring more staff, and expanding their clientele. They can also broaden their skills by writing articles for trade publications and teaching or lecturing.

Education and Training

A four-year degree in illustration is recommended, but may not be required. Many Architectural Illustrators gain exposure to architecture by taking classes in school and while working in architectural firms. While some Architectural Illustrators have undergraduate and even graduate degrees in architecture, not all firms require this. What is becoming more important is versatility and flexibility among illustration media. Architectural Illustrators must be trained and talented in drawing, painting, and sketching and must also know computer design software such as Adobe Photoshop and Illustrator.

Experience, Skills, and Personality Traits

Architectural Illustrators need to have an appreciation for and love of architecture to truly enjoy and thrive in their work. Because they have the huge responsibility of expressing someone else's ideas, with the purpose of winning project bids, they must be excellent listeners who have a rare combination of technical and creative skills. They must be able to follow detailed plans and have the vision to transform those plans into appealing illustrations that sell the proposal. In addition to strong drawing and painting skills, some Architectural Illustrators may need to be well versed in design software such as Adobe Illustrator and Photoshop. Independent, self-motivated, deadline-driven individuals do well in this field.

Unions and Associations

Architectural Illustrators can become members of the American Institute of Architects, the American Society of Architectural Illustrators, and the New York Society of Renderers for discounts on conferences and educational workshops, trade publications, professional advice and representation, and networking opportunities.

Tips for Entry

1. Get your foot in the door by taking a freelance or staff position as an in-house illustrator in an architectural firm. You'll have the opportunity for on-the-job training and networking. You can find names of firms by doing a search on the Internet or through the phone book.

2. Read everything you can about architectural illustration. Make sure you are always learning throughout your entire career; it will help you stay inspired and keep your artwork fresh and creative. Research and learn about different illustration designs and styles and architectural projects. Read about the illustrators and architects behind the projects, also, to understand their approaches to their work.

3. Join associations and attend meetings. It's important to keep abreast of issues and trends in the architectural field. Networking with architects as well as with Architectural Illustrators will help people remember you when projects come up. It's also especially beneficial to form connections because if an Architectural Illustrator is too busy to handle incoming projects, he or she may refer work to you.

4. Take courses in small business management. Architectural Illustrators need to understand not only creative techniques, but the day-to-day tasks involved in running a business, such as pricing, terms of agreement, negotiating, billing, self-promotion and marketing tactics, and more.

MEDICAL ILLUSTRATOR

CAREER PROFILE

Duties: Provides scientifically accurate images for clients on demand; manages business of medical illustration

Alternate Title(s): None

Salary Range: $40,000 to $100,000+

Employment Prospects: Fair to Good

Advancement Prospects: Good to Excellent

Best Geographical Location(s): Major urban areas with teaching hospitals; areas equipped with broadband Internet service

Prerequisites:

Education or Training—Bachelor of fine arts; master of arts in medical illustration

Experience—None required

Special Skills and Personality Traits—High degree of skill as draftsman and painter, whether analog or digital; ability to adhere to rigid standards of accuracy; good business sense; flair for self-promotion

CAREER LADDER

```
┌─────────────────────────────┐
│     Medical Illustrator     │
└─────────────────────────────┘

┌─────────────────────────────┐
│      Graduate Student       │
└─────────────────────────────┘

┌─────────────────────────────┐
│    Undergraduate Student    │
└─────────────────────────────┘
```

Position Description

Medical illustration is a centuries-old and highly respected profession that supports the advancement of medicine. Neither the photograph nor modern strides in medical imaging have diminished the role of the Medical Illustrator. These artists distill complex visual information into didactic and beautiful illustrations and are integral contributors in disseminating medical knowledge. Medical Illustrators' work appears in a variety of venues: textbooks for medical students and surgeons, medical journals, brochures, consumer health magazines, pharmaceutical advertising, in courts of law, and in film.

When crafting images to appear in medical texts, Medical Illustrators employ a great degree of specificity and detail. Medical texts support medical education for medical students and CME (continuing medical education) for board-certified practicing professionals.

Medical journals often require imaging to further describe new scientific theory, new surgical procedures, and new drug therapy modalities for evolving disease. Articles of this sort, including Medical Illustrators' images used as visual aids, are subjected to review by a peer group of medical professionals prior to publication.

When a physician teaches patients about a medical test, disease, or prescription, he or she often requires written material and visual aids to help describe the subject discussed. These cases present the Medical Illustrator with a very different task than providing imaging for instructional texts for medical students and professionals. When creating images for viewing by patients, a different degree of careful editing takes place. Illustrators create patient-friendly brochures that include simpler anatomical renditions in soft colors to provide an informed understanding of the procedure required. In this same way, charts lining the wall of a physician's examination room may offer a patient an easy view to understand the part of the body he or she is there to have investigated.

Medical Illustrators also compose images for consumer-level health magazines. A fascination with health and a greater desire for awareness about the workings of one's body has bloomed in contemporary American culture, giving rise to the popularity of such publications. Medical

Illustrators operate much on the same level here as they do above, keeping in mind the layperson audience when designing the imagery.

Medical Illustrators have long worked directly with pharmaceutical companies and medical device manufacturers and with their medical advertising agencies. When new drugs and products enter the market, advertising to prescribing physicians and practicing surgeons is instrumental to building awareness and understanding of new benefits from medical breakthroughs. Medical advertising must pass review by the Food and Drug Administration (FDA). Accustomed to having his or her work subject to great scrutiny coupled with expertise in the medical field, the duty of providing imaging for these advertisements falls almost exclusively to the certified Medical Illustrator.

In perhaps the most surprising use of medical illustration to those not working in the field, a good deal of Medical Illustrators' work passes through the nation's courtrooms. Lawyers call expert witnesses to the stand to testify in cases of medical malpractice or personal injury, as medical professionals are the only people qualified to give testimony about the accepted standards of medical practice or medical evaluation of injury. In many cases, the extreme finer points of medical procedure are entered into the court record, and much of that testimony can be too large to digest for juries when taken on its own. In such cases, expert witnesses rely upon the skills of a Medical Illustrator to provide clear, understandable imagery that is entered as demonstrative evidence to support the experts' sworn testimony. By pointing to the parts of a medical illustration that supports what he or she is saying, an expert witness stands a much greater chance of getting his of her point across.

In addition to providing still-image depictions, Medical Illustrators also create animations—the newest area of exploration for Medical Illustrators, which is growing rapidly. Projects ranging from short Web-based animations for health information sites, to scientific conference exhibitions, to instructional films for network or cable transmission, to recreational Hollywood movies employ the services of Medical Illustrators.

In years past, Medical Illustrators relied upon traditional painting techniques and airbrush to render their images. As digital technologies became available, many Medical Illustrators were drawn to their greater degree of flexibility and edibility. Armed with these powerful imaging technologies, Medical Illustrators began building fully realized three-dimensional models in the virtual environment of digital space to deliver their imagery. As this occurred, artists also began to take advantage of the animation capabilities built into these new programs.

No longer bound by the limitations of cel-to-cel animation, these newly equipped Medical Illustrators began delivering three-dimensionally modeled animations. Instructional films broadcast on television and shown in classrooms and hospitals and a whole host of other venues now exhibit the expert imaging of the Medical Illustrator as motion pictures. Similarly, feature films rely on Medical Illustrators to provide a degree of accuracy and believability unavailable by any other means. A great deal of emphasis is placed upon verisimilitude in contemporary mainstream filmmaking, and there's no better authority than Medical Illustrators to provide this in the area of visualizing the inner workings of the human body.

Salaries

There are two ways to measure the salary expectations of the professional Medical Illustrator: salaried staff positions and independent freelance Medical Illustrators. Salaried staff positions for Medical Illustrators are available at some hospitals (typically teaching hospitals) and medical illustration houses that employ several certified medical illustrators. In this latter circumstance, which is an increasingly rare occurrence, independent freelance Medical Illustrators usually constitute the ownership of such groups. A Medical Illustrator so employed can expect to start in the $40,000 range, depending upon factors such as cost of living in the surrounding area. This income is also bolstered in most cases by assuming freelance duties in off-hours, which typically leads to a fully independent freelance medical illustration career.

Independent freelance Medical Illustrators, who are the majority of those employed in this field, start around $40,000 and can fetch more than $100,000, depending upon the individual's skills at the crafting of images, promoting the business to buyers of medical illustration, and managing the business aspects of the trade. As with many other independent contractors listed herein, ambition and work ethic greatly increase one's likelihood for success in this field.

Employment Prospects

Most Medical Illustrators receive their master of arts or master of science from one of five accredited graduate programs in the United States and Canada. (Undergraduate bachelor degrees are available from the Cleveland Institute of Art and Rochester Institute of Technology. These two schools are currently working to attain accreditation to offer graduate degrees.) Board certification attained after earning this specialized graduate degree demonstrates the completion of a peer-accepted portfolio and assures current competency. According to the Association of Medical Illustrators, there are between 800 and 900 certified Medical Illustrators actively working in the United States. With the United States leading the world in the advancement of medical knowledge, the continued role of the Medical Illustrator will be valued.

Advancement Prospects

While one may not have a clear career ladder in medical illustration as one would in a typical corporate environment, the prospects of advancing one's income and position in the field are good. The primary requirements for advancement are business skills, including copyright management and contract negotiation, management of cash flow and investment, advertising and marketing of skills, flexibility in learning new methods of execution, excellence in skill level, and dedication to personal continuing education. A motivated, certified Medical Illustrator who's prone to making good business decisions while keeping track of developing technological advancements in imaging technology stands a very good chance at increasing his or her billings and client base.

Education and Training

Given that this profession supports written material conceived by medical professionals in the overwhelming majority of circumstances (Hollywood notwithstanding), it stands to reason that a Medical Illustrator requires the same education and training given to prospective medical professionals. As with any prospective candidate for a medical degree, a bachelor's degree is the first step. Most Medical Illustrator hopefuls complete a bachelor of fine arts degree from an accredited degree-granting institution, along with all the science prerequisites necessary for admission to medical school. Conversely, a bachelor of science is acceptable, with core and advanced art courses in drawing, painting, and design. Meeting these requirements nearly constitutes a double major, and graduate school candidates typically spend five to seven years in undergraduate studies to complete all required prerequisites in these two disparate disciplines. A personal interview, a high GPA, and a portfolio are required for acceptance into a graduate program. The five graduate programs for Medical Illustrators are connected to the respected teaching hospitals at the Medical College of Georgia, the University of Illinois at Chicago, the Johns Hopkins School of Medicine, the University of Texas Southwestern Medical Center at Dallas, and the University of Toronto's Faculty of Medicine's Division of Biomedical Communications.

The prospective Medical Illustrator graduates from one of these specialized programs with either a master of arts or a master of science in medical illustration. A Medical Illustrator completes the same academic coursework as his fellow medical students. When the medical students begin seeing patients on rounds, the Medical Illustrators begin drawing and observing in surgery and autopsy.

This is an intense regimen, one that graduates about 40 candidates per year collectively among all five degree-granting institutions. Programs are generally six semesters or nine quarters, plus an internship and thesis. Medical Illustrators can choose to pursue the optional Certified Medical Illustrator (CMI) credential offered by the Board of Certification of Medical Illustrators.

Experience, Skills, and Personality Traits

Business knowledge is important for success. (One of the requirements for quinquennial CMI recertification is contin-

ued education in business courses.) A Medical Illustrator must understand the ins and outs of managing copyrights. A freelance Medical Illustrator owns title to the work he or she creates. Many staff Medical Illustrators also maintain an active freelance business, and many Medical Illustrators fluidly pass in and out of staff and self-employed status throughout their careers. Staff Medical Illustrators must manage and license the copyrights owned by their institutions, as well as those they have retained as independent authors. Whether managing a biomedical communications department within an institution, running a studio, or acting as an independent contractor, a Medical Illustrator must also manage cash flow well and understand how investments made in the business amortize over a period of years.

Given the precise nature of the work and the standards to which it is held, a Medical Illustrator must possess a very high degree of visual art skill. Whatever the application—traditional pen and ink, paint, airbrush, or digital imaging programs—a Medical Illustrator has to be able to deliver precise results. The nature of the material demands it, as does the expectation of the medical profession that it supports.

Unions and Associations

While there are several trade associations to which Medical Illustrators belong, there are no unions in the traditional labor union sense. This owes to a provision in the current labor relations laws that prohibits an individual who takes place in collective bargaining from retaining any individual copyrights to work executed under the collective bargaining arrangement.

The chief association to which Medical Illustrators belong is the Association of Medical Illustrators (AMI). AMI offers several benefits to the practicing Medical Illustrator, chief among them a certification credential that must be renewed every five years. Additionally, AMI offers networking and continuing education opportunities including annual seminars and scholarships.

Since Medical Illustrators primarily operate as independent contractors, it behooves them to consider membership in the two leading organizations devoted to the practice: the Illustrators Partnership of America (IPA) and the Society of Illustrators (New York). Additional information can be had by investigating the Guild of Natural Science Illustrators (GNSI), Health Sciences Communications Association (HeSCA), and the Association of Biomedical Communications Directors (ABCD).

Tips for Entry

1. Sharpen your observational drawing and painting skills.
2. Earn your accreditation.
3. Seek employment through a school's job placement program.
4. Advertise your skills and accreditations.

CUSTOM PRINTER

CAREER PROFILE

Duties: Creates high-quality prints for visual artists, photographers, collectors, and art representatives and buyers; often corrects color and in some cases retouches artwork in the prints; meets with clients to discuss projects and advises on appropriate printing techniques and materials

Alternate Title(s): Fine Art Printer

Salary Range: $40,000 to $150,000+

Employment Prospects: Good

Advancement Prospects: Fair

Best Geographical Location (s): Large metropolitan areas

Prerequisites:

Education or Training—Four-year degree in art recommended with some coursework in art, such as art history, drawing, or painting

Experience—Two to three years of experience as an apprentice or assistant in a service bureau critical

Special Skills and Personality Traits—Technologically savvy; solid knowledge of printing software, equipment, and materials; strong appreciation for and understanding of artists and artwork; entrepreneurial; creative thinker; good business management skills; excellent communicator; organized and able to meet deadlines

CAREER LADDER

```
┌─────────────────────────────────┐
│   Manager (Quality Control)     │
└─────────────────────────────────┘

┌─────────────────────────────────┐
│        Custom Printer           │
└─────────────────────────────────┘

┌─────────────────────────────────┐
│    Apprentice or Assistant      │
└─────────────────────────────────┘
```

Position Description

People who value high-quality prints and personal attention hire Custom Printers to handle reproducing their images. Custom Printers work with artists, photographers, art representatives, collectors, and even consumers who want high-quality prints of their favorite artwork. Artists and photographers who need prints for their portfolios, copies of the original artwork for their records, prints to ship out to galleries, and additional prints of their artwork to sell use Custom Printers to get the job done.

A Custom Printer first meets with a client in person to review the project. The client often brings the artwork to the meeting in one of several formats: on disk, as a transparency or slide, in its original form (e.g., canvas painting), or as a reproduction if the original is not available. The Custom Printer will advise the client if he or she can actually com-

plete the work requested and how well he or she can do the work with the materials provided. Sometimes another process outside the Customer Printer's realm may serve the artwork better. If that is the case, it is the Customer Printer's responsibility to have the integrity and professionalism to recommend that process instead.

Many Custom Printers can also create Giclée prints for the highest-quality reproduction of fine art. There is no dot screen pattern in Giclée prints, and the light-fast inks used in the process have been cited to last upwards of 25 years if the prints are kept out of the sun. Giclée ("to spray or squirt" in French) is often the closest thing to the original artwork, as its images closely match the original in colors, tones, and textures. Giclée prints can be made on any type of paper, including canvas, and are frequently done in large formats. Giclée prints enable artists to extend the market for their work. They can create limited-edition prints, double their output, and increase their income. Once the image is scanned, they can order any number of prints. All they have to do is create that original piece.

Custom Printers discuss printing processes, the best materials to print the image on, and color schemes to get a sense of their clients' expectations. If needed, they will bring to the meeting portfolios of their print work to give examples of the quality of their work. They may also have color swatches on hand to compare with the artwork and help the client decide what works well with the image. Printers will occasionally flag an area within the image that can use improvement (e.g., color correction or retouching), but they will only do this when appropriate and in a manner that is merely suggestion. The ultimate decision on the course of the image rests with the client. Printers will then discuss the price for the project and the deadline.

After project details are finalized, the printer takes the image back to his or her studio and gets to work. He or she scans the image on a flatbed scanner and tweaks the color on a computer using the reference materials from the meeting with the client. (Transparencies sometimes have helpful color scales.) The printer works on the screen to get the image as close to the original as possible, often using software such as Adobe Photoshop. Scanner software is also important because it's critical to start out with a good scanned image.

The Custom Printer then produces a proof for the artist to review and either approve or make changes to. Some printers allow for two proofing sessions in the cost for the project. The proof is usually $8'' \times 10''$. If the client is concerned about resolution, the printer will create a strip of the image (perhaps $3'' \times 20''$) or an $8\frac{1}{2}'' \times 11''$ that incorporates everything. Usually, the printer will not show the first proof her or she produces, but rather a proof closest to what the client wants. The client will proof the work for color and resolution. Once approved, the Custom Printer delivers the final product to the client. Framing, matting, and all presentation aspects are typically left to the client to handle. Sometimes the Custom Printer works on a laptop at meetings to make adjustments to the print if the client requests any changes.

Self-employed Custom Printers are responsible for setting their prices and invoicing their clients, and well as handling their bookkeeping and taxes or hiring a bookkeeper to manage that end of the business. They are also responsible for creating their brand image, marketing themselves, and networking. Many attend gallery openings, trade shows, and art expos and regularly telephone or e-mail former clients. They also make cold calls to promote their business. Word-of-mouth is the most effective advertisement, so it's important to have a solid reputation for quality work. Custom Printers can work from their homes or open storefronts anywhere. Most printers own high-end scanners, Macintosh computers, wide-format printers, cutting mats, rulers, packing materials, and other peripheral necessities. Keep in mind that you will need some space to store your inventory. You will also need working capital to keep your business afloat.

Salaries

The salary for a self-employed Custom Printer can range anywhere from $40,000 to more than $150,000, depending on a number of variables. As in any entrepreneurial business, an individual's income correlates to the amount of time and energy he or she commits to the work. The clientele and the focus of the work also drive a Custom Printer's salary. Retouching and color correcting tend to generate more money. Straight printing in volume can also be profitable. And, naturally, the more clients, the higher the income. Artists don't need printers every week, so it is critical for Custom Printers to market themselves and grow their customer base as much as possible.

Employment Prospects

According to the U.S. Department of Labor's *Occupational Outlook Handbook,* employment of artists and related workers is expected to grow about 10 to 20 percent, or as fast as the average, from now through 2012. Artists will need Custom Printers to enhance and market their work, and as the demand for artists grows, so too will the demand for Custom Printers. Improvements to technology coupled with dramatic drops in prices are enabling more people to start and successfully run their own custom printing businesses. Additionally, although there is heated discussion in the arts community about the merits of the Giclée process, an increasing number of artists and collectors are turning to Giclée prints to preserve their artwork. This interest in Giclée is expected to grow. Custom Printers who add Giclée printing to their service menu will consequently enjoy more business in years to come.

Advancement Prospects

Independent Custom Printers run their own businesses and are frequently so enmeshed in the day-to-day operation there is no time to think about "advancement." After committing years to the field and building a loyal clientele, some Custom Printers may consider expanding their niche or opening new stores in other locations. Some may advance by moving into management and/or quality control roles and hiring and overseeing other printers for their clients.

Education and Training

A four-year degree in art is recommended for a better-rounded education, but it's not critical. Art courses, however, are very helpful, particularly art history, painting, and drawing classes. It's important for Custom Printers to be able to speak the same language as artists and also to see things through artists' eyes. (You can also always take these classes on a continuing education level.) Art classes will help you gain an appreciation of good versus bad art. Art is subjective work, so having a trained, educated eye helps. It's also important for Custom Printers to know digital software processes for printing (e.g., Adobe Photoshop and various scanner software). Some of this can be self-taught, but classes are also available at universities and art, trade, and technical schools.

Experience, Skills, and Personality Traits

Fine artists are oriented to high quality; they want the best but are still cost conscious. To be a successful, sought-after Customer Printer, you need to be tuned in to artists, and you must love working with them. Your work with artists can actually be seen as a "collaboration." Thus, you must be able to speak their language, communicate clearly, and ask the right questions so that you completely understand what is expected of you. Integrity is also key; you must know how and when to advise your clients about appropriate printing materials and techniques to best enhance their work. This type of work is not about taking control of projects and doing only what you want to do, but partnering with artists to help them realize their vision. Custom Printers must be honest, trustworthy, accurate, and factual, particularly with equipment and the results. They must follow through on their promises.

Unions and Associations

Custom Printers can join such organizations as the Amalgamated Lithographers of America, Printing Industries of America (also Graphic Arts Information Network on the Internet), National Association for Printing Leadership (NAPL), Print Image International (PII), and the Giclée Printers Association for networking, education, business tips, market updates, workshops, and discounts on various products.

Tips for Entry

1. Have strong knowledge of all of the equipment you will be using in your work, and make sure your skills are up to speed and that you are ready at all levels to handle this job.

2. Work at least one to two years as an apprentice or in any other foot-in-the-door capacity in a service bureau. Learn the equipment, workflow, and software. It's important to see firsthand the real world use of the equipment and how the Customer Printer business runs.

3. Be an expert in the process. Know exactly what you are going to offer, and know the solutions that you can provide to your clients. You must have a product that you can show, and whatever it is, you must do it at a high-quality level.

4. Sometimes you'll have only one chance to speak with a prospective client, so always be professional, informed, and honest. A Custom Printer's business is driven by his or her integrity and quality of work. A good reputation will help you secure repeat business as well as gain new clients through referrals.

CERAMIST

CAREER PROFILE

Duties: Creates ceramic objects, ranging from functional (e.g., plates, bowls, and cups) to decorative (e.g., vases and sculptures); chooses and purchases clay; mixes and sculpts clay into desired shapes by using various hand techniques or premanufactured molds; uses kilns or fire techniques to heat and solidify objects; glazes objects; may create collections for exhibitions and installations; may sell directly to stores; may attend and participate in art fairs and crafts shows; handles all business-related duties, from self-promotion to office and staff management

Alternate Title(s): Ceramicist, Potter

Salary Range: $10,000 to $75,000+

Employment Prospects: Good

Advancement Prospects: Good

Best Geographical Location(s): Major metropolitan areas

Prerequisites:

Education or Training—B.F.A. not required, but four-year degree helpful; coursework or training in sculpture and ceramic art recommended

Experience—One to three years of experience as an intern or apprentice helpful; gallery or studio experience helpful

Special Skills and Personality Traits—Creative; strong hand-eye coordination; excellent communication skills; patient; flexible; solid knowledge of clays, kilns, sculpting techniques, and sculpting materials; physical ability to work with clay

CAREER LADDER

```
┌─────────────────────────────────┐
│         Gallery Owner           │
└─────────────────────────────────┘

┌─────────────────────────────────┐
│           Ceramist              │
└─────────────────────────────────┘

┌─────────────────────────────────┐
│    Apprentice Ceramist or       │
│  Studio or Gallery Assistant    │
└─────────────────────────────────┘
```

Position Description

Ceramists are freelancers who create a variety of clay products, from decorative to functional, either for exhibition and sale to collectors and domestic customers or for designers, interior decorators, or retail stores. Ceramists are responsible for choosing the types of clay needed for their work, as well as the colors (brown, gray, red, etc.), based on the textures they want to create, the glazes they plan to use, and the temperatures at which they plan to fire (meaning heat and harden) the object.

Some Ceramists sketch their designs first; others start creating immediately by working with the clay. Some of the diverse techniques Ceramists use in their work include:

- wheel throwing, or throwing, which is building an object by strategically throwing wedges of clay onto a pottery wheel
- coiling, or hand building, which entails hand-rolling the clay into long strands, then winding or coiling the strands and attaching them atop each other to create objects such as vases and bowls
- press-molding, or slipcasting, which is reproducing original artwork by creating molds of the objects

Work can be studio glazed, Raku fired (a Japanese low-fire technique), or wood fired. Kilns, or ovens, can be gas, oil, electrical, or they can also be simple brick boxes or pits in which the work is layered amid sawdust and newspapers and wood is used for the fire. The fire burns from the top to the bottom. This firing technique creates softer, more natural looking objects that can be black and white or brown and white and usually appear burnt. The Anagama technique, the oldest in Japan, entails firing work continuously for anywhere from one day to up to several weeks in a kiln. Natural ash glazes the objects, creating interesting and unique designs.

Some Ceramists create work for exhibitions in galleries. Collectors, designers, and decorators may commission Ceramists to create either one-of-a-kind objects or lines for sale in stores or catalogs. Retailers also commission specific lines of either functional or decorative objects to sell in stores, catalogs, and on the Internet. Ceramists may also exhibit and sell their work at gift, trade, art, and crafts shows. Unless they have representation, they manage all aspects of their business, from having a business logo, stationery, and Web site to maintaining both their ceramic art equipment and their business equipment. They handle administrative tasks or delegate them; they network to promote their business.

Salaries

Ceramists can earn salaries ranging from $10,000 to $75,000 or more, depending on the quality and/or quantity of the work they produce and the caliber of their clients. Ceramists who create decorative products (such as vases, wall sconces, masks, etc.) for celebrities, designers, and interior decorators may earn higher incomes. Those who create functional products that are mass-produced (such as plates, cups, bowls, etc.) for retail also earn higher incomes. Be aware that salaries vary annually depending upon orders and sales. Ceramists new to the field will most likely earn lower salaries until they establish themselves and attract a steady clientele. Often, Ceramists supplement their income with other types of work, such as teaching or freelancing in galleries or museums.

Employment Prospects

According to the U.S. Department of Labor's *Occupational Outlook Handbook,* employment of artists overall is expected to increase by about 10 to 20 percent through 2012. Talented Ceramists who create marketable and desirable products and who have excellent communication skills and know how to promote themselves will succeed in finding work and building their businesses. Ceramists located in major cities such as Chicago, Miami, New York City, San Francisco, and Washington, D.C., will have greater opportunity to find work and secure clients.

Advancement Prospects

As with many freelance artists, there is no definitive career ladder, per se, for freelance Ceramists. Many are self-taught, and some even start working as Ceramists without formal training or apprenticeships. Many, however, intern or apprentice with Ceramists, or work in galleries or studios as

a way to learn the business from the ground floor. Most aspire to reach a level within their field at which they are a recognized name, where their style stands out because they create work that is self-directed and self-expressive. Once a Ceramist is working for himself or herself, meaning creating work he or she desires as opposed to work specifically commissioned and controlled by clients, the next step is often owning a gallery. Other means of advancement include experimenting with different materials and techniques, collaborating with other artists on projects, and teaching, lecturing, and/or writing.

Education and Training

While a B.F.A. is not required to become a Ceramist, a four-year degree with coursework in sculpture, ceramic art, design, and art history is recommended. Some classes in business management and/or small business ownership are helpful. Many Ceramists are self-taught but do take classes along the way to help hone their skills. Ceramic art is a combination of art and science. Beyond being creative, Ceramists need to understand how the materials work together and which materials are safest to use. They also need to understand how to work the kiln and which temperatures to use with the clays and the glazes. A one- to three-year apprenticeship with a Ceramist or working in a gallery or studio is an excellent way to learn firsthand about techniques, equipment, and how to run a small business.

Experience, Skills, and Personality Traits

Successful Ceramists have a deep understanding of the materials and techniques needed to create specific effects for end products (e.g., smooth glazes, rough textures, dark or light colors, and undertones). They must be knowledgeable about clays, glazes, firing techniques, and how to use different types of kilns. They must also be able see beyond the clay and visualize the shape and form they plan to create. Ceramists need to be patient, both in their creative process and with their clients. Clay is not always easy to work with; having an open mind helps overcome glitches quickly and easily. Patience also helps when dealing with clients, who will not always understand the intricacies and challenges involved in creating certain pieces. It's up to the Ceramist to communicate clearly yet professionally what can and cannot be done when commissioned to create certain works. They must also have the physical strength to work with the clay. Ceramists must be proactive and determined to succeed. Until they establish a name for themselves and build their clientele, they must promote their work by using a variety of methods, from open studios to direct mailings.

Unions and Associations

The National Council on Education for the Ceramic Arts (NCECA) provides industry news, journals, educational publications and conferences, as well as access to exhibitions, awards, and other resources and support to Ceramists. Ceramists also have opportunities to exhibit their work, attend conferences and workshops, and have access to networking and educational opportunities through membership to such associations as the Society of Arts and Crafts (SAC) and the National Association of Independent Artists (NAIA).

Tips for Entry

1. Be patient. It takes time to build a ceramics business, so learn everything you can while interning or apprenticing at a gallery or studio.
2. Hone your interpersonal skills. Unless you have a rep handling your business, it is up to you to interact with your prospective clientele and to foster relationships. Your art is all-important, but your ability to communicate clearly and your overall "bedside" manner will ultimately make or break your business. Also, having a good sense of humor helps.
3. Read and research as much as you can about ceramic art. Read about other artists. Even experienced Ceramists make sure that they are always learning something new by regularly reading books and magazines and visiting Web sites. Read about contemporary or classic art, whatever interests and inspires you. Learn how the work is created and about the thinking behind it.
4. Visit galleries and museums regularly. Attend art shows and crafts fairs when you can. It's important to stay inspired.
5. Share studio space with other Ceramists. It's an excellent way to partner on projects, build community, learn and share techniques, and reduce overhead.

PAINTER

CAREER PROFILE

Duties: Composes images through personal exploration; promote work to galleries; maintain studio

Alternate Title(s): None

Salary Range: $17,000 to $100,000+; in extraordinarily rare circumstances, $500,000+

Employment Prospects: Poor

Advancement Prospects: Poor to fair

Best Geographical Location(s): Major urban areas that support fine art galleries

Prerequisites:

Education or Training—No degree requirement but B.F.A. is helpful; knowledge of painting techniques, fundamental art principles

Experience—None

Special Skills and Personality Traits—Creative mind geared toward generating personal visual imagery; patience for the vagaries of art criticism; ability to manage one's own business

CAREER LADDER

```
+-------------------------------------+
|              Painter                |
+-------------------------------------+

+-------------------------------------+
| Graduate Student or Artist's Assistant |
+-------------------------------------+

+-------------------------------------+
|              Student                |
+-------------------------------------+
```

Position Description

Nowhere else in the visual art industry does the division between high culture and popular culture exist in more hotly contested extremes. In order to properly discuss the parameters of a job description for a Painter, we must first examine this divide in brief.

On the broad face of things, high-culture minded Painters explore academic and philosophical principals in their work on a very personal level. Popular-culture Painters practice a more commercially viable or commodity-oriented brand of painting aimed at a broader audience. These latter typically work within well-defined modes of depiction—a representational lean toward a specific subject, a decorative approach to painting, or sticking to a distinct type of abstraction, for example. Their modes of expression tend toward more universally readable and accepted uses of iconography and methods of application. (While the preceding is vastly oversimplified for the purposes of introduction to the basic ideas surrounding the divide, more can be learned by reading contemporary art criticism and some of the suggested readings in this volume's bibliography.)

In either case, the basics of the job remain the same: generate works of art, either by traditional methods and media of painting or one of the various mixed-media works accepted as paintings in the contemporary art world; promote these works to a receptive audience; and manage one's studio, including business expenses, appointments, and so on.

The methods of painting are so numerous that a comprehensive listing exists outside the parameters of this volume: traditional media, including transparent watercolor, opaque watercolor, casein, encaustic, acrylic and oil paint to name just a few; the several methods of collage; mixed-media applications; and combinations thereof have all been touted and accepted as paintings in contemporary culture. Whatever the method or mode of expression, generating the work comes first.

Once a large body of work has been constructed, a Painter acts as his or her own advocate in seeking representation and promoting the work. To this end, the Painter more interested in a high-culture paradigm seeks gallery representation in which original works are sold to smaller audiences. A more commercially minded Painter typically seeks a gallery that doubles as a limited edition–print publisher that markets to a broader, more popular culture–oriented clientele. In this latter arena, one usually faces a greater prospect of bigger financial returns, especially at the beginning stages of one's career.

Finally, a Painter in either area of focus must maintain a studio; this means managing cash flow (balancing accounts payable and accounts receivable), keeping stores of items necessary to the execution of one's art, organizing available space to optimal use, gathering reference materials, and so on. In this regard, a successful Painter differs very little from other independent contractors in the visual arts industry.

Salaries

While some big-name painters command prices in the solid six figures for individual paintings, the odds of becoming one of them are akin to buying a winning lottery ticket while being struck by lightning. This is true of both Painters with high-culture aspirations and the more commercially oriented ones. According to the U.S. Department of Labor's Bureau of Labor Statistics (BLS), median incomes for fine artists (including Painters, sculptors, and illustrators) were $35,000 in 2002.

Painters interviewed for this listing provided the following general benchmarks. As a high culture–oriented Painter, pricing for original works starts between $3,000 and $5,000 each, including gallery commission. (Galleries vary in commission percentage based upon different factors, among them: amount of promotional expenses they front to generate interest in a new Painter; the level of prestige the gallery has earned over the years; location of the gallery's space; etc. However, a good average is around a 50–50 split between artist and gallery.) At this level, one typically sells between three and 10 pieces per year. As one's prices goes up with increased demand over a period of years, one usually sees a greater number of pieces moving at these higher prices (usually between $7,000 and $20,000 per painting).

On the popular-culture side, prices per painting are typically lower, ranging from $600 to $1,200 for original art. Limited-edition Giclée prints or mass-market prints made from these paintings, however, can generate more than 10 times that amount per image, depending upon the quality of promotional support provided.

Employment Prospects

Since Painters are by nature independent contractors, it's not a position one easily rates in terms of employment prospects. Painters execute their works and earn their living through the sale of the originals or a combination of sales of originals bolstered by limited-edition prints retailed by publishers. While specific data on the number of Painters earning a living solely through their art are difficult to nail down, a very telling piece of information comes from the

BLS: "Only the most successful fine artists are able to support themselves solely through the sale of their works. Most fine artists must work in an unrelated field to support their art careers."

Given that so many of the factors leading to earning a successful living as a Painter are beyond the artist's control (one's work catching on with an audience, favorable reviews by critics, the ebb and flow of the market being in one's favor, etc.), expectations for earning a living at this vocation are at best a long shot. As of 2002, the most recent year's statistics available at this writing, the BLS stated that 23,000 workers were employed as fine artists, and this includes Painters, sculptors, and illustrators. Additionally, these positions are projected to see a growth of only 4,000 job openings over the succeeding 10 years, a very low growth rating.

Advancement Prospects

As in many other aspects of this position, what's typical in the usual working world doesn't directly apply to advancing as a Painter. While one may have a clear-cut path to climbing a corporate ladder in a position within a large company (as a designer moving all the way up to creative director, for example), advancement within the working world as a Painter moves a little more organically.

As a more commercially oriented Painter, one may find advancement by moving laterally from one gallery/publisher to another that promises to promote the work more aggressively and expose it to larger markets. This may require a larger commission percentage on the part of the gallery/publisher, but the overall earnings on the part of the artist may net out higher.

The same applies to the more high-culture minded Painters. At some point, a gallery's influence and exposure may plateau, and a move to another gallery may prove profitable. (For instance, submitting work for a group show can lead to exposure to larger collectors or development of relationships with foundations receptive to one's work.)

Education and Training

While the only educational requirement one has in order to paint is the ability to paint, which can be learned through exhaustive self-exploration and by doing, earning at least a bachelor's of fine art gives the prospective Painter a leg up toward earning a living for several reasons. First, instruction available at reputable colleges and universities is designed to strengthen an artist's skills. While certainly not the sum total of what one requires in order to succeed as a Painter, a sharp skill set does rate high on the requirement list.

Postsecondary education also exposes one to likeminded artists, and this benefits a prospective Painter in many ways. Getting a sense of what one's peers consider positive about one's work helps sharpen focus and broaden one's perspective. It also prepares the soon-to-be Painter to discuss aspects of his or her work and familiarizes him or her with the discussion process that will be a large component of promotional efforts.

Additionally, college and university curricula included broad surveys of what's been done throughout art history. This typically leads one toward an awareness of what avenues exist in the larger art world for self-expression.

Another important note about completing a course of study: Having to schedule classes, meet deadlines, and organize one's time prepares the fledgling Painter for the working world. This job requires a great deal of time management, as one has to juggle self-promotion along with generating one's work (and, most typically, at least a part-time job to subsidize one's living while starting out); planning and completing a course of study sows the seeds of practicing organizational discipline.

Finally, completing a fine arts degree (which tops out at the master's level) puts one in a position to more easily qualify for a teaching position at a college or university. This path is a time-honored one traveled by many professional Painters on their way to becoming successful Painters.

Experience, Skills, and Personality Traits

Aside from the obvious need for a creative mind interested in exploring visual imagery, one must also have a thick skin and a high degree of stick-to-itiveness. Rejection letters from juried exhibitions, constant retooling of one's portfolio for presentation to galleries, and long hours of reading about the current markets in periodical publications await anyone seriously pursuing a career in painting. One must have the patience to deal with the prospective buying/representing public's preconceived notions about one's mode of expression and the ability to network within fine art circles (attending gallery openings, opening up one's studio for local studio tours, attending workshops sponsored by artist associations, etc.).

Networking plays a very key role in promoting one's work to prospective galleries and publishers. Without exception, every professional interviewed for data on this profession put networking near the top of the list of necessary requirements for success.

One must also develop at least a minimum of organizational skill when it comes to time management. While balancing books and keeping track of one's business expenses may seem to run counter to a person of artistic temperament, it's only the most unusually successful Painter who can afford to hire someone to manage the business end of workaday life.

Unions and Associations

While no union exists to protect the labor practices of Painters across the nation, there are several associations that provide networking opportunities, the ability to buy into group-rate medical insurance plans, opportunities to apply for grants, and the like. Primary among these is the National Endowment for the Arts; online you can find grant applications as well as listings for the categories in which one can apply: http://www.nea.gov.

Similarly, many states fund fine arts organizations. For instance, the Ohio Designer Craftsmen (http://www.ohiocraft.org) offers networking opportunities, publications, workshops, marketing assistance, referral services, and opportunities for selling work through retail outlets and fairs. (A state-by-state listing of arts organizations would be too lengthy to include here; more information can usually be found by contacting individual states' councils for the arts.) In addition, the New York Foundation for the Arts (http://www.nyfa.org) offers nationwide listings of awards, services, and publications for artists, and the College Art Association has opportunities for individual artists as well as those who teach art, including group-rate medical insurance information (http://www.collegeart.org).

Tips for Entry

1. Learn as much as possible about the craft of painting—supports, vehicles, pigments, applications, etc.
2. Continue to sharpen your skills in your chosen mode of expression.
3. Establish relationships with working professionals; apply for artist assistant positions.
4. Be objective when reviewing your work and submit work to reputable regional, state, and nationwide juried exhibitions.

PRINTMAKER

CAREER PROFILE

Duties: Creates high-quality prints for singular or multiple use for self or clients; may use variety of techniques, such as etching, lithography, screenprinting, or relief printing; chooses ink types and colors; chooses materials to print to; may use design software to manipulate photographs; handles or delegates administrative tasks related to running a business; may promote and market self, unless represented by a gallery or an agent

Alternate Title(s): Screenprinter, Etcher, Lithographer

Salary Range: $1,000 to $50,000+

Employment Prospects: Good

Advancement Prospects: Good

Best Geographical Location(s): Major urban areas, but can work anywhere

Prerequisites:

Education or Training—B.F.A. recommended, either with specification in printmaking or coursework in fashion and textile design; master's coursework in printmaking helpful

Experience—One to three years of experience as apprentice or intern

Special Skills and Personality Traits—Creative; patient; motivated; organized; excellent communication and interpersonal skills (particularly if working with clients); ability to have a vision and follow through on it (especially if work is self-directed); some design software knowledge (e.g., Adobe PhotoShop)

CAREER LADDER

```
┌─────────────────────────────────────┐
│     Book Publisher, Owner of         │
│  Printmaker Gallery, Educator        │
└─────────────────────────────────────┘

┌─────────────────────────────────────┐
│            Printmaker                │
└─────────────────────────────────────┘

┌─────────────────────────────────────┐
│  Apprentice or Assistant Printmaker  │
└─────────────────────────────────────┘
```

Position Description

Printmaker is a broad job title that can cover different types of Printmakers who work in specific media, such as etchers, lithographers, and screenprinters. Overall, Printmakers create high-quality prints either for their own creative purposes, for commercial purposes, or specifically for clients. Artists sometimes want multiple copies of their artwork and seek out Printmakers to meet that need. Printmakers create printed images either from their own original designs or from artists' or clients' artwork. They decide which method will most effectively capture the artwork in reproduction. Some artwork will look best flat, as in a lithograph, while others will be most accurately portrayed in intaglio (recessed) or relief (raised). Printmakers choose the types of inks, the ink colors, and the materials to transfer the print onto, such as fabric, clothing, marble, mirror, wood, linoleum, tile, and more. Depending on the material, they will prepare the image for transfer by using different tools to carve, etch, paint, engrave, or draw. One- to five-color prints can be created; five-color prints are not as common, because the more colors used, the more complicated and expensive the process becomes.

Printmakers, or screenmakers, use a photographic process in their work. They may photocopy the image onto acetate or film. They use a screen that they first coat with photo emulsion, then burn the photocopy directly onto it. They may initially use computer design software, such as Photoshop, to digitally manipulate the image and fine-tune the details. They may also print the image onto paper from the computer. Printmakers may use either a machine press or create the prints manually by using a squeegee to push ink through a wood-framed screen. Screens are available in varying degrees of courseness. Screenprinters can make the screens themselves, or save on the labor by either having screens custom made or by buying them in a store or through the Internet.

Because equipment and studio space can be expensive, many Printmakers often share their workspace with other Printmakers. Being part of an on-site collective is an excellent way to pool resources, reduce overhead costs, and create a work team. Printmakers often teach and offer workshops either on their own premises or in schools. Printmakers who are not represented by galleries or agents are responsible for promoting and marketing their work. They will network by attending gallery openings and exhibitions and arts events, announcing their own shows through mailings as well as hosting (and attending) open studios.

Salaries

Salaries for Printmakers can range anywhere from as low as $1,000 to more than $50,000, depending on the quality of a Printmaker's work and the market demand. Printmakers who create high-quality prints and promote and market themselves aggressively, and intelligently can expect to earn higher salaries. Those who cater to well-known, established artists may also realize larger salaries. Printmakers whose end products (e.g., shirts, tiles, etc.) are presented and sold through galleries or agents may also net higher incomes. Many printmakers, whether new to the business or entrenched for many years, will at some point in their careers need to supplement their incomes by either working in other areas of art (e.g., graphic design, textile design) or teaching.

Employment Prospects

Independent Printmakers who have products that are in demand and who are excellent at self-promotion and networking have greater opportunities to find work. Be aware, however, that competition will be keen. According to the U.S. Department of Labor's *Occupational Outlook Handbook,* there will be more artists and related workers than there will be jobs, with employment growing only about as fast as the average through 2012.

Advancement Prospects

Independent Printmakers can advance by honing their skills and expanding into different techniques and different materials. They can also expand into teaching and leading workshops or by applying their skills to book publishing or opening their own printmaking gallery. A Printmaker's advancement will depend on his or her degree of motivation and available resources.

Education and Training

A bachelor's degree in fine arts, with a specification in printmaking, is recommended. Coursework in fashion, textile design, and fine art is also helpful. While not critical, a master's course in printing will enhance skills. A one- to three-year apprenticeship or internship, either directly with a senior Printmaker or in a printmaking gallery, will offer in-depth education not only into the creative process and techniques involved in printmaking, but also shed light on what it takes to successfully run an independent business.

Experience, Skills, and Personality Traits

Successful Printmakers have a unique combination of creativity and business savvy. If they own their own businesses, they understand the importance of networking and building community as well as spending time on their art. Their studios are organized, and they balance their time well. Printmakers need to be motivated if they're creating work for themselves, their portfolios, or for galleries. They must have a vision and be able to follow that vision through to completion. Interpersonal skills are also key, particularly if Printmakers plan to share workspaces and create collectives. Building community is often the best way to increase work and enhance the creative process along the way. Working alone in a studio can sometimes create a vacuum. Having on-site peer support can often inspire new ideas that otherwise might not have existed, as well as help improve and hone techniques.

Unions and Associations

The American Print Alliance offers networking, advocacy, lectures, demonstrations, journal subscriptions, exhibitions, and opportunities to take part in exhibitions and printmaking projects.

Tips for Entry

1. Apprentice with a Printmaker. It's the best way to get firsthand experience and to learn if this type of work suits you. And seek out a mentor if you're not apprenticing. An artist more senior in the field can be extremely helpful.
2. Network! Get involved in an artists' community. Peer support and encouragement will help you gain confidence and hone your skills.
3. Remember to keep an adventurous spirit when you approach your artwork. Have fun with it, because your work will reflect your state of mind.
4. Even if you haven't been commissioned to create prints, keep working and keep printing. It's important to always be creating and exploring, even when business is slow. Stay inspired by going to museums and galleries.

SCULPTOR

CAREER PROFILE

Duties: Creates original or commissioned work using different materials (e.g., wood, stone, marble, metal, glass, plastic, fabric, etc.) and techniques; carves, shapes, molds and/or joins materials to form objects; exhibits in and/or sells to galleries, museums, or stores; may handle production and merchandising; may work with an agent or representative; may handle self-promotion and marketing; purchases or finds materials and tools

Alternate Title(s): Modeler

Salary Range: $1,000 to $100,000+

Employment Prospects: Fair

Advancement Prospects: Fair

Best Geographical Location(s): Large metropolitan areas

Prerequisites:

    Education or Training—While not critical, a four-year degree in fine art is recommended; an M.F.A. is also helpful; if working with models, anatomy classes beneficial.

    Experience—Two to three years of experience as an assistant or apprentice to a Sculptor strongly recommended

    Special Skills and Personality Traits—Strong knowledge of sculpting materials, equipment, and techniques; extremely creative and visual; some physical strength may be required (especially wrist strength) if working with large and/or dense materials; persistent; outgoing (if self-promoting and marketing)

CAREER LADDER

```
┌─────────────────────────────────────┐
│   Gallery or Museum Sculptor         │
└─────────────────────────────────────┘

┌─────────────────────────────────────┐
│             Sculptor                 │
└─────────────────────────────────────┘

┌─────────────────────────────────────┐
│   Apprentice or Assistant Sculptor   │
└─────────────────────────────────────┘
```

Position Description

Sculptors can specialize in creating portraits or architectural sculptures or they can be moldmakers, glass carvers, or etchers. Sculptors create original three-dimensional work, or work as commissioned by clients, using a wide range of materials and techniques. At some point in their careers, Sculptors may decide to hone their skills in one particular medium and become known for their craft with that material. Ideas, forms, textures, and colors matter most in the sculpting field. Sculptors might work with clay, wood, stone, concrete, marble, metal, glass, plastic, paper, foam, or fabric. If working with large blocks of solid material (e.g., wood or stone), Sculptors need to use tools such as chisels, mallets, or power tools to cut, carve, and shape. If using metal, they need welding tools and protective gear to cut and bend. Some Sculptors create mixed-media objects by joining together different types of materials, while others might even bring motion, light, and sound to their work. Some Sculptors create bas-relief tiles with clay. On a smooth block of clay, they draw their figure and mold the clay around the drawing. Sculptors who create bronze pieces often start sculpting in Styrofoam or wax. Sculptors can purchase their own materials or use found materials and recreate them to follow their vision. Materials, tools, and foundry costs can add up; cost-conscious Sculptors need to know how to comparison shop and negotiate prices.

To save their work and have the option to create copies, Sculptors of smaller projects often create molds and casts of their pieces. Molds are made only after the piece has dried. Sculptors use various materials and methods to make molds, such as plaster, liquid rubber, resin, and wax. Some Sculptors turn their soft clay sculptures into bronze by using what's referred to as the "lost wax process." They make two molds of the piece. The first mold is of plaster and rubber to create a wax cast, and the second is created by soaking the wax cast into liquid ceramic. Once that dries, it's able to stand up to the extremely high temperature of molten bronze. The Sculptor then heats the mold, the wax melts out (thus the *lost wax* process), and he or she fills the empty space with the bronze.

Sculptors either work at their own studios or at a foundry, depending on the size of their piece and the materials and techniques required. When the molds are completed and the piece is ready for finishing touches, the Sculptor decides which patina or color to use. Some options include watercolor, acrylic or metallic paint, gold leaf, and even coffee.

Sculptors often work with assistants and apprentices, delegating administrative work and sharing advice and tips about the creative process. Early career Sculptors need to spend time networking and mingling at places and events where people interested in sculpture flock. If exhibiting at galleries or museums, they will also be on hand at openings to meet their fans and prospective clients. Some Sculptors also either hire grant writers or apply for grants themselves to help fund their work.

Salaries

The U.S. Department of Labor's *Occupational Outlook Handbook (OOH)* lists the salary range for fine artists (including painters, Sculptors, and illustrators) from less than $16,900 to more than $73,560. Realistically, Sculptors can expect to earn anywhere from $1,000 to more than $100,000 per year. Their salaries depend on a number of factors, for example the types of sculptures they create (the size, the materials used, whether they are one-of-a-kind pieces or intended for mass production); the caliber of their clientele (museums, galleries, wealthy collectors, the general public); and whether they self-promote or have representation. A Sculptor's salary also depends on his or her manufacturing and production choices. Some Sculptors who mass market their pieces have their artwork molded in other countries and then handle the finishing touches themselves. Some Sculptors often do well selling their work at crafts fairs, in stores, and through such online markets as eBay. Their salaries also depend on the quality of their work and their reputations.

Employment Prospects

Employment prospects for Sculptors are only fair because competition is fierce in this field. Typically, only famous Sculptors can earn their livings by sculpting alone. Those Sculptors striving for recognition in the marketplace will need to find ways to supplement their income. Until you become well known, supporting yourself solely as a Sculptor is extremely challenging. According to the *OOH,* through 2012 employment of artists and related workers is expected to grow about 10 to 20 percent, which is as fast as average. The handbook predicts "acute" competition for gallery showings and sponsorships, but still foresees those artists who display "outstanding talent, creativity, and style" having the best opportunities to find work. If you are just starting out as a Sculptor, you may need to find work in a gallery, museum, or other arts-related organizations. Sculptors are either hired by clients to create certain pieces based on a line they already have, or they sell their work through private galleries or dealers, or to the general public.

Advancement Prospects

Most Sculptors work on a freelance or commission basis. Advancement prospects are only fair and don't necessarily apply to them. Sculptors can advance by honing and expanding their skills and techniques and by taking on new and different projects. They can also advance from working with a variety of clients to working solely with a museum or gallery.

Education and Training

While it is not critical for Sculptors to have formal college degrees, those with bachelor's and master's degrees may have more well-rounded educations, which can enhance their work. Many sculpting schools offer training and degree programs in specific sculpting methods and media, some more classically based than others (e.g., Art Students League, National Academy of Design, New York Academy of Art). Sculptors who work with models need to understand how the body works, and therefore anatomy classes are most beneficial. Drawing classes can also be useful. Whether degreed or not, it is also highly recommended that Sculptors first apprentice or assist a Sculptor for at least two to three years to learn the details of the craft and the business. As assistant or apprentice, you will help make molds and learn how to work with foundries. You will also learn the techniques involved in handling commissioned work and working with various clients.

Experience, Skills, and Personality Traits

Sculpting can be aggressive, physical, and tactile. Depending on the type of materials and tools you use, you will need to have wrist strength, and you must like the physicality of the work. If you're working with metal, you'll be using torches and welding tools, and you must be comfortable and creative and still remember to be safe throughout the whole process.

Also, until you establish a strong reputation in the market-place, you will need to market your work and therefore must have some business savvy and strong communication skills.

Unions and Associations

Sculptors can find job listings, agents, events and workshops, educational articles, and other resources at www.Sculptor. Org. Organizations such as the Sculptors Guild offer net-working and exhibit opportunities to Sculptors; membership is by invitation only, but twice a year the Guild reviews Sculptors' membership applications. Sculptors can also join the International Sculpture Center and the National Sculpture Society and learn technical tips, secure career advice, find out about grants and competitions, get discounts on educational literature, and take advantage of networking opportunities.

Tips for Entry

1. It's not easy being a Sculptor. Be clear and sure this is exactly what you want to do, but also be flexible. Because it's hard to earn a living solely as a Sculptor, you may have to work at other jobs to supplement your income until you establish a solid reputation for your work.
2. Apprentice with a Sculptor whose work you admire. It's the best way to learn and also to find out if this is really for you. You can also assist at foundries.
3. Ask a lot of questions. Sculptors tend to share infor-mation easily. Learn from them!
4. Find a way to express yourself uniquely and individu-ally. Different materials will help you keep your work fresh.

RETOUCHER

Duties: Improves photographic images (both film and digital) for advertising agencies, publishers, photographers, photography studios, production houses, private clients, and others; follows client suggestions and makes own recommendations for changes; may retouch images on site at photography shoots; uses computer design software such as Adobe Photoshop to manipulate images, correct color, etc.; may scan images, coordinate film processing, and maintain records and files; may manage staff

Alternate Title(s): Digital, Photograph, or Color Corrector/Retoucher, Imaging Specialist, Airbrush Artist

Salary Range: $40 to $100+ per hour

Employment Prospects: Good

Advancement Prospects: Good

Best Geographical Location(s): Major urban areas

Prerequisites:

Education or Training—Bachelor's degree in art recommended; trade school degree may be sufficient for some companies; coursework in drawing, painting, photography, and photography design software helpful

Experience—Two- to three-year apprenticeship or internship with photography studio or in-house retouching department of advertising agency recommended

Special Skills & Personality Traits—Creative, with a solid understanding of color (CMYK/RGB) and light; basic understanding of film and digital photography; knows how to look at illustrations; some experience in drawing and painting helpful; technically adept and detail oriented; adept at working with PC and Macintosh systems; good grasp of prepress and how images will look once printed; skilled in Adobe Photoshop, Illustrator, QuarkXPress, and/or other photography design software programs; excellent communication and listening skills; able to take directions as well as suggest directions; strong management and organizational skills; professional and ethical

```
┌─────────────────────────────────────────┐
│   Lead Retoucher or Senior Retoucher     │
└─────────────────────────────────────────┘

┌─────────────────────────────────────────┐
│               Retoucher                  │
└─────────────────────────────────────────┘

┌─────────────────────────────────────────┐
│   Junior Retoucher, Photographer's       │
│   Assistant, or Photo Lab Assistant      │
└─────────────────────────────────────────┘
```

Position Description

Retouchers enhance photographs and scanned images for such clients as advertising agencies, magazine and book publishers, photographers, photography studios, and private clients. Once the client delivers the images (usually scanned or digital), Retouchers review and make notes about the colors, lighting, and other elements that need to be adjusted. Often, the client has specific instructions about the image and will ask for either color or lighting to be improved or altered or for certain objects to be removed. For instance, if the skin color of a model in a photograph appears too yellow, or if there is a dark splotch on a shirt, the Retoucher will be asked to make the skin appear healthier and to remove the splotch on the shirt. In some instances, the client will have specific directions in mind; in others, he or she will have a general idea of the change and will leave it to the Retoucher to decide on the specifics. Retouchers can work on scanned images as well as on original prints.

Image restoration is another area in which Retouchers work. Many people have old family photographs that they want restored and will seek out Retouchers for assistance. For example, if a photograph has been folded for many years, parts of the image may be missing or faded along the fold mark. Retouchers can either create a new image by photographing the original and retouching by hand, using ink, paint, stencil, or pencil, or they can scan the image and retouch in a computer using Adobe Photoshop or Illustrator.

Because of technological advances, images can now be improved and enhanced to the point they are practically unrecognizable when compared to the original photographs. Great debate has arisen among Retouchers, clients, and the general public alike about what is acceptable in alterations and what is taking it too far. There is no official industry policy regarding the extent to which Retouchers should and should not go in their work. Many seek support and advice through Web site forums and chat boards. Until associations are created for Retouchers and standards established, it is left to Retouchers and the companies they work with to find an ethical balance.

Salaries

Several industry experts state that Retouchers can earn hourly wages ranging from $40 to $100 or more, depending on experience, client, complexity of the work, end product, and usage. According to the *Graphic Artists Guild Handbook of Pricing & Ethical Guidelines* (11th edition), hourly fees for digital photo illustration/retouching work can range from $65 to $200 for the national/general consumer market; $60 to $150 for regional/trade; and $65 to $150 for the Web. Retouchers generally charge higher fees when rush jobs are requested and when they are asked to work through weekends and holidays.

Employment Prospects

The majority of clients who hire Retouchers are advertising agencies and publishing houses. The U.S. Department of Labor's *Occupational Outlook Handbook* predicts that the advertising industry will stay strong and continue to grow to meet the demand of "intense domestic and global competition in products and services offered to consumers." While some advertising agencies and publishers have in-house retouching departments, most work through outside studios. Retouchers will most likely find greater opportunities for freelance, as opposed to staff, work. However, those who specialize in portraiture may not fare as well because of the advances in digital photography. More lay people are using digital cameras and adjusting their own images with the software that is frequently sold with the cameras.

Advancement Prospects

With years of experience, Retouchers can start their own image retouching studios and hire staff to help carry the workload and expand the client base. They can also advance within photography labs and studios to become lead or senior retouchers, overseeing more complex projects and managing staff. Retouchers can also teach the art of retouching to college-level and trade school students.

Education and Training

A four-year degree in art is recommended, with courses in illustration, photography, painting, and computer design software. For some companies, a trade school degree and two to three years of training in a photography lab or apprenticing to a photographer may also be sufficient. Retouchers must be well versed in color and color correction techniques. Most Retouchers are trained and have a solid knowledge of such software programs as Adobe Photoshop and Illustrator. A working knowledge of 3-D programs may also be helpful in creating certain effects. While an undergraduate degree is helpful, it is by no means required. On-the-job training is invaluable in this field.

Experience, Skills, and Personality Traits

Several years of experience in a photography lab or studio, or assisting a photographer, is helpful in securing work as a Retoucher. A great deal of the work involves correcting color, so Retouchers must understand how color works and how it looks in print. They must know how to adjust it using computer design software as well as other methods to meet the client's goals and must also have good hand-eye coordination for the detail work. Excellent communication skills will also be called upon regularly in this work. When meeting with a client, Retouchers must be good listeners to follow specifically what the client wants, and they must also be knowledgeable enough to clearly point out what is feasible and what is not, as well as provide their own suggestions for changes that may enhance the final product. Typically, Retouchers with years of experience are permitted greater input.

Unions and Associations

There are no associations or unions specifically for Retouchers. Membership in photographers' associations, such as the American Society of Media Photographers (ASMP), as well as organizations for digital and graphic artists, such as the American Institute of Graphic Arts (AIGA) and the Association of Graphic Artists (AGA), can provide Retouchers with access to networking opportunities, educational resources, and discounts on various services. Retouchers can also find educational resources and participate in online forums by registering with RetouchPro (http://www.retouchpro.com).

Tips for Entry

1. Be persistent. Maintain a positive, flexible attitude. This approach will help you in the job market and is especially needed in the retouching field.
2. Try to secure an apprenticeship. It's the best way to learn the business and see if this is the type of work that you will enjoy. Do your research first. Find the advertising agencies that have in-house retouching departments and the retouching studios you want to work for, and check their Web sites for employment listings. If they have no job or internship openings, call the main number to get the names of the people you need to contact. Then call or write to briefly introduce yourself and inquire about apprenticing.
3. Network as much as possible. The more people you meet and speak with, the more avenues you may have for referrals to work.
4. Stay tuned to what's going on in the industry by reading trade publications, such as *Advertising Age,* visiting industry-related Web sites, and signing up for e-newsletters. Prospective clients will be impressed by your knowledge of their projects and the people who are responsible for them.

GRAPHIC DESIGNER

CAREER PROFILE

Duties: Depending on specialty, designs logos, business cards, stationery, product packaging, publications, signage, flyers, invitations, brochures, e-newsletters, content for Web pages, and more

Alternate Title(s): Designer

Salary Range: $36,680 to $90,000+

Employment Prospects: Good

Advancement Prospects: Good

Best Geographical Location(s): Large metropolitan areas

Prerequisites:

Education or Training—A four-year degree in art recommended, with coursework in graphic design, composition, and various computer software programs; some business management coursework helpful

Experience—Two to three years of experience as an assistant or intern in a design firm recommended

Special Skills and Personality Traits—Strong design and composition skills; solid computer software skills; business management ability; multitasker; flexible; able to put clients' needs first; creative thinker; problem solver; ability to handle deadlines; extremely organized and efficient

CAREER LADDER

```
┌─────────────────────────────┐
│     Creative Director       │
└─────────────────────────────┘

┌─────────────────────────────┐
│     Graphic Designer        │
└─────────────────────────────┘

┌─────────────────────────────┐
│    Intern or Assistant      │
└─────────────────────────────┘
```

Position Description

Graphic Designers strategize with clients and help them create brand identities by designing logos and other visuals to promote products, events, and ideas. Designers are responsible for much of what we see in the world every day. They design annual reports, menus, CD packaging, catalog sheets, posters, billboards, and more. They meet with clients to discuss projects and find out the specific objectives so they can estimate the amount of time needed to complete the work and the fees involved (known as a job estimate). Designers find out who the target audience is, the tone and manner of the product, how the product will be used, and the competition.

Graphic Designers understand composition. For print materials, they carefully choose colors, text fonts and sizes, column widths, artwork, and other facets and combine them to produce effective, appealing visuals. They use various software programs (e.g., Adobe Photoshop and Illustrator), but they may initially sketch their concepts by hand before investing time on the computer. Designers interact frequently with clients and may also be responsible for securing and/or overseeing other consultants' involved in the project. They may also work closely with printers.

Self-employed Graphic Designers are responsible for all aspects of their business. They invoice clients, handle accounts receivable and payable, and may even do light bookkeeping. They oversee tax reporting and payments and maintain their office supplies and equipment. Designers also spend time creating their own brand identity (e.g., logos, business cards, stationery, brochures, promotional products, Web sites, e-newsletters, etc.) and creating and implementing advertising and marketing campaigns to get word out about their work. They tailor their portfolios for prospective client meetings by choosing certain visuals and past projects that reflect their skills and interests and relate to the client's mission.

Salaries

Depending on their area of expertise, their client base, and the location of their business, salaries for Graphic Designers can range from $36,680 to more than $90,000. In 1999 the American Institute of Graphic Artists (AIGA) reported median earnings of $50,000 for Graphic Designers who worked independently. Graphic Designers who work with management and public relations firms earn an average of $37,570, while those who design for newspapers earn only about $28,170, according to the U.S. Department of Labor's *Occupational Outlook Handbook (OOH)*.

Employment Prospects

Overall, design jobs are increasing by about 10 to 20 percent, about as fast as average according to the *OOH*. The good news is that the demand for Graphic Designers specifically is growing and should continue to increase because of new and existing technologies. More companies than ever before are broadening their reach by turning to the Web and video entertainment markets and will be calling upon Graphic Designers to create and enhance their visuals.

Advancement Prospects

Graphic Designers who work independently can advance by increasing their business and hiring staff to help meet demand. They can also expand into new areas by hiring and working with designers who have a different clientele or a different area of expertise. After three to five years of working independently, Graphic Designers may be able to take on larger, more complex projects in creative director roles.

Education and Training

A four-year degree in art is recommended in order to understand different aspects of graphic design. Some Graphic Designers learn while apprenticing and also take design and computer software courses in their spare time. Graphic Designers also continue learning about computer and software developments and industry issues to keep their skills sharp. They read books and magazines, attend panel discussions, and take courses at local art schools or trade and vocational schools. Certification is not required in the United States, but many designers believe it would enhance their careers, earning them increased respect and higher salaries. Canadian Graphic Designers can receive certification from the Association of Registered Graphic Designers of Ontario (RGD Ontario) by passing the registered Graphic Designers qualification examination.

Experience, Skills, and Personality Traits

Graphic Designers need to be technologically savvy. They need to have computer software skills for both Macintosh and PC platforms. To create and maintain a strong client base, they need to have good interpersonal skills. They need to be able to clearly communicate with clients about projects, the work that is expected, and the reasons for their design choices. Designers must also be professional and ethical, able to meet deadlines and deliver the quality of work that is promised. In addition to design skills, Graphic Designers must have good negotiation skills and be aware of standard industry practices in order to draft fair contracts.

Unions and Associations

Graphic Designers join arts associations for membership benefits that can include networking, educational programs and literature, discounts on various products, and group health insurance. A sampling of organizations where they can enjoy some if not all of these benefits includes the American Institute of Graphic Arts (AIGA), the Art Directors Club, the Graphic Artists Guild, the Society of Illustrators, the Society of Publication Designers, and the Type Directors Club.

Tips for Entry

1. Identify the area of design you want to pursue.
2. Consider the beginning of your design career part of the learning curve and be open to the education. Don't be discouraged! Imitate and learn from your idols and heroes. Take classes.
3. Pay attention to the commercial and business world. Design often stems from and kicks off trends.
4. Commit 20 to 30 percent of your time to promoting your business by doing a variety of things: advertising, contacting people you know for references, using a mailing list or database, networking at events, and speaking at associations and even Rotary clubs.

INDUSTRIAL DESIGNER

CAREER PROFILE

Duties: Researches the marketplace to determine needs for new products or redesigns currently existing products; works in industrial, environmental, and product fields; sketches designs for anything from hairdryers, mobile phones, toothbrushes, and toys to sneakers, medical equipment, and cars; creates designs by hand with drafting tools and/or with computer-aided design software (e.g., AutoCad); establishes packaging requirements by consulting with engineers, salespeople, and marketing managers; uses hand tools to create plaster, wood, metal, paper, or clay models of products

Alternate Title(s): Product Designer, Commercial Designer

Salary Range: $28,820 to $82,130+

Employment Prospects: Good

Advancement Prospects: Good

Best Geographical Location(s): Depends on design specialization

Prerequisites:

Education or Training—Four-year degree in industrial design or related field; graduate degree may be required by some companies; coursework in drawing, design, and computer-aided design software (e.g., AutoCAD)

Experience—Three- to five-year apprenticeship, or several years of on-the-job training

Special Skills and Personality Traits—Strong drawing, sketching, and designing skills; able to clearly communicate ideas; mathematically inclined and able to incorporate technical details into designs and drawings; ability to work independently and with variety of staff and consultants; strong research skills; detail and deadline oriented

CAREER LADDER

```
┌─────────────────────────────────────┐
│   Chief Industrial Designer or       │
│         Project Leader               │
└─────────────────────────────────────┘

┌─────────────────────────────────────┐
│        Industrial Designer           │
└─────────────────────────────────────┘

┌─────────────────────────────────────┐
│     Industrial Design Assistant      │
└─────────────────────────────────────┘
```

Position Description

Industrial Designers help design and develop products that meet customers' needs as well as heighten product sales for manufacturing clients. Industrial Designers work closely with research staff, marketing personnel, engineers, product managers, production experts, and machine operators to determine designs that make products convenient, easy to use, and appealing to customers. They either redesign currently existing products or create designs for products that are new to the market. Most Industrial Designers specialize in certain areas of manufacturing, such as airplanes, computer equipment, automobiles, toys, sports equipment, home appliances, and medical and office equipment, to name a few.

Industrial Designers first meet with clients to discuss the product and clarify the design specifications. They may work either independently or as part of a specialist team in developing the design. They sketch their designs, from initial to final, by hand or using computer-aided design (CAD)

software and computer-aided industrial design (CAID) software, incorporating all the technical specifications and the appropriate and available materials. They provide a list of all parts required as well as cost estimates. They also discuss and clear costs, productions processes, and commercial issues with engineers and other responsible staff. Industrial Designers may need to be present at manufacturing plants and production facilities to decide on the feasibility of the product and the process. They make design presentations to clients, displaying samples, models, budgets, slides, and films, to secure design approvals and project commissions.

Industrial Designers use a wide variety of tools in their work, including drafting instruments, air brushes, pens, pencils, inks, watercolors, pastes, and glues. They create samples of their work by hand in clay, plastic, wax, or wood or use computerized prototyping equipment to test their designs. Industrial Designers also use math tools for calculating designs, such as calculators, T-squares, triangles, charts, and graphs. Computer-aided design and computer-aided industrial design equipment is a must in their work. Industrial Designers use CAD to design and analyze products prior to manufacture; CAID allows designers to create designs and convey them to automated production tools. CAD and CAID speed the production process and improve product reliability.

Freelance Industrial Designers oversee all aspects of the administration of their own business, from advertising and promoting their work to invoicing clients, handling accounts receivable and payable, purchasing and maintaining office equipment, and managing staff.

Salaries

Salaries for Industrial Designers vary depending on their geographical location, types of products they design, and the budgets of their clients. According to the U.S. Department of Labor's *Occupational Outlook Handbook (OOH)*, $52,260 was the average income for industrial and commercial designers in 2002, with about 50 percent earning between $39,240 and $67,430. Less experienced designers may earn in the lower 10 percent range of $28,820, while more experienced designers can earn upwards of $82,130. Some Industrial Designers receive flat fees or retainers for their work for certain time periods; others may receive per-design payments. Freelance Industrial Designers may work for several companies, under contract for a set fee. The work for each company is typically proprietary and is therefore designed exclusively for that company.

Employment Prospects

Consumers are more interested in product safety and quality than ever before, and as a result, the need for Industrial Designers is expected to rise. The *OOH* predicts a 10 to 20 percent growth through 2012 because of this heightened demand for safe, easy-to-use products in areas ranging from entertainment, transportation, and recreation to sports, medicine, and more. Cities around the country are often known for certain industries (e.g., Detroit for cars). Industrial Designers will do best to research those areas that feature industries they specialize in before they begin their hunt for employment.

Advancement Prospects

With experience, Industrial Designers can advance to become design managers or design leaders on certain projects. They can assume more responsibilities by working on larger, more complicated projects. Industrial Designers can also enhance their skills by teaching at colleges, writing educational articles, growing their client bases, and changing their design specializations.

Education and Training

Most people entering the industrial design field have a four-year degree in industrial design, architecture, applied design, or industrial engineering. Some companies may require a master's degree. Coursework in design, sketching, and CAD and CAID are required.

Experience, Skills, and Personality Traits

Generally, three to five years of apprenticeship or prior experience is required. Industrial Designers must understand market and production research and have a solid understanding of production processes and materials. They must be able to visualize creative, functional designs based on product descriptions. Industrial Designers need to have a combination of creative skills and engineering talent, mathematical abilities, and solid verbal and written communication skills. Industrial design is rooted in solving problems; only those designers who enjoy testing their design theories and creating models and samples to determine what will or won't work will thrive in this field.

Unions and Associations

Designers can become members of the Industrial Designers Society of America for educational resources, networking opportunities, and more.

Tips for Entry

1. Secure an apprenticeship to get your foot in the door. It's the best way to learn industrial design firsthand. If you can find a mentor while you're apprenticing, an Industrial Designer with a few years under his or her belt, that will take your experience to the next level.
2. Join associations, network, and pursue all avenues possible to find work, from classified advertisements

in print publications to online employment Web sites.

3. Volunteer at an agency if you can afford to and if you can't initially find a paying position in industrial design. Volunteering is often the best way for management to see your skills firsthand and learn that you are a valuable asset to the company.

4. Be prepared to supply samples of your work when you are applying for jobs. Companies will expect to view your work as slides, drawings, or electronic files (e.g., PDFs), and possibly in a print portfolio. Ask first which format they would like to receive it in if they don't mention it.

INTERIOR DECORATOR

Duties: Decorates interior spaces or areas within offices, homes, retail stores and windows, show rooms, hospitals, schools, commercial buildings, and more; works closely with clients to help them create appealing environments that function and suit their style; chooses wall coverings, fabrics, color schemes, paints and textures, textiles, furniture, lighting, plants, accessories, and fixtures; creates design and decoration proposals and presents them with samples and cost estimates to clients for approval; creates budgets; oversees purchase, delivery, and installation of materials and products ordered; may maintain research and sample library; handles all business management tasks (e.g., invoicing clients, scheduling meetings, maintaining office equipment, accounts payable and receivable); promotes business; manages staff

Alternate Title(s): Home Stylist, Decoration Designer

Salary Range: $21,240 to $69,640

Employment Prospects: Good

Advancement Prospects: Good

Best Geographical Location(s): Major urban areas and suburbs across the country

Prerequisites:

Education or Training—Four-year degree in design required; coursework in art history, illustration, drawing, and working knowledge of design software (e.g., Auto-CAD) recommended

Experience—Two to three years of experience as interior design coordinator or assistant

Special Skills and Personality Traits—Creative; strong sense of aesthetics; well connected to vendors and contractors, knows where and how to shop to meet budgets; highly organized; solid business, marketing, and negotiating skills; excellent interpersonal and management skills; able to juggle projects, work under pressure, and meet deadlines; able to present a professional image

Special Requirements—Interior design is subject to government regulations; 22 states and the District of Columbia require licensing

> **Senior Interior Decorator or Project Manager**

> **Interior Decorator**

> **Assistant Interior Decorator**

Position Description

Interior Decorators help clients create environments that are appealing and functional and that best suit their styles. They help design and choose furnishings and decorations for homes, offices, retail stores, show rooms, restaurants, theaters, concert halls, and more. Television networks also hire Interior Decorators for home improvement shows. Decorators pay attention to the size and scale of the space. Some even work with feng shui, the Chinese practice of decorating and placing certain objects and colors in specific locations to improve energy, health, happiness, and prosperity. Many Interior Decorators focus their skills on specific industries or specific interiors. Some work strictly with private homeowners, others design and decorate for commercial practices, and some may even specialize solely in bathrooms or kitchens.

Interior Decorators meet with clients to discuss the work that's needed and to get a sense of the clients' goals and tastes. They take notes, create proposals and budgets, then meet again to present ideas as well as share fabric samples and possibly pictures of furnishings and accessories for review and approval. An increasing number of Interior Decorators are using AutoCAD and other design software programs to save time and money and reduce stress. The interior design process tends to be fraught with changes. Clients can change their minds at any point, and design software makes it easy to incorporate their ideas.

Interior Decorators keep a library of samples and materials and often conduct a great deal of research for design and decoration concepts. They choose color schemes, materials, furniture, wall hangings, and so on, then contact vendors, suppliers, and contractors to get prices and negotiate fees. On the more administrative side, Interior Decorators are also responsible for paying all service providers, keeping an inventory of bills, and even ensuring that decorations and designs are in accordance with federal, state, and local building codes and laws.

Salaries

Salaries for Interior Decorators vary by specialty, client, project budget, and region. In 2002, annual salaries ranged from $21,240 to more than $69, 640, according to the U.S. Department of Labor's *Occupational Outlook Handbook*. Interior Decorators working with architectural, engineering, and related services earned approximately $41,680, while those working with furniture stores earned $36,320.

Employment Prospects

The outlook for the employment of Interior Decorators is bright. Owners of private homes, restaurants, offices, and other commercial establishments are relying more on Interior Decorators and other designers to create specific environments that suit their needs and attract more customers. Interior Decorators can work independently as freelance consultants, on staff with decorating or multidiscipline firms, in furniture stores, or in home furnishing departments of retail stores. Television networks have also been adding more home improvement shows to their lineups, raising public awareness of Interior Decorators even further and improving employment opportunities.

Advancement Prospects

Interior Decorators can advance to become senior Interior Decorators, project managers, product specifiers, or product sales representatives. Some may choose to open their own design firms or even head back to school to meet the requirements to become an architect. Interior Decorators can also write articles and columns for trade publications, teach classes at universities or trade schools, and lecture.

Education and Training

A four-year degree in interior design is required, preferably in a program accredited by the Foundation for Interior Design Education and Research (FIDER). Depending on the program, some schools may offer five-year degree programs. Coursework in design, architecture, and drawing is recommended, and a working knowledge of Adobe Photoshop and Illustrator, as well as AutoCAD, is beneficial. Classes in small business management and budget-creating software such as Quickbooks will also help.

Special Requirements

Many states require Interior Decorators to be licensed. In the states where licensing is not required, Interior Decorators will have greater professional recognition by belonging to trade organizations such at the American Society of Interior Designers (ASID). Members must meet education and work experience requirements (usually two years of postgraduate work in the field) and pass the National Council for Interior Design qualification examination.

Experience, Skills, and Personality Traits

Interior Decorators are expected to have a strong sense of aesthetics, a good eye for balance and composition, and great familiarity with textiles, fabrics, materials, fixtures, furnishings, and home design accessories. They must also understand architecture and building structures when designing interior spaces and have an awareness of scale. Interior Decorators need strong interpersonal skills because they work closely with a range of people: clients, contractors, vendors and suppliers, stores, architects, as well as other consultants. Interior Decorators juggle clients, meetings, proposals, samples, fabrics, and more; solid organizational and time management skills help them stay on track and meet deadlines. Interior Decorators must also present a professional image to gain clients' confidence.

Unions and Associations

Interior Decorators can become members of such organizations as the American Society of Interior Designers (ASID) and the International Interior Design Association (IIDA) for educational resources, access to design competitions, networking opportunities, and discounts on credit cards, office supplies, and more.

Tips for Entry

1. Network as much as possible, and take business cards with you wherever you travel. Many Interior Decorators get work through word of mouth, so it's important to be prepared to talk up your work. Also, always be sure to remind people to refer their friends to you.

2. Create a business and marketing plan, and create a list of the companies and clients you want to target. Prepare a short script for cold calls, advertise in magazines and publications your target clients read, write and place press releases, and create flyers and brochures to promote your business. Pursue all avenues.

3. Specialize. Find a niche and focus your skills in that area. Develop contacts with shops, service providers, and others that serve this niche. Becoming known as the go-to person for a specific area in interior design can be the best way to build a successful business and secure an excellent reputation.

INTERIOR DESIGNER

CAREER PROFILE

Duties: Designs interior spaces for homes, offices, stores, hospitals, schools, libraries, etc.; works closely with clients, architects, and project managers to assess needs and review plans; creates and reviews production drawings; may use design software and computer-aided design software (e.g., AutoCAD) to create designs; estimates costs and products needed; visits sites to oversee work and ensure construction is meeting design specifications; may create and manage budgets and schedules; may manage interior design staff; handles accounts receivable and payable and other administrative tasks inherent to running a small business

Alternate Title(s): Interior Planner

Salary Range: $30,000 to 75,000+

Employment Prospects: Good

Advancement Prospects: Good

Best Geographical Location(s): Major urban areas, but can work anywhere depending on specialty

Prerequisites:

Education or Training—Four-year degree in art, specialization in interior design preferred by most companies

Experience—Three to four years of design experience preferred; apprenticeship helpful

Special Skills and Personality Traits—Excellent design skills; creative yet analytical, able to visualize interior spaces and create proposals and designs to meet clients' needs; well connected to industry service providers and vendors; detail oriented; able to juggle projects; solid management skills; works well with variety of people to meet deadlines; calm and professional under pressure

Special Requirements—Interior design is subject to government regulations; 22 states and the District of Columbia require licensing

CAREER LADDER

```
┌─────────────────────────────┐
│   Senior Interior Designer   │
└─────────────────────────────┘


┌─────────────────────────────┐
│      Interior Designer       │
└─────────────────────────────┘


┌─────────────────────────────┐
│  Assistant Interior Designer │
└─────────────────────────────┘
```

Position Description

Interior Designers plan new interior spaces and redesign existing spaces to improve and enhance appearance and functionality. They create plans for homes, office buildings, hospitals, hotels, schools, theaters, and more. Interior Designers usually specialize in either residential, business, or commercial design, or in specific rooms or areas, such as kitchen/baths, furniture, or lighting. Specializing enables designers to hone their skills, maintain long-term and close relationships with service providers and vendors, as well as track trends and products more readily.

Interior Designers meet with clients, usually on-site, to see firsthand the project the client has in mind. Interior Designers learn what the client's main goals are in the design and discern their specific needs, their style, and, most importantly, their budget constraints. They consider how the space will be used in their design. If the space already exists, they look it over to determine if it needs renovations to match the client's needs. Once the details are clarified, Interior Designers create initial rough drawings for interior construction. They may design by hand or with computer-aided design (CAD) software, which makes it easier to save documents and quickly make changes. Interior Designers may also design lighting, fixtures, and architectural details such as cabinets, bookshelves, crown molding, and more. They usually include remodeling plans as well as proposals for lights, furnishings, and color recommendations. Interior Designers who specialize in commercial and office buildings take into account whether the space is to be used for meetings, conferences, selling merchandise, or simply working. All Interior Designers are required to create design specifications that meet with local building codes and disability access requirements.

Once the client approves the rough designs, Interior Designers use CAD software to create detailed designs. They present these along with cost estimates for furnishings, materials, and labor. Some Interior Designers may hire and oversee the construction and renovation crew as well as the painters, the carpet or light installation, the delivery of the furnishings, and more. They may track the purchase orders and keep records of all invoices and transactions throughout the project.

Salaries

Interior Designers' salaries vary widely depending on their specialty, years of experience, and the client's budget. Interior Designers who specialize in commercial buildings may command higher salaries, as may those designers with exceptional reputations who are in high demand. According to the American Society of Interior Designers (ASID), surveys reveal that neophyte Interior Designers earn approximately $30,000 per year, while designers who are principals or partners in well-respected firms can earn annual incomes of $75,000 or more.

Employment Prospects

Interior design is in high demand and expected to grow. According to the U.S. Department of Labor's *Occupational Outlook Handbook (OOH),* construction activity will continue to rise both by level and complexity, and thus the need for Interior Designers will rise to meet clients' needs. While the *OOH* predicts that employment of designers overall will grow about as fast as the average for all occupations through 2012, Interior Designers will fare better compared to other designers. An added boon is the rise in media coverage of home renovation and construction projects. "Makeover" shows continue to appear on television network lineups,

with new ones being added each season. The television show *This Old House* paved the way for the home improvement programs that grace the networks. Many of these shows feature home and business owners who allow Interior Designers to help them create new or redesigned living and work spaces. Once Interior Designers have established themselves in the business and grown their reputations, they may be able to secure work in television and film, either as on-screen talent or as behind-the-scenes consultants.

Freelance Interior Designers are also responsible for creating their business image through a company logo, stationery, brochures, Web site, and e-newsletters. They handle advertising and marketing for their business, as well as accounts receivable and payable and general office management tasks.

Advancement Prospects

With years of experience, Interior Designers can advance to become senior or chief Interior Designers if they work for large firms. Freelance Interior Designers can expand by moving into new areas of design. If they specialize in residential, they may want to explore commercial, and vice versa. Trade and mass-market publications are always seeking insights from Interior Designers, so there are always opportunities to write articles and columns about the field. Interior Designers can also teach and participate in public speaking engagements.

Education and Training

Companies prefer Interior Designers to have, at minimum, a bachelor's degree in art with a specialization in interior design. Interior Designers will have an edge in the job hunt if their school's design program is accredited by the Foundation for Interior Design Education and Research (FIDER). Coursework in design, engineering, architecture, drawing (e.g., drafting and perspective), model building and rendering, color theory, art history, as well as Adobe Photoshop, Illustrator, and AutoCAD is highly recommended.

Special Requirements

Interior Designers are required to be licensed or certified in 22 states as well as in the District of Columbia. Licensing requirements vary by state. To obtain a license, Interior Designers must pass a written exam given by the National Council for Interior Design (NCID), and to be eligible to take the exam, they must have a minimum of six years of education and experience, combined, in interior design, two years of which is postsecondary design education.

Experience, Skills, and Personality Traits

Most companies prefer Interior Designers to have two to three years of prior design or interior design apprenticeship experience. Interior Designers must have excellent design skills as well as a strong customer service approach to business. Their mission is to create interior spaces that clients will be happy with, so they must be good listeners to clearly understand what a client wants. They must also have the ability to analyze the clients' specifications, compare them with the actual space and purpose of the space, and visualize what is feasible and what will not work. Along with knowledge of color, textiles, fabrics, and furnishings, Interior Designers must also understand electrical capacity and safety and construction. They must be good managers to see projects through from beginning to end. They work with a wide range of people, from clients, architects, and project managers to service providers, vendors, staff, consultants, and more. Strong communicators with solid organizational skills and leadership abilities will thrive in this field. Interior Designers often work under intense deadline pressure. Only levelheaded professionals achieve respect that earns them referrals and a larger client base.

Unions and Associations

The American Society of Interior Designers (ASID), the Foundation for Interior Design Education Research (FIDER), and the International Interior Design Association (IIDA) offer Interior Designers educational resources, networking opportunities, and other membership benefits. ASID requires members to meet specific educational and work experience requirements. Members must also pass the National Council for Interior Design qualification examination.

Tips for Entry

1. Join a professional interior design association and take the National Council for Interior Design qualification examination. You may work in a state that has no licensing requirements, but passing the exam coupled with membership in an association will impress and instill confidence in your clients.

2. Secure an internship or apprenticeship with an Interior Designer who specializes in the area you want to work in and whose work you admire. Make a list of the studios that interest you most, and contact them to introduce yourself and inquire about job opportunities.

3. Attend trade shows, expos, exhibitions, and conferences. Network as much as possible. Even joining your local chamber of commerce can be an excellent opportunity to spread the word about your work and the types of clients you're seeking.

FASHION DESIGNER

CAREER PROFILE

Duties: Designs clothing and accessories for apparel manufacturers, private clients, or specialty or department stores; creates one-of-a-kind outfits or lines for mass production; researches trends by reading fashion magazines, attending fashion shows, and networking at conferences and exhibitions; draws rough sketches by hand and with computer design software; sews pattern sections together to form sample garments; tests patterns on models; chooses colors, cloths, fabrics, and textiles for designs; coordinates sample garment presentations for fashion shows and presentation to clients; may oversee and manage staff

Alternate Title(s): Clothing Designer, Accessory Designer

Salary Range: $25,350 to $105,280+

Employment Prospects: Fair

Advancement Prospects: Fair

Best Geographical Locations(s): Major urban areas

Prerequisites:

Education or Training—Four-year degree in fashion design required; coursework in art history, drawing, sewing, clothing and textiles, design, and computer-aided design (CAD) recommended

Experience—One to three years of experience as assistant Fashion Designer or cutting assistant required

Special Skills and Personality Traits—Strong design skills; good eye for color and beauty; understands materials and fabrics and how they move; extremely detail oriented and precise, particularly when measuring cloth; able to solve problems quickly; works well under pressure; strong management and supervisory skills; solid written and verbal communication abilities; knows how to work with models, clients, and staff

CAREER LADDER

```
┌─────────────────────────────────┐
│     Senior Fashion Designer      │
└─────────────────────────────────┘

┌─────────────────────────────────┐
│        Fashion Designer          │
└─────────────────────────────────┘

┌─────────────────────────────────┐
│  Assistant Fashion Designer or   │
│        Cutting Assistant         │
└─────────────────────────────────┘
```

Position Description

Fashion Designers design clothing and accessories for private clients, manufacturers, and specialty or department stores. Fashion Designers may work for pattern, textile, or apparel manufacturers or high-end fashion shops and salons. After years of experience and exposure in the business, some may work exclusively with celebrities and wealthy clients. A handful are able to succeed in creating their own lines of clothing and achieve name recognition and stardom.

Fashion Designers design everything from jackets and sweaters to business suits and evening gowns. Some specialize in particular areas and become known for their skills, such as Vera Wang (wedding dresses) and Calvin Klein, who initially designed jeans and casual attire. Fashion Designers participate in all areas of design, from conception, presentation, and production to the fashion shows. They devote a portion of their day to reading magazines and trade publications to track current trends and predict future styles. They meet with clients, head designers, or heads of manufacturing firms to discuss projects, then sketch designs by hand or using design software (such as CAD) and present the designs for approval. They may also bring fabric, clothing, and/or garment samples to presentation meetings.

Once designs have been approved, Fashion Designers measure and map out the garment or accessory patterns by drawing sections to scale on paper and fabric. Cutting assistants then cut the sections, with Fashion Designers overseeing their work. Either the cutting assistants or Fashion Designer then sew the sections together to form the sample garments. Fashion Designers then test the garments on models by having them wear them. Designers make notes of measurements that need adjusting or any other aspects that need to be changed. Fashion Designers make final changes to garments and then present them at sales meetings and fashion shows. Fashion Designers are more than artists; they are savvy business and marketing people who know how to create exciting designs that will sell and set new trends. A combination of creative flair, intuition for what will be popular among certain groups, and excellent technical skills is what it takes to thrive in this position.

Salaries

Depending on experience, region, and customer, Fashion Designers can earn salaries ranging from $25,350 to more than $105,280, according to the *Occupational Outlook Handbook*. Designers who own their own firms and clothing lines earn higher salaries. Those who have celebrity clients, work with high-end fashion shops or department stores, or host or consult with television networks also see larger paychecks.

Employment Prospects

The design industry overall is expected to grow about as fast as the average through 2012. While consumer demand for fashion is expected to remain steady and strong, the declining apparel manufacturing industry may hamper the Fashion Designer's quest for work. To make matters worse, many people are attracted to the fashion design field because of the lure of glamour, so the competition is fierce. Fashion Designers can expect to start in entry-level positions that will be true testing grounds. Only those who truly have the passion to be in the fashion design field will endure. On a slightly brighter note, however, the spate of makeover and self-improvement shows on television the past few years has turned the spotlight on Fashion Designers and created some fresh employment opportunities for the few who have the right connections and image.

Advancement Prospects

With experience, Fashion Designers can advance to become senior or head designers, design managers, or move on to start their own clothing lines and own their own design firms. Fashion Designers can also teach in colleges and high schools and write for fashion magazines and newspapers. Some who have established themselves and already have name recognition or are well connected may also be able to move into television and either host fashion-related shows, make guest appearances, or serve as consultants.

Education and Training

Companies prefer to hire Fashion Designers who have a four-year degree in fashion design and one to two years of design or cutting experience. Coursework in art history, clothing and textiles, drawing, painting, sewing, and small business management is highly recommended. Fashion Designers also need to have a working knowledge of CAD software and other design software programs such as Adobe Photoshop and Illustrator.

Experience, Skills, and Personality Traits

Successful Fashion Designers have exceptional design skills, a solid knowledge of fashion trends, fabrics, textiles, and accessories, as well as strong management and interpersonal abilities. They have the ability to listen to what clients want and the knack to translate their specifications into creative and attractive clothing and accessory designs. Fashion Designers need to know how the body works and how fabrics and materials move with the body. They research and test materials before creating designs. They have a great interest in trends and keep up with the marketplace by regularly reading fashion magazines and attending fashion shows.

Unions and Associations

Fashion Designers can join the International Association of Clothing Designers and Executives for information on trends, business practices and education, networking opportunities, and updates on design technology. Designers who specialize in particular industries can find similar benefits through membership in such trade groups as the Childrenswear Marketing Association, the Professional Apparel Association, or the Sporting Goods Manufacturing Association. State and city organizations such as New York City's Garment Industry Development Corporation also provide Fashion Designers with access to job listings and educational resources

Tips for Entry

1. Many people have the misconception that the fashion design world is all glamour, all the time. Get ready for

reality. Depending on where you work, there may be some glamour, but entry-level positions are universally rigorous. Be prepared for long hours, low pay, and high pressure in the first few years. Make sure you have a thick skin and excellent interpersonal skills; each will help you survive and thrive in the early days.

2. The best way to learn is to find a mentor. Join associations for Fashion Designers and see if they have mentorship programs.

3. Once you land an entry-level position, take advantage by asking lots of questions. Keep a running list of questions and answers in a notebook or on your computer. Now is the best time to get on-the-job training, so research and learn everything you can.

4. It's important for Fashion Designers to keep abreast of trends. Make it your habit to regularly read fashion magazines, such as *Vogue,* as well as trade publications, such as *Women's Wear Daily.* Stay tuned in also by attending classes and lectures and networking as much as possible.

FURNITURE DESIGNER

CAREER PROFILE

Duties: Designs furniture for domestic, commercial, and industrial clients; hand sketches designs and/or renders designs and models using computer software; chooses and purchases lumber and all woodworking materials; maintains shop and shop equipment; uses hand and power tools; interacts with manufacturers and general contractors; may either manage a staff of designers and woodworkers or hire consultants as needed; negotiates fees; establishes production schedules; oversees accounts payable and receivable; may handle business promotion and marketing

Alternate Title(s): Woodworker

Salary Range: $30,000 to $85,000+

Employment Prospects: Good

Advancement Prospects: Fair

Best Geographical Location(s): Urban and suburban areas

Prerequisites:

Education or Training—B.F.A. in furniture design or product design or B.A. in architecture helpful but not required; coursework in design history recommended; vocational school or on-the-job training in woodworking and welding machinery required; some computer-aided design software knowledge recommended

Experience—Several years of carpentry experience beneficial; one to three years of experience as apprentice Furniture Designer recommended

Special Skills and Personality Traits—Creative; entrepreneurial; manual dexterity and physical strength; an eye and feel for wood, as well as an understanding of and appreciation for furniture design history; strong knowledge of woodworking materials, such as paints and finishes; deadline oriented; organized; persistent; flexible; patient; sketching ability; computer savvy

CAREER LADDER

```
┌─────────────────────────────────┐
│  Furniture Design Studio Director, │
│        Gallery Owner, or         │
│  Museum Furniture Conservator    │
└─────────────────────────────────┘

┌─────────────────────────────────┐
│       Furniture Designer         │
└─────────────────────────────────┘

┌─────────────────────────────────┐
│        Apprentice or             │
│  Assistant Furniture Designer    │
└─────────────────────────────────┘
```

Position Description

Furniture Designers either create designs for their own product lines, or they design to their clients' specifications. They create such items as chairs, tables, beds, bookcases, benches, cabinets, bureaus, wall units, and desks for homes, hotels, interior design studios, retailers, and various businesses. If working with clients, they schedule meetings to discuss the pieces requested and help clients decide upon styles, wood types, other materials and accessories, colors, and finishes. They also solidify production schedules and negotiate fees.

Furniture Designers hand draw and/or use computer-aided design (CAD) software to map out their design plans. They sketch individual components of the piece (e.g., desk legs, drawers), as well as the piece as a whole. CAD eases things because the designer can key in changes (for example, height adjustments), and the software automatically adjusts the design to fit the edits. Furniture Designers can also layer their designs using CAD. It's similar to sketching various aspects of the design onto different sheets of transparencies, then placing them atop each other, with the top sheet displaying the complete design, with the difference being the ease of saving the document in the computer and making changes as needed.

Once the client approves the design, the Furniture Designer either hires a furniture builder or craftsman or builds the piece him- or herself. He or she will use a variety of hand and power tools to cut wood to the dimensions and shapes needed; glues, screws, nails, and other materials to join pieces together (such as legs, drawers, tabletops, etc.); and wood cleansers, paints, and finishes once the piece is constructed. Most Furniture Designers follow the construction details that they included in the design. In building the piece, they make sure that materials and their properties, such as strength of the piece being worked on (such as a table leg or cabinet door) match the tool requirements and types of equipment. They might weld steel parts or drill and bolt them together. They might join wood parts together with glue if they want a seamless appearance, or use screws and nails if the piece will function better that way. In the design and building phase, Furniture Designers make decisions that directly affect the look and functionality of the final product.

Furniture Designers usually keep wood on stock in their shops and visit lumberyards frequently. They work either out of basement shops or set up separate studios or workshops. Shop sizes depend on their furniture specialty (e.g., small cabinets or large wall units), the number of clients, and the numbers of pieces they're commissioned to produce. If they work alone, they purchase and maintain all equipment and supplies in their shops, handle the accounts payable and receivable, business promotions and marketing, and other administrative tasks, or they may hire and manage consultants and staff.

Salaries
Furniture Designers can earn salaries ranging from $30,000 to more than $85,000. The range will depend heavily upon the furniture's marketability, types of wood and materials used in the pieces, as well as the Furniture Designer's business savvy, persistence, and communication skills.

Employment Prospects
The the U.S. Department of Labor's *Occupational Outlook Handbook* predicts a 10 to 20 percent growth in overall employment of designers through 2012. Furniture design, as in most design disciplines, is a competitive field. Furniture Designers who are highly creative and imaginative, whose designs are functional and have market value, and who have business skills and persevere will do well in their careers.

Advancement Prospects
Furniture Designers can advance by exploring new areas of design. They may choose to experiment with different types of wood that they've never used before, or try out a different style. If they specialized in chairs, they may move onto desks. They can also enhance their careers by lecturing, teaching, or writing. Some may wish to become museum furniture conservators or restorers. If working solo, another way Furniture Designers can take on new challenges is by hiring staff or opening and managing galleries.

Education and Training
Some Furniture Designers gain valuable experience by attending vocational schools and apprenticing with carpenters and other Furniture Designers. While a four-year college degree is not required, a B.F.A. in furniture design can help provide a well-rounded education and a solid base to draw from when entering the field. Coursework in CAD, creating and rendering models, and building pieces to scale is helpful. Some schools also offer studio classes in such beneficial areas as carving, design history, and traditional and historical detail and ornament. Training in the use of hand and power tools is critical, and experience working with manufacturers or consultants is a plus.

Experience, Skills, and Personality Traits
Self-employed Furniture Designers must be creative to originate designs that are both visually appealing and physically functional. Their pieces must appeal to clients, and they must work. The chair must support the sitter; the desk must support the writer. Furniture Designers must understand how different types of wood age and what materials, finishes, and paints work best with specific woods. Furniture Designers who run their own businesses must also have strong interpersonal skills; they must be able to attract and maintain a clientele as well as manage a staff. They must also be flexible, persistent, and patient. It is a given that Furniture Designers must also enjoy working with their hands and building furniture. The work requires great thought, but physical strength is a must, particularly when lifting lumber, turning large pieces of wood on table saws, and moving finished products.

Unions and Associations
The American Society of Furniture Designers (ASFD) provides such membership benefits as updates on new products and developments in hardware, materials, and systems, as well as networking opportunities, professional support, and a designer referral system. ASFD also offers student members access to mentors.

Tips for Entry
1. Apprentice with a Furniture Designer you respect, or find a mentor or teacher.
2. Perfect your design and woodworking skills, but don't neglect to work on your business management skills, also.
3. Familiarize yourself with CAD. You can either learn it on your own or take a class.

JEWELRY DESIGNER

CAREER PROFILE

Duties: Designs jewelry; maintains quality control of designs; sets retail prices of jewelry; may repair and/or alter jewelry; meets with clients to discuss custom work; chooses materials (e.g., gems, stones, settings, etc.); communicates with contractor in regard to design specifications; tracks inventory; negotiates rates; may handle payables and receivables; hires and manages staff

Alternate Title(s): Jeweler, Precious Stone (or Metal) Worker

Salary Range: $30,000 to $125,000+

Employment Prospects: Fair

Advancement Prospects: Fair

Best Geographical Location(s): Large metropolitan areas

Prerequisites:

Education or Training—Bachelor's in fine arts; master's in fine arts with specification in jewelry design is helpful; certification in gemology is beneficial

Experience—Three- to five-year apprenticeship in jewelry shop

Special Skills and Personality Traits—Strong design, drawing, and sculpting skills; steady hands; solid knowledge of stones, gems, benchwork, polishing, wax making, and fabrication; responsible; detail oriented; excellent business management skills; excellent communicator who cares about the client and the job; entrepreneurial; strong interest in and awareness of fashion

CAREER LADDER

```
┌─────────────────────────────┐
│      Master Jeweler         │
└─────────────────────────────┘

┌─────────────────────────────┐
│      Jewelry Designer       │
└─────────────────────────────┘

┌─────────────────────────────┐
│        Apprentice           │
└─────────────────────────────┘
```

Position Description

Jewelry Designers design jewelry. They choose and purchase all the materials and equipment needed to accomplish the job. They know specifically the type of stones and gems they want, the number of carats, the size and thickness, the types of metals (gold? silver? platinum?), and they track their orders with a calendar. When the materials arrive, Jewelry Designers make sure the order and quality of the materials is exactly as they had requested. They also track costs of the items to help determine retail prices for the designs.

Jewelry Designers either design the jewelry themselves or assign the design to staff and oversee the project. They can specialize in fine jewelry or costume jewelry; they can create individual one-of-a-kind pieces or line collections, which consist of 30 to 40 pieces for mass production. They keep their eye on fashion because when they're dreaming up designs they must also aim for what is in demand. Designers use specialized hand tools and equipment to cut, set, and polish gemstones or repair and adjust jewelry. Designers often sketch their ideas first, making sure the materials and the mechanisms (e.g., clasps for bracelets and necklaces) they have in mind will perform well together and not affect the integrity of the design. They create models for the jewelry out of wax and metal for casting, solder together the rest of the parts, and mount the stones or gems. Some jewelers may specialize in finishing, which means they will set and polish the stones.

Jewelry Designers who own their own businesses oversee all administrative aspects of their business, from hiring and managing staff to keeping the books and maintaining office supplies and equipment. They also design the layout of their stores, choosing lighting and display cases to effectively showcase their work and making sure everything is covered by insurance.

Salaries

Jewelry Designers can expect to earn salaries between $30,000 and $125,000 or more, depending on years of experience, location, and specialty. Designers just starting out will earn closer to $30,000, while those with many years of experience and advanced education and certification can earn higher salaries.

Employment Prospects

In 2002 about 40,000 jewelers and precious stone and metal workers held jobs, according to the the U.S. Department of Labor's *Occupational Outlook Handbook.* Employment for Jewelry Designers is expected to grow more slowly than average until 2012, with only a 3 to 9 percent increase. As the economy improves and people have more expendable income, jewelry sales will rise, as will the need for new Jewelry Designers.

Advancement Prospects

Jewelry Designers who own their own businesses typically do not advance to higher positions because there is no career track. They may grow their staff and branch out by opening stores in other locations. Designers who work for larger shops may be able to move up to master jeweler, though this may take years, as Jewelry Designers tend to stay in the same position for years.

Education and Training

A bachelor of fine arts degree is recommended in this position and a master's is helpful but not required. Jewelers who own small stores prefer to hire gemologists and designers.

Thus, certification in gemology is highly recommended. To further their gemological grading and identification skills and potentially earn higher incomes, Jewelry Designers can earn their graduate gemology degrees (G.G.) at the Gemology Institute of America (GIA). Jewelry Designers who run their own businesses should also take courses in small business management.

Experience, Skills, and Personality Traits

Jewelry Designers must have a thorough knowledge of materials for their designs to succeed. They need to have good interpersonal skills to interact with their staff and also to discuss the design or repair work needed with their clients. They must be persistent and persuasive when presenting their ideas to clients. Jewelry Designers need to be fashion conscious and aware of trends, particularly when they are designing collections. They must be very detail oriented in both their design work and the administrative management of their business. Jewelry Designers also need very steady hands, because they often work with extremely small stones and gems; one small tremor and the whole design can be thrown off.

Unions and Associations

Jewelry Designers can participate in educational and networking programs by joining such organizations as the Gemology Institute of America and Jewelers of America. The Jewelers Vigilance Committee also educates jewelers and the trade about industry standards and jewelers' rights and provides mediation and arbitration services.

Tips for Entry

1. Be willing to take a position that offers great learning possibilities, even if it pays less than you were hoping for. Eventually it will pay off.
2. Work in all aspects of the business. The more knowledge the better. Learn about diamonds, gemstones, bench work, polishing, wax making, fabrication, and the business overall. Take some business courses, too. This will make you an asset to any company or to your own business.
3. Be interested in and care about your clientele.

PACKAGE DESIGNER

CAREER PROFILE

Duties: Designs packaging for products, from food and toys to cosmetics and medicines; works closely with product managers and sales, research, and marketing staff; reads product proposals and considers how product is to be positioned and presented when designing packaging; designs by hand and using computer design software; may oversee staff; invoices clients and handles other small-business owner–related tasks (from bookkeeping to office equipment maintenance); promotes business through advertisements, press releases, and networking

Alternate Title(s): Graphic Designer

Salary Range: $25,000 to $65,000

Employment Prospects: Fair

Advancement Prospects: Fair

Best Geographical Location(s): Major cities

Prerequisites:

Education or Training—Four-year degree in package design or graphic design recommended but not required; solid knowledge of Adobe Photoshop and Illustrator required

Experience—One to two years of internship at design firm or corporate design department; one to three years of design experience in a design firm or design department

Special Skills and Personality Traits—Strong design skills and product awareness; solid understanding of 3-D concepts; ability to grasp advertising and marketing concepts; flexible; patient; team player as well as independent thinker; good eye for what makes products appealing to target markets; ability to take instructions and follow through; good listener; detail and deadline oriented

CAREER LADDER

```
┌─────────────────────────────────────┐
│   Creative Director or Art Director  │
└─────────────────────────────────────┘

┌─────────────────────────────────────┐
│          Package Designer            │
└─────────────────────────────────────┘

┌─────────────────────────────────────┐
│       Junior Package Designer        │
└─────────────────────────────────────┘
```

Position Description

Package Designers create packaging for just about every product that is displayed and stocked in stores. They design packages for dolls, games, CDs, beverages, food, candy, cosmetics, fragrances, medicines, detergents, and more. Package Designers can specialize in retail package design, designing packages for such things as coffeemakers, toasters, blenders, and sports equipment. They may either work directly with large retailers or with design firms or corporate design departments who create packages for such clients. Package Designers read research and marketing proposals to help them understand how to design packaging that is functional, attractive, and meets customers' needs.

Package Designers first meet with product managers and sales, marketing, and possibly engineering staff to discuss the product, how it will be positioned in the marketplace, who the competition is, who the customer is, and the packaging requirements. Package Designers learn everything they can about the product before beginning design work. They must know the size of the product, the color of the product and the packaging (if specified), the texture, the graphics, and so on. After the product specifications and packaging requirements are clarified, the Package Designer then sketches an initial package design or creates a prototype, usually using Adobe Photoshop or Illustrator. When making design choices, Package Designers consider all the following factors: how the product will store on shelves; how the packaging will make it easier for customers to use or handle the product; what will make this product "pop" or stand out from the competition; and what is the most feasible, cost-effective design.

Package Designers use brushes, paints, pencils, and markers as well as computer design software to create package designs and graphics. Depending on the product and the materials used for packaging, they also create three-dimensional models using plastic, metal, paper, wood, glass, and other materials. Package Designers either present their initial design work at meetings or e-mail it to appropriate staff for review. Once they have gathered all comments and suggestions, they make appropriate changes and secure final approval.

Package Designers who own their businesses are responsible for creating their own brand image, from company logo and business stationery to print literature and a Web site. They handle accounts receivable and payable, maintain their office equipment, and may also manage staff. They network and promote their businesses by a variety of avenues, creating target client lists and cold-calling, networking through association memberships, creating advertisements, purchasing mailing lists and sending out direct mailings, and via the Internet.

Salaries

Salaries for Package Designers can range from $25,000 to $65,000, depending on the product and the budget of the design firm or design department. Package Designers who work with high-end products may earn higher salaries, as may those who work with corporate design departments. Package Designers who are more established in the field also command higher salaries.

Employment Prospects

The market is saturated with designers, so employment prospects are fair, at best, for Package Designers. Design work is exciting and diverse, and as a result, many individuals without prior experience are flocking to these positions. Competition is keen for Package Designer jobs. According to the the U.S. Department of Labor's *Occupational Outlook Handbook,* employment of designers overall is expected to increase about as fast as the average through 2012, which is about 10 to 20 percent. There will be fewer jobs, however,

for Package Designers than there are designers to fill them. Package Designers who are interning or working as junior Package Designers in design firms or design departments will have the advantage by already having a foot in the door.

Advancement Prospects

There is no specific career ladder for Package Designers. Those who work in more structured and/or corporate environments can advance after several years to become either senior Package Designers or creative directors. Others can branch out into areas of package design they may not yet have explored and expand their client base.

Education and Training

While a four-year degree in package design or graphic design is recommended, it is not a requirement. What is required is that Package Designers understand graphics and package design, which can be learned while interning with a design firm or in a corporate design department, as well as taking courses at design schools. Package Designers must know how to design using computer design software. Coursework in Adobe Photoshop and Illustrator, the two design programs companies most frequently require, is a must.

Experience, Skills, and Personality Traits

Strong design skills and a solid understanding of sales and marketing concepts are critical in this position. Retail Package Designers will do well to have several years of experience in such areas as branding and packaging. Package Designers work closely with diverse staff and consultants and therefore must be professional, flexible team players. They must take direction well, but also be capable of thinking independently and making creative, feasible suggestions regarding package design when it is in the best interest of the product. Because products come in all shapes and sizes, Package Designers must have a solid grasp of three-dimensional design, as well as the ability to distinguish what makes a product and its packaging appealing to specific customers. Package Designers must also be fast, creative thinkers who are able to keep cool heads. Turnaround times on designs are often fast, and design firms and corporate design departments can be stressful at times. Package Designers who are quick on their feet and deadline driven but who also keep their wits about them will do well in this type of work.

Unions and Associations

Package Designers often join such associations as the American Institute of Graphic Arts (AIGA) and the Graphic Artists Guild (GAG) as well as local and regional art directors' clubs for educational and networking opportunities, design competitions and exhibitions, employment listings, conferences, newsletters, discounts from design-related service vendors, and more.

Tips for Entry

1. Make sure you love package designing before committing to the field. Work as an intern first to see if this type of work is for you.
2. Be open-minded and be a good listener. Ask a lot of questions and learn everything you can while you have the opportunity.
3. Finding a job in package design will be challenging. Use every avenue that's out there to job hunt, from employment agencies to Internet job sites. Network as much as you can, and join associations.
4. Make sure your package design work is in electronic file format (e.g., PDF). Prospective clients frequently request work be sent to them as PDFs.

TEXTILE DESIGNER

CAREER PROFILE

Duties: Designs original prints for textiles, garments, curtains, bedding, ceramics, etc.; may also reconfigure existing designs so that they work with particular textiles and products; chooses colors, sizes of designs, and types of materials; meets with manufacturers and buyers to discuss and negotiate projects; may license original work

Alternate Title(s): Surface Designer

Salary Range: $25,000 to $60,000+

Employment Prospects: Fair

Advancement Prospects: Fair

Best Geographical Location(s): Large metropolitan areas

Prerequisites:

Education or Training—A four-year degree in art is recommended, with coursework in textile design and various computer software programs; some illustration classes may be helpful

Experience—Two to three years of experience as an assistant or intern in a design firm recommended

Special Skills and Personality Traits—Strong design and composition skills; excellent color sense; solid computer software skills; business management ability; creative thinker; problem solver; ability to handle deadlines; extremely organized and efficient; detail oriented

CAREER LADDER

```
┌─────────────────────────────┐
│        Studio Owner         │
└─────────────────────────────┘

┌─────────────────────────────┐
│      Textile Designer       │
└─────────────────────────────┘

┌─────────────────────────────┐
│     Intern or Assistant     │
└─────────────────────────────┘
```

Position Description

Textile designers create two-dimensional designs that "repeat" (meaning one design will repeat throughout the material) for a variety of textiles, garments, bed linens, curtains, ceramics, home and office furnishing fabrics, rugs, wall hangings, wallpapers, tiles, and more. Some create designs for greeting cards, wrapping paper, and even tableware. Textile Designers work in or with such industries as interior design, fashion, technical textiles, and automotive. Some Textile Designers take existing designs and figure out how to make them work with particular textiles and garments. They may also provide clients with color separations and reductions. Other designers may create only original designs. Original designs are typically not commissioned, so it's up to the Textile Designer to shop his or her creative portfolio work around to appropriate buyers. To successfully pitch and sell even the smallest percentage of original work, Textile Designers must thoroughly research the market by staying tuned in to trends and forecasts, reading industry magazines and attending trade shows and association meetings.

Textile Designers have a strong understanding of patterns, colors, textures, and quality of materials, as well as the production process. They need to know all of this for their textile design to succeed and for it to fit within the buyer's budget. Clients who hire Textile Designers are typically manufacturing companies, fashion and clothing retailers, design studios, and interior design and decorating companies. After the initial meeting with clients, Textile Designers may either sketch their ideas on paper or on the computer to create samples for presentation and approval.

Many, but not all, use computer-aided design (CAD) systems in their work. Depending on the clients' specifications, Textile Designers decide the surface patterns, types of materials, and weights of materials for the products, and they will proof for color and quality before going to final print.

Self-employed Textile Designers are responsible for all aspects of their business. They invoice their clients and either handle their own bookkeeping or hire someone (usually part-time) to manage their accounts. They oversee tax reporting and payments and maintain their office supplies and equipment. Textile Designers also create their own brand identities (e.g., logos, stationery, brochures, promotional products, Web sites, e-newsletters, etc.) and promote and advertise their work. They tailor their portfolios for prospective client meetings, making sure the design pieces best reflect their interests and skills, and also closely match the client's body of work.

Salaries

Annual salaries for Textile Designers can range anywhere from $25,000 to more than $60,000, depending on the markets they work in, their clients' budgets, the materials and products they design, and their skill levels and years of experience. Textile Designers may also increase their salaries by licensing their artwork.

Employment Prospects

Although the textile industry has been slowly yet steadily declining due to increased production overseas, manufacturers will continue to need Textile Designers to create the designs, patterns, and color schemes for their products. Design jobs overall are expected to increase by 10 to 20 percent, about as fast as average, from now through 2012, according to U.S. Department of Labor's *Occupational Outlook Handbook.* And while there will be work for Textile Designers, the job hunt will remain competitive. Those designers who have sharp portfolios, solid design and computer skills, and who have done their research on the marketplace will have the edge needed to secure steady work and grow their reputations in the business. Textile Designers may also find work and grow their mark by selling their work directly to the general public. They can exhibit in galleries and set up booths at craft fairs and trade shows.

Advancement Prospects

Textile Designers can advance by increasing their staff, delegating more work to other staff members, working with new and different products and materials and/or software, and working with a completely different type of clientele.

Education and Training

A four-year degree in art is recommended in order to understand different aspects of textile design. Some courses that are helpful include design construction and repeat printed textile design, color theory, color design and forecasting, silk screen printing and dyeing, block printing, and computer-aided design. Textile Designers can also learn textile design skills through apprenticeships, assisting in a design studio or working for a manufacturer or even a printing mill. Textile Designers must continue to stay apprised of trends in the industry, such as what colors and types of products are selling, who's manufacturing and selling them, which designs and prints are top sellers, and so on. They stay abreast by reading magazines such as *Women's Wear Daily* and *Home Textiles Today,* regularly visiting Web sites such as techexchange.com, attending trade fairs and exhibitions, and participating in arts associations and unions.

Experience, Skills, and Personality Traits

Textile Designers need to have a combination of strong drawing and visualization skills. They must understand colors and how and when to use them in designs, particularly since the designs must sync up with the type of materials, shapes, and sizes of the products they're being printed on. To truly enjoy this work, Textile Designers must be innately curious about textiles and patterns, always exploring what is being marketed to keep up with trends. Smart designers regularly visit popular stores, read magazines, and talk to manufacturers and buyers to see what's selling. As with all self-employed artists, freelance Textile Designers must have strong communication and interpersonal skills as well as solid business management savvy and ethics. Knowledge of some design software (e.g., Adobe Illustrator and Photoshop) will also be useful.

Unions and Associations

Textile Designers attend trade shows (e.g., Surtex) and exhibitions for networking, education, and marketing. They join arts associations and unions such as Unite Here!, the Computer Integrated Textile Design Association (CITDA), the Textile Society of America (TSA), the Textile Artists and Designers Associations (TADA, Canada), and the Surface Design Association (SDA) for membership benefits that can range from assistance in negotiating and securing fair contracts and workers' rights to networking, educational programs and literature, discounts on various products, and group health insurance.

Tips for Entry

1. Research the companies that are buying designs and find out what they're buying and why they're buying it. Look at the designs, prints, and colors that are selling. Find the places where your work fits in and create a portfolio that matches. And remember to always keep your portfolio updated!

2. Learning industry-specific software is critical. Taking an internship in a design studio or manufacturing company that has this software can be the best way to hone your skills as well as see firsthand how the business runs.

3. Visit the stores that are selling the products and textiles you want to create designs for, and pay attention to the color schemes. Color is a huge driving force in the textile industry, and it is critical you stay aware of what's hot each season.

4. Network! Job hunting is competitive in the textile industry, and often the best way to find a job is through word of mouth. The more people you meet along the way, the better your chances of getting work through referrals. Join associations, and go to trade shows and exhibitions. See what other designers are doing. Don't be afraid to talk to them and ask questions. A small word of advice can sometimes have the most dramatic and important impact on a career.

VIDEO GAME DESIGNER

CAREER PROFILE

Duties: Conceives and designs video games; defines what games will contain (e.g., characters, environments, objects, skill levels, etc.) and how everything will interact to create "gameplay"; works closely with programmers, artists, and other designers, and possibly with publishers and game owners; may write game text; manages design team; studies and tests games to test theories and determine design problems

Alternate Title(s): None

Salary Range: $25,830 to $85,260+

Employment Prospects: Fair

Advancement Prospects: Fair

Best Geographical Location(s): California (Los Angeles, San Diego)

Prerequisites:

Education or Training—Four-year degree in art

Experience—Two to three years of studio design experience preferred

Special Skills and Personality Traits—Extremely creative; enjoys video games; detail oriented; problem solver; strong communication skills; excellent writing skills; skilled in mechanical drawing; knowledgeable about 2-D and 3-D software programs; good listener; solid management abilities

CAREER LADDER

```
┌─────────────────────────────────┐
│      Senior Game Designer        │
└─────────────────────────────────┘

┌─────────────────────────────────┐
│       Video Game Designer        │
└─────────────────────────────────┘

┌─────────────────────────────────┐
│            Artist                │
│ (Concept or Texture Artist, Modeler) │
└─────────────────────────────────┘
```

Position Description

Duties will vary depending on the company and the game. Typically, Video Game Designers create, design, and develop the concepts, stories, and structures behind video games. They usually work for design studios or in-house for such video game companies as Microsoft, Hasbro, and others. Game designers decide the look and feel of the video games and come up with the designs for the game. They are responsible for maintaining the original vision of the games.

Game owners are sometimes involved in the game design process and have their own ideas that they want designers to pursue. If this is how the work relationship is structured, Video Game Designers find themselves coordinating projects more than designing games. Publishers also have their own varying degrees of input. According to one veteran Video Game Designer, however, designers work less directly with publishers these days. Because of fierce competition for shelf space, many publishers are not picking games up until those games become solid players and therefore have little direct contact with Video Game Designers.

The first stage of game design is brainstorming. When coming up with ideas for designs, one of the first things Video Game Designers consider is the target audience. They need to know the age groups the game is geared toward as well as where the game will be marketed and sold. Once the idea solidifies, Video Game Designers do a great deal of 3-D work and create rough layouts, which they then pass on to artists to finesse. The Video Game Designer decides how everything in the game will look and provides a general overview and direction for size and style to the artists, who then expand on the ideas and illustrate the characters and props. Video Game Designers also work with programmers and provide them with lists of hit points on objects and characters, as well as points needed to advance to higher levels. Depending on the company, Video Game Designers may also be responsible for writing all the text that appears in the game, from the storyline itself and the script to pop-up boxes, game help and instructions, and more. Video Game Designers may also create the game levels themselves or work closely with level designers.

Designers are very technical, "almost like movie directors," as one industry expert put it. Because so many people are interested in video games and also play the games, designers get a great deal of feedback and input from everyone—design teammates, owners, publishers, and even family and friends. It's up to the Video Game Designer to filter the ideas, paying close attention to the ones that are feasible and in-line with the game's mission and look. Video Game Designers allow people to add their thoughts on the game designs because there is always the possibility that the ideas or even portions of the ideas may be helpful and worth pursuing. Good Video Game Designers know that it's critical to keep an open mind, stay curious, and listen carefully.

Design technology is changing constantly, and Video Game Designers need to keep abreast of these changes. They work long hours, particularly during the last few weeks before a game is due to release, and usually don't have time to take design software and graphics classes. Most are self-educated when it comes to design software skills, learning from books, tutorials, game design magazines, and Web sites.

Salaries

Video Game Designers can earn salaries ranging from $25,830 to $85,260 or more, depending on the company, the game, and the designer's years of experience and reputation. Designers who have shipped many games command higher salaries. In 2002, according to the the U.S. Department of Labor's *Occupational Outlook Handbook (OOH)*, salaried multimedia artists and animators who worked in motion pictures and video industries earned median annual incomes of $58,840.

Employment Prospects

According to the *OOH*, employment of artists overall will grow by about 10 to 20 percent, or as fast as the average, through 2012. Video Game Designers may find some increase in opportunities due to expected growth in the video and motion picture industries. The video game design field attracts many people, however, and is expected to remain highly competitive. Its small geographical hub (Los Angeles and San Diego mostly) further narrows employment opportunities. Game companies and design studios prefer to promote artists or programmers from within to Video Game Designers, so getting a foot in the door by taking one of those positions is a smart career move. While on the job, you will learn 3-D backgrounds and how to create environments, which will come in extremely handy in designing games.

Advancement Prospects

With years of experience, Video Game Designers can advance to become senior Video Game Designers. They can also expand their writing base by contributing articles to game magazines and Web sites and writing and publishing books. If they are on staff, they can work as consultants to game companies, publishers, and design studios. Video Game Designers can also teach and lecture at colleges and through professional associations.

Education and Training

A bachelor's degree in art, with coursework in illustration, graphic design, sculpture, drawing, painting, composition, and 2-D and 3-D software is preferred. Design software programs that may be useful to know include Adobe After Effects and Photoshop, Kinetix 3-D Studio Max, and Maya. For writing, it's important to know basic MS Word.

Experience, Skills, and Personality Traits

Video Game Designers play a key role at game companies and have many responsibilities and stressors. While the job can be creatively rewarding, there are tasks that are inherent to the job that can also be tedious (e.g., creating lists of game objects, levels, etc.). Attention to detail and follow-through are important skills in this field. Video Game Designers must be responsible team players who can do it all—manage their designers, stay true to the game's vision, write engaging game text, create clear, detailed, and accurate lists, meet deadlines, keep everyone in the loop, and more. They must be dedicated and committed to the design process and the product, willing to work long hours, and able to put their lives on hold when called upon to meet deadlines. They must also be good listeners and strong communicators. Most of all, they must truly love video games!

Unions and Associations

Video Game Designers can join the International Game Developers Association (IGDA) for networking opportunities and educational resources. Video Game Designers frequently find and share information through industry Web sites such as http://www.gamasutra.com and http://www.gignews.com and by reading such publications as *Game Developer Magazine*.

Tips for Entry

1. Find a mentor, someone who is willing to support and advise you in your career.
2. Make sure you attend a good school and have a strong background in art or programming before you enter the field.
3. Put together a good reel of your 3-D art, and study and play as many games as you can so you understand what makes them work and where there is room for improvement. Always approach the games with the critical eye of a designer and of a gamer.
4. Game companies want designers who have flexible art styles and philosophies. Designers who aren't fixated on a single type of game design will find the most work.

WEB DESIGNER

CAREER PROFILE

Duties: Creates and designs Web sites and Web pages; chooses color, text, and artwork for Web sites; writes and codes Web pages; updates and refreshes Web sites and pages as needed

Alternate Title(s): Multimedia Programmer

Salary Range: $35,000 to $90,000+

Employment Prospects: Good

Advancement Prospects: Fair

Best Geographical Location(s): Large metropolitan areas

Prerequisites:

Education or Training—A four-year degree in art is recommended, with coursework in Web design, graphic design, and various computer software programs; some business management coursework helpful

Experience—Two to three years of experience as an assistant or intern in a Web design firm recommended

Special Skills and Personality Traits—Strong design knowledge; technologically savvy, knows wide variety of software and coding programs; creative thinker; clear communicator; organized

CAREER LADDER

```
┌─────────────────────────────┐
│     Creative Director       │
└─────────────────────────────┘

┌─────────────────────────────┐
│        Web Designer         │
└─────────────────────────────┘

┌─────────────────────────────┐
│ Assistant Web Designer or Intern │
└─────────────────────────────┘
```

Position Description

Web Designers create Web sites and Web pages for a wide variety of clients. They are responsible for the design, layout, and coding of Web pages, which is also known as the front end. They strategize with clients to decide on the look of the site and the content to be included based on the site's target audience, its purpose, its goals, and the competition. Clients may provide Web Designers with text, logos, and color choices, and it is up to the designers to translate it all into a comprehensive Web site that works. They may need to skim through company brochures and other print literature to further assimilate information for the site. Web Designers may also create banner advertisements and other Web marketing tools.

Web Designers work with clients on the layout of the site or site map. Web Designers focus not only on the look of the site but its navigation as well. Web users need to be able to get from page to page, link to link, and then back home again easily and seamlessly. It all has to make sense, and it is the Web Designer who is responsible for making it so. The Web site must be intuitive, and to ensure this, designers need to understand the user interface (UI) and human-computer interaction (HCI).

After negotiating the terms and securing a signed contract, Web Designers create a draft Web site for client approval. Web Designers usually allow for a certain number of modifications in their contracts. Designers create Web pages using hypertext markup language (HTML), Dreamweaver or GoLive, Javascript, Flash, PHP (if working with a programmer), XML, CSS, and others. They make sure the Web site works in different browsers at different resolutions. Once approved, they upload the Web site to the Internet and make modifications or refresh the site in accordance with the terms of their contract. Web Designers who own their own businesses manage the day-to-day office operations, which include everything from accounts payable and receivable, overseeing staff, invoicing clients, opening mail, and maintaining office equipment and supplies.

Salaries

Web Designers who responded to the American Institute of Graphic Artists (AIGA)/Aquent Survey of Design Salaries 2000 stated that their salaries ranged from $35,000 to $50,300, with a median salary of $42,600. The survey also showed that owners and partners at design firms earned significantly higher salaries, the median being $90,000. It would be safe to predict that Web Designers who are owners or partners of a firm can expect to also earn higher salaries.

Employment Prospects

The demand for Web Designers should parallel if not exceed the demand for graphic designers. An increasing number of companies and individuals are starting Web sites to expand their businesses and will need to hire Web Designers to get the work done right. The the U.S. Department of Labor's *Occupational Outlook Handbook (OOH)* predicts that through 2012, design jobs overall will grow by about 10 to 20 percent, which is as fast as the average. However, the *OOH* does not currently show a specific forecast for Web Designers.

Advancement Prospects

With experience, Web Designers who work for design firms can advance to handle more complex projects and oversee more staff in the creative director role. Designers who own their own firms and have successful businesses can increase their staff, delegate more work, and take a vacation now and then.

Education and Training

It is recommended that Web Designers have a four-year degree in art with coursework in graphic design and computer software programs. They should have a thorough understanding of HTML, Dreamweaver, GoLive, Javascript, Flash, PHP, XML, CSS, and so on. Two to three years as an intern or working as an assistant to a Web Designer is highly recommended.

Experience, Skills, and Personality Traits

Web Designers need to be passionate about design and understand how it relates to the overall look and function of a Web site, and they must love to surf the Web. They need to be extremely comfortable using lots of different software. It's also critical that they be interested in and open to learning new software because programs upgrade and change every day. To accurately translate a client's vision into an effective Web site, Web Designers must be clear communicators. They need to be confident enough to ask many questions to find out exactly what the client wants. They must be able to meet deadlines and have solid negotiation and business management skills. Like many artists, Web Designers work long, offbeat hours and must be flexible to meet deadlines. They need to have a grasp of how long the work will take and be able to visualize timelines.

Unions and Associations

For networking, educational programming, and discounts on products and services, Web Designers can join such organizations as the American Institute of Graphic Arts (AIGA), the Graphic Artists Guild, the Association of Graphic Communicators (AGC), the Society for News Design, and the Society for Technical Communication.

Tips for Entry

1. Interning is a great way to hone your skills and get comfortable with the work. Volunteering to work for organizations that interest you is another excellent way to learn and possibly get a foot in the door.
2. Network with fellow Web Designers who are at your level and more experienced. Ask lots of questions and share. Everyone is usually happy to share tips and tricks, and this will help you stay sharp.
3. You have to continually learn, so be a voracious reader and Web surfer. You must also have an interest in the back end. More Web sites are integrated now, and Web Designers need to know how to design appropriately.
4. Self-promotion is important. Get your portfolio together online so that you can have it on your laptop to show to clients. You should also keep a print portfolio. It's also an excellent idea to put your work onto CDs. You can also send e-mails with PDFs of, or links to, your work.

MUSEUMS AND GALLERIES

CONSERVATOR (MUSEUM)

CAREER PROFILE

Duties: Examines artwork to gather information about construction, materials and ingredients; searches for reasons for deterioration or alteration; through scientific and historical research, determines and applies procedures to best conserve and preserve the artwork; documents research; oversees packing and shipping of artwork; delegates work to assistant or apprentice.

Alternate Title(s): Preservation Specialist, Restorer

Salary Range: $20,010 to $66,050+

Employment Prospects: Fair

Advancement Prospects: Fair

Best Geographical Location(s): Major urban areas

Prerequisites:

Education or Training—Master's degree in conservation; coursework in art history

Experience—Minimum several years of experience as volunteer technician in conservation studio required; five to six years of experience as apprentice Conservator; museum experience recommended

Special Skills and Personality Traits—Extremely detail oriented; steady hands and manual dexterity; focused; inquisitive; foreign language skills may be helpful; organized; professional and ethical; serious about the importance of one's work; respectful, cautious and fastidious in the treatment of the artwork

CAREER LADDER

```
┌─────────────────────────────────┐
│        Museum Director           │
└─────────────────────────────────┘

┌─────────────────────────────────┐
│     Conservator or Restorer      │
└─────────────────────────────────┘

┌─────────────────────────────────┐
│      Apprentice Conservator      │
└─────────────────────────────────┘
```

Position Description

A museum Conservator is a combination of artist, historian, scientist, and archaeologist. He or she is responsible for conserving and preserving various types of artwork, depending upon his or her specialty. Some Conservators specialize in restoring paintings, others in sculptures, papers, books, photographic materials, wood, textiles, metals, or ethnographic materials. The reasons Conservators are needed range from obvious physical changes to objects, such as faded or peeling paintings, to discolored, tarnished, chipped sculptures, tattered books, and so on. Conservators are also needed to help create environments that will protect the longevity of the objects.

Conservators research the artwork, learning everything they can about the design work, the actual construction of the piece itself, materials and ingredients used, and the original colors. They also conduct historical and scientific research, finding out what kinds of materials were typically used in the years the piece was created. They learn how the environment impacts the artwork and the effects of temperature, humidity, light, and pollutants. Knowing the chemical composition of the artwork is key; this knowledge enables Conservators to determine the techniques and chemicals to apply that will either successfully restore the artwork to the creator's original intention or prevent further deterioration and alteration.

Conservators document and record their findings and share them with fellow conservators and other museum professionals by publishing reports and articles in association journals. They may hire staff and work closely with apprentices or assistants.

Salaries

According to the U.S. Department of Labor's *Occupational Outlook Handbook (OOH),* salaries for Conservators and other museum technicians and professionals ranged from as low as $20,010 to more than $66,050 in 2002. Freelance Conservators often work with multiple museums with varying budgets. Those who work with smaller, less well-funded museums often supplement their incomes by lecturing, writing articles and books, and/or working in other areas of museum and cultural institutions where their skills are transferable.

Employment Prospects

Conservation work is extremely interesting and crucial, yet employment opportunities are few and far between for Conservators. Competition is fierce. Graduates who have specialized in conservation programs and those with technical backgrounds will have an edge on their competitors. Those who are multilingual and have the flexibility to move may also have greater chances of finding work. According to the *OOH,* employment of Conservators is expected to grow as fast as the average for all occupations through 2012. Jobs may grow as public and private organizations emphasize establishing archives and organizing records and information. Museum attendance is also, consequently, on the rise and is expected to grow, potentially generating more jobs. However, while art conservation and restoration will always be needed, many museums still do not have sufficient budgets to compensate Conservators. Some Conservators may need to supplement their incomes by working in other areas of art, such as teaching or writing. Another issue to keep in mind is that arts and cultural institutions are subject to funding and staffing cuts during recessions.

Advancement Prospects

Conservators can advance by becoming museum directors. They can also move into education by teaching, lecturing, or writing. They can also expand their businesses by increasing their staff and by branching out into other areas of conservation.

Education and Training

Conservators must have a master's degree in conservation, several years of internship, then a minimum of six years of experience as an apprentice in a museum or on a historical site. Not only is competition fierce for Conservator jobs, it's intensely keen to get into graduate school for conservation education. Foreign language skills may give graduate school prospects an edge. Other prerequisites for graduate school are courses in organic chemistry, archaeology, anthropology, natural history, studio art, and art history and tangible examples of manual dexterity, such as your own artwork. Grad school hopefuls can also gain an edge by having prior volunteer or technician experience in an art conservation studio, working with reputable conservation professionals. Graduate programs are two to four years, with the last years focusing on internship training. Very few people are able to become Conservators through the more difficult route of strictly apprenticing. Note that if you choose this path, it may take years before you become a full-fledged Conservator, and you still must take the courses previously recommended.

Experience, Skills, and Personality Traits

Caring for works of art is a tremendous responsibility. Conservators must be extremely serious about their work. Attention to detail is crucial, as is a steady hand, manual dexterity, a design and artistic sense, and an ethical approach to the work. Because their job is to prevent and protect against further damage and deterioration, Conservators must also have a deep knowledge of materials and how they interact with the environment.

Unions and Associations

Most states have conservation associations that provide various resources to Conservators and conservation technicians. Organizations such as the American Association of Museums (AAM), the American Institute for Conservation of Historic & Artistic Works (AIC), the Association for Preservation Technology (APT), the International Centre for the Study of the Preservation and Restoration of Cultural Property (ICCROM), the Getty Conservation Institute (GCI), the International Council of Museums (ICM), and many others offer conservation and museum professionals educational resources and networking opportunities.

Tips for Entry

1. Conservation schools are hard to get into. Become a volunteer technician in a conservation studio first to make certain that this is the type of work you want to do before investing your time and money.
2. There are more Conservators specializing in paintings than there are jobs. Consider specializing in paper conservation or working in the library field. Also explore ethnographic materials.
3. See what kinds of jobs are out there by subscribing to and reading conservation association newsletters. You'll have a better idea of the areas of conservation that are in demand.

EXHIBITION DESIGNER (MUSEUM)

CAREER PROFILE

Duties: Designs exhibitions of artwork for museums; coordinates all aspects of exhibitions with curators, conservators, art handlers, and other museum professionals; creates budgets for exhibition design work; creates blueprints for exhibition space; oversees carpenters, painters, electricians, and others involved in creating exhibition space; prepares exhibition for deinstallation; visits other museums and galleries; reads and researches artwork; attends events and show openings; manages staff

Alternate Title(s): Gallery Designer

Salary Range: $25,000 to $85,000+

Employment Prospects: Fair

Advancement Prospects: Fair

Best Geographical Location(s): Major urban areas

Prerequisites:

Education or Training—B.F.A. with coursework in exhibition, graphic, and/or set design, illustration, and art history; training in computer software such as Vectorworks and AutoCad; M.F.A. may be preferred by some museums

Experience—Three to five years of experience as assistant Exhibition Designer; museum internship recommended

Special Skills and Personality Traits—Strong design and illustration skills; working knowledge of building materials and set construction; detail oriented; flexible; patient; excellent communication skills; strong organizational and management abilities; team player and independent thinker; deadline oriented; design software knowledge

CAREER LADDER

```
┌─────────────────────────────────┐
│   Chief Exhibition Designer     │
└─────────────────────────────────┘

┌─────────────────────────────────┐
│      Exhibition Designer        │
└─────────────────────────────────┘

┌─────────────────────────────────┐
│  Assistant Exhibition Designer  │
└─────────────────────────────────┘
```

Position Description

Exhibition Designers work closely with curators and other museum executives to determine the best and most interesting ways to exhibit artwork to the general public. Exhibition Designers take into account all aspects of the artwork when creating the exhibition design. They consider such factors as the design and weight of the artwork, the lighting needed, the best ways to mount the work, and the actual environment in which the artwork will be exhibited. Before beginning the design, they also must find out the style the museum prefers, which can range from minimalist to historically-accurate exhibitions. They often research and learn about the artwork, then make design presentations for approval, and create budgets for exhibition design work.

Once the specifics are discussed, clarified, and a direction is set, the Exhibition Designer maps out the space and makes drawings for wall construction and paint schemes and specific spacing measurements for artwork, lighting, graphics placement, seating, video areas, and more. He or she ensures that signature images and titling are accurate and that the exhibition is in keeping with the museum's other collections and mission. The Exhibition Designer also reviews layouts with conservators and art handlers and collaborates with curators on the artwork's arrangement.

Exhibition Designers create and review blueprints and installation drawings for carpenters, painters, electricians, art handlers, and audiovisual personnel. They are present for and oversee the building, painting, wiring, and lighting of the space and the final installation of artwork, the graphic elements, and protective barriers, to ensure that the work is completed to spec. When the exhibition ends, they prepare for deinstallation and coordinate demolition of fabricated walls, graphics, and so on to prepare the space for the next exhibition.

Exhibition Designers frequently attend press previews, exhibition openings, and other events. They also visit other museums and galleries. Depending on the size and structure of the museum, they may also manage staff and handle some administrative tasks directly related to their work.

Salaries

Salaries for Exhibition Designers can range from $25,000 to more than $85,000. Well-funded museums in major cities pay larger salaries. Freelance Exhibition Designers can earn large rates for single exhibitions, depending on the reputation and budget of the museum, the artist and the artwork, and the scope of the exhibition. Exhibition Designers often supplement their incomes by freelancing as retail or trade show display designers or even as set designers.

Employment Prospects

Designer positions overall are expected to grow about as fast as the average, or by about 10 to 20 percent, through 2012. The exhibition design field is a small niche, though. According to the U.S. Department of Labor's *Occupational Outlook Handbook* few job openings exist, and competition for those jobs is keen. Major cities with numerous museums and galleries offer greater opportunities for exhibition design work. Exhibition Designers are often referred to curators and museum directors, so networking and building contacts is an excellent way to hunt for work in this field.

Advancement Prospects

Exhibition Designers can advance to become chief Exhibition Designers after five to 10 years of experience. They may also expand their skills by freelancing for other clients in the arts, such as galleries and theaters.

Education and Training

Most museums require a B.F.A. with a specialization in exhibition design or design. Some museums may prefer a master's degree. Exhibition Designers must have design experience and know how to create two- and three-dimensional designs, both by hand and by using design software such as Vectorworks or AutoCad. An internship in a museum or gallery is the best way to learn firsthand how exhibitions are created. At least three to five years of on-the-job training while working as an associate Exhibition Designer is crucial.

Experience, Skills, and Personality Traits

Exhibition Designers need to be passionate about and have a broad interest in art. Because they work with a variety of museum professionals, changes are often made to their designs, so patience, flexibility, and professionalism are extremely useful. Exhibition Designers must also be excellent researchers and readers. Artwork is often exhibited in keeping with the era in which it was created, so Exhibition Designers must know how to locate information about that timeframe to accurately design the exhibition. Exhibition Designers must have strong design and drawing skills, both by hand and using computer software. They must understand lighting techniques and have strong color and tonal awareness. Because they are responsible for so many aspects of the exhibition, they must also be detail oriented and extremely organized. Exhibition Designers collaborate with a wide variety of people, from curators to carpenters; having excellent interpersonal and communication skills will ease their jobs.

Unions and Associations

The American Association of Museums (AAM) offers Exhibition Designers and other museum professionals such membership benefits as networking opportunities, job listings, and educational workshops and conferences.

Tips for Entry

1. Travel! See art in its original settings. Visit Italy to see Italian sculptures. Go to Egypt to see Egyptian art. Absorb the environment and the culture. It will make a difference in how you approach your exhibition design work.
2. Persevere. The exhibition design field is specialized and small, but if you have the talent and the drive, you will find work. Make as many connections as you can. Go to show openings and exhibitions. Get your foot in the door by interning, whether it's paid or not.
3. Do your research and confirm that your information is accurate before you begin design work. Make sure you know such aspects as the dimensions of the artwork and the measurements of the space the artwork is to be exhibited in. Know the types of lighting involved and the flooring and find out what's permanent and what can be changed.
4. Be relaxed, keep an open mind, and have fun. Listen to music when you're designing, and remember to pay attention to your body, also. Many designers advocate stretching exercises to limber the body and the brain.
5. Stay inspired by visiting other exhibitions, and go beyond the museum world. Look at stage sets for theater or dance. You can learn a lot by seeing what professionals in other arts fields are doing. Department store windows are rich in creativity. Films also have elaborate and well-conceived sets.

PUBLIC RELATIONS MANAGER (MUSEUM)

CAREER PROFILE

Duties: Steers the image of the art museum by overseeing all printed materials; develops and maintains relationships with the press and all media; oversees advertising; may participate in various aspects of marketing; writes and places press releases, e-mail and e-newsletters, and other communiques; maintains database of media contacts; serves as a conduit to all departments within the museum, as well as to outside organizations; hosts press conferences; attends exhibitions and events; oversees public relations staff; creates and manages department's budget

Alternate Title(s): Director of Public Relations, Press Director

Salary Range: $30,000 to $75,000+

Employment Prospects: Good

Advancement Prospects: Good

Best Geographical Location(s): Major metropolitan areas

Prerequisites:

Education or Training—Bachelor's degree preferred (degree may be in public relations or journalism, with coursework in art history strongly recommended); some museums may prefer a master's degree

Experience—At minimum, three to five years of experience as associate or assistant Public Relations Manager or public relations coordinator

Special Skills and Personality Traits—Excellent written and verbal communication skills; strong interpersonal abilities; organized; computer savvy; passionate about art and artists; motivated; decisive yet flexible; solid leadership skills; able to handle stress constructively and professionally

CAREER LADDER

```
┌─────────────────────────────────┐
│   Public Relations Director or   │
│    Communications Director       │
└─────────────────────────────────┘

┌─────────────────────────────────┐
│    Public Relations Manager      │
└─────────────────────────────────┘

┌─────────────────────────────────┐
│  Public Relations Coordinator or │
│    Communications Associate      │
└─────────────────────────────────┘
```

Position Description

The Public Relations Manager (PR Manager) is responsible for ensuring that the museum's image stays true to its mission. The PR Manager is literally the eyes and ears of the museum, interacting regularly with nearly every department within the museum, from curatorial and educational to advertising and Web. By being aware of what each department is working on as well as what interests the public, the PR Manager cultivates stories about the museum and crafts press releases with specific publications and television shows in mind for placement. He or she is responsible for maintaining lists of relevant media and either managing the database directly or delegating it to an appropriate staff member. He or she may also develop and implement advertising campaigns.

Public Relations Managers must be thoroughly informed about the industry they represent. They need to intelligently converse at exhibitions and events. More specifically and critically, they need to be aware of trends that might affect the museum's direction in order to make informed recommendations to the museum director and/or other executive managers. To keep abreast, they regularly read a wide variety of literature, such as magazines, newspapers, books, other museum catalogs and literature, and Web sites. PR Managers may also create and produce internal company communications (e.g., staff newsletters) and other literature to accompany the institution's reports. They may help the museum director and other executives in drafting speeches and maintaining other forms of public communication.

Public Relations Managers guide contact with the public, making sure that the staff communicates consistent and accurate information in adherence to the museum's brand. They are also responsible for maintaining the museum's archive of public relations materials, including photos and published materials for exhibitions and events. Some PR Managers may handle special events, parties, or other activities to generate public attention through the press. Because they are key representatives of the museum, PR Managers attend many of the museums events as well as those of other organizations. PR Managers are also responsible for creating annual budgets and may need some familiarity with computer spreadsheet software.

Salaries

Public Relations Managers in art museums can anticipate salaries ranging anywhere from $30,000 to $75,000 or more, depending on the size of the museum and the state of the economy. Larger, well-known museums may pay higher salaries. If a recession is in effect, however, funding to all museums diminishes, and museums, in turn, scale back on salaries and staff to survive. Public Relations Managers who have years of successful art museum experience or corporate public relations experience are more likely to command higher salaries.

Employment Prospects

According to the U.S. Department of Labor's *Occupational Outlook Handbook (OOH)*, employment of Public Relations Managers throughout all industries, is expected to grow by about 36 percent (faster than the average) through 2012. Job opportunities will be directly linked to the economy, as museum budgets often depend on grants and government funding. Although jobs in this field are growing, competition is keen for Public Relations Manager positions. Museums prefer candidates who have strong knowledge of the specific artwork and artists the museum features, related or transferable work experience, and strong computer skills.

Advancement Prospects

Public Relations Managers with at least five years of experience can advance to communications director, depending on the size and budget of the museum. Advancement prospects are usually brighter in larger museums and cultural institutions, where career ladders are more defined. According to the *OOH,* because Public Relations Managers have such highly visible jobs, those who are successful in their work have the greatest opportunities to advance within their field. Other options for advancement fall outside the typical career ladder and pertain more to the nature of expanding work experience. A Public Relations Manager can apply his or her expertise by becoming a freelance public relations consultant.

Education and Training

Most museums prefer Public Relations Managers to have a bachelor's degree. Although the degree need not necessarily be in public relations or journalism, coursework in art history is a must. Public Relations Managers need to have a solid knowledge and understanding of the art world, and an art history background is extremely helpful. Some museums prefer a master's degree. Public Relations Managers need a familiarity with advertising, business administration, public affairs, public speaking, political science, and writing. Several years of experience as either a public relations coordinator, associate, or assistant and an internship in a public relations firm, museum, gallery, or arts-related organization are extremely beneficial. Because more public relations work is being done via the Internet, PR Managers must be familiar and comfortable with various software programs and accustomed to surfing the Web. Depending on the museum, some bilingual PR Managers may find greater work opportunities.

According to the *OOH,* certification is available through some associations, though this may not pertain directly to PR Managers who work with art museums. The *OOH* states, "While relatively few advertising, marketing, promotions, public relations, and sales managers currently are certified, the number of managers who seek certification is expected to grow. For example, Sales and Marketing Executives International offers a management certification program based on education and job performance. The Public Relations Society of America offers a certification program for public relations practitioners based on years of experience and performance on an examination."

Experience, Skills, and Personality Traits

Public Relations Managers must have excellent written and verbal communication skills. They are the face and voice of the museum; they therefore must have a professional appearance and solid public speaking skills. It is critical that they be passionate about the art and artists featured in their museums, because it is this energy that they will bring to the media and to the public. Their interest and their message will attract the public and increase attendance at the museum, which can also lead to increased funding. Public Relations Managers must be naturally outgoing, because they interact with a wide variety of people on various levels, from the museum's staff, directors, and trustees to the press, media, staff at other organizations and museums, and the general public. Public Relations Managers juggle many tasks and must be organized to be successful. They must know the status of their projects, production deadlines, press deadlines, and key contacts. In addition to computer software knowledge and agility working on the Internet, PR Managers should have some understanding of graphic design, as they work closely with graphic designers on the creation of various museum materials.

Unions and Associations

Public Relations Managers for art museums have access to networking opportunities, lectures and other educational resources through membership in such organizations as the American Association of Museums (AAM) and the Public Relations Society of America.

Tips for Entry

1. Get work experience by interning in a museum or gallery. Be sure that you want to do this kind of work before taking the job. You must be passionate about artwork and artists.

2. Network. You need to know what's going on in the industry. Meeting other museum and/or gallery staff, as well as the artists, will help you increase your knowledge and potentially create inroads to work that might not otherwise be advertised to the general public.

3. Do your research. Find and create a list of the top 25 public relations firms in your area. Contact one to three heads of these firms and set up informational interviews. You can also contact the public relations departments of the museums you're most interested in working for, set up informational interviews, and see if they have internship opportunities available. Even if it means working for free, having your foot in the door will be a worthwhile investment in your public relations career.

GALLERY DIRECTOR

CAREER PROFILE

Duties: Chooses artists to exhibit in gallery; creates and plans shows; if working for small galleries, handles promoting artists and sales, creating show announcements, and writing and placing press releases; may participate in cleaning and organizing the gallery, managing staff and payroll, accounting, and other business administrative tasks

Alternate Title(s): Exhibition Director

Salary Range: $30,000 to $60,000+

Employment Prospects: Good

Advancement Prospects: Good

Best Geographical Location(s): Major cities

Prerequisites:

Education or Training—B.F.A. required, with coursework in art history recommended; M.F.A. helpful but not required; arts business management coursework is recommended

Experience—One to two years of experience interning at a gallery; two to three years of experience assisting Gallery Director

Special Skills and Personality Traits—Good eye and intuition for choosing artists and subject matter for exhibitions; strong problem solving abilities; able to form successful partnerships; amicable; organized; solid interpersonal and communication skills; rational, clearheaded

CAREER LADDER

```
┌─────────────────────────────────┐
│         Gallery Owner           │
└─────────────────────────────────┘

┌─────────────────────────────────┐
│        Gallery Director         │
└─────────────────────────────────┘

┌─────────────────────────────────┐
│      Gallery Manager or         │
│   Assistant Gallery Director    │
└─────────────────────────────────┘
```

Position Description

Gallery Directors create and plan exhibitions that feature specific artists, have specific messages or themes, focus on specific media and/or styles, and generate interest, conversation, and sales from both the general public and collectors. Directors decide the focus of each show in accordance with the overall mission of the gallery. For instance, one New York–based gallery features only artists who have never exhibited before. The gallery's mission is to help introduce new and promising artists to the general public, as well as to provide greater accessibility to the artwork. Gallery Directors keep apprised of new artists and trends in the field by attending art shows regularly as well as visiting art fairs. There they review the artwork, meet and speak with artists, and keep track of the work that most interests them.

A Gallery Director's responsibilities vary from gallery to gallery. It is common for the Gallery Director to wear many hats. He or she is responsible for promoting artists and handling and negotiating sales. In promoting artists, the Gallery Director thoughtfully targets appropriate media to announce show openings as well as creates and mails show invitations to specific individuals and organizations. He or she writes and places the press releases, based on the in-house media list. The Gallery Director handles consignments and makes sure that all the press packets are sent out.

Artists are often referred to Gallery Directors by word of mouth and through artists who have previously exhibited.

The Gallery Director looks at slides and online and in-print portfolios, meets with artists, and decides whether to pursue them. He or she also reviews artists' exhibition queries and follows up with the artists when work stands out and has exhibition potential. Gallery Directors may also handle administrative tasks or delegate them to appropriate staff and/or consultants. They manage payroll and accounting, oversee business machinery maintenance, as well as make sure that the gallery is clean, organized, and the best environment for the artwork. They also oversee staff, meet with clients regularly, and may also be involved in researching and applying for grants for the gallery.

Salaries

Gallery Directors can expect to earn annual salaries ranging anywhere from $30,000 to $60,000 or more, depending on the size of the gallery, the staff size and budget, the type of work exhibited and sold, and the clientele. Galleries that feature high-end artwork and recognized artists attract collectors and a greater audience and therefore also attract more money. Some Gallery Directors also earn commissions on the sales they make. Gallery Directors can always supplement their incomes by teaching or writing.

Employment Prospects

The U.S. Department of Labor's *Occupational Outlook Handbook* states that there has been an upsurge of interest in art and art museums that will continue through 2012. As long as people continue to need and enjoy art, galleries will thrive, and Gallery Directors will find employment. Major cities and areas of the country that are rich in the arts (such as Santa Fe) will offer greater opportunities for Gallery Directors. Galleries are always in need of help, and the best way to get into this field is by starting at the bottom and working your way up. Sweeping a gallery floor can often be the best way to learn what it takes to run the business.

Advancement Prospects

There is no specific, structured career ladder for Gallery Directors. Gallery Directors often advance by opening their own galleries or, if they already own a gallery, opening another. They can also advance by exploring new artists and new art styles and/or changing the message that their exhibitions convey. They may also grow professionally by teaching at institutions and associations as well as writing for print and Internet publications.

Education and Training

Galleries often require their Gallery Directors to have a B.F.A., with an emphasis in art history. A fine arts back-

ground may also be helpful, particularly if the background is in the medium and style of the artwork featured in the gallery. Coursework in small arts business management is also highly recommended.

Experience, Skills, and Personality Traits

It's critical that Gallery Directors be excellent problem solvers. Every day, new issues crop up that need to be resolved. Whether it's a snafu regarding shipping the artwork, trying to schedule a photography session of one installation around the opening night of a new exhibition, or resolving a payroll issue, Gallery Directors need flexibility, open minds, and the ability to communicate clearly and efficiently. They need to be great visualizers as well as solid business managers. Because they are dealing regularly and consistently with artists, they must have a passion for the artwork and an understanding of what was involved in creating it. As they also deal with a wide variety of people, from staff and the general public to artists, collectors, and even the press, Gallery Directors must have exceptional speaking skills, patience, and a friendly, inviting manner. Prior experience working as an intern or assistant at a gallery is recommended. Some Gallery Directors move into the position from gallery manager roles. Gallery Directors must have a clear idea of the message they want the gallery to convey and the artists and artwork that will best convey that message to the viewing public.

Unions and Associations

The Art Dealers Association of America (ADAA) provides invited and accepted members the opportunity to reach a wider, global audience through participation in its exhibitions as well as access to networking, education, and other resources. Gallery Directors also have access to networking opportunities, lectures, and other educational resources through membership in such organizations as the American Association of Museums (AAM).

Tips for Entry

1. You must be prepared to pay your dues. You may need to start at the lowest level, but use your position to your advantage. This is the best opportunity to observe and absorb what's going on around you. Learn, be patient, and don't be afraid to ask questions.
2. Be proud of your own accomplishments. Don't focus on reviews and what other people think, as this will impact your choices going forward. Stay true to your original mission and intention with the gallery.
3. Have a business partner. It helps to be able to share the workload as well as to brainstorm and solve problems together.

CURATOR (MUSEUM)

CAREER PROFILE

Duties: Researches, reviews, and chooses art to display in museums; depending on museum structure, may collect materials and write proposals for art exhibitions for exhibition or corporate committee review; interacts with artists; may participate in fund-raising, grant writing, and other tasks related to promoting the museum; attends gallery openings, art exhibitions, open studios, and various social functions; may negotiate art acquisitions; authenticates artwork; works particularly closely with conservators, archivists, museum's education department, and more generally with all departments within the museum; manages staff

Alternate Title(s): None

Salary Range: $33,720 to $70,100+

Employment Prospects: Fair

Advancement Prospects: Fair

Best Geographical Location(s): Major urban cities

Prerequisites:

Education or Training—M.F.A., with coursework in curatorial studies; some museums prefer doctoral degrees; coursework in business management and computer software programs recommended

Experience—Museum internship and minimum three to five years of experience as apprentice or assistant Curator required

Special Skills and Personality Traits—Knowledgeable and passionate about art; strong communication and interpersonal skills; inquisitive; solid research skills; creative and visual thinker; business savvy; some knowledge of computer software and office programs; awareness of fund-raising, grant writing, and promotion techniques and trends; flexible

CAREER LADDER

```
┌─────────────────────────────────────┐
│   Chief Curator or Museum Director   │
└─────────────────────────────────────┘

┌─────────────────────────────────────┐
│              Curator                 │
└─────────────────────────────────────┘

┌─────────────────────────────────────┐
│   Apprentice or Assistant Curator    │
└─────────────────────────────────────┘
```

Position Description

A Curator's main responsibility is to choose art to exhibit in a museum for new shows or to enhance collections. The Curator reviews and researches artwork by visiting artists' open studios, attending gallery and museum shows, looking at art, and reading articles in various publications and on the Internet. He or she also reviews literature and art that artists submit for consideration and contacts the artists directly if interested in pursuing them. The Curator's job is to create exhibitions that highlight specific artists or focus on certain motifs, styles, and/or themes as well as to raise awareness about specific issues. To do this, the Curator must be well read and have both a global and local perspective. In creating a plan for an exhibition, a Curator may read literature from a certain era or newspapers from a particular part of the world. The goal is to create shows that generate conversation, controversy, and/or contemplation.

Curators who work for private and corporate collectors help them purchase artwork by doing the legwork for them. Curators research the artwork and artists, collect materials, create and maintain lists of the materials collected, and make recommendations to aid in the final decision.

Some Curators may also be involved in purchasing, selling, exchanging, or loaning artwork, maintaining or overseeing the maintenance of the archives, as well arranging for storage of the artwork in collaboration with conservators. Many Curators also evaluate and verify, or authenticate, that the artwork is truly created by the artist.

Curators work alongside other museum staff on fundraising and promotion projects. They may help write grant proposals, lecture at workshops and conferences, socialize at exhibition openings and other events, and help write promotional literature. Curators in smaller museums have a wider range of responsibilities; in addition to their curatorial duties, they may also have more administrative tasks. They are responsible for hiring and managing staff and creating budgets.

Salaries

Art Curators can expect to earn salaries ranging from $33,720 to $70,100 or more. According to the U.S. Department of Labor's *Occupational Outlook Handbook (OOH)*, several variables determine a Curator's income: the size and type of the museum and the specialty. Large, well-known, and well-funded museums will, naturally, offer higher salaries.

Employment Prospects

Employment of Curators is expected to grow about as fast as the average for all occupations through 2012, according to the *OOH*. However, competition for Curator positions is keen. Graduates with master's degrees in curatorial studies, solid full-time internships in relevant museums or galleries, as well as strong computer skills will have the advantage.

Advancement Prospects

Curators in large museums can move up to become chief curators. Those who have been in their positions for years can advance to become museum directors, or they can move beyond the museum to freelance curate, lecture, and/or write. Some may choose to specialize in the field of art that most inspires them and open their own museums or galleries.

Education and Training

Most Curators have master's degrees in art, art history, museum studies, or the specific area of art that the museum specializes in (e.g., contemporary, modern, etc.). Some museums may prefer doctoral degrees. Smaller museums may require only four-year undergraduate degrees but will lean toward candidates with coursework in the areas of art that the museum features. Several years of experience interning full time for a gallery or museum is preferred by many museums. Coursework in conservation as well as business management is highly recommended. Curators must have a working knowledge of computer programs and electronic databases and be Internet savvy.

Experience, Skills, and Personality Traits

Curators must be committed to the arts. Their work is varied and demanding, so flexibility is also called upon. Curators who work for smaller museums may be involved in setting up exhibits, and thus steady hands and manual dexterity are important. Successful Curators are inquisitive and enjoy reading and research. They are always learning about art, history, news, trends, and everything that relates to exhibits and prospective exhibits on both a local and international scale. Many Curators are involved in museum fund-raising and must have strong writing skills for grant writing projects. They also must have solid verbal and interpersonal skills for public presentations, networking, and training staff and volunteers.

Unions and Associations

The American Association of Museums (AAM) offers Curators and other museum professionals such membership benefits as networking opportunities, job listings, and educational workshops and conferences.

Tips for Entry

1. Internships are important. Some Curators enter museums through their internships at galleries, and vice versa. Interning is an excellent way to gain experience and see what interests you most.
2. Engage and be interested in broader cultural issues. Stay abreast of the world's art market; it's as important to your work as art history.
3. Hone your writing skills.
4. Socialize as much as possible. Networking can open doors to artists you may want to exhibit, issues you may want to create exhibits around, and other ideas and opportunities that may otherwise never have existed.
5. Read everything. Constantly challenge yourself to learn something new.

PUBLISHING

SEQUENTIAL ARTIST

CAREER PROFILE

Duties: Composes a sequence of images consisting of drawings and text that tell a story

Alternate Title(s): Cartoonist

Salary Range: $0 to $100,000+

Employment Prospects: Poor

Advancement Prospects: Poor

Best Geographical Location(s): Areas with broadband Internet access; New York metropolitan area

Prerequisites:

Education or Training—While no specific degree is required, one must have the ability to draw characters with a consistent appearance and tell a story through pictures

Experience—None, though it furthers one's chances of success to begin as an artist assistant to a working professional Sequential Artist

Special Skills and Personality Traits—Ability to work with others and accept criticism

CAREER LADDER

```
┌─────────────────────────────┐
│      Sequential Artist      │
└─────────────────────────────┘

┌─────────────────────────────┐
│       Artist Assistant      │
└─────────────────────────────┘

┌─────────────────────────────┐
│           Student           │
└─────────────────────────────┘
```

Position Description

Sequential Artists craft comic books and graphic novels, mostly for print publication but increasingly for Web publication as well. These pieces of art, referred to as sequential narratives for purposes of this listing, combine words and pictures in a sequence to tell a story visually. In several ways, sequential narratives read like still-image movies. As such, many of the visual storytelling devices of film—straight narrative, flashback, future narrative, changing point of view—are employed by the Sequential Artist when crafting his or her work.

In the United States, the field of sequential art has undergone dramatic changes in the last 60 years, since DC Comics' Action Comics #1 introduced Superman in 1938. At that time, public demand for sequential narratives was very great, often leading to sales upward of 1 million copies per issue at its height. In the current marketplace, sales of 60,000 copies per issue of a mainstream sequential narrative publication are considered highly successful. In the independent arena, sales of 20,000 copies per issue is similarly considered a huge success. A Sequential Artist wears many hats in his or her working life in order to draft successful works of sequential narrative. A story comes first, and a Sequential Artist may at times write his or her own material. The writing considerations for sequential narratives are rigorous, as they involve many characters and settings. These stories often have subplots that relate to prior stories and set the stage for future ones as well. Due to these considerations, in many cases a Sequential Artist works with a writer. After being fitted with a story to tell, a Sequential Artist begins translating the written description into a series of relating pictures that tell the story as best it can be told without words.

In the best examples of the medium, the work of Sequential Artists can impart the narrative aspect of a story without the aid of a single word of dialogue or caption. While not a hard and fast rule, dialogue appears in sequential narratives in word balloons, and captions filled with illuminating text appear in boxes elsewhere in the individual images. To craft this visual telling of a story, the Sequential Artist begins by making thumbnail sketches. These sketches are typically done in pencil on a small scale, proportionate to the final print size of the published work. During this stage, a Sequential Artist acts as a pseudo–film director, using still visual images to move the story along, set pacing, and create tension. He or she also begins considering the visual layout of the individual pages, designing them in interesting ways that will enhance the flow of the story and leaving appropriate space for inclusion of dialogue and narration.

After completing thumbnails, the artist then begins to flesh these very rough sketches out on the final drawing surface. This fleshing-out phase of the work takes place almost universally in pencil. Though some artists prefer to use non-reproductive blue pencil, most use some sort of graphite, ranging from 4H (a very hard lead, good for very light marks) to 2B (a very soft lead, good at generating heavy black lines).

With the rough-cut direction complete in the thumbnail stage, the Sequential Artist begins acting as a set decorator, casting director, costume designer, and lighting director as he or she fleshes out the thumbnails. While he or she may have had many of these considerations in mind while roughing out the story, it's during this tightening phase of the work that he or she begins refining these decisions. He or she sets dramatic lighting to enhance mood, adorns characters with visual personality traits that enhance their place in the story, and sets the virtual stage with props and places that add to the story's mood and tension.

The finalization of the fleshed-out pencil drawings takes place in a few different manners. In most mainstream publishing environments, these pencils drawings get handed off to another artist, who letters the dialogue and narrative. A third artist then applies ink to firm up the forms indicated in pencil, add texture, and enhance the positive-to-negative contrast. (Increasingly, the lettering stage takes place after the penciled pages are inked, as more and more letterers use personal computers to generate letterforms.) Finally, a fourth artist applies color to these finalized, inked, and lettered pages either digitally or by hand.

This assembly-line approach exists in many cases by necessity—there is simply too much work for a single artist to handle and still meet deadlines. Sometimes publishers take this approach because one artist may be particularly skilled at one aspect of generating the final product while being deficient in one or several others. Whatever the circumstances, when working with most mainstream sequential narrative publishers, the Sequential Artist can expect to be part of a team.

In a very few special cases at the mainstream level and in many at the independent and Web level, a lone Sequential Artist can expect to steer the entire ship. This takes a particularly motivated and dedicated artist, as finishing all aspects of a sequential narrative requires an enormous investment of time and energy as well as a very well-rounded skill set.

The newest aspect of delivering a finished work of sequential narrative is also the last duty with which a Sequential Artist is charged—book design. This duty applies only in rare circumstances, when a higher-end product is printed. In most sequential narratives, a standard book size and company design style govern the overall packaging of the material. More and more, however, many Sequential Artists seek to set their work apart from usual standards, leading them to consider book size, style of binding, and paper on which the material gets printed, among other aspects. Additionally, as the higher-end products gain more respect in mainstream popular culture, an expectation for more sophisticated book design comes along with the expectation for the more sophisticated content. In these cases, a Sequential Artist who designs the final package would be called upon to act as a graphic designer for publishing.

The final item to keep in mind when considering the pursuit of a career as a Sequential Artist is the unusually large amount of work involved with the creation of sequential narratives. Whether working in a fairly representational style, one requiring a lot of references and/or models, or applying a more stylized sensibility, the steps are the same. A Sequential Artist will find himself or herself creating upward of 100 individual pictures for a complete sequential narrative of average length (the current mainstream sequential narrative publishers have that set between 22 and 24 pages plus cover), most or all images containing text. Only the most committed artists make a serious go of this occupation.

Salaries

Beginning Sequential Artists in many cases can expect no payment other than contributor copies, most typically in independent publishing. On the extremely rare occasions that an independent book strikes a chord with a large audience, salaries can reach above $100,000 if tied into licensing deals.

Usually, Sequential Artists aren't paid a salary. Whether on the independent level or mainstream, a Sequential Artist is paid by the page, and rates for pages differ between type of work done and, sometimes, the level at which a Sequential Artist works. (e.g., a highly skilled Sequential Artist who has worked in the industry for mainstream publishers will have a page rate as high as triple that of an entry-level artist.) Entry-level Sequential Artist rates run between $300 and $500 for a completed page—pencils, finishes, colors, and letters—at the mainstream level. These rates are divvied among artists when work gets completed by a team. At the high end of the mainstream, an artist who works solely on the pencil stage can earn that same page rate for his or her specialty alone. If in high demand, a Sequential Artist who works relatively quickly can earn between $50,000 and $100,000.

A second type of recompense that has fallen largely by the wayside is royalties. While working for most mainstream publishers of sequential narratives, an artist sells the a copyrights to his or her work, as the characters and distinctive likenesses thereof are owned by the companies. The publishers do, however, work a royalty consideration into the contracts to which they sign artists and pay out sums of money that vary based upon sales figures.

Independent publishers have rates that vary far too dramatically to accurately list, as do Web publishers. The rates range from contributor copies up to rates that rival those of the mainstream publishers.

Employment Prospects

The sequential narrative industry has shrunk wildly in the years between 1990 and 2004. Experienced professionals with several years of steady work from mainstream publishers have taken offers from independent publishers at dramatic cuts in pay just to stay working. Additionally, a steady flow of interested newcomers keep knocking on the doors of any publisher of sequential narrative. This is a highly competitive field with more skilled artists than vacancies to fill.

Some prospective professionals find entry-level positions with established professionals as artist assistants. The duties performed by these assistants vary from keeping reference files organized to assisting the experienced artist in the drafting of final art. These positions are very rare in the current market, as many experienced professionals scramble to find enough paying work to support themselves.

Advancement Prospects

Even working fairly steadily does not guarantee that one's rates will go up or that book sales will drive higher and earn a compensatory bump in royalties.

Education and Training

While there are many self-taught artists working as Sequential Artists, the most successful tend to have completed courses in drawing, painting, design, and narrative storytelling.

Experience, Skills, and Personality Traits

When selecting a Sequential Artist to fulfill an assignment, an employer cares most about the quality of work presented by the prospective candidate. It does, however, help one's chances to show a track record of meeting deadlines in this and other related fields such as illustration, animation, and design. It helps, too, to provide references from established professionals with good reputations in the business who the candidate has assisted.

Since the position requires an artist to draw a very large number of pictures per project, a high level of draftsmanship skill is paramount. Whether stylized or representational, the Sequential Artist must be able to place figures into believable spaces and draw a variety of sets, props, and costumes. Thus, a candidate must demonstrate a familiarity with drawing figures, environments, and objects in proper perspective.

The old saw "Nothing is created in a vacuum" applies mightily to the creation of sequential narratives. Even an artist who crafts his or her own stories and personally handles every visual phase of the work must interact with others for the work to reach the public. An ability to work well with others, especially in the most common application of this trade, wherein other artists will execute different phases of the final product, comes in very handy.

One other item about character bears note: Sequential narratives are products aimed at a large popular audience. As such, the work will be read and judged by the whim of popular culture. A Sequential Artist must have a degree of patience in accepting this often subjective response to the work.

Unions and Associations

Like a great many vocations within the visual art industry, there is no specific union to which Sequential Artists belong. However, there are some organizations that offer networking opportunities and further education. The first among these is the Society of Illustrators (New York). Since it has added sequential art to the category list for its annual exhibition, this offers Sequential Artists a new showcase for the best work of the year in one of the most notable and prestigious competitions in the visual art industry. It is a terrific resource for networking.

Tips for Entry

1. Become the absolute best craftsperson possible—draw all the time.
2. Learn to observe visual storytelling devices in film and sequential narratives and apply them to your craft.
3. Develop relationships with employers and established professionals and seek their input into how you can sharpen your skills.

CHILDREN'S BOOK ILLUSTRATOR

CAREER PROFILE

Duties: Illustrates book interiors and covers for children's books

Alternate Title(s): None

Salary Range: $20,000 to $50,000+; in rare circumstances, $100,000+

Employment Prospects: Fair to Good

Advancement Prospects: Fair

Best Geographical Location(s): Major urban areas with clusters of book publishing companies or areas equipped with broadband Internet connection

Prerequisites:

Education or Training—Good sense of design; highly developed illustrative skill, be it stylized or representational

Experience—Entry-level, well-developed portfolio reflecting illustrative abilities; mid-level, well-developed body of published work; master-level, body of work representing high sales and/or awards

Special Skills and Personality Traits—Ability to translate written word into imagery attractive to child audiences; ability to work with others

CAREER LADDER

```
┌─────────────────────────┐
│    Master Illustrator    │
└─────────────────────────┘

┌─────────────────────────┐
│       Illustrator        │
└─────────────────────────┘

┌─────────────────────────┐
│         Student          │
└─────────────────────────┘
```

Position Description

Whether flights of fancy, retellings of classic fairy tales, or brightly colored instructional texts, most young people begin their reading lives with children's books, most of these being picture books. These books are illustrated in most cases by craftspeople who focus solely on working in this very specialized medium.

Children's books appeal to several different age ranges, from nine months to toddler/pre-K, toddler/pre-K to easy readers, all the way up through young adult novels aimed at adolescents. In almost all cases—the chief exception being young adult novels—Children's Book Illustrators play a large role in making the final book, as they craft the "picture" part of picture books.

The process begins with a story. In most cases, the writer and illustrator work independently of one another, but there are a great many author-illustrators who generate their own content from beginning to end. The story, having been selected by a children's book publisher's acquisitions department, is handed off to a creative director or art director in order to find an illustrator best suited to craft the imagery. Once contacted and selected by the children's book publisher as the illustrator of choice, contract negotiations begin. Once the business arrangements are made, including setting of deadlines for both art and payment deliveries and copyright considerations, the work on the book begins.

The book starts off by binding rough pencil sketches (or rough pencils) drafted by the illustrator together with text in position into what's called a dummy book. As the rough pencils are polished into final sketches, all parties involved—illustrator, creative/art director, and designer—refer to the dummy book to assure that text and imaging maintain a relationship.

Once the final pencils have been cleared, the illustrator begins crafting the final imagery. To this end, there are as many techniques for executing finals as there are illustrators, most of them derived from classic painting and drawing techniques. Pen and ink; pen and ink with transparent watercolor; graphite renderings, with or without color applied manually through colored pencil or watercolor; watercolor as a stand-alone medium; tempera; acrylic; and oil paint are just the top of the list. Additionally, desktop computers—most typically the Macintosh platform—have made significant inroads into the working lives of Children's Book Illustrators. For some, manual applications of traditional media begin the working process, and it's finished off by running the images through image-editing software such as Adobe Photoshop and Illustrator.

Once the final images for an entire book have been completed, it's time to deliver the goods. The delivery method will vary by publisher and illustrator. It has become increasingly common to deliver high-resolution images electronically, either via the Internet or as scans on removable media such as CDs.

Starting out in this field, an illustrator commands very little advance money when assigned a book. Publishers pay up-front money as advances on expected sales of the book, and entry-level illustrators seldom work on the books that sell in the many tens of thousands. As an illustrator's reputation grows both inside the publishing world and with the buying public, greater numbers of books get moved and the bigger the up-front investment the publisher is willing to make. This describes what's considered a mid-level Children's Book Illustrator's career—solid sales, consistent quality of work, and an increasing body of published books. Many illustrators make a whole career of being at this level and enjoy producing five to 10 books a year.

Children's Book Illustrators who climb to the top of the food chain, however, arrive at master status. Several criteria exist for this distinction: an unusually high number of book sales; name recognition with the buying public; and winning one or more of various industry awards, including the Coretta Scott King Award, the Newbery Medal, and the heavyweight champ of children's book awards, the Caldecott Award. While it's possible to find this type of success early in one's career, it is far more the exception than the rule. Many illustrators spend years, if not decades, honing their craft to achieve this level.

Salaries

Except in very rare circumstances, Children's Book Illustrators work on an assignment basis, so there is no salary per se. Earnings are determined by the number of books one illustrates in the course of a year and how well those books sell. While this circumstance bodes well for their intellectual property rights, as most illustrators retain copyrights to their work, it can be financially harrowing.

Starting out one's career as an entry-level Children's Book Illustrator, one can expect to earn between $15,000 and $20,000, depending upon how many books one is assigned. Frequently, a beginning Children's Book Illustrator supplements this income by holding a full- or part-time job as his or her career gets rolling.

As the number of assignments per year and list of published books increase, the illustrator moves to mid-level classification. At this stage, he or she can expect to earn between $20,000 and $50,000 annually. This jump represents not only an increased number of assignments per year, but also higher book sales figures and larger advances. Additionally, many mid-level illustrators who begin to make a name for themselves within the business find opportunities for paid speaking engagements at colleges and universities around the country.

Master-level earnings are more difficult to nail down, as the ranges vary. Some wildly popular and commercially successful books can earn more than $100,000 in a single year, but these are very rare occurrences. In the current cultural climate, books written by celebrities have high market value and larger than average print runs. Fittingly, advances and royalties are higher.

Employment Prospects

More than 5,000 children's books are published each year in the United States, so opportunities abound. While one cannot predict the whim of popular trend, the number of children under the age of nine increased by more than 3.27 million between 1990 and 2000 (by the U.S Census Bureau's calculations), which means there are increasingly more children who need books.

There is, however, some heavy pavement-pounding to do at the outset of an illustrator's career. Whether you compile lists of publishers and the art-buying contacts there yourself or purchase commercially available lists, the beginning illustrator must expect to make lots of phone calls, send out scores of mailings, and be diligent in his or her attempts to break into the industry.

Advancement Prospects

Given that much of what determines an illustrator's climb in the world of children's book publishing depends upon factors outside one's direct influence (e.g., awards and popular sales), a specific formula for advancement is difficult to draft. One illustrator may find tremendous success with his or her first book and ascend to what amounts to master level very quickly; another may labor away for 20 years and slowly build his or her popularity and reputation in the business.

The one sure factor within the illustrator's control is reliability; editors, creative directors, and art directors will assign books to illustrators who have proven themselves dependable far more readily than they will to unknowns. The more consistent work one is capable of producing in a timely manner, the more assignments he or she is able to field in a given year, thereby increasing earnings. Additionally, as one's body of work grows over time, it's reasonable to expect that royalties, money earned from continued sales of a particular book, will begin to substantially augment an illustrator's annual earnings.

Education and Training

The primary selling point for editors, creative directors, and art directors is the prospective illustrator's portfolio, pure and simple. The greater the body of work one presents to a prospective employer, the better one's chances of landing an assignment. And while there is no specific degree or certification requirement, an illustrator is best served by completing a course of study at a postsecondary professional art school, professional art college, or degree-granting institution. At these places, a prospective illustrator gets hands-on instruction about areas he or she is strong in, where he or she needs to concentrate, and how best to put the whole package together as he or she gets ready to enter the job market.

Additionally, he or she will be forced to acquire organizational skills and learn how to prioritize tasks in an effort to manage deadlines. This becomes key when working as a professional, especially since the most successful Children's Book Illustrators must juggle more than one assignment at a time.

In addition to sharpening one's illustrative skills and developing time-management abilities, a degree-granting course of study familiarizes one with art history and affords the opportunity to meet and work with those who will be assigning book contracts in the future. It's never too early to begin networking.

Experience, Skills, and Personality Traits

No matter how brilliant a body of work may be, it does the creator of that work no good unless he or she is able to find the appropriate audience and get it to market. To that end, an illustrator must be able to work with others, particularly the creative professionals assigning the work. He or she must be able to communicate and exhibit diplomacy, especially when it comes time to discuss changes to a book (which are inevitable). Being easy to work with goes a long way toward being seen as reliable in the eyes of editors, creative directors, and art directors, and the easier one is to work with, the longer and more productive one's career can be.

A Children's Book Illustrator must also understand design principals and have a sense of how type and pictures relate to each other. Since most children's books are picture books, text and imaging work together and appear on the same page more often than not. Leaving enough room for the specific text called out and gracefully addressing the area under which the text lies begins to separate the merely competent illustrators from the soon-to-be successful ones.

The two final items to discuss here relate to one another: patience, especially starting out in one's career, and a love of the medium. It's extremely rare that young illustrators break into children's books and hit the ground running; it's far more typical that a few assignments per year trickle in, and he or she begins to build a body of published work. Patience for this process will help stave off discouragement. Additionally, a true love of the medium helps the prospective illustrator overcome discouragement and disillusion. If one is having fun while executing the work, whether for an assignment or to build one's portfolio, he or she is likely on the right track.

Unions and Associations

While there are no specific unions to which illustrators belong—as many of them are independent contractors, they're barred from collective bargaining by antitrust and copyright laws—there are several organizations that cater to illustrators as a whole and Children's Book Illustrators specifically. For anyone involved with the production of children's books, the Society of Children's Books Writers and Illustrators (SCBWI) remains an excellent resource. With annual networking opportunities, 70 regional chapters, regular events, and member-specific benefits that include grants, awards, and conferences, there simply is no better resource for those specifically interested in the craft of making children's books. Additionally, the Society of Illustrators (New York) and Graphic Artists Guild offer additional networking and educational opportunities.

Tips for Entry

1. Learn to organize your time and prioritize tasks.
2. Continually sharpen your illustrative skills and learn as much as possible about the interaction of shape, type, and text.
3. Apply for internships with children's book publishers while in school.
4. Maintain contact with like-minded classmates after graduation.
5. Keep an eye on current trends in the children's book publishing field; compile contact lists and keep a polite correspondence with publishers.

ART DIRECTOR (CHILDREN'S BOOKS)

| CAREER PROFILE | CAREER LADDER |

CAREER PROFILE

Duties: Designs book interiors and covers while managing efforts of outside vendors and collaborating with editorial and marketing department

Alternate Title(s): Designer

Salary Range: $20,000 to $50,000+; in rare circumstances, $100,000+

Employment Prospects: Fair to Good

Advancement Prospects: Fair to Good

Best Geographical Location(s): Major urban areas with book publishing companies

Prerequisites:

    Education or Training—Two-dimensional design expertise; knowledge of typography; facility with digital environment, chiefly the Macintosh platform

    Experience—Entry-level, education reflecting concentration on book design; mid- to senior-level, two to five years of book design

    Special Skills and Personality Traits—Ability to manage large number of projects and delegate tasks; awareness of how design and typography relate to the written word; ability to work with others

CAREER LADDER

```
┌─────────────────────────────┐
│      Creative Director       │
└─────────────────────────────┘


┌─────────────────────────────┐
│        Art Director          │
└─────────────────────────────┘


┌─────────────────────────────┐
│    Assistant Art Director    │
└─────────────────────────────┘
```

Position Description

Almost everyone begins reading life with picture books and easy readers aimed at children—given this, these works often conjure warm feelings of nostalgia. An Art Director who specializes in the design and production of children's books typically seeks out this position because of a true fondness for this time-honored book form and considers the efforts labors of love. In many cases, the positions do not offer the same type of compensation available to the corresponding titles in the mass-market adult publishing world.

There are several permutations this job description can have, and the hierarchy varies among the many publishers of children's books. In some environments, the hierarchy directly mirrors that of larger book publishing companies in that the labor is divided among entry-level designers (assistant art directors), mid-level designers/managers (Art Directors), and a senior-level designer/manager (creative director).

These are typically book publishing companies that sport a robust book list and publish books aimed at a mass market and a wide range of ages, from toddler through young adult readers. In many cases, however, publishers specializing in children's books print smaller runs aimed at a more targeted niche audience. In these cases, as well as some others in between the niche and large publishers, a children's book Art Director can expect to wear many hats at once.

Children's book Art Directors occupying a senior position often act much like creative directors in book publishing. They have many responsibilities, some of which include managing a staff of junior- and entry-level children's book Art Directors; seeking out and negotiating contracts with outside vendors who provide design, illustration, or, in rare cases, photography; and designing books themselves. A junior-level position resembles the position held by many Art Directors in the larger publishing world in that they split time between supervisory duties and design duties, with the larger portion of time spent executing children's book design. And those holding entry-level positions act much in the same way as assistant art directors in the larger publishing world in that they spend nearly all their time designing books.

No matter what level at which a children's book Art Director works, the day-to-day design responsibilities are ever-present. Children's book Art Directors tend to be all-in-one book designers in that they see a book through interior and exterior design, and they must always have the reading level of the target audience in mind when designing books.

When discussing children's books, the most common type to which people refer is the picture book. These books target audiences that range in age from toddlers through pre-teen and are the best example of the design and production issues faced by a children's book Art Director. Art Directors who craft books aimed at teen and young adult readers work in much the same way as those who occupy positions in the larger publishing world, as these books tend to be more text-driven.

Once the acquisitions department accepts a story for publication (in some cases, a senior-level children's book Art Director will be party to this decision), an illustrator is selected to bring the story to visual life. (In some cases, books are written and illustrated by the same person, so the next step gets skipped.) A children's book Art Director has many tools at his or her disposal when seeking an image provider: Several Web sites offer on-line portfolio hosting; printed source books in which illustrators advertise their wares are often sent directly to publishing houses by the companies that print them; and independent illustrators and their artist representatives continually send out promotional mailings. After sifting through all these resources and settling on an image provider, the children's book Art Director offers the job and presents the contract.

Once the contract is resolved, the children's book Art Director and image provider work together to create what's called a dummy book, consisting of rough design drawings with the text in place that will serve as a model for the completed book. This collaborative effort takes time and patience on both parts (sometimes there's some back-and-forth about how best to design a page with imaging and type), but once completed, there exists a very solid map of what the book will be once completed. Refinements along the way often occur. As a designer, the children's book Art Director may think that a particular line of type needs to break differently, just as an illustrator may want to move an object to clarify focus, but the dummy book serves as a pretty solid representation of what to expect from the book once all the art is finished.

The last bit of design comes into play when drafting the cover. Working closely with the illustrator again, text and imaging are married on the page to create visual impact in an effort to attract potential buyers. In this area as in all others, the children's book Art Director takes a design approach appropriate to the material and reading level of the book. It wouldn't do, for instance, to employ the same design approach for a book chronicling historical figures aimed at children as for a humorous book about friendly aliens from space. This appropriateness must also be communicated to the illustrator and comes into play when selecting the right artist for a project.

The final duty for a children's book Art Director usually falls into place fairly quickly, and that is preparing the book for print. When drafting the book's design, one may work with low-resolution, for position only (FPO), images, as this saves some time in the digital environment. If this is the case, swapping out these images for high-resolution scans of the art seals the deal and completes the project.

Salaries

A great many variables affect what a children's book Art Director can expect to make—size of the publishing company and its success at reaching a large audience, cost of living in the area surrounding the publishing company, and the experience level of the children's book Art Director. In any event, most children's book Art Directors accept these positions out of a great fondness for the material and not for the great chase for the buck.

Employment Prospects

Even in small companies that publish children's books that reach relatively modest audiences, a children's book Art Director position exists. In smaller companies the design typically is contracted out to independent graphic designers, and the job of the children's book Art Director on staff is to act as a manager of projects. Adbase, Inc., an online resource that tracks creative job positions in many industries, puts the number at more than 200 nationwide. However, there are an inestimable number of people interested in holding these positions, so the competition remains high.

Advancement Prospects

One climbs the ladder of children's book publishing somewhat more slowly than one does in traditional publishing. Turnover is slow, and, as stated, many people take the positions out of a love for the material. Several factors can speed the climb. For instance, there are several industry-specific awards (International Reading Association, Coretta Scott King Award, and the Caldecott Award, the holy grail of children's book awards, among them). Producing a book that claims any of these prizes can earn one a fast track toward greater compensation.

Education and Training

One has to have a highly developed sense of two-dimensional and type design to be an effective children's book Art Director. While a highly motivated individual can acquire these skills by reading books and taking night courses, the best preparation is completing a course of study that earns at least a bachelor's degree, either in arts and sciences or fine arts (B.A.S. or B.F.A.). In addition to acquiring the manual skills of desktop design and sharpening one's intuitive design sensibilities, a degree-granting course of study familiarizes one with art history (and in some cases histories specific to traditional book and children's book publishing) and some of the skills used by vendors who will supply imaging.

Experience, Skills, and Personality Traits

In any publishing environment, many hands go into creating a work for print. To that end, a children's book Art Director has to be able to work with others, and a basic component of that is an ability to communicate. For instance, when it comes to signing an illustrator to work on a book, the publisher typically has a boilerplate contract into which an image provider's pertinent information is inserted. In many cases, contract negotiation goes rather smoothly but there are occasions when an illustrator seeks to improve upon the contract based on prior experience with other publishers or his or her own usual mode of doing business. It's at times like these that a children's book Art Director employs diplomacy. Working between the company's best interests and the illustrator's expectations can be very taxing, but patience and an ability to communicate calmly come in handy.

This is merely one example. When working on a children's book with a high-profile author, a children's book Art Director may come in contact with that author throughout the production of the book as imaging is produced. (This is most typical at the senior level.) Some authors desire a step-by-step involvement with the execution of books they write, and this can place a great deal of extra strain on the children's book Art Director. Patience, commitment to the work, and knowing when to be flexible versus when to take a polite stand all come into play in circumstances such as these.

One must also have a love of the medium. While not as taxing as the schedule maintained by artists working in the advertising field, the odd book here and there will occasion the need to spend extra hours, either weekends or late nights, to see it through to completion. Making one's way through such times becomes an easier prospect when one loves the material.

Unions and Associations

The primary national association to which design professionals can belong is the American Institute of Graphic Arts. With its headquarters in New York City and 47 local chapters around the United States, it offers significant networking and educational benefits unavailable elsewhere. The country's leading designers write essays available to members in the on-line library, an online directory of like-minded professionals is available, and events too numerous to list here are offered throughout the year that educate designers about all aspects of the business.

Additionally, the Art Director's Club (New York) and Graphic Artists Guild offer additional networking and educational opportunities. While chiefly an organization aimed at the generators of children's book content, the Society of Children's Books Writers and Illustrators (SCBWI) is an excellent way to stay in touch with the industry.

Tips for Entry

1. Learn to organize your time and prioritize tasks.
2. Sharpen your design skills, and learn as much as possible about the interaction of shape, type, and text.
3. Apply for internships with book publishers while in school.
4. Maintain contact with like-minded classmates after graduation.
5. Keep an eye on current trends in the children's book publishing field.

BOOK DESIGNER

CAREER PROFILE

Duties: Designs book interiors and covers

Alternate Title(s): Assistant Art Director

Salary Range: $25,000 to $40,000+

Employment Prospects: Fair to Good

Advancement Prospects: Good

Best Geographical Location(s): Major urban areas with large numbers of book publishing companies

Prerequisites:

Education or Training—Two-dimensional design expertise; knowledge of typography; facility with digital environment, chiefly the Macintosh platform

Experience—A strong portfolio of work exhibiting a well-honed sense of design, built through college courses or at small publications (free weeklies, etc.)

Special Skills and Personality Traits—Awareness of how design and typography relate to the written word; diplomacy and ability to work with others

CAREER LADDER

```
┌─────────────────────────────┐
│        Art Director         │
└─────────────────────────────┘

┌─────────────────────────────┐
│    Assistant Art Director    │
└─────────────────────────────┘

┌─────────────────────────────┐
│        Book Designer        │
└─────────────────────────────┘
```

Position Description

Most creative directors and art directors for book publishing break into the field as a book designer. This entry-level position focuses on the mechanics of laying out and designing book interiors and covers (or jackets for hard-bound books). After some time at this position (the time varying by publisher, individual ambition, and aptitude), one begins to get involved with more management-oriented decision making. At the start, however, this is solely an entry-level position in which the decisions one makes have as much to do with taking direction as with an individual's creative instincts.

A Book Designer is responsible for two different aspects of book design, interiors and exteriors. In many publishing environments, designers focus on a single area. Designers who craft book interiors keep several factors in mind as they're laying out their work, and the primary ones are legibility (the ease with which one reads the words made by the letterforms), consistency (having a unified look throughout the book's interior), and compatibility (choosing a design scheme and selecting fonts that complement the "voice" of the material).

In most cases, book interiors consist solely of written material. When laying out the interiors of these books, a designer chooses a font for the headlines (chapter numbers and names, if applicable) and body copy (including the indicia information, ISBN information, etc.). Often, several production-related issues factor into the choices a designer makes. Among them are word and page counts. Books published in hard cover are bound in signatures, collections of folded sheets sewn together, which requires that a page count fall within a specific multiple (typically a factor of 8). Paperback books afford a greater degree of flexibility, as they're loose sheets bound by glue to the wrap-around cover. (More about the specifics of binding and page counts can be learned in classes specializing in book design, either as part of a degree-granting course of study or night school courses).

With the advent of desktop publishing, the tools available to the Book Designer have become nearly limitless. Available font selections are now virtually infinite, pages can be laid out in a digital environment that allows for endless editing, and computers afford a degree of precision previously unavailable. These advances have also paved the way for a much easier task of resolving many of the production challenges designers face. For instance, it's no longer necessary to use a ruler and calculator to determine how a specific font will lay out when composing the text component of a book's interior. Many page layout programs—QuarkXPress and Adobe InDesign are the industry leaders—offer tools that can calculate these variables in seconds.

In certain circumstances—historical texts, text supported by graph and chart material, and classroom texts, to name just three—a large imaging component may be present. In such cases, a designer may work closely with outside vendors who have been tapped by the art director or creative director to deliver these images. In some cases, particularly when it comes to generating charts and graphs, the duty may fall to the designer or the supervising art director.

A designer specializing in cover design or jacket design for hard-bound books must consider a very different set of criteria. While legibility remains a primary goal, the design of a book's cover seeks to get an immediate response from a potential consumer. Whether the book's content calls for a subtle approach or bold visual statement, a designer specializing in this particular craft must be able to determine which approach serves the book better and be able to execute an appropriate layout. Often, a designer will have a slate of projects to complete that cover a wide range of stylistic content and must be able to switch back and forth between them with relative ease.

An additional factor for the cover designer to consider is imagery. In most cases, photographic or illustrative imaging accompanies the text design, and it falls to the cover designer to work this imaging into the overall scheme. In most cases with this entry-level position, the designer isn't empowered to select the image provider. Direction on this matter often is handed down from an art director or creative director, but the designer may have a say in some circumstances. In any case, a successful designer will be able to wield the tools of page layout to marry text with imaging in an eye-catching way that attracts attention.

While the two duties described above have been presented as tasks performed by two different artists, in some cases Book Designers are called upon to deliver both aspects of a book's layout. Job descriptions and titles vary from publisher to publisher, and it behooves the prospective designer to have a working vocabulary in all aspects of book design. Preparing oneself for such versatility while developing one's design skills greatly improves one's chances of landing a job and climbing the career ladder once employed.

Salaries

As with many jobs in the visual art field, location plays a great part in determining what a Book Designer can expect to make. In major urban areas where many book publishers compete for available candidates, salaries often start higher than in areas where fewer publishers exist. Additionally,

larger publishing houses tend to generate higher sales revenues and can offer more robust compensation packages—more comprehensive medical benefits, retirement, paid vacation time—and most of these exist in major urban areas, such as the New York City metropolitan area. Similarly, the cost of living in such areas is typically higher, so one must carefully consider these factors when choosing where to work.

In many smaller book publishing companies, however, a designer may take on a much larger role than in a larger publishing environment. In such cases, the job begins to blur the edge between designer and art director in that one may be called on to have a greater role in selecting image providers and so on. When saddling a designer with these added duties, many smaller publishers often compensate the designer with a salary higher than is typical of the jobs in the surrounding market.

Finally, many Book Designers are offered compensation packages that can include 401(k) benefits, retirement fund–matching policies, and medical insurance. These packages vary by employer, though, as there is no unionized standard across the industry.

Employment Prospects

As a book has to be designed before it's printed, there are Book Designer positions available at virtually every book publishing company in the United States, even if the designer's position is listed as art director. There are a great many positions available at this level nationwide.

Advancement Prospects

Once a Book Designer has proven himself or herself by delivering consistent work, working well with others, and taking direction well, he or she finds many opportunities to move up the ladder. It's fully expected that one move up the ladder, as a matter of fact, as this is an entry-level position.

Education and Training

Familiarity with computer programs that facilitate graphic design and an excellent two-dimensional and type design sense top the list of criteria for Book Designers. While it is true that a highly motivated individual can acquire these skills by reading books and taking night courses at a local community college, the best preparation is completing a course of study that earns at least a bachelor's degree in either arts and sciences or fine arts. As with the several other jobs that involve time management and directing the efforts of other professional artists, one of the many advantages of completing a degree-granting course of study is learning to manage one's time and prioritize tasks. Showing an aptitude for these skills facilitates a designer's upward career movement.

Many colleges offer job-placement programs, which is another advantage of seeking a formal postsecondary education. In many colleges, most particularly professional art colleges, instructors are working professionals and can bolster these job-placement programs by providing leads and making introductions for ambitious, hard-working students as they're preparing to graduate. At the minimum, surrounding oneself with like-minded students gets one's networking abilities established, and this comes in handy throughout one's professional life.

Becoming acquainted with other facets of professional art is another decided advantage to completing a course of study at a degree-granting institution. As a designer begins to set his or her sights on career advancement, being familiar with the other disciplines associated with book publishing helps a great deal. Knowing the ins and outs of professional image-makers' crafts allows a forward-thinking designer to schedule projects and keep a consistent workflow.

Experience, Skills, and Personality Traits

The job title says it all—design. Knowing the intricacies of shape and type design can be a lifelong pursuit; there's always a new way to solve a design problem, and there are as many solutions as there are Book Designers. A thirst for knowledge in this area can never be too overdeveloped. The most successful Book Designers always keep an eye out for what's being done in book design, advertising design, and editorial design.

Similarly, keeping up to date on what enhancements software developers make to their page layout programs helps. Updates to existing programs are made by the software publishers themselves and by third-party developers. Knowing which enhancements are useful to one's workflow and which developments aren't will continually streamline one's processes.

Unless working in the smallest of print houses, a Book Designer works with several other people in completing projects, most of them superiors. To this end, a designer must

have a highly developed ability to work with others and take direction from superiors. Not only does this allow a designer to get through day-to-day duties, but allows him or her to further his or her career. He or she must also be able to communicate with other professional artists. Working with others quite often boils down to communicating verbally.

Aptitude for keeping several projects cooking at once also serves the working designer well. Being able to keep track of the varying needs of several projects in the works and organize one's efforts prepares an entry-level designer for upward movement and a fruitful career.

Unions and Associations

Leading the field in organizations for design professionals in all fields is the American Institute of Graphic Arts. Headquartered in New York City, it has 47 local chapters around the country and offers networking and educational benefits not available elsewhere. Design industry leaders offer essays about the craft available only to members, a directory of working professionals is available online, and the group sponsors events and seminars around the country in major urban areas throughout the year. Additionally, the Art Director's Club (New York) and Graphic Artists Guild offer networking and educational opportunities.

Tips for Entry

1. Sharpen your eye for design; learn as much as possible about shape, type, and text and how they interact.
2. Develop the ability to organize your time and prioritize tasks.
3. Apply for internships with book publishers while in school.
4. Build relationships and stay in touch with like-minded classmates after graduation.
5. Learn as much as possible about the specifics of the book publishing field.

ART DIRECTOR (BOOKS)

CAREER PROFILE

Duties: Designs book interiors and covers while managing efforts of assistant art directors and outside vendors

Alternate Title(s): Designer

Salary Range: $30,000 to $60,000+

Employment Prospects: Fair to Good

Advancement Prospects: Good

Best Geographical Location(s): Major urban areas with book publishing companies

Prerequisites:

Education or Training—Two-dimensional design expertise; knowledge of typography; facility with digital environment, chiefly the Macintosh platform

Experience—Two to five years of book design

Special Skills and Personality Traits—Ability to manage large number of projects and delegate tasks; awareness of how design and typography relate to the written word; diplomacy and ability to work with others

CAREER LADDER

```
┌─────────────────────────────┐
│      Creative Director      │
└─────────────────────────────┘

┌─────────────────────────────┐
│         Art Director        │
└─────────────────────────────┘

┌─────────────────────────────┐
│   Assistant Art Director    │
└─────────────────────────────┘
```

Position Description

An Art Director holds a mid-level position in most book publishing companies. Reflecting this, duties are often split between managing the creative endeavors of others (assistant art directors and designers on staff and outside contractors who provide design and imaging) and executing the director's own creative output (designing the books sold by the publishing company). The balance between these two tasks varies from circumstance to circumstance, but most often the job leans more heavily toward the design end. When an Art Director is groomed to assume a creative director position, this balance starts to tip the opposite way, but this happens only after several years of experience in most cases.

An Art Director is responsible for two different types of book design: interiors and exteriors. When crafting the interior of a book, the Art Director is mainly concerned with type design. In many cases, these design duties are split between Art Directors and the assistant art directors who report directly to them. Each publishing company has its own specific hierarchal structure, but we'll examine the most typical for this listing.

Even when a book's interior must include imaging (whether photographic material that supports specific passages or illustrations that begin or end individual chapters), the main concern when crafting a book interior remains the type design. When setting about designing the interior text design, an Art Director has to keep a some primary text design principals in mind: legibility, that is, the ease with which one reads the letterforms and the words they make; appropriate choice of font for the book's content; and overall unity. Whether designing the interior alone or directing the efforts of an assistant art director, he or she must always focus on this primary concern.

Additionally, an Art Director bears several production-related issues in mind when crafting a book's interior, among them word count and page count when a book is bound in signatures, lining up color plates so they fall into appropriate spaces for binding in signatures, and making sure interior images are press-ready. This last task includes making sure ink coverage falls within acceptable levels for the type of printing used and has a high enough resolution in terms of lines per inch to print clearly.

An Art Director who specializes in cover design—or jacket design for hardbound books—has a wholly different task to perform. The cover designer seeks to get an immediate response to the book. This doesn't always mean bold strokes or high contrast, however. In some cases, the Art Director employs a more subtle approach to create an eye-catching cover that will spark an interest in a prospective buyer. What drives the differing approaches is always the book's content. An artist designing a book cover must have an awareness of the book's subject and style. For example, an Art Director may be working on two wholly different types of book at the same time, say, a thriller and a self-help book dealing with professional issues. His approach to laying out the title design and seeking imagery will, by necessity, differ if he's going to successfully put a face on these two very different subjects.

When crafting a book cover, image plays a large role. In some circumstances, a powerful-enough title treatment, coupled with an intriguing design, may do the trick—the design-driven book cover is still very fashionable after being popularized in the late 1970s—yet cover imaging still pervades the book publishing world. When cover imagery is either photographic or illustrative, the image that accompanies the type and shape design of the overall book most typically comes from outside. When selecting a provider of imaging and even when choosing what type of imaging to use, an Art Director will work closely with a creative director.

While the two types of design have been described here as separate duties, in some cases an Art Director will be called upon to design an entire book, inside and out. This happens most often in smaller companies with more modest publishing lists. An Art Director assuming such responsibilities has a faster track toward advancing to a creative director position, as this more well-rounded experience better prepares him or her for handling those broader duties.

Salaries

Location is one of the primary drivers behind what an Art Director can expect to make. In areas where the concentration of available jobs and cost of living are higher, an Art Director can expect to earn larger salaries than where the demand for such skills is lower. Additionally, areas with higher concentrations of book publishers tend to see opportunities open at the large publishing houses, which can offer larger compensation packages based upon their higher revenues.

In many cases at smaller print houses, however, an Art Director may be called upon to shoulder greater responsibility than is typical of the position at a larger publisher, so much so that the duties begin to cross over to the realm of creative director. In such scenarios, most employers reward an Art Director who assumes these tasks with a salary higher than is typical for the market.

Finally, most Art Director positions come replete with compensation packages that may include 401k benefits,

retirement fund–matching policies, and medical insurance. These packages vary by employer, though, as there is no unionized standard across the industry.

Employment Prospects

The Art Director position being ubiquitous to the book publishing field, there are a great many jobs available at this level. There is nearly always an on-staff Art Director, even in small print houses that publish relatively short lists. In cases such as these, the duties performed by an Art Director may well resemble those of a creative director in that much of the actual design described above will be jobbed out to independent contractors, and the staff Art Director will manage these contractors.

Advancement Prospects

Once entrenched in the publishing world—meaning at least three years of experience with a sharp portfolio of printed works that show a wide range of subjects—an Art Director often finds many opportunities to move up the ladder. Since the position is a mid-level one, it's expected that an Art Director will want to move up the ladder. In most cases, the table is set for an Art Director to advance by his or her employer by tailoring the Art Director's duties toward upward movement (examples of this include assigning more support staff to oversee, allowing the Art Director greater flexibility in seeking outside vendors, etc.).

Education and Training

The primary requirements for this position are a familiarity with computer programs that facilitate graphic design and an excellent two-dimensional and type design sense. It is true that a highly motivated individual can acquire these skills by reading books and taking night courses at a local community college, but the best preparation one can have for this job is completing a course of study that earns at least a bachelor's degree, in either arts and sciences or fine arts.

One of the many advantages of completing a degree-granting course of study is learning to manage one's time and prioritize tasks. Setting aside time to contact one's outside resources while maintaining a schedule that allows for the meeting of one's own design deadlines is a balancing act a successful Art Director accomplishes every day.

Many colleges offer job-placement programs, which is another advantage of seeking a formal postsecondary education. In many colleges, particularly professional art colleges, instructors are working professionals and can bolster these job-placement programs by providing leads and making introductions for ambitious, hardworking students as they're preparing to graduate. At the minimum, surrounding oneself with like-minded students gets one's networking abilities established, and this comes in handy throughout one's professional life.

Additionally, while a degree-granting course of study is tailored to concentrate on design principals, the best schools expose a prospective Art Director to the many facets of professional art. This helps round out one's vocabulary and experience and allows a future Art Director to be aware of the ins and outs of the crafts supplied to him by outside vendors (chiefly, photography and illustration).

Experience, Skills, and Personality Traits

Design, design, design—any Art Director will state this ad infinitum. One can never be too good a shape and type designer, and one never stops looking for new ways to solve a design problem. Keeping an eye out for what's clever but still legible maintains one's creative edge, and staying sharp increases one's likelihood of advancement. One must also have the ability to translate the design principals to the printed page through desktop publishing programs and keep up with the advances software publishers make in designing their programs.

Typically, publishers have dozens of projects being brought to print at any given time during the year. For instance, Simon and Schuster alone will brought roughly 1,700 new titles to market in 2004. Given this, it's impossible for any Art Director to expect to handle any but the smallest publisher's entire book list alone. This means he or she must be willing to work with others. Whether the assistant art directors and creative director with whom he or she works on a daily basis or the outside vendors supplying design and imaging, an Art Director has to be able to communicate.

An Art Director must also have the ability to juggle several projects in differing stages of completion and manage the stress well. While not as pressured as the working life of an advertising art director, there still exists a level of strain that comes in any job in which having to meet continual deadlines is the norm.

Unions and Associations

The leading association for design professionals is the American Institute of Graphic Arts. With its headquarters in New York City and 47 local chapters around the United States, it offers significant networking and educational benefits unavailable elsewhere. The country's leading designers write essays about trends in design available to members, a directory of like-minded professionals is available online, and a robust list of AIGA-sponsored events take place year-round. Additionally, the Art Director's Club (New York) and Graphic Artists Guild offer networking and educational opportunities.

Tips for Entry

1. Learn to organize your time and prioritize tasks.
2. Sharpen your design skills, and learn as much as possible about the interaction of shape, type, and text.
3. Apply for internships with book publishers while in school.
4. Maintain contact with like-minded classmates after graduation.
5. Learn as much as possible about the specifics of the book publishing field.

CREATIVE DIRECTOR (BOOKS)

CAREER PROFILE

Duties: Oversees creative department of book publishing company; designs book jackets and interiors; interacts with editorial and marketing departments

Alternate Title(s): Art Director; Designer

Salary Range: $50,000 to $100,000+

Employment Prospects: Fair

Advancement Prospects: Poor

Best Geographical Location(s): Major urban areas with book publishing companies

Prerequisites:

Education or Training—Two-dimensional design expertise; knowledge of typography; facility with digital environment, chiefly the Macintosh platform

Experience—Managing a support team; book or editorial design

Special Skills and Personality Traits—Ability to manage large number of projects and delegate tasks; ability to organize and design workflow; awareness of how design and typography relate to the written word; diplomacy and ability to work with others

CAREER LADDER

```
┌─────────────────────────────┐
│      Creative Director      │
└─────────────────────────────┘

┌─────────────────────────────┐
│         Art Director        │
└─────────────────────────────┘

┌─────────────────────────────┐
│    Assistant Art Director   │
└─────────────────────────────┘
```

Position Description

A Creative Director in book publishing has a very prominent role in preparing materials that are ready for print, especially in large print houses that publish a great many books in any given year. While it's typical that a staff of designers, art directors, illustrators, photographers, and imaging specialists field most of the actual nuts and bolts of the physical work, a Creative Director's influence is exercised over all facets.

The largest part of the Creative Director's day is spent overseeing a staff comprised chiefly of designers, assistant art directors, and art directors, though in most cases there are also one or more secretarial positions. Typically, publishers have dozens of projects being brought to print at any given time during the year. Simon and Schuster alone, one of the United States' largest publishers, with several imprints, planned to bring roughly 1,700 new books to market in 2004. With such a terrific workload, it would be impossible for any one person to field the job of preparing

the designs of interiors and jackets across the whole line. Thus, Creative Directors manage these staffs of support people to make sure publishing schedules are kept.

Art Directors make up the first level of support. In most cases, art directors are the primary direct reporters to a Creative Director. (In a single division of Simon and Schuster, for example, one Creative Director has four direct reports out of a support staff of 27). Art directors have jobs that involve managing support persons as well, including assistant art directors (sometimes labeled designers) and independent contractors who deliver imaging or design. Among the duties an art director assumes are interior design, including all typesetting chores, chapter division, and maintaining an interior cohesiveness; and jacket design, which includes title design, cover imaging design, blurb placement, and flap copy design.

When crafting the interior of a book, in most cases the chief duty boils down to type design. While in special circumstances the interior design may include imaging (whether photographic material that supports specific passages or illustrations that begin or end individual chapters), the primary duty remains the design of the text that the reader encounters when digesting the material the author composes. Additionally, the interior designer has to keep in mind several production-oriented concerns, such as word count and page count when drafting books bound in signatures. Any Creative Director working for a book publisher has to have a handle on these issues in order to manage the projects under his or her supervision effectively.

The jacket design—or cover design when working on a paperback release—has its own set of criteria to be considered. The artist drafting a jacket or cover design concentrates more on generating an immediate response to the package to lure a viewer into taking a closer look at the book. The cover designer seeks impact. Whether employing a subtle approach or a direct, in-your-face one, a cover designer's chief concern is getting a consumer interested in picking a book up off a shelf. A savvy cover designer must be able to segue from one type of cover design to the next, and the Creative Director must also have the ability to recognize the success a designer achieves and also to offer informed criticism and encouragement.

Imaging acts as a primary driver of the cover design, and often this aspect is delivered by an outside resource, whether photographic or illustrative. To that end, a Creative Director works closely with the art director in selecting the outside resource that will provide this imaging. In these cases, another aspect of the Creative Director's job comes into play: negotiating contracts. While those working on-staff for a company own no copyrights to the works they produce, outside vendors are not bound to selling copyrights to their work by default. In some cases, book publishers make selling all copyrights a requirement for providing imaging—Scholastic, Inc., for example. Most, however, do not. A Creative Director has to understand what the company policy is in dealing with contracts for outside vendors and must relay these terms when hiring out.

A Creative Director must have a working knowledge of all facets of book design for several reasons. First, he or she must be aware of what the two different artists are drafting on the same project to ensure that a unified whole comes together. Second, it may fall to the Creative Director to jump in on a project should one of the staff take ill or leave the company prior to the project's completion. Similarly, a Creative Director may have to bring in another designer to complete a task left unfinished in such a state. In any case, the Creative Director bears the responsibility of bringing a complete, unified product to market; having the ability to understand how the disparate parts work together ensures success.

In addition to the crafting of individual books and the management skill to make these books become unified wholes, a Creative Director must work with the editorial and marketing departments and, in special circumstances, the acquisitions department. When working with the editorial and acquisitions departments, a Creative Director makes informed observations about how proposed written materials would translate into finished books. For instance, an author proposing a fictional thriller involving in-depth research into some historical events may pique the interest of the editorial and acquisitions staff. The Creative Director's job in a meeting that weighs the pros and cons of bringing such a project to market is to point out the particulars of designing such a package, what resources would be required in terms of outside suppliers, and how best to draft an effective presentation that will attract consumers.

In much the same way, a Creative Director works with the marketing department to sharpen a book's image. Marketing plays a key role in presenting the book to the public, and a conscientious Creative Director stays involved in this process. Marketers keep a close eye on what's current and effective in attracting a buying public. Often, these departments conduct surveys or purchase survey results from firms that specialize in this area to augment what they personally observe and read about. Suggestions made by the marketing department on the visual aspects of a book, particularly the cover design, play a large part in how direction is handed down to the creative professionals involved.

Salaries

As with many of the positions available in the visual art field, location serves to drive salary expectation. When living and working in an area that has a large number of publishing houses, such as New York, competition and cost of living drive salary expectations higher. In addition, larger publishers that have very robust print lists tend to be able to pay better.

That isn't to say that some smaller publishers aren't equipped to pay well by their market standards for Creative Directors. Since the position requires such a highly polished skill set and well-rounded experience, even smaller publishers are willing to pay well for seasoned Creative Directors. Given that, a Creative Director working in a smaller market in the Midwest making $60,000 a year would net roughly the same standard of living as someone earning $100,000 a year in an area where the cost of living is higher, such as New York City. Additionally, the Creative Director position is a high-level one that often comes with additional perks. Retirement funds, annual bonuses, and competitive benefit packages usually accompany the salary earned by the Creative Director.

Employment Prospects

While still a very common position in the book publishing arena in that most publishers, large and small, have at least one Creative Director position, the competition for these high-level positions is great. There are many more qualified applicants for every job opening than there are openings available. In many cases, senior-level art directors with several years of book publishing experience attempt to fill any available vacancy, whether with a company for which they've worked or one across town (figuratively speaking). The level of competition for Creative Director positions is always high, and the prospective candidate must have a resume that proves a minimum of 10 years of experience in the publishing industry (in most cases) and a portfolio of printed work that exhibits excellence in shape and type design.

Advancement Prospects

Once someone is in the position of Creative Director, it's difficult to advance in most circumstances, because this job tends to be the top of the ladder. In special circumstances, a Creative Director may be offered an officer's position in the company (typically, a vice president position). Officer positions often come with larger bonuses and stock options.

Education and Training

The primary requirements for this position are a facility with layout and design and computer programs, excellent two-dimensional and type design sense, and an ability to manage an active art department. While these skills can be learned by intense individual exploration and reading or continued postsecondary education, it's very rare that someone reaches the Creative Director level without at least a bachelor's degree, in either arts and sciences or fine arts.

One of the many advantages of completing a degree-granting course of study is learning to manage one's time and prioritize tasks. Any successful Creative Director uses these skills on a daily basis. Faced with setting up meeting times with other department heads, delegating design and management of independent contractor duties, and leaving time to work on one's own creative tasks, a Creative Director performs a continual juggling act.

In addition to learning these organizational skills, completing a degree-granting course of study typically exposes a Creative Director hopeful to a variety of creative endeavors, from hands-on observational painting and drawing, to photography, to writing. The more well-rounded a Creative Director's education, the better he or she is prepared to speak intelligently about the several facets that go into making a complete book.

Experience, Skills, and Personality Traits

As stated above, the primary skills required to be a Creative Director are the design considerations. Knowing how a viewer responds to typography and shape is key.

As with any managerial position, one must have prior experience in delegating tasks and supervising the work of others in order to qualify for a Creative Director position. To this end, a successful Creative Director exhibits diplomacy and flexibility and is able to maintain a firm stance when needed. This comes into play particularly when dealing with contract issues with outside vendors. He or she must possess organizational and creative skills in equal proportion.

While the world of book publishing typically doesn't operate under the rigid time constraints of the advertising world, there still exists a good deal of stress and pressure at the Creative Director level. Book publishers invest large sums of money in bringing material to print; to that end, a great deal rides on the efforts of those artists a Creative Director oversees. It's these efforts that put a face on the overall package and are the first part of the book a potential reader encounters. Thus, a Creative Director has to work well under pressure.

Unions and Associations

While there is no union protecting the rights of Creative Directors, there are several national associations that offer networking opportunities and keep a finger on the pulse of what's current in the design field. Chief among these is the American Institute of Graphic Arts, which offers educational benefits and an online library and directory and lists many of the leading designers in the country as its members. It works on both a national and local level, as it supports 47 local chapters in addition to its national headquarters in New York City. Additionally, the Art Director's Club (New York) and the Graphic Artists Guild offer networking opportunities.

Tips for Entry

1. Learn to organize your time and prioritize tasks.
2. Sharpen your design skills, and learn as much as possible about the interaction of shape, type, and text.
3. Apply for internships with book publishers while in school.
4. Maintain contact with like-minded classmates after graduation.
5. Learn as much as possible about the specifics of the book publishing field.

ASSISTANT ART DIRECTOR (EDITORIAL)

CAREER PROFILE

Duties: Works within overall publication design drafted by Creative Director; takes direction from Art Directors; at times in larger publishing environments, oversees efforts of entry-level designers; works with editorial department to ensure marriage of editorial content and pictorial content; works with and hires vendors to supply imaging

Alternate Title(s): Designer

Salary Range: $35,000 to $60,000+

Employment Prospects: Fair to Good

Advancement Prospects: Good

Best Geographical Location(s): Major urban areas with magazine/newspaper publishing companies

Prerequisites:

Education or Training—Two-dimensional design expertise; knowledge of typography; facility with digital environment, chiefly the Macintosh platform

Experience—A portfolio of editorial or book design samples

Special Skills and Personality Traits—Ability to manage large number of projects and delegate tasks; ability to organize one's time; awareness of how design and typography relate to the written word; diplomacy and ability to work with others

CAREER LADDER

```
┌─────────────────────────────────┐
│       Creative Director         │
└─────────────────────────────────┘

┌─────────────────────────────────┐
│         Art Director            │
└─────────────────────────────────┘

┌─────────────────────────────────┐
│ Assistant Art Director/Designer │
└─────────────────────────────────┘
```

Position Description

While publishing environments vary of necessity (some publications run daily, such as newspapers; some run as infrequently as bimonthly), there are enough overlapping duties and operations to paint a broad picture of this position. Chiefly, an Assistant Art Director in an editorial environment designs pages of copy and lays out spaces for accompanying imagery. In some arenas, an Assistant Art Director has some minor management duties in that he or she oversees the efforts of entry-level designers as well as the authority to source the imagery that accompanies articles.

Creative directors compose the overall layout and look of publications, so a rough template of page style exists when the Assistant Art Director sets out to compose the work. Additionally, input is given to the Assistant Art Director by his or her immediate superior, the art director. The amount of artistic freedom afforded an Assistant Art Director varies from publication to publication. For instance, a daily newspaper has stricter guidelines than a funky pop-culture magazine. This ensures that a publication put together by a team of creative professionals, of which the Assistant Art Director is but one member, still has a unified look and maintains the brand identity of the publication. Working within these guidelines, an Assistant Art Director takes copy provided by the editorial department—often accompanied by notes, either written or spoken, about the gist of the piece to expedite the assignation of imagery—and works it into a layout with the other pieces needed to complete the page (advertisements, headlines, subheads, etc.). In many cases, the notes from the editorial department are fleshed out further by the art director.

An important aspect of the Assistant Art Director's duties involves the actual print production of the final pages. Knowing how the process works from digital layout through film to plate production for Web printing is a must. This mechanical concern involves all aspects of the printed page, from resolution requirements for printed imagery all the way down to the number of inks on the page.

On occasion, an Assistant Art Director will have some management duties to perform. This takes place most often for publications with very tight deadline schedules, such as a daily newspaper, and in these cases entry-level designers take direction from Assistant Art Directors. In such cases, the designer's chief duties boil down to nuts-and-bolts composition—sizing type, importing text into predetermined columns, and so on. In these cases, Assistant Art Directors are often charged with composing a slate of individual pages within a larger section overseen by an art director, and the designer subordinate to the Assistant Art Director works on very basic parts within these pages.

In these more atypical circumstances, the Assistant Art Director assumes some of the responsibility for managing the creative budget by assigning or sourcing the imagery that accompanies the articles. Assistant Art Directors charged with these duties must therefore have a working knowledge for the appropriate types and styles of imagery to accompany the articles being laid out. In such cases, an Assistant Art Director has very little authority to deviate from set parameters concerning funds allocated to the pages, and any proposed changes to this—an illustrator whose work seems particularly appropriate to the written material, for instance—must be approved by his or her supervisors.

As do other design professionals, any good Assistant Art Director stays abreast of what's current in popular culture. Keeping an eye out for what's current in the advertising and book publishing worlds, not to mention what takes place in other competing publications, helps sharpen the Assistant Art Director's design sense. Having a sharp eye and discussing such trends with peers and superiors helps an Assistant Art Director move upward on the career ladder.

Another important aspect of staying up to date includes keeping an eye out for what changes in the technical application area of the design world. Software and hardware advances in personal computing technology have taken place at an unprecedented pace since 1980, and these advances have literally changed the entire process of composing publication designs. Assistant Art Directors who are ambitious and take their careers seriously keep up to date with these advances.

Salaries

As the cost of living and competition on publishers' parts for available candidates varies across the nation, so do salaries for Assistant Art Directors. One's earnings in areas that support large clusters of newspaper and magazine publishers will be higher than those of someone in a region of the United States with fewer publishers. Newspapers and magazines in these more heavily concentrated areas—the New York metropolitan area, for instance—tend to have greater circulation, often nationwide coverage, and this drives up advertising rates. With higher revenues from circulation and advertising, the publishers have greater financial resources and an ability to pay larger salaries. Larger publishers with these greater resources seldom pay less than $45,000 annually for Assistant Art Directors, even at the beginning level.

In the U.S. Department of Labor's *Occupational Outlook Handbook,* statistics gleaned from the American Institute of Graphic Arts serve as a benchmark for print design professionals (including designers, Assistant Art Directors, and art directors). In 2002, design professionals holding positions that include the duties described above earned a median income between $40,000 and $55,000 nationwide.

Employment Prospects

There are a great many Assistant Art Director positions available in the United States, and while competition runs high, they are easier to acquire than jobs higher up the ladder. One disturbing trend to look out for that has been reported as fairly prevalent is companies offering a position that pays commensurate with lower-level Assistant Art Directors but asks for candidates to perform tasks more in line with high-level Assistant Art Directors or full art directors.

Advancement Prospects

It's almost a matter of course that an Assistant Art Director move up the career ladder, as it's truly an entry-level or low-level position. Once one is entrenched in the editorial publishing world—at least three years of experience, a large body of work on which to draw, significant contacts within the editorial publishing world—one's way is paved toward upward movement. In some cases, this means retaining the same title while assuming larger management duties and getting commensurate hikes in pay and benefits.

Education and Training

Any candidate considered for an Assistant Art Director position must exhibit knowledge of and facility for typographic and graphic design. While these skills can be acquired through intense individual investigation and application—reading texts about the primary tenets of design and typography and how the primary design applications work—seldom does one rise to this level without at least a bachelor's degree, in either fine arts or arts and sciences.

Completing a course of study that grants a bachelor's degree teaches not only the technical knowledge and application of design and typography, but acquaints one with the ability to organize one's time to meet deadlines. Making sure that classes are attended and assignments are completed prepares the soon-to-be Assistant Art Director to arrange extremely limited time in the most effective way possible. Juggling courses in design with other academic requirements paves the way for the constant back-and-forth one performs in daily working life.

A degree-granting course of study also provides a design professional with a well-rounded education, ensuring that he or she is exposed to many of the facets that go into editorial publications. He or she will encounter courses in literature and composition, spend time around those studying other aspects of the visual art world upon whom he or she will rely when hiring subcontractors (photography, illustration, etc.), and likely be exposed to actual practicing professionals in the form of instructors or guest speakers.

Experience, Skills, and Personality Traits

Assistant Art Directors usually begin their careers at the entry level—in the rarer environments in which an Assistant Art Director has to ply some management duties, this is not the case—and as such must present a good portfolio, often of work completed as a student. In the best-case scenario, this student work is bolstered by some work done for small publications or even college newspapers. A more mid-level management person must have some prior management experience or a good deal of experience at the entry level.

Additionally, as with virtually any position in a publishing environment, one encounters a great deal of stress at times in the day-to-day working world. Working with other creative professionals, tight deadlines (especially in daily publications), editorial content changing at the last minute, vendors not coming through for whatever reason, needing to work within budget constraints—all these and many other factors conspire to make the job difficult at times. Successful Assistant Art Directors manage these situations and lead by example, maintaining a high degree of flexibility and, even in tough times, a sense of humor.

Unions and Associations

In rare circumstances, an Assistant Art Director may be called upon to hold a union position. These occur when working in a union town on a publication, typically a newspaper, that has collective bargaining requirements to fulfill. In most cases, however, these positions aren't union. There are, however, several trade associations to which an Assistant Art Director can belong to enhance his or her career, chiefly for networking and educational purposes.

The American Institute of Graphic Arts (AIGA) heads the list of associations aimed at enhancing the working lives of design professionals. The AIGA offers frequent educational seminars, keeps a running address book of members (among whom are many of the leading designers in the country), and has an online library of essays and publications that explore the many finer points of two-dimensional and typographic design. With 47 local chapters around the country and a headquarters in New York City, the AIGA covers a great portion of the United States and is a good barometer for regions with larger numbers of job opportunities. Additionally, the Art Director's Club (New York) and the Graphic Artists Guild offer networking opportunities.

Tips for Entry

1. Learn to organize your time and prioritize tasks.
2. Sharpen your design skills, and learn as much as possible about the interaction of shape, type, and text.
3. Apply for internships with editorial publishers while in school, and work on student or local publications to enhance your portfolio.
4. Maintain contact with like-minded classmates after graduation.
5. Learn as much as possible about the specifics of the editorial publishing field.

ART DIRECTOR (EDITORIAL)

CAREER PROFILE

Duties: Works within overall publication design drafted by creative director; manages staff of assistant art directors and Designers; works with editorial department to ensure marriage of editorial content and pictorial content; works with and hires vendors to supply imaging

Alternate Title(s): Designer

Salary Range: $40,000 to $120,000+

Employment Prospects: Fair to Good

Advancement Prospects: Fair

Best Geographical Location(s): Major urban areas with magazine and newspaper publishing companies

Prerequisites:

Education or Training—Two-dimensional design expertise; knowledge of typography; facility with digital environment, chiefly the Macintosh platform

Experience—Managing a support team; editorial or book design

Special Skills and Personality Traits—Ability to manage large number of projects and delegate tasks; ability to organize and design workflow; awareness of how design and typography relate to the written word; diplomacy and ability to work with others

CAREER LADDER

```
+-------------------------------------+
|         Creative Director           |
+-------------------------------------+

+-------------------------------------+
|            Art Director             |
+-------------------------------------+

+-------------------------------------+
|   Assistant Art Director/Designer   |
+-------------------------------------+
```

Position Description

While publishing environments vary of necessity (some publications run daily, such as newspapers; some run as infrequently as bimonthly), there are enough overlapping duties and operations to paint a broad picture of this position. Chiefly, an Art Director in an editorial environment designs pages of copy and accompanying imagery and manages both support staff and outside vendors who supply imaging. Additionally, the Art Director works with input from the editorial department to ensure that the imaging paired with the text matches the intent of the copy and balances an overall art budget attributed to his or her pages or section.

Since the overall publication design is composed by the creative director, a rough template of page style exists when the Art Director sets out to compose his or her work. The amount of wiggle room afforded an Art Director varies from publication to publication. For instance, a daily newspaper has stricter guidelines than a funky pop-culture magazine. This ensures that a publication put together by a team of creative professionals still has a unified look and maintains its brand identity. Working within these guidelines, an Art Director takes copy provided by the editorial department, often accompanied by notes, either written or spoken, about the gist of the piece to expedite the assignation of imagery, and works it into a layout with the varying other pieces needed to complete the page (advertisements, headlines, subheads, etc.).

When it comes to imagery, Art Directors have two main resources: independent contractors and stock agencies. Independent contractors supply original art (be it illustration or photography) and stock agencies sell licenses to preexisting art (typically photography, but stock agencies have been aggressively entering the illustration market). Having a grasp on the written material goes a long way toward selecting an image supplier. For instance, a hard news article usually calls for a newswire photograph, whereas an opinion piece typically calls for illustration. (These distinctions have been exaggerated and simplified for this entry. Many additional variables factor into decision making when it comes to selecting imagery, including budget, overall visual style of the publication, deadline for print, etc.)

In addition to working with the editorial staff, the Art Director has to manage the efforts of assistant art directors and designers in his or her department. Again, the amount of management will vary by publication, owing to many factors, including size of the publication, both in page count and circulation; frequency of publication; amount of editorial content; and visual brand identity, which determines how much imagery and design support the written content. In a typical environment, Art Directors are responsible for large sections of a publication and have a support staff dedicated to assisting them with the execution of individual page layouts. The type of assistance varies. In some environments, assistant art directors have a large hand in assigning illustration or sourcing imagery; in others less so. Similarly, assistant art directors may have duties limited to importing and sizing text to columns before the Art Director takes the pages for a final run-through (including image placement, sizing and placement of headlines, etc.).

Art Directors also manage a creative budget, and publications address this component of the job in various ways. In some cases, publications assign the creative department an annual budget on which it draws over the course of a year. In others, a budget exists on a per-issue basis. Yet other publications have sectional budgets determined by differing advertising rates by section. In any case, one of the Art Director's main duties is managing these budgets.

Additionally, any good Art Director keeps an eye out for what's current in popular culture. Staying abreast of what happens in the advertising world, in the book publishing arena, and at other editorial publications helps keep him or her sharp and informs design decisions. Knowing how traditional design principals are applied in other areas of the visual art world is an ongoing process, and Art Directors who understand this responsibility are able to adapt and tweak their designs to stay with the times.

Another aspect of staying up to date includes keeping an ear out for changes in the technical application area of the design world. Software and hardware advances in personal computing technology have taken place at an unprecedented pace since 1980, and these advances have literally changed the entire process of composing publication design. Gone are the paste-up mechanicals and wax machines that once dominated the physical process of assembling pages for print. Now, layout is done in the virtual digital universe. As technology changes, Art Directors who continue to stay employed at high levels adapt to these changes and adopt these worthwhile advances.

Salaries

As the cost of living and competition by publishers for available candidates varies across the nation, so do salaries for Art Directors. One's earnings in areas that support large numbers of newspaper and magazine publishers will be higher than they would be if one lived in a region of the United States with fewer publishers. Newspapers and magazines in these more heavily concentrated areas—the New York metropolitan area, for instance—tend to have greater circulation and often nationwide coverage, and this drives up advertising rates. With higher revenues from circulation and advertising, the publishers have greater financial resources and an ability to pay larger salaries. Larger publishers with these greater resources seldom pay less than $55,000 annually for Art Directors, even at the beginning level.

In the U.S. Department of Labor's *Occupational Outlook Handbook,* statistics gleaned from the American Institute of Graphic Arts (AIGA) serve as benchmark for print design professionals (including designers, assistant art directors, and Art Directors). In 2002, design professionals holding positions that include the duties described above earned a median income of $85,000 nationwide in 2002.

Employment Prospects

There are a great many Art Director positions available in the United States, more than 51,000 as of 2002, but competition runs hot for them. Assistant art directors and designers vie for these jobs as well as Art Directors from other publications looking to make lateral moves.

Advancement Prospects

While there is some room for advancement at the level of Art Director (for instance, one can advance within the position by assuming more managerial duties, overseeing larger groups of assistant art directors and designers, and working more closely with the creative director, etc.), the only job remaining after ascending to the most senior level of Art Director is creative director. While ascending within the position offers greater recompense and benefits in most cases—there are some odious publications that will saddle its creative professionals with added responsibilities without a commensurate bump in pay, but those are more the exception than the rule—there's only a single title to be had above Art Director.

Education and Training

Any candidate considered for an Art Director position must exhibit knowledge of and facility for typographic and graphic design in addition to prowess as a manager. While these skills can be acquired through intense individual investigation and application, reading texts about the primary tenets of design and typography, seldom does one rise to this level without at least a bachelor's degree in either fine arts or arts and sciences.

Completing a course of study that grants a bachelor's degree teaches not only the technical knowledge and application of design and typography, but acquaints one with the ability to organize one's efforts in a timely fashion and meet deadlines. Making sure that classes are attended and assignments are completed prepares the prospective Art Director to arrange extremely limited time in the most effective way possible. Juggling courses in design with other academic requirements paves the way for the constant back-and-forth one performs daily as an Art Director.

A degree-granting course of study also provides the eventual Art Director with a well-rounded education, ensuring exposure to many of the facets that go into editorial publications. He or she encounters courses in literature and composition, spends time around those studying other aspects of the visual art world upon which he or she will rely when hiring subcontractors (photography, illustration, etc.), and likely is exposed to actual practicing professionals in the form of instructors or guest speakers.

Experience, Skills, and Personality Traits

Art Directors are primarily managing designers and as such need an excellent grasp of typographic and graphic design. Additionally, they must exhibit excellent managerial traits and habits.

Typically, one must have prior experience managing creative professionals in order to qualify for an Art Director's position. The specific requirement in years varies by publisher and job circumstance, but without at least three years of experience in such a management position, it's nearly unheard of to achieve this status. Often, this can come from being in a more senior position as an assistant art director, whereby one has managed the efforts of vendors and perhaps entry-level designers.

Additionally, as with virtually any management position, one encounters a great deal of stress at times in the day-to-day working world. Working with other creative professionals, tight deadlines (especially in daily publica-

tions), editorial content changes at the last minute, vendors not coming through for whatever reason, needing to deal with budget constraints—all this and half a hundred other factors conspire to make the job difficult at times. Successful Art Directors manage these situations and lead by example, maintaining a high degree of flexibility and, even at tough times, a sense of humor.

Unions and Associations

In rare circumstances, an Art Director may be called upon to hold a union position. These occur when working in a union town on a publication, typically a newspaper, that has collective bargaining requirements to fulfill. In most cases, however, these management positions aren't union. There are, however, several trade associations to which an editorial creative director can belong to enhance his or her career, chiefly for networking and educational purposes.

The American Institute of Graphic Arts (AIGA) heads the list of associations aimed at enhancing the working lives of design professionals. The AIGA offers frequent educational seminars, keeps a running address book of members, among whom are many of the leading designers in the United States, and has an online library of essays and publications that explore the many finer points of two-dimensional and typographic design. With 47 local chapters around the country and a headquarters in New York City, the AIGA covers a great portion of the United States and is a good barometer for regions with larger numbers of job opportunities. Additionally, the Art Director's Club (New York) and the Graphic Artists Guild offer networking opportunities.

Tips for Entry

1. Learn to organize your time and prioritize tasks.
2. Sharpen your design skills, and learn as much as possible about the interaction of shape, type, and text.
3. Apply for internships with editorial publishers while in school.
4. Maintain contact with like-minded classmates after graduation.
5. Learn as much as possible about the specifics of the editorial publishing field.

CREATIVE DIRECTOR (EDITORIAL)

CAREER PROFILE

Duties: Designs and oversees the implementation of the design of an editorial publication; manages an entire department of creative professionals

Alternate Title(s): Art Director; Designer

Salary Range: $60,000 to $150,000+

Employment Prospects: Fair

Advancement Prospects: Poor

Best Geographical Location(s): Major urban areas with magazine and newspaper publishing companies

Prerequisites:

Education or Training—Two-dimensional design expertise; knowledge of typography; facility with digital environment, chiefly the Macintosh platform

Experience—Managing a support team; editorial or book design

Special Skills and Personality Traits—Ability to manage large number of projects and delegate tasks; ability to organize and design workflow; awareness of how design and typography relate to the written word; diplomacy and ability to work with others

CAREER LADDER

```
┌─────────────────────────────────────┐
│         Creative Director           │
└─────────────────────────────────────┘

┌─────────────────────────────────────┐
│            Art Director             │
└─────────────────────────────────────┘

┌─────────────────────────────────────┐
│   Assistant Art Director/Designer   │
└─────────────────────────────────────┘
```

Position Description

The lion's share of a Creative Director's day-to-day duties consists of overseeing the creative department(s) charged with putting a publication together in a timely fashion to meet expected publication deadlines. Senior art directors, their juniors, assistant art directors and designers, and imaging specialists (such as photographers and illustrators) all have parts to play in delivering key components to the makeup of a page. Ensuring that all these individual pages add up to a consistent, unified whole is the primary function of the Creative Director. It is a unified look with which he or she is very familiar, as, in most cases, he or she is the design professional who drafted it.

Art directors and assistant art directors and designers constitute the majority of a Creative Director's staff. These creative professionals primarily compose the magazine or newspaper the Creative Director helms—they are the Creative Director's hands. They use virtual templates based upon the Creative Director's design decisions and work the specific editorial content into the spaces allotted on the page. By sizing type, sourcing out and placing imaging, and composing the relationships among disparate parts within parameters set by the Creative Director, the creative staff drafts the pieces that make the whole.

All the various aspects of page and publication design have to be set down in the Creative Director's template: headlines, subheads, spaces for body copy, margins, credit lines, allocations for imaging space, and various other aspects have to be addressed. Even in publications in which differing types of content are published—reviews of stylish eateries and hard-news stories, for instance—a brand identity must unify the publication. To this end, a Creative Director must have an extremely highly developed sense of page design and typography. After all, different fonts have different "voices," and using these "voices" goes a long way toward defining how a publication reads.

So, too, does the type of imaging one selects to accompany written content. Photography included with hard-news stories, for example, tends to give a sense of being in the moment. Illustration often goes a long way toward enhancing opinion or subjective pieces. All of these considerations are taken into account when a Creative Director sets the parameters for an overall publication's brand identity and the specific departments therein.

A Creative Director often acts as a go-between for the editorial departments and the creative departments, as well. Though many upper-level art directors have one-on-one contact with editors due to time constraints in a daily workflow, a Creative Director bears the ultimate responsibility of making sure the translation between the written and visual content takes place smoothly. Day-to-day working life often involves meetings with members of both departments to ensure that nothing's being lost in the transition from what's expected by editorial.

Additionally, a Creative Director who enjoys continued success keeps an eye out for what's current in popular culture. Staying abreast of what happens in the advertising world, the book publishing arena, and at other editorial publications helps keep the visual brand identity of the publication that he or she stewards fresh and contemporary. Knowing how traditional design principals are applied in other areas of the visual art world is an ongoing process, and Creative Directors who understand this responsibility are able to adapt and tweak their overall publication design to stay with the times.

Another aspect of staying up to date includes keeping an ear out for changes in the technical application area of the design world. Software and hardware advances in personal computing technology have taken place at an unprecedented pace since 1980, and these advances have literally changed the entire process of composing publication design. Gone are the paste-up mechanicals and wax machines that once dominated the physical process of assembling pages for print. Now, layout is done in the virtual digital universe. As technology changes, Creative Directors who continue to stay employed at high levels adapt to these changes and adopt these worthwhile advances.

Salaries

As the cost of living and competition by publishers for available candidates varies across the nation, so do salaries for Creative Directors. One's earnings in areas that support large numbers of newspaper and magazine publishers are higher than they would be if one lived in a region of the United States with fewer publishers. Newspapers and magazines in these more heavily concentrated areas—the New York metropolitan area, for instance—tend to have greater circulation and often nationwide coverage, and this drives up advertising rates. With higher revenues from circulation and advertising, the publishers have greater financial resources and an ability to pay larger salaries. Larger publishers with these greater resources seldom pay less than $150,000 annually for Creative Directors.

When choosing an area to target, however, careful consideration about the cost of living versus the higher compensation must be made. For instance, housing costs in New York City are far higher than those in the Cleveland, Ohio, metro area. Should a job in New York pay $150,000 to a person shelling out more than $3,000 a month in rent or mortgage, a figure considered a bargain to many New Yorkers, especially those living in the borough of Manhattan, housing alone will account for nearly half of posttax earnings. A counterpart in a smaller city earning $100,000 yet paying only $1,500 a month in rent or mortgage would be ahead of the game in terms of percentage of annual earnings devoted to housing expense.

One last consideration: Creative Directors have executive management positions, and as such typically have compensation packages that reflect this status. Medical insurance, retirement funds, expense accounts, annual bonuses, and stock options usually bolster one's compensation. These added perks vary by publisher.

Employment Prospects

Though this position exists at nearly every publication—the name of one's job title may be art director in smaller publications, but the duties for the top creative design professional will be the same—it's still a difficult one to attain. Many years of experience precede any ascent to the level of Creative Director, not to mention years of networking within one's own work environment and the editorial publishing world at large. A candidate for this job faces stiff competition, and résumés for the position seldom reflect less than 10 years of experience as a senior-level art director.

Advancement Prospects

Once ascended to the position of Creative Director, it's difficult to advance in most circumstances, because this job tends to be the top of the ladder. In special circumstances, a Creative Director may be offered an officer's position in the company (typically, a vice president position), which is a way to advance one's place after becoming Creative Director. Officer positions often come with larger bonuses and stock options among its perks.

Education and Training

Any candidate considered for a Creative Director position must exhibit knowledge of and facility for typographic and graphic design in addition to prowess as a manager. While these skills can be acquired through intense individual investigation and application—reading texts about the primary tenets of design and typography—seldom does one rise to this level without at least a bachelor's degree in either fine arts or arts and sciences.

Completing a course of study that grants a bachelor's degree teaches not only the technical knowledge and application of design and typography, but acquaints one with the ability to organize one's efforts in a timely fashion and meet deadlines. Making sure that classes are attended and assignments are completed prepares the prospective Creative Director to arrange his or her extremely limited time in the most effective way possible. Juggling courses in design with other academic requirements paves the way for the constant back and forth one performs daily as a Creative Director.

A degree-granting course of study also provides the eventual Creative Director with a well-rounded education, ensuring exposure to many of the facets that go into editorial publications. He or she encounters courses in literature and composition, spends time around those studying other aspects of the visual art world upon whom he or she will rely when hiring subcontractors (photography, illustration, etc.), and likely is exposed to actual practicing professionals in the form of instructors or guest speakers.

Experience, Skills, and Personality Traits
While the absolute primary skill one employs when designing the overall look of a publication remains typographic and shape design, there are several other factors running a close second. This being an executive management position, one must possess the skills and personality traits of a good executive manager.

One doesn't ascend to the position of Creative Director without having managed creative professionals. The specific requirement in years varies by publisher and job circumstance, but without at least five years of experience in such a management position, it's nearly unheard of to achieve this status. A Creative Director must know the ins and outs of handling situations diplomatically, organizing time extremely well and delegating authority when necessary. In this position, one utilizes creative skills and management skills in equal measure.

Additionally, as with virtually any upper management position, one encounters a great deal of stress at times in the day-to-day working world. This pressure typically doesn't run as hot as it does in the advertising world, but deadlines are tight and rigid. Periodicals have strict publishing schedules that cannot be altered without extreme financial consequence. Changes to topical stories take place regularly at deadline times, necessitating quick thinking and changes made under high pressure. A successful Creative Director manages this stress deftly, getting the team to operate efficiently.

Unions and Associations
Creative Directors hold management positions, so even in union towns where publications are run with union labor, Creative Directors don't occupy union positions. There are, however, several trade associations to which an editorial Creative Director can belong to enhance his or her career, chiefly for networking and educational purposes.

The American Institute of Graphic Arts (AIGA) heads the list of associations aimed at enhancing the working lives of design professionals. The AIGA offers frequent educational seminars, keeps a running address book of members, among whom are many of the leading designers in the United States, and has an online library of essays and publications that explore the many finer points of two-dimensional and typographic design. With 47 local chapters around the country and a headquarters in New York City, the AIGA covers a great portion of the country and is a good barometer for regions with larger numbers of job opportunities. Additionally, the Art Director's Club (New York) and the Graphic Artists Guild offer networking opportunities.

Tips for Entry
1. Learn to organize your time and prioritize tasks.
2. Sharpen your design skills, and learn as much as possible about the interaction of shape, type, and text.
3. Apply for internships with editorial publishers while in school.
4. Maintain contact with like-minded classmates after graduation.
5. Learn as much as possible about the specifics of the editorial publishing field.

PHOTO EDITOR

CAREER PROFILE

Duties: Solicits photography portfolios to review for prospective assignments; reviews and chooses photographs to accompany articles, or to use in text-free spreads to convey messages or themes; commissions photographs either directly from photographers or through photographers' representatives; negotiates fees and contracts with photographers; meets regularly with creative directors and editorial staff; reviews photographs to ensure quality; may coordinate with printers; maintains photography files and database of photographers; may manage staff

Alternate Title(s): None

Salary Range: $32,000 to $60,000+

Employment Prospects: Good

Advancement Prospects: Good

Best Geographical Location(s): Major cities, such as New York, Chicago, Los Angeles, Boston, Philadelphia, and San Francisco

Prerequisites:

Education or Training—Four-year degree with specialization in photography recommended; coursework in publishing and printing processes helpful

Experience—One to three years of experience as associate photo editor; photography background beneficial

Special Skills and Personality Traits—Knowledgeable about composition and balance; solid understanding of printing processes in order to choose photos that will translate accurately to the end product; strong visual sense; creative; excellent communication and business management skills; patience; flexibility; good listener; deadline oriented; extremely organized; solid knowledge of Adobe Photoshop and other computer design software

CAREER LADDER

```
┌─────────────────────────────┐
│      Creative Director      │
└─────────────────────────────┘

┌─────────────────────────────┐
│         Photo Editor        │
└─────────────────────────────┘

┌─────────────────────────────┐
│    Associate Photo Editor   │
└─────────────────────────────┘
```

Position Description

Photo Editors choose photographs for associations, magazines, newspapers, books, trade publications, and Web sites. They meet and work closely with editorial staff, creative directors, and clients to discuss upcoming projects. They learn specifics about the editorial direction for each project, find out what is expected visually, make recommendations, and decide on the photographers or photographers' representatives who are most appropriate to approach.

Photo Editors devote part of their day to researching photographs, photographers, agencies, and representatives. They contact photographers or their representatives to solicit portfolios, review and consider the work, and decide on the photographers whose work closely matches the clients' vision. Photo Editors negotiate contracts and fees in accordance with the clients' budgets. Most Photo Editors set up photo shoots and create shoot and production schedules. In setting up shoots, they may occasionally be responsible for contacting the people who will be photographed as well as securing certain licenses or permissions for shoot locations. When it's feasible, they attend shoots to make sure assignments are on track and everything is running smoothly. Once the shoot ends, they review and choose photographs that best match the assignment and will work well with the end product. If a photograph needs to be reformatted or retouched, they typically first discuss the adjustments required with the photographer. They either offer him or her the opportunity to reformat or retouch the photograph in Photoshop or other such design software programs, or if necessary secure permission to make the adjustments themselves.

Photo Editors are also responsible for handling photographers' bills and returning work to photographers. They organize and maintain databases of photographers (including contact information, rates, style synopses, etc.) as well as digital files of photographs. They also keep a library of photographs on CD. Photo Editors are responsible for fact checking, making sure photographers' information is accurately given in publications and online, and ensuring that models or the people being photographed sign release forms, meaning they've given permission for their images to appear in print or online.

Freelance Photo Editors, like all freelance artists, also need to have a business image that best represents them, from a company logo, business literature, and a Web site to promotional and advertising campaigns. They handle their own business accounting and payroll, if it applies, or delegate it to a financial consultant. They also maintain their business equipment.

Salaries

Salaries for Photo Editors vary widely depending on the size and budgets of the organizations. Salaries can range from $32,000 to $60,000 or more. Nonprofit associations and publications offer lower rates but may extend other benefits as compensation. Photo Editors may be able to secure higher rates with advertising agencies, public relations firms, and major media.

Employment Prospects

Employment of editors overall is expected to increase by about 10 to 20 percent through 2012, which is about as fast as the average, according to the U.S. Department of Labor's *Occupational Outlook Handbook.* More magazines are being published each year, and a growing number of organizations are creating newsletters and Web sites to attract wider audiences. Photo Editor positions are popular because the work is so interesting, and as a result competition is fierce. Talented Photo Editors will be able to secure work with associations and organizations that publish print literature and Web content. They can also find work with organizations that are archiving photos, as well as with book publishers, maga-

zines, newspapers, broadcasting companies, advertising agencies, and public relations firms. Photo Editors who have a photography background, are knowledgeable about design software and printing processes, and have prior publishing experience will have an edge on the competition.

Advancement Prospects

Photo Editors with five or more years of experience can move up to become senior Photo Editors or creative directors for entire creative departments. They can also advance by moving into other areas of photography, such as archival and curatorial work for museums or galleries or lecturing, writing, and teaching.

Education and Training

While it is not critical, many Photo Editors have B.F.A.'s in photography, with coursework in photographic techniques and technology, publishing, printing processes, and art history. Some design experience is also helpful. Several years of experience interning in the creative department of a publication or association, as well as one to three years of experience working as an associate Photo Editor, is recommended.

Experience, Skills, and Personality Traits

Publications and associations usually prefer Photo Editors with some publishing experience, a solid knowledge of Photoshop and other design software, and a deep understanding of printing processes. Photo Editors with photography and art direction backgrounds typically best understand photographic techniques and usually have a strong visual sense of composition and balance. Flexibility, diplomacy, creativity, and decisiveness are called upon in this job. Photo Editors must also have strong interpersonal skills. They must be able to work well with a variety of staff and clients, as well as photographers, photographers' representatives, and in some instances printers and other service providers. Because they will be assigning work, negotiating contracts, managing schedules, and maintaining records and photograph files, excellent communication and organization skills are important.

Unions and Associations

The American Society of Media Photographers (ASMP) provides photographers and professionals working in the photography field with educational workshops and literature and networking opportunities. The ASMP is an active advocate and lobbyist for photographers in areas such as copyright, work-for-hire, and improved working conditions. Membership organizations such as the National Press Photographers Association (NPPA) and Editorial Photographers (EP) also provide educational publications, conferences, membership directories, networking opportunities, discounts from various service providers, and more for photographers and photography professionals.

Tips for Entry

1. Learn as much as you can about different photographic processes and current technology.
2. As a Photo Editor, it's your responsibility to know how to choose photographs that will hold up well in the printing process and best meet the clients' expectations. It is critical that you have a solid grasp of printing techniques, inks, and papers.
3. No matter the level you are at in your career, research and knowledge is key to your success. Keep up with what's going on in the industry by reading magazines, Web sites, and visiting galleries and museums.
4. Photo Editors need to have fresh eyes and perspectives for each project. Get inspired by reading books about photographers as well as about artists. Even perusing old family photos can spark ideas.

THEATRICAL

ANIMATOR

CAREER PROFILE

Duties: Designs characters, backgrounds, and props for television, movies, videos, Web sites, and computer software; reads scripts and breakdowns of elements needed for animation; researches references for drawings; draws by hand or uses computer design software; works closely with art directors, creative directors, supervisors, and other animators; invoices clients and handles other freelance business management tasks

Alternate Title(s): Animation Designer; Backdrop, Character, or Prop Designer

Salary Range: $25,830 to $85,160+

Employment Prospects: Fair

Advancement Prospects: Fair

Best Geographical Location(s): Major cities such as Los Angeles and New York

Prerequisites:

Education or Training—B.F.A. in animation or illustration recommended; coursework in computer design software (e.g., Adobe PhotoShop and Illustrator), drawing, painting, and art history recommended; small business management classes helpful

Experience—One- to two-year internship in a studio recommended; illustration background beneficial

Special Skills and Personality Traits—Strong illustration and drafting skills; good eye for form and composition; solid figure drawing abilities; background Animators need to know perspective; character Animators should understand how to draw figures in action; extroverts and introverts are welcome in this field, as are hard workers who can think like kids and can draw what kids want to see

CAREER LADDER

```
┌─────────────────────────────────────────┐
│  Lead Animator, Animation Director, or   │
│               Supervisor                 │
└─────────────────────────────────────────┘

┌─────────────────────────────────────────┐
│                Animator                  │
└─────────────────────────────────────────┘

┌─────────────────────────────────────────┐
│       Animator Assistant or              │
│        Production Designer                │
└─────────────────────────────────────────┘
```

Position Description

Animators create various aspects of animated artwork for television, film, video, advertising, and computer design services. Animators are often hired to work on specific areas of the production, such as props, characters, and backdrops. Backdrop, or background, Animators design the background scenery and must have an eye for composition and perspective. Prop Animators design and illustrate objects in scenes, such as boxes, cell phones, and weapons. Some Animators work specifically in the development area of the show. By experimenting with different paints and styles of drawing, they create the moods and styles that work best with the storyline and characters. Animators regularly attend meetings with directors and other animators to share ideas, scene structures, and designs.

Animation directors usually review scripts first, analyze and imagine every aspect within each scene, then create a breakdown of the elements that need to be animated. They then give Animators the script and breakdown (which sometimes is in storyboard format) so they can read it through and get a feel for the story, characters, props, and background scenery. Animators sketch the elements they've been assigned. Most prefer to draw by hand, using color erase and graphite pencils or even watercolors or paints. They present their rough drawings, or "thumbnails," to the animation director, who reviews them, makes notes, then passes them back to the Animator. If working on a large, big-name production with a more structured staff, an Animator's work may then be passed on to a "cleanup" artist, who, as the title suggests, cleans up the work and tightens the lines. If working for a smaller studio, one Animator typically does it all. Many Animators use design software such as Adobe Photo-Shop and Illustrator to design and illustrate such things as logos, maps, or bit screens where the images must be concise. Many television animation studios have the characters and poses drawn in the United States, and the final animation work is completed overseas.

Salaries

Depending on the studio and its budget, annual salaries for Animators can range from about $25,830 to $85,160 or more, according to the U.S. Department of Labor's *Occupational Outlook Handbook (OOH)*. Studios often hire Animators for each season the show is in production. Animators can be hired for up to three seasons, which is about the time when most shows go into syndication (unless they are an exception to the rule, such as *The Simpsons*). Many Animators are paid on a weekly basis, with paychecks ranging from $800 to $1,200 or more per week.

Employment Prospects

Employment of artists overall is expected to grow by about 10 to 20 percent through 2012, according to the *OOH*. Competition for Animator positions, though, is expected to remain fierce. There are few jobs available, and the field is extremely small and highly specialized. Unless they have strong connections, many art school graduates seeking entry to this field may find the job hunt daunting, particularly because assistant animator jobs are scarce. Based on their own job-hunting experiences, some Animators recommend getting a foot in the door by taking whatever job is available, even if it means working in a department outside animation. Once in, the key is to work hard, network strategically, and make opportunities to show your work to people with the right connections.

Companies often test Animators before hiring them. They give a prospective employee a portion of the script with a breakdown of the characters and props as well as some design examples and a deadline by which to create the animation (usually one to two days). Once the Animator completes and submits the test, if studios are interested, they will then ask to see the Animator's portfolio. Many

Animators have print portfolios with about 15 pieces of their best work included.

Animators who have flexible, adaptable styles may also be able to secure more work than those who have a very distinct and singular style. Each production will be different. The stories and characters will vary, as will the style of drawing. Being able to adapt your drawing style to suit the production may make you more marketable.

Advancement Prospects

Talented, hardworking Animators with several years of experience can advance to become animation directors or supervisors. If they work for small studios, they can transition to animate for larger studios. Animators may even choose to open their own animation studios and production companies, hire staff, and/or explore animating different aspects of productions. For instance, if they focused on prop design, they may try character or background design, depending on their skills and interests. Animators can also expand their skills by writing and teaching.

Education and Training

Animators do not need to have a four-year degree, but attending art school is an excellent way to hone illustration and animation skills, learn perspective, finesse figure drawing abilities, and access design software classes for Adobe Photo-Shop, Illustrator, and others. Talent is especially important in the animation field because it is so highly competitive. And while it cannot be taught anywhere, natural ability is an absolute requirement. Animators should keep their skills fresh by drawing and painting whenever possible, even when work is slow. Many Animators continue to take art classes throughout their careers, and some production companies even require Animators to attend model-drawing, figure-drawing, painting, and other animation-related classes.

Experience, Skills, and Personality Traits

Animators must be highly creative, be excellent illustrators, and have a working knowledge of Adobe PhotoShop and Illustrator. Graphic design and painting experience is also helpful. Animators must be creative under pressure, able to take directions from art directors and supervisors, and deadline oriented. They must be independent thinkers who also work well on a team. And, naturally, a vivid, childlike imagination helps, particularly if drawing for children's shows.

Unions and Associations

Animators can join such groups as the Broadcast Designers Association (PROMAX & BDA, http://www.bda.tv), American Institute of Graphic Arts (AIGA), Animated Film Association (ASIFA, Association Internationale du Film d'Animation), and Society of Illustrators for educational resources, conferences, access to animation festivals, and more.

Tips for Entry

1. You will need to have a lot of patience if you plan to work in this field. The work is cyclical, it's hard to get a foot in the door, and you may have to start either at the bottom or in a completely different department or studio than you had originally planned. Work hard, work well, hone your skills, and again, be patient!

2. There will be times when work is slow. If a production has ended and you haven't yet secured another job, you will be unemployed. Although it will be tough, make sure you have a backup plan at the ready. Whether it's temporary employment through an agency or a former employer who can slate you in for last-minute projects, having a safety net will ease your stress.

3. Keep your portfolio updated with your strongest pieces, and make sure they're suitable for the studios you're pitching to. Most Animators keep 15 pieces, at most, in their portfolios.

ART DIRECTOR
(FILM, TELEVISION, THEATER)

CAREER PROFILE

Duties: Creates the look and mood of sets for film, television, or theater; reads scripts and works closely with wide range of staff, from directors, costume designers, and set designers to props managers, lighting crew, and others; may create or oversee storyboards; conducts research if stories are based in historic times; creates and maintains schedules, oversees staff progress to ensure deadlines are met; may create budgets for design work and staff needed; works in studios as well as on location at shoots

Alternate Title(s): Creative Director

Salary Range: $32,410 to $115,570+

Employment Prospects: Good

Advancement Prospects: Fair

Best Geographical Location(s): Major cities where television and film studios are based and theaters abound, such as Chicago, Los Angeles, Miami, New York City, San Francisco

Prerequisites:

Education or Training—B.F.A., with courses in design, illustration, painting, drawing, art history, and design software; some coursework in theater design helpful

Experience—Four to five years of experience as assistant art director or designing for theater, television, or film sets

Special Skills and Personality Traits—Able to read and interpret scripts to successfully and accurately translate into sets; decisive yet flexible; extremely creative with a strong visual sense; excellent communication skills; organized; able to work with variety of people; deadline and detail oriented; interested in history; good research abilities; budget conscious; knowledge of design and illustration software programs; energetic and able to work long hours

CAREER LADDER

```
┌─────────────────────────────────────────┐
│          Senior Art Director            │
└─────────────────────────────────────────┘

┌─────────────────────────────────────────┐
│              Art Director               │
└─────────────────────────────────────────┘

┌─────────────────────────────────────────┐
│  Assistant Art Director or Set Designer │
└─────────────────────────────────────────┘
```

Position Description

Art Directors are responsible for creating the look and feel of sets for movies, television shows, and theater productions based on scripts and storylines. Art Directors who work in television may design or oversee the design of sets for soap operas, police dramas, sitcoms, or commercials. Theater Art Directors work closely with set designers to create sets for plays, ballets, musicals, and concerts. Art Directors collaborate with and oversee a wide range of freelancers, staff members, consultants, and service providers such as scenic artists, illustrators, model makers, carpenters, painters, electricians, laborers, decorators, costume designers, and makeup and hairstyling artists.

Art Directors review scripts and visualize how things will look on camera and on screen. After reading the scripts, Art Directors typically start projects by making rough sketches, either by hand or using design or illustration software. They meet with show directors and producers to review and confirm directions before proceeding to full-color drawings. They meet with set and prop designers, costume designers, and other artists to discuss the specific settings and styles, what is expected from each person, and the deadlines. Art Directors oversee design schedules, making sure artists are following their work assignments within the allocated time frames. If the story is set in a historical period, Art Directors as well as costume and set designers are responsible for ensuring that the fashions, designs, accessories, and props are consistent with and accurate for that era. Art Directors conduct heavy research by reading books, visiting museums and art galleries, and, possibly, speaking with curators and other experts.

Art Directors who specialize in animation and technology oversee the special effects and supervise animators, 3-D model-makers and clay designers, and makeup artists. Art Directors also help directors in their work from the storyboard phase through to the actual shoot. They discuss each shot in each scene, planning the composition, frame, angle, and movement of the camera. Film and TV Art Directors often work on shoots, also, either at the studio set or on location.

Theater Art Directors oversee every aspect of stage settings and effects. They work closely with stage managers, choreographers, costume designers, set designers, prop artists, lighting crew, and others, keeping everyone on track with work assignments and deadlines as well as the original vision and interpretation of the storyline.

Salaries

In 2002, the median annual earning of Art Directors was $61,850; salaries ranged from as low as $32,410 to $115,570 or more. Art Directors who work in television and movies usually earn higher wages due to higher budgets as well as the support of their unions. While theaters tend to pay lower wages overall, theater Art Directors with years of experience and excellent reputations command higher rates.

Employment Prospects

The U.S. Department of Labor's *Career Guide to Industries* predicts a 31 percent growth rate through 2012 for overall employment in the motion picture and video industries. New programming will be needed for cable and satellite television channels in the United States and oversees. Also, the increased demand for in-home films on the Internet as well as DVDs and videos will create more opportunities in the film and video business. Employment of Art Directors will paral-

lel this growth, though competition will continue to be fierce, as the niche is small and many clamor for this type of work. Art Directors who are talented, meet deadlines, have excellent reputations, and are well connected will find employment and thrive in this field. In the entertainment business, networking and word of mouth are the crucial elements in securing employment. A slight twist to the old adage is, "It's not only *what* you know, but *who* you know." Art Directors who know who to contact, how to tailor their portfolios and resumes, and who have excellent presentation and communication skills will find the most opportunities for work.

Advancement Prospects

Because the Art Director field is small and specialized, advancement can sometimes take years. Also, in the entertainment industry, many jobs are temporary and on a project-by-project basis, making it a true challenge for Art Directors to grow their reputations and advance to higher levels. With years of experience, Art Directors can eventually advance to become lead or senior art directors. Theater Art Directors can move into film or television, and vice versa. Some can apply their experience and take on more complex projects. Art Directors can also expand their expertise by branching out into filmmaking.

Education and Training

While a four-year degree is recommended, it is not required in the art direction field. Of utmost importance are creativity, a strong visual sense, and the ability to work with a variety of people toward a shared goal. Art Directors can often get a foot in the door by starting in entry-level roles in documentary film houses or by working on educational or industrial films.

Experience, Skills, and Personality Traits

Art Directors must be creative and versatile to succeed in the entertainment field. They work with and oversee many people, and strong interpersonal skills as well as leadership abilities are needed. They must also be able to work under a great deal of pressure, juggle projects and people, and meet deadlines. Art Directors need to have a good eye for sets that will work well with the story lines and the ability to visualize designs that will engage audiences. Depending on their specialty, Art Directors must have not only theater set design experience but strong knowledge of television, movie, and/or theater history and technique as well.

Unions and Associations

Art Directors in the entertainment industry are usually required to be union members. Film, television, and theater companies may hire nonunion Art Directors who have certain specializations and are known in the field, but more often than not, Art Directors belong to unions. This helps them secure work and decent wages. Typically, Art Directors are members of the Art Directors Guild, Local 800, a part of the International Alliance of Theatrical Stage Employees, Moving Picture Technicians, Artists and Allied Crafts (IATSE), or the United Scenic Artists Association.

Tips for Entry

1. Internships are an excellent way to get in on the ground floor. The career ladder for Art Directors in the entertainment field isn't a straight line; many move freely between theater, television, and design studios. An internship provides the best opportunity to see firsthand how things work and what interests you most while learning valuable on-the-job skills.

2. Stay tuned to what's going on in the industry. Read not only the arts section of newspapers, but the business section also. Read trade publications such as *Backstage*. Watch the television shows and stage productions that most interest you. Take notes on what works and what doesn't. Challenge yourself to create sets that can improve the look and best portray the stories and characters.

3. You can see which film and television shoots are coming to your city by visiting the Web site of the film department of your city's mayor's office. Production companies are required to secure permits and licenses when they shoot on location in cities. Mayors' offices typically list upcoming television, film, and commercial shoots and job opportunities on their Web sites. If you don't know the specific URL of your city's mayor's office, you can always use a search engine, such as Google, to find it. Key in the name of your city, then "mayor's office film department."

COSTUME DESIGNER

CAREER PROFILE

Duties: Researches and designs costumes for theater, film, and television; reads scripts and researches costumes if production is historically based; works closely with artistic directors, producers, technical managers, lighting designers, and set designers; chooses materials, fabrics, and colors for costumes; handles and chooses bids from costume shops; may assign and oversee tailoring of clothes; creates and presents budgets; invoices clients; handles administrative tasks necessary to run own business

Alternate Title(s): Theatrical Designer

Salary Range: $25,350 to $105,280+

Employment Prospects: Fair

Advancement Prospects: Fair

Best Geographical Location(s): Major cities (Chicago, Hollywood, Los Angeles, New York, Philadelphia, San Francisco)

Prerequisites:

Education or Training—B.F.A. in costume design or fashion design; courses in sewing and art history recommended; small-business management classes helpful

Experience—Three to five years of experience designing clothes or costumes recommended; background in theater, television, or film helpful

Special Skills and Personality Traits—Strong design and dressmaking skills; creative; knowledgeable about materials, fashion history, and art history; excellent communication and research skills; solid hand-eye coordination; deadline oriented; strong interpersonal abilities

CAREER LADDER

```
┌─────────────────────────────────┐
│   Chief Costume Designer or      │
│       Creative Director          │
└─────────────────────────────────┘

┌─────────────────────────────────┐
│        Costume Designer          │
└─────────────────────────────────┘

┌─────────────────────────────────┐
│   Assistant Costume Designer     │
└─────────────────────────────────┘
```

Position Description

A character's costume is the first impression audiences have before the lines are spoken. A Costume Designer plays a key role in helping production companies successfully tell stories and make impressions about actors and performers with their attire. Costume Designers create costumes for movies, plays, operas, musicals, concerts, dance productions, television programs, parades, masquerade balls, sporting events, and more. They can work for small local theaters, regional production houses, or large production

companies and networks. They work closely with producers, creative directors, lighting, set, and technical managers to discuss and decide the creative direction for shows.

Costume Designers read scripts and make notes about scenes for costume details. They keep an eye on such details as events (e.g., black-tie dinner party, lunch date in a small-town diner, etc.), characters (e.g., ages, fashion styles), seasons and geographical locations, years in which the production is based, and cultural influences. For instance, if the production is a period piece, they need to conduct thorough research to make sure that the costumes are historically accurate. They meet with lighting, set designers, and technical directors to learn the specific lights and colors that will be used, how and when specific characters will be lit, the details about the scenery, and any other technical aspects of the production in order to determine the fabrics and colors that will work best.

Costume Designers are responsible for choosing fabrics, materials, and accessories for costumes. They often adapt costumes to enhance a performer's physical assets or to camouflage certain flaws that may distract from the performer's character. Costume Designers often sketch designs by hand and bring the rough sketches as well as samples of fabrics and garments to meetings and for try-on sessions. After they sketch the designs, they create lists of the items needed and cost estimates to present to appropriate production executives for approval. They also present budgets to various costume shops, which in turn bid on the projects. Costume Designers hire dressmakers and tailors and oversee sewing and fitting sessions with cast members.

Costume Designers are responsible for invoicing their clients, maintaining their design and business equipment and tools, managing their office, hiring and overseeing staff, and all other duties related to small business ownership.

Salaries

Costume Designers can earn salaries ranging from $25,350 to more than $105,280, depending on years of experience and type of production (e.g., stage concert, off-Broadway, Broadway, film, television). Costume Designers are often paid per production. While entry-level designers may receive about $500 per production, experienced and renowned designers can be compensated as much as $100,000 or more. Costume Designers who work in film usually receive higher salaries and weekly paychecks. Those who work in theater are typically paid a flat fee as opposed to a regular paycheck. Most Costume Designers are expected to belong to unions, and it is those unions that help determine the fees.

Employment Prospects

Employment of designers overall is expected to grow by about 10 to 20 percent through 2012, which is about as fast as the average. Competition for Costume Designer positions will be keen, however, as the niche is small and many people are attracted to the entertainment field. Most theater production companies, which are typically based in New York and other large cities, are seasonal and offer more employment opportunities in the fall and spring. Regional theaters tend to offer more year-round shows and may provide greater opportunity for steady costume design work. Costume Designers can also secure work in film, television, and video. Work for larger productions will be based, for the most part, in Los Angeles and New York, although many studios can be found across the country. Independent film and TV production company growth may also spark an increased need for Costume Designers.

Advancement Prospects

Depending on years of experience, talent, and reputation, Costume Designers can advance to work in larger, well-known theaters, move from off-Broadway to Broadway, or transfer their skills from theater to film or television. If they work with larger, more structured theatrical departments, they can advance to become chief Costumer Designers or creative directors. They may also lecture and write about the costume design field.

Education and Training

Most Costume Designers have a four-year degree in costume design or fashion. Courses in sewing are helpful, particularly when overseeing dressmakers and tailors and if last minute changes need to be made. Because many Costume Designers are freelance, coursework in small business management is also beneficial.

Experience, Skills, and Personality Traits

Several years of experience as an assistant Costume Designer is usually required in this field. On-set experience may also be required if working in film, television, or video. Costume Designers must be interested in film and theater to enjoy and be successful in their work. They need great creativity, excellent design and drawing skills, and a solid knowledge of fabrics, textures, colors, and styles. They also need to know costume shops and service providers. They must know how to read scripts and how to match appropriate costumes to characters, scenes, and time frames. Many costumes must be related to the era in which the story line is based, so Costume Designers need a strong appreciation and understanding of history. They must also have solid research skills and know where to find information about clothing and accessories from certain time frames. The entertainment field is highly pressurized, and Costume Designers must be able to work creatively and quickly to deliver quality costumes on time. If working in larger productions, Costume Designers may be expected to manage a creative staff and therefore must have strong management and leadership skills, as well as the ability to juggle projects. They also must be budget conscious when creating designs and choosing materials.

Unions and Associations

Theatrical Costume Designers can apply for membership to the Costume Designers Guild, Local 892, of the International Alliance of Theatrical and Stage Employees (IATSE).

Membership requirements are one screen credit and a presentation before the guild's membership committee. Membership benefits include contract negotiations, educational publications and resources, networking opportunities, and discounts on industry-related services. Many Costume Designers also belong to United Scenic Artists, Local 829, for contract negotiation help, educational resources, group health insurance, and discounts on various services.

Tips for Entry

1. Make sure your portfolio includes your best and most current design work. Have both a print portfolio and you work in electronic file format (PDF) so that you can provide your prospective employer format options.
2. Costume design is a highly competitive field. Be patient when you're job hunting, and be prepared to start at the bottom of the ladder. Keep an open mind. If you know the names of the Costume Designers you would like to work with and learn from, make a list and call them. See if you can apprentice with them for free, if you must. Do whatever it takes that is reasonable and feasible for you to get your foot in the door.
3. Never turn work down, especially when you're just starting out. The more work you do, the more people will see your work, and the more references you'll receive. It's especially important because of the intense competition in and cyclical nature of this field. Keep working as much as possible!
4. If you haven't yet gone to school, choose one where you'll meet like-minded directors, producers, artists, and actors. This will be your base community for networking for future work.

DIGITAL ANIMATOR

CAREER PROFILE

Duties: Works closely with producers, art directors, and creative director on film and television projects, Web sites, CD-ROMs, and more; uses design software to create animated images or special effects; chooses images, graphics, and colors and weaves them together to create 2-D (two-dimensional) or 3-D (three-dimensional) animations; may hand sketch, paint, and/or mold models

Alternate Title(s): Animator

Salary Range: $25,830 to $85,160+

Employment Prospects: Good

Advancement Prospects: Good

Best Geographical Location(s): Major cities such as New York City and Los Angeles

Prerequisites:

Education or Training—B.F.A. with specialization in animation; coursework in design software, illustration, painting, typography, and design history recommended

Experience—Several years of internship experience in television or film; several years of graphic design experience recommended; illustration background helpful; thorough knowledge of design software critical

Special Skills and Personality Traits—Creative, independent thinker; may need to have team-player and interpersonal skills (depending on organization's staff size, structure, and approach to business); strong design software skills and computer savvy; solid knowledge of typography and color; good understanding of and eye for motion and movement; illustration and painting skills; flexible; deadline oriented

CAREER LADDER

```
┌─────────────────────────────────────┐
│         Creative Director           │
└─────────────────────────────────────┘

┌─────────────────────────────────────┐
│   Digital Animator (2-D or 3-D)     │
└─────────────────────────────────────┘

┌─────────────────────────────────────┐
│         Graphic Designer            │
│     (commercial advertising)        │
└─────────────────────────────────────┘
```

Position Description

Digital Animators add dimension, color, and movement to designs, photographs, images, typography, and more. They work with a variety of media clients, ranging from film and video production to Web sites and CD-ROM. Animators who work for television programs, film and video production companies, advertising agencies, and other related businesses work closely with producers and creative and art directors to discuss the programs and decide upon the elements to pull from the show to highlight in the visual message. They may also work on teams with photographers, copywriters, account executives, and printers. Their mission is to draw the viewer in with appealing images that catch the eye and best represent the show.

Digital Animators create animations by creating "cells," or pictures that, when put together in sequential order, appear to be animated. Other Digital Animators use design software and animation programs such as Adobe PhotoShop, Maya, and Macromedia's Director in their work. Television news Digital Animators often receive lists of written instructions, or work orders, for animation from producers and/or creative directors. They must then decipher and translate these instructions into animation that fits the request. They may create the charts used for financial reports, choosing the colors and the symbols, or they may weave graphic design and special effects throughout a series of photos and images to create such things as animated show openers.

Because technology is constantly improving, Digital Animators must stay on top of their game by regularly reading industry magazines and visiting Web sites, such as http://www.designinmotion.com. Successful Digital Animators need to keep abreast of new developments in the industry, the latest trends in animation, and news about animation software technology itself.

Salaries

Freelance Animators can expect to earn salaries ranging from about $25,830 to $85,160 or more. According to the U.S. Department of Labor's *Occupational Outlook Handbook (OOH),* animators and other multimedia artists earned median annual salaries of about $43,980 in 2002. Most Digital Animators charge hourly rates based on their years of experience as well as their software specialty. For example, one industry expert notes that while Digital Animators who work specifically with After Effects may charge approximately $50 per hour, those who use more expensive machinery such as PaintBox may charge from $80 to $150 per hour.

Employment Prospects

While employment prospects for artists in general are expected to increase through 2012 about as fast as the average, according to the *OOH,* animators and multimedia artists may fair slightly better. The *OOH* foresees a 40.1 percent increase in opportunities to meet the growing demand for printed or electronic media as well as the growth in motion picture and video industries. Competition will be keen, because these are considered "glamour" jobs, and people clamor to secure them. Only those Digital Animators with internships in relevant fields and top companies and exceptional graphic-design, illustration, typography, and computer-software skills will stand out in the crowd.

Advancement Prospects

Depending on their talent and business acumen, Digital Animators with anywhere from five to 10 or more years of experience can advance to become creative directors or art directors. Digital Animators can always move on to other areas of animation and expand their fields of expertise. Some may choose to become independent film producers or own their own animation companies.

Education and Training

To break into the animation field, an animator must have a bachelor's degree in fine art, with a specialization in animation or television graphics. Some organizations may even require a master's degree. Coursework in and strong knowledge of graphic design, color, typography, illustration, and painting are highly recommended. While animators are always learning on the job and honing their skills, it's still key to have a repertoire of software design programs (for both Mac and PC) under your belt before pitching reels and portfolios. Some useful programs to know include After Effects (3-D), Maya (3-D), Adobe Photoshop and Illustrator (2-D), Vizrt, and Liberty. Many Digital Animators also get a foot in the door by interning at the networks and shows they're most interested in working with.

Experience, Skills, and Personality Traits

Digital Animators must be highly creative and fluent in design software. Depending on their area of focus, they need varying degrees of illustration and/or painting skills, both traditionally as well as with a computer. Some Digital Animators may also need to have hand sculpting and model-making abilities. All animators should have strong color awareness, a solid knowledge of typography, and a good sense of motion and movement. If working on a team, they must be flexible, communicative, and able to share ideas. Most challenging may be that they must also stay creative (and calm) under deadline pressure. Film and television animators must also be deadline oriented and open to suggestions if work needs alteration.

Unions and Associations

The Broadcast Designers Association (PROMAX & BDA, http://www.bda.tv) provides animators, designers, producers, and others who work in television, radio, and digital media with educational resources, national and international conferences, employment opportunities, and more. The Animated Film Association (ASIFA, Association Internationale du Film d'Animation) offers such membership benefits as monthly newsletters, screenings, and links to international events such as animation festivals and seminars. Digital Animators can also join the American Institute of Graphic Arts (AIGA) for networking opportunities and educational and professional support and resources.

Tips for Entry

1. Be persistent. The animation field is highly competitive; to find work, you'll need determination, perseverance, and a thick skin.
2. Whatever medium you plan to animate for, get as much internship experience as you possibly can in

diverse organizations. For instance, if you're aiming to be an animator for TV, intern at as many TV networks as you can.

3. Create a strong portfolio, and make sure you include examples that show you understand typography.

4. You'll also need to create a reel for your job hunt. Keep your reel between two and three minutes long, and put only your best work on it. Prospective employers don't have the time to watch long reels, and the first images will have the most impact.

5. Once you have your reel completed, create a list of the production companies you'd like to work for, call or email them, and see if you can set up meetings to show your reel.

PRODUCTION DESIGNER

CAREER PROFILE

Duties: Works with director and producer to draft overall vision of film or television project; manages staff of creative professionals to realize this vision; manages expenditures within a set budget

Alternate Title(s): Art Director (in years past)

Salary Range: $100,000 to $500,000+

Employment Prospects: Poor to Fair

Advancement Prospects: Poor

Best Geographical Location(s): New York City and Los Angeles

Prerequisites:

Education or Training—Bachelor of fine arts or arts and sciences

Experience—Five to 10 years as creative professional in film/television

Special Skills and Personality Traits—Ability to communicate visually, verbally, and in writing; self-motivation; ability to manage tight deadlines and stress; dramatic imagination; affinity for reading scripts and distilling them into visual concepts

CAREER LADDER

```
┌─────────────────────────────────────┐
│        Production Designer           │
└─────────────────────────────────────┘

┌─────────────────────────────────────┐
│   Set Designer/Costume Designer      │
└─────────────────────────────────────┘

┌─────────────────────────────────────┐
│  Draftsman/Set Dresser/Prop Assistant│
└─────────────────────────────────────┘
```

Position Description

Production Designers have very important jobs in the film and television industry. They are responsible for determining the overall visual look of a film, including oversight of all sets, locations, and costume design. While this vision ultimately becomes a collaboration between producer, director, and Production Designer—and the scores of creative professionals who support each of them—the Production Designer drafts the look, composes the designs, and oversees their execution.

Once a Production Designer is picked for a project, a conference takes place among him or her, the director and the producer of the project. At this meeting, the team goes over the script at hand, and some preliminary talk is had about the overall visual "feel" of the project. From there, the Production Designer takes the script, does careful study of the settings described, and researches any and all materials required to pull off whatever illusion is necessary. For instance, if the script calls for a contemporary setting with flashbacks to a specific period, the Production Designer needs to reference architectural, clothing, and popular culture styles of the time described.

At this early stage, the Production Designer also begins to plot location settings. He or she begins to weigh cost considerations, roughly gauging what the savings would be between building sets and visiting a locale (factoring in such expenses as travel, location fees, boarding for actors and crew, etc.). For instance, a project that calls for extensive shooting in an outdoor setting and very limited interiors would likely be a project for which sets would be constructed for the interior shots and a trip to Vancouver scheduled for the film crew.

After careful consideration of all visual elements called for by the script, the Production Designer begins the process of composing images and hiring an art staff. This art staff includes draftsmen to execute finished sketches of the rough ideas proposed by the Production Designer, a costume designer (who will hire a staff of craftsmen dedicated to sourcing or constructing costumes), a set designer (who will hire a staff of craftsmen dedicated to building and decorating sets), and a prop manager (who will hire a staff of craftsmen dedicated to sourcing and constructing props used by the actors). In addition to considering the hiring of staffs, careful attention is paid at this point to the outside vendors required. For instance, if there are any special effects shots needed to pull off a particular scene or location photographers to shoot scene-setting material, the Production Designer puts this into the mix at this time. Additionally, a bookkeeper comes on board to start tracking the expenditure of funds allocated to the project. This bookkeeper becomes a vital partner to the Production Designer throughout the shoot; keeping tabs on how money gets spent is a vital aspect of making a project, especially toward the end, when the budget starts to stretch thin.

Once this rough draft begins, the Production Designer meets again with the director and producer to discuss progress and set budgets. After all parameters have been set and design directions approved, final execution of the Production Designer's vision begins. He or she will be on set at the beginning of each scene to make sure the sets, costumes, and props are all in keeping with what was conceived and then move on to oversee the construction of materials for the scene shooting next. In the meantime, a staffer who reports either directly to the Production Designer or to one of his or her direct reports (e.g., costume designer) stays with the shoot to ensure props, costumes, and sets all stay consistent.

An additional aspect of the job is working with vendors. Those creative professionals or agencies that supply special effects or photographs for backdrops or even stock reels of scene setting fall under the purview of the Production Designer. He or she scouts locations and is be present if the project calls for location photography, and he or she works directly with the special effects vendors to ensure that the effects provided fit within the overall scheme of the project's visuals.

Salaries

The range of salaries for Production Designers varies widely due to a great many factors, first among them one's workload in any given year. Production Designers are not salaried employees but rather work on a project-by-project basis. Production Designers who find themselves working on films that wrap rapidly can find themselves taking on more projects, thereby earning higher incomes in any given year.

Another important factor that determines one's fees is experience and reputation within the business. A Production Designer with a proven track record of working on large motion pictures for major studios commands very large salaries (exact numbers on these aren't available, but the range was given by several interviewees as being between $300,000 and $1,000,000). These positions are extremely rare, and the chances of arriving at such a lofty height are akin to hitting the lottery.

The type of project on which one works is another key component in determining income. Big budget studio motion pictures that rely heavily on the visual aspects of the product pay considerably higher than television originals. Additionally, works completed for not-for-profit organizations have lower pay scales. Minimum standards for these project fees have been set by the United Scenic Artists Union (USAU) and begin at $1,000 a day at the low end.

This brings up nonunion or independent projects. Ironically, independent films have become a rather mainstream commodity in recent years, and these are often completed outside of union oversight. As expected, the protections afforded by union projects don't exist and as such, they have a case-by-case nature. In many scenarios, prospective Production Designers who are trying to break into the position will take work of this sort for relatively little pay to earn the credit.

Employment Prospects

This is a tough area to enter. As with any high position in the filmmaking business, there are far more applicants for jobs than jobs available. Hard statistics on the number of Production Designers working in the United States are difficult to nail down for several reasons: The U.S. Department of Labor (DOL) does not give them a specific category (actors, directors, and producers are even lumped into a single category); statistics reported in its *Occupational Outlook Handbook* are lower than the U.S. DOL estimates for executive-level creative positions, as many are between projects in any given year; and the number of Production Designers working on nonunion projects makes it impossible for even the USAU to track.

That stated, however, every interviewee answering questionnaires and providing time for interviews for this volume brought up the dearth of openings compared to the number of qualified applicants and hopefuls. As one Production Designer who also taught at Carnegie Mellon for decades put it, "Nearly every set dresser and draftsman already working in film aspires to the top job, not to mention all the qualified students who graduate every year." Competition runs high in the film industry, and it only stiffens as one seeks the higher echelons.

Advancement Prospects

Anyone working at the level of Production Designer has pretty much reached the pinnacle of the profession. For professional visual artists, this is the top rung on the ladder. One can advance in this position, however, by working on higher-profile projects.

Many of the key factors that lead to advancement within this job are within one's own control: being easy to work with and running a very efficient workflow, having a sharp eye for talent when it comes to hiring a creative team, paying strict attention to detail, and continually sharpening one's creative edge. Two of the main components are not within one's own control, sadly, and they can loom large in one's prospects for advancement toward larger projects and fees: luck (getting in good with a director and/or production company on the rise), and timing (working on a project that somehow captures a great deal of public attention).

Education and Training

One cannot understate the benefits of earning at least a bachelor's degree in set or costume design in seeking employment as a Production Designer. Not only does one acquire the skill to manage one's time and deadlines by juggling a full-time course load, but there are other benefits. First, a well-rounded education primes the potential Production Designer to solve problems involving research specific to a particular project. For instance, survey courses in history come in handy when a film project calls for period authenticity.

Second, many of the professors teaching these courses are practicing professionals and can offer very specialized instruction on the nuts and bolts of performing this job. Additionally, when it comes time for these professors to staff their creative teams when working on a project, it's not uncommon for undergraduate students to find entry-level employment opportunities on the professor's projects.

Finally, alumni networks go a long way toward getting graduates of a particular program started in the business. A graduate of New York University's film school stands a good chance of landing work on a project headed by another alum. After all, a working Production Designer looking to fill out his or her staff knows what kind of education the entry-level worker has gotten and often comes with recommendations from professors he or she knows.

Experience, Skills, and Personality Traits

As with any collaborative effort, the more open the lines of communication are, the greater the chances for a successful

project. This goes double for film projects, as so many sets of hands go into making the final product. Production Designers have to communicate with a great many people and perform this task at a very high level, both in speech and writing.

Production Designers must be able to read film scripts, distill them down to visual imagery, and compose an overall mood for the project through the composition of special effects, sets, locations, props, and costumes. They must then work with the various creative professionals on the art staff to oversee the realization of this vision. To this end, the Production Designer must have highly developed draftsmanship skills in addition to verbal skill. Additionally, it's becoming more and more critical for Production Designers to have a grasp of computer imaging programs such as Adobe Photoshop, Adobe Illustrator, Final Cut Pro, and Maya. Management skills must also be very keen to oversee a large team of creative professionals.

Unions and Associations

The United Scenic Artists Union sets minimum standards for Production Designers' earnings and working conditions, and provides medical benefits through a group plan. It also provides a resource for resolving grievances with employers. While membership in this union is not mandatory, given the popularity of independent films, it is highly advisable. The vast majority of major film and television projects are union jobs, and one must be a union employee to work on them.

Tips for Entry

1. Attend a college with a very well-developed and highly regarded theatrical department, and stay in touch with your peers and faculty after graduation.
2. Work on films while in college to build a body of work and list of credits.
3. Take positions on independent films or lesser-paying films that move you vertically up the ladder in title and responsibility level.
4. Network. In few places in the visual art world is the need to be friendly with a lot of people more important.

SET DESIGNER

CAREER PROFILE

Duties: Designs sets for movies, television shows, plays, musicals, concerts, and other forms of stage entertainment; reads scripts; if historical productions, researches materials, construction, and design for accurate portrayals; creates models of sets; oversees set construction; works closely with directors, lighting designers, carpenters, prop masters, and costume designers; delegates work to and manages staff; may create budgets

Alternate Title(s): Theatrical Designer

Salary Range: $17,830 to $63,280+

Employment Prospects: Good

Advancement Prospects: Good

Best Geographical Location(s): Major cities for major networks (e.g., New York, Los Angeles); anywhere in the country for local and regional production work

Prerequisites:

Education or Training—Four-year degree in theater design recommended; M.F.A. in set design helpful

Experience—One- to two-year internship in theater, television, or film recommended

Special Skills and Personality Traits—Creative; excellent eye for composition, color, and balance; strong research, design, and drawing skills; deadline oriented; strong interpersonal skills; management and leadership abilities; knowledge of set-building materials and construction techniques; solid knowledge of Adobe Photoshop, Illustrator, and AutoCAD

CAREER LADDER

```
┌─────────────────────────────┐
│      Artistic Director       │
└─────────────────────────────┘

┌─────────────────────────────┐
│        Set Designer          │
└─────────────────────────────┘

┌─────────────────────────────┐
│    Assistant Set Designer    │
└─────────────────────────────┘
```

Position Description

Set Designers create the sets, or environments, for plays, movies, musicals, television shows, concerts, and other forms of stage entertainment for audiences. They work closely with directors to conceive the visual styles, color schemes, materials, and designs that will help set the mood for viewers. They play a pivotal role in laying the foundation for a viewer's experience of the story and characters and draw upon their rich knowledge of history, painting, architecture, engineering, and literature in their set design work.

Set Designers first read scripts and then create rough sketches, usually by hand in black and white or color, of the sets for each scene or act within the show. If the production is based in a certain time in history, they research that era to ensure that designs and building materials are accurate and consistent. They take a lot into account in their drawings and have to keep a variety of perspectives and technical details in mind. They typically include ground plans, elevations representing the audience's view, cross sections of walls or set units, center-stage cross sections, and possibly more, depending on the production house's set design requirements.

Once the director approves the sketches, Set Designers create sketch models based on input from production directors, writers, actors, light technicians, costume designers, and other technical and creative staff. They may initially sketch the model by using pencil on white board, then move on to create larger scale models will texture and color for use in rehearsals. After they receive final approval, Set Designers then oversee the construction of the set, making sure that the materials that are delivered are accurate and that the builders, carpenters, lighting and sound technicians, and all others involved are working according to specifications and deadlines.

Salaries

Salaries for Set Designers can range from as low as $17,830 to more than $63,280, depending on years of experience, union status, and the budget of the production house. With more than five years of experience and union status, Set Designers can expect to earn higher salaries. Major film and television companies and Broadway productions tend to pay higher salaries.

Employment Prospects

Like many jobs in the entertainment business, it takes a while for new Set Designers to establish themselves and gain recognition for their work. A Set Designer just entering the field will find the job hunt challenging and highly competitive. Set design is a small, specialized niche, and more people are clamoring to get into it than there are jobs to fill. In the beginning, a four-year degree in technical theater or film design might give a Set Designer the extra edge he or she needs to land jobs and start adding firsthand experience to the resume. Los Angeles and New York are the hubs for big-name production houses, though Set Designers can find work in smaller theaters and studios throughout the country. Set Designers may also find work in production firms that specialize in set conception and construction.

Advancement Prospects

Set Designers with three to five years of experience in small theater companies can advance by working for larger production houses; this may mean moving from local theater to regional or national projects. Depending on their interests and talents, Set Designers can also transition to become directors or stage managers or even open their own production houses. Other skill-expanding steps can be teaching, lecturing, and writing.

Education and Training

While it is not required, a four-year degree in technical theater or film design can give Set Designers an advantage. Designers who choose to work in academia, however, will be required to have a graduate degree in set or theater design. Many Set Designers gain valuable set-building skills when first starting out in local theater productions or while working on low-budget films. Set Designers must know Adobe Photoshop and Illustrator. A working knowledge of computer-aided design (CAD) software and previsual software programs (which provide directors with a 3-D tour of the set) is also recommended.

Experience, Skills, and Personality Traits

Set Designers must have an exceptional eye for composition, perspective, and style. They must have solid manual and computer drafting skills and be able to draw and sketch using everything from charcoals to oils. Set Designers work closely and regularly with a range of staff, freelancers, and consultants. Their ability to interact with people on all different levels helps them achieve their goals as well as secure a reputation in the business for being a professional who is an excellent team player. Getting gigs in this field is not easy, and word of mouth can make or break a career. To succeed, Set Designers must have a combination of technical, artistic, creative, and people skills. Set Designers must be able to stay calm and creative under deadline pressure. No easy task! They need to know how to prioritize their own work and time while simultaneously delegating work to staff and overseeing their projects. The ability to stay focused and meet deadlines will frequently come in handy.

Unions and Associations

Many production houses require Set Designers to be union members. Set Designers with union cards may also be able to secure higher wages and fairer treatment. United Scenic Artists, Local 829, provides theater, television, and film designers and other related workers with labor representation, contract negotiation help, educational resources, group health insurance, and discounts on various services.

Tips for Entry

1. Say yes to all theater- and entertainment-related work, regardless of whether it's a design job or not. When you are just starting out, you need to work as much as possible to get your name out there and make connections. And wherever you work and at whatever level, absorb everything. Ask lots of questions. This is your chance to learn by observation.

2. If you're going to school for set design, be sure you learn other skills, also. Theaters, like many organizations these days, are leaning more toward hiring designers who are capable of crossing into other creative disciplines. You will increase your marketability by having lighting and technical skills under your belt and on your resume.

3. AutoCAD is important and helpful in this field. If you don't know it yet, sign up for a class, and make sure you have a working knowledge of it.

4. Wherever you work, be professional and flexible. The entertainment business bases much of its hiring practices on references, so word of mouth plays an important role in the Set Designer job hunt. It's a smaller world than you realize, and how you conduct yourself can dictate your career. Your reputation is important, so do everything you can to make yours stellar.

STORYBOARD ARTIST

CAREER PROFILE

Duties: Reads and interprets scripts by illustrating stories in visual sequences; works with such clients as advertising agencies, sales promotion houses, film and video production companies, and other related business; draws, sketches, and paints by hand and with illustration software

Alternate Title(s): Production Illustrator

Salary Range: $20,000 to $100,000+

Employment Prospects: Fair

Advancement Prospects: Fair

Best Geographic Location(s): New York City, Los Angeles, and other major cities

Prerequisites:

Education or Training—B.F.A. in illustration, film, cartooning, or related disciplines; coursework in advertising may be helpful; training in illustration software beneficial

Experience—One to three years of experience as assistant or intern in advertising agency, publishing firm, television network, or video or film production company

Special Skills and Personality Traits—Excellent illustration skills; ability to draw realistically; deadline oriented; must work well and quickly under pressure; team player; visual problem solver; flexible; patient

CAREER LADDER

```
┌─────────────────────────────┐
│      Creative Director       │
└─────────────────────────────┘

┌─────────────────────────────┐
│      Storyboard Artist       │
└─────────────────────────────┘

┌─────────────────────────────┐
│  Assistant Storyboard Artist │
└─────────────────────────────┘
```

Position Description

When advertising agencies are planning television commercials, or when film and video production companies are in the early stages of preproduction on movies, documentaries, public services announcements, or other films or videos, they often hire Storyboard Artists. Storyboard Artists read scripts then meet with various creative directors and producers to decide how best to tell the story visually. They interpret scripts visually by illustrating the stories frame-by-frame, much like comic strips. The "strips" in this art discipline, however, are known as "storyboards." And while the comic strip guides the reader, the sequence of the storyboard helps film and video directors figure out the best ways to map out scene details and angles to shoot from. Storyboards also help ensure continuity between shots. If a character has black hair in the first frame (or shot), the Storyboard Artist

makes sure the character has black hair in the final frame (unless, that is, the story line is about changing haircolor). Storyboards help creative directors see the movie from beginning to end, before they invest time, labor, and, most important, money into film and shooting. They can make changes in the storyboards easily. Storyboards also help special effects artists and other creative consultants working on the project understand the approach they should take in their work to match the creative director's vision.

This kind of work often requires a quick turnaround, sometimes even drawing and turning in sketches on the spot amidst meetings and pitches. Storyboard Artists create fast black-and-white sketches using pencils, pens, or markers on paper. They incorporate details and directions from the creative directors and producers. They work sequence by sequence, getting approval each step of the way before moving on to the next shot and the next scene. To facilitate changes, a growing number of Storyboard Artists are using software design programs, such as Adobe Photoshop, to illustrate their work.

Storyboard Artists either self-promote through direct mail, the Internet, and networking or by hiring a representative. Having representation is not critical, but it frees Storyboard Artists to devote more time to being creative. Independent Storyboard Artists without representation manage all administrative aspects of their businesses, from bookkeeping to maintaining office equipment and supplies, unless they hire consultants. They handle the promotion and marketing of their work, as well as creating their own brand image, complete with logo, business card, letterhead, and Web site.

Salaries

Storyboard Artists can earn annual incomes ranging from $20,000 to $100,000 or more, depending on the project, the client, and their years of experience in the field. According to the U.S. Department of Labor's *Occupational Outlook Handbook (OOH)*, artists working in motion picture and video industries earned median annual salaries of $58,840 in 2002. Storyboard Artists who are established in their fields and those with representation earn higher salaries.

Employment Prospects

Employment of artists overall is expected to grow by only about 10 to 20 percent through 2012, according to the *OOH*. The Storyboard Artist field is highly competitive, but predicted motion picture and video industry growth may open new opportunities to illustrators and other artists in the years to come. Storyboard Artists can increase their marketability by learning and enhancing their computer design software skills.

Advancement Prospects

Independent Storyboard Artists can advance by becoming creative directors at film or video production companies. They can also enhance their brand images and change how they spend their workday by increasing their staff and delegating administrative tasks. They may also improve their work experience and their salary levels by having representation.

Education and Training

A B.F.A. in illustration, film, cartooning, or related disciplines is the minimum requirement for Storyboard Artists. Many take courses in computer illustration software, such as Adobe Photoshop, or teach themselves through training manuals and online support. Depending on the area of focus, Storyboard Artists would do well to take courses in advertising, film, video, or documentary production.

Experience, Skills, and Personality Traits

One to three years of experience as an intern in an advertising agency, publishing firm, television network, or film or video production company is recommended. Several years of full-time or freelance work experience as an apprentice or assistant Storyboard Artist is extremely beneficial. Storyboard Artists must be fast, creative visualizers. Clients depend upon them to create the foundations for their projects. There is often tremendous stress and deadline pressure in this field, so Storyboard Artists must know how to stay professional and unflappable, yet still deliver the artwork as requested and to the clients' specifications. Changes to the artwork will be frequently requested, so flexibility, patience, and strong communication skills help. Storyboard Artists must have excellent illustration skills and be able to work both independently and on teams. Computer savvy and knowledge of illustration software programs are becoming increasingly important in this area.

Unions and Associations

Storyboard Artists can join such organizations as the Graphic Artists Guild and the Society of Illustrators for networking opportunities and professional support and resources. Storyboard Artists specializing in television and film can join such unions as the International Alliance of Theatrical Stage Employees, Moving Picture Technicians, and Artists and Allied Crafts of the United States and Canada (IATSE) for contract negotiations and professional support.

Tips for Entry

1. Be persistent and patient. This is an extremely competitive field. If you really want to break into it, hone your skills, network as much as you can, and get a portfolio together of your best work.
2. Whatever medium you plan to work in, whether it's documentaries or commercials, spend as much time as you can watching and absorbing that medium so that you can learn the types of shots that are being used.
3. Sketch as much as you can in your free time. Keep a sketchbook and take it with you wherever you go. Practice making fast sketches of park scenes, train commutes, and other daily life experiences.

MAKEUP ARTIST

CAREER PROFILE

Duties: Using various cosmetics, prepares people's faces for public appearances; may also prepare wigs, hair pieces, and/or special effects; may specialize in celebrities (e.g., politicians, television actors, theater performers, models, musicians, etc.), may specialize in weddings (e.g., brides, bridesmaids), or may help ready people for special events (e.g., conferences, photo shoots, dinners, etc.); analyzes skin, complexion, eye color, and hair and chooses makeup textures, colors, and combinations to enhance or change individual's features and translate best to the medium used (photography, film, theater stage, etc.); discusses makeup preferences with client; may work directly with individual, through a salon, or be commissioned by an agency for a particular project; purchases and maintains makeup, applicators, cleaners, lights, and carrying cases; handles invoicing and accounts payable and receivable; responsible for self-promotion and networking for business

Alternate Title(s): Cosmetologist, Stylist

Salary Range: $20,000 to $100,000+

Employment Prospects: Good

Advancement Prospects: Good

Best Geographical Location(s): Major urban areas (particularly if working in entertainment field); smaller cities (for local entertainment, conferences, weddings, events, etc.)

Prerequisites:

Education or Training—Certified by cosmetology school; state licensed (requirements vary by state); four-year degree not required but may be helpful; business classes recommended

Experience—Three to five years of experience as apprentice or assistant in a salon; some experience in department store also useful

Special Skills and Personality Traits—Creative; personable; extremely comfortable with people; confident; knowledgeable about cosmetics, applications, and fashion trends; organized; clean; steady hands

CAREER LADDER

Salon or Agency Owner

Makeup Artist

Apprentice or Assistant Makeup Artist

Position Description

Makeup Artists help enhance or transform a person's appearance with cosmetics. They work either directly with a client or they are commissioned by an agency or salon to perform cosmetic services for different types of projects. If they work directly with a client, they work either at that client's home or place of business or at their own salon. If commissioned, they may find themselves working with models behind the scenes of a fashion show, at a movie shoot making up actors, or even on the road transforming musicians for concerts.

Makeup Artists who work directly with clients have a greater ability to express themselves creatively than do those commissioned by agencies for specific projects. Often with such projects as fashion shows and film shoots, the agency wants the models to look a specific way, and it's up to the Makeup Artist to follow the rules to a certain degree and adhere to that look. When working independently with individual clients, however, the Makeup Artist has more choices. He or she first speaks with the client to find out what the client likes and dislikes about makeup and what features the client would like to enhance. The Makeup Artist analyzes the client's face and preferences and makes recommendations. The Makeup Artist chooses the makeup and application, and as he or she applies the makeup, tells the client what he or she is doing to engage the client as well as keep the client at ease with what is being done.

Applying makeup requires confidence, a deft touch, a sensitivity to people, and an ability to have a vision for the client's final appearance and the tools to realize that vision. Unlike a canvas oil painting, the final product is a human being who is quite capable of telling you that he or she either loves what you have done or wants changes to what you have done. To get a better idea of what the client prefers, Makeup Artists sometimes ask clients to bring pictures of celebrities or people whose makeup appeals to them. This helps the Makeup Artist grasp whether the client wants to be heavily made up or prefers a more natural appearance, as well as the color schemes the client leans toward. Makeup Artists who work with wedding parties often have "test" appointments before the wedding day. They meet with the bride and bridal group in advance to do a trial run of the makeup that will be used on the wedding day. This enables the bride to create the look she wants for her wedding day during a less stressful time. She'll be able to discuss her options with the Makeup Artist, the Makeup Artist will record everything they use in the trial that the bride likes, and come the wedding day, the makeup session will be a calmer, more streamlined experience for all.

Makeup Artists use the following in their work (brands vary depending on clientele and projects): facial cleansers, moisturizers, foundations and concealers, blushes, eye liners, eye shadows, mascaras, lip liners, lip glosses, lipsticks, brushes and wands of all shapes, sizes and textures, makeup lights and light stands, hairbrushes, and makeup carrying cases for traveling to and from work.

Some Makeup Artists may give scalp and facial treatments as well as clean and style wigs and hairpieces. An esthetician is one type of Makeup Artist whose focus is to clean skin with facials and who may also provide body treatments, head and neck massages, and hair removal. Another type of Makeup Artist is the special effects artist, who works specifically for television, film, and theater. Special effects artists are responsible for designing makeup and often prosthetics that transforms actors to suit their roles,

such as aging, illness, scars, injuries, blood, and so on. Many special effects artists use computer-generated images in the design process.

Makeup Artists who work independently are also responsible for all administrative aspects involved in running a business. In addition to keeping records of the work completed with clients (including types of makeup and colors chosen in the past), they self-promote through their own Web sites and the Internet as well as via networking, direct marketing, and cold-calling. They schedule appointments, manage their own schedules, handle the invoicing as well as the accounts receivable and payable, or delegate this to a bookkeeper. They maintain their makeup tools and equipment, clean all of their applicators, and check their makeup supplies constantly to ensure quantity, quality, and freshness. If running their own salons, they manage staff and handle the inventory as well as the salon maintenance (e.g., cleaning services, equipment maintenance, etc.).

Salaries

Makeup Artists can expect to earn $25,000 to more than $100,000 per year, depending on their specialties. Makeup Artists who work in the entertainment field command higher salaries. They typically charge a flat fee per day if working on a film set or with models or any groups of people for a particular project. Those who work with individuals outside the entertainment field usually charge a flat fee per makeup session, with client tips enhancing their salaries.

Employment Prospects

Job opportunities are best for Makeup Artists who are licensed to practice in their state. (License requirements vary state by state.) The U.S. Department of Labor's *Occupational Outlook Handbook* predicts that the employment of Makeup Artists (or "personal appearance workers") will grow by about 10 to 20 percent through 2012, which is about as fast as the average for all occupations. While employment prospects are good for Makeup Artists, the competition will still be fierce. These jobs are highly desirable because artists can theoretically create their own schedules, travel, be creative, and, if working in the entertainment field, rub shoulders (and maybe cheeks) with the stars. The work can be glamorous, and those Makeup Artists with the skills, expertise, and exceptional communication powers will secure the jobs.

Advancement Prospects

Independent Makeup Artists who hone their skills over the years and build solid reputations as quality service providers can advance to become salon or agency owners. They can move on to more managerial roles, delegating work and overseeing a staff of Makeup Artists while still keeping their hands in the business when they choose. Those who prefer to stay independent and unburdened by salon ownership can expand their knowledge by exploring other areas of makeup artistry, such as special effects.

Education and Training

Each state has different educational and training requirements, but regardless, Makeup Artists must be licensed to practice their craft. If you are considering the field of makeup artistry, contact the state board of cosmetology examiners in your state capital for details on licensing requirements and approved schools. You can also learn more about licensed training schools and requirements from the National Accrediting Commission of Cosmetology Arts and Sciences (http://www.naccas.org) and find career information at the National Cosmetology Association Web site (http://www.salonprofessionals.org).

Experience, Skills, and Personality Traits

Makeup Artists must be creative, have a keen knowledge of fashion and makeup, and enjoy working with a wide variety of people. For many burgeoning Makeup Artists, one to two years of experience at the cosmetics counter of a department store or apprenticing in a salon is an excellent way to learn the craft firsthand, gain an understanding of the general public, and get discounts on products. Successful Makeup Artists are not only decisive about the products they use and the vision they are aiming for, but they are flexible and open enough to listen to their clients and to create looks that match what their clients want. They are good listeners and excellent communicators, always keeping their clients informed of the makeup products and techniques they are using and always asking questions to make sure their clients are comfortable and at ease. Because the Makeup Artist's business is all about appearance, Makeup Artists themselves must present an image that appeals to their clients and to prospective clients. They must be presentable and fashionable, their equipment and facilities (if they own a salon) must be clean and neat, and they must be organized. All of these

skills coupled with the ability to keep appointments in a timely manner will help ensure repeat business as well as referrals to new clientele.

Unions and Associations

Makeup Artists who work in entertainment and related fields can benefit from membership in the union IATSE (International Alliance of Theatrical Stage Employees, Moving Picture Technicians, Artists and Allied Crafts of the United States, Its Territories and Canada). Primary benefits include representation at the negotiating table for acceptable wages, benefits and working conditions, in addition to networking and educational resources. Independent Film Project (IFP, http://www.ifp.org) is a not-for-profit service organization that provides such resources as education, job listings, networking opportunities, and more to its members, who are independent filmmakers, industry professionals, and independent film enthusiasts.

Tips for Entry

1. If you are working independently, be diligent in staying organized and taking your work seriously. Keep records of your clients, and be on time to all of your appointments.
2. Word of mouth is the best way to get work in the Makeup Artist business, so network as much as possible. It's up to you to sell yourself!
3. Be persistent. This is an extremely competitive field, so don't let any initial rejection stop you from going out there and selling yourself.
4. You need to show your work to get work, so volunteer your services if you're just starting out. Make a list of the fashion and people photographers, theaters, and modeling agencies in your area. Call them, introduce yourself, and tell them you're interested in volunteering your services. Working for free can pay off in the long run. You'll get a taste of what the work is like, and you'll be able to get photos of your work from an actual job to include in your portfolio.

APPENDIXES

APPENDIX I
ART SCHOOLS

POSTSECONDARY SCHOOLS

Below is a list of postsecondary schools that offer diplomas or certificates of completion. While not degree-granting courses of study, they can provide a great deal of hands-on knowledge about executing visual art.

CONNECTICUT

Connecticut Institute of Art
581 West Putnam Avenue
Greenwich, CT 06830
http://www.artinstitute.com

MASSACHUSETTS

Butera School of Art
111 Beacon Street
Boston, MA 02116
http://www.buteraschool.com

NEW JERSEY

duCret School of Art
1030 Central Avenue
Plainfield, NJ 07060
http://www.ducret.edu

Gloucester County College
1400 Tanyard Road
Sewell, NJ 08080
http://www.gccnj.edu

**Joe Kubert School of Cartoon and
   Graphic Art**
37 Myrtle Avenue
Dover, NJ 07801
http://www.kubertsworld.com

Somerset County Technology Institute
P.O. Box 6350
Bridgewater, NJ 08807
http://www.scti.org

WASHINGTON

School of Visual Concepts
500 Aurora Avenue North
Seattle, WA 98109
http://www.svcseattle.com

A. ASSOCIATE DEGREE (TWO-YEAR)

UNDERGRADUATE PROGRAMS

This list of undergraduate programs includes two- and four-year degree-granting institutions selected for excellence in art and art-related courses of study.

ARIZONA

Glendale Community College
Art Department
6000 West Olive Avenue
Glendale, AZ 85302
http://www.gc.maricopa.edu

Pima Community College
Art Department
4905 East Broadway Boulevard
Tucson, AZ 85709-6619
http://www.pima.edu

Yavapai College
Art Department
Prescott, AZ 86301
http://www2.yc.edu

ARKANSAS

Garland County Community College
101 College Drive
Hot Springs, AR 71913
http://www.gccc.cc.ar.us

CALIFORNIA

Antelope Valley College
3041 West Avenue K
Lancaster, CA 93536
http://www.avc.edu

Butte College
3536 Butte Campus Drive
Oroville, CA 95965
http://www.butte.edu

El Camino Community College
Division of Fine Arts
16007 Crenshaw Boulevard
Torrance, CA 90506
http://www.elcamino.edu

Los Angeles Trade Tech College
400 West Washington Boulevard
Los Angeles, CA 90015
http://www.lattc.cc.ca.us

Rancho Santiago College
2323 North Broadway
Santa Ana, CA 92706
http://www.rsccd.org

COLORADO

Arapahoe Community College
5900 South Santa Fe Drive
Littleton, CO 80160-9002
http://www.arapahoe.edu

Colorado Mountain College
831 Grand Avenue
Glenwood Springs, CO 81601
http://www.coloradomtn.edu

Pikes Peak Community College
5675 South Academy Boulevard
Colorado Springs, CO 80906
http://www.ppcc.cccoes.edu

CONNECTICUT

**Quinebaug Valley Community
   Technical College**
Department of Art

742 Upper Maple Street
Danielson, CT 06239-1440
http://www.qvctc.commnet.edu

FLORIDA

**Miami Dade Community College
North**
11380 NW 27th Avenue
Miami, FL 33167
http://www.mdc.edu

Pensacola Junior College
1000 College Boulevard
Pensacola, FL 32504
http://www.pjc.edu

GEORGIA

Portfolio Center
125 Bennet Street
Atlanta, GA 30309
http://www.portfoliocenter.com

ILLINOIS

Prairie State College
Department of Arts and Sciences
202 South Halsted Street
Chicago Heights, IL 60411
http://www.prairie.cc.il.us

IOWA

Northeast Iowa Community College
Calmar Campus
P.O. Box 400
Calmar, IA 52132
http://www.nicc.edu

KENTUCKY

Lexington Community College
Cooper Drive
Lexington, KY 40506
http://www.uky.edu/LCC

MASSACHUSETTS

Quinsigamond Community College
Applied Arts Department
670 West Bolyston Street
Worcester, MA 01606
http://www.qcc.mass.edu

MICHIGAN

Kirtland Community College
1077 North St. Helen Road
Roscommon, MI 48653
http://www.kirtland.cc.mi.us

MISSOURI

**St. Louis Community College at
Florissant Valley**
3400 Pershall Road
St. Louis, MO 63135
http://www.stlcc.cc.mo.us/fv

NEVADA

**Community College of Southern
Nevada**
Art Department
3200 East Cheyenne Avenue
North Las Vegas, NV 89030
http://www.ccsn.nevada.edu

NORTH DAKOTA

Turtle Mountain Community College
Art Department
P.O. Box 340
Belcourt, ND 58316
http://www.turtle-mountain.cc.nd.us

OHIO

Art Institute of Cincinnati
2528 Kemper Lane
Cincinnati, OH 45206
http://www.theartinstituteofcincinnati.com

Cuyahoga Community College
11000 Pleasant Valley Road
Parma, OH 44130
http://www.tri-c.edu/art

Davis College
Design Department
4747 Monroe Street
Toledo, OH 43623
http://www.daviscollege.edu

School of Advertising Art
2900 Acosta Street
Kettering, OH 45420
http://www.saacollege.com

PENNSYLVANIA

Bradley Academy for the Visual Arts
1409 Williams Road
York, PA 17402
http://www.bradleyacademy.edu

NEW YORK

Bronx Community College
Art Department
P.O. Box 243
Bronx, NY 10465
http://www.bcc.cuny.edu

Dutchess Community College
53 Pendell Road
Poughkeepsie, NY 12601
http://www.sunydutchess.edu

Monroe Community College
1000 East Henrietta Road
Rochester, NY 14623
http://www.monroecc.edu

Niagara County Community College
3111 Saunders Settlement Road
Sanborn, NY 14132
http://www.niagaracc.suny.edu

Onondaga Central College
4941 Onondaga Road
Syracuse, NY 13215
http://www.sunyocc.edu

TEXAS

Collin County Community College
Fine Arts Division
2200 West University Drive
McKinney, TX 75074
http://www.ccccd.edu

Kingwood College
Art Department
20000 Kingwood Drive
Kingwood, TX 77339
http://kcWeb.nhmccd.edu

B. BACHELOR'S DEGREE (FOUR-YEAR)

ALABAMA

Auburn University
College of Liberal Arts
Auburn, AL 36849
http://www.auburn.edu

University of Alabama
College of Arts and Sciences
Clark Hall Box 870293
Tuscalossa, AL 35487
http://www.as.ua.edu/as

University of North Alabama
College of Arts and Sciences
UNA Box 5011
Florence, AL 35632
http://www.una.edu

ALASKA

University of Alaska Anchorage
College of Arts and Sciences
3211 Providence Drive
Anchorage, AK 99508
http://www.uaa.alaska.edu

University of Alaska Southeast
Arts and Sciences
11120 Glacier Highway
Juneau, AK 99801
http://www.uas.alaska.edu

ARIZONA

Art Institute of Phoenix
2233 West Dunlap Avenue
Phoenix, AZ 85021-2859
http://www.aipx.edu

Northern Arizona University
College of Arts and Letters
South San Francisco Street
Flagstaff, AZ 86011
http://www.nau.edu

University of Arizona at Tucson
School of Art
P.O. Box 210002 J. Gross Gallery
Tucson, AZ 85721
http://www.arizona.edu

ARKANSAS

Arkansas State University
College of Fine Arts
P.O. Box 1920
State University, AR 72467
http://www.astate.edu

Arkansas Tech University
School of Liberal and Fine Arts
Witherspoon 240
Russellville, AR 72801
http://www.atu.edu

Henderson State University
Matt Locke Ellis College of Arts and
    Sciences
1100 Henderson Street
Arkadelphia, AR 71999
http://www.hsu.edu

CALIFORNIA

Academy of Art College
540 Powell Street
San Francisco, CA 94108
http://www.academyart.edu

Art Center College of Design
1700 Lida Street
Pasadena, CA 91103
http://www.artcenter.edu

**Art Institute of California Orange
    County**
3601 West Sunflower Avenue
Santa Ana, CA 92651
http://www.aicoac.artinstitutes.edu

Art Institute of California San Diego
7650 Mission Valley Road
San Diego, CA 92108
http://www.aicasd.artinstitutes.edu

California College of the Arts
5212 Broadway
Oakland, CA 94618
http://www.cca.edu

California College of the Arts
1111 Eighth Street
San Francisco, CA 94107
http://www.cca.edu

California Institute of the Arts
24700 McBean Parkway
Valencia, CA 91355
http://www.calarts.edu

California State University Chico
College of Humanities and Fine Arts
Chico, CA 95929
http://www.csuchico.edu

California State University Davis
College of Letters and Science
Humanities, Arts, and Cultural Studies
    Department
1 Shields Avenue
Davis, CA 95616
http://www.ucdavis.edu

California State University Fullerton
College of the Arts
Fullerton, CA 92634
http://www.fullerton.edu

California State University Long Beach
401 Golden Shore
Long Beach, CA 90840
http://www.calstate.edu

California State University Los Angeles
5151 State University Drive
Los Angeles, CA 90032
http://www.calstatela.edu

**Fashion Institute of Design and
    Merchandising**
919 South Grand Avenue
Los Angeles, CA 90015
http://www.fidm.com

San Jose State University
School of Art and Design
One Washington Square
San Jose, CA 95192-0089
http://www.sjsu.edu

University of the Pacific
Department of Visual Arts
3601 Pacific Avenue
Stockton, CA 95211
http://www.uop.edu

Whittier College
Department of Art and Art History
13406 Philadelphia
Whittier, CA 90608
http://www.whittier.edu

COLORADO

Colorado Institute of Art
1200 Lincoln Street
Denver, CO 80203
http://www.aic.artinstitutes.edu

Colorado State University
College of Liberal Arts
Fort Collins, CO 80523
http://www.colostate.edu

Metropolitan State College of Denver
Art Department
Campus Box 59, P.O. Box 173362
Denver, CO 80217-3362
http://clem.mscd.edu/~art_cs

**Rocky Mountain College of Art and
    Design**
1600 Pierce Street
Lakewood, CO 80214
http://www.rmcad.edu

**University of Colorado at Colorado
    Springs**
College of Letters, Arts, and Sciences
1420 Austin Bluffs Parkway
Colorado Springs, CO 80933
http://www.uccs.edu

CONNECTICUT

Central Connecticut State University
School of Arts and Sciences

1615 Stanley Street
New Britain, CT 06050
http://www.ccsu.edu

Paier College of Art
20 Gorham Avenue
Hamden, CT 06514-3902
http://www.paierart.com

Sacred Heart University
College of Arts and Sciences
5151 Park Avenue
Fairfield, CT 06430
http://www.sacredheart.edu

South Connecticut State University
College of Education, Humanities, and
    Social Sciences
501 Crescent Street
New Haven, CT 06515
http://www.scsu.edu

University of Bridgeport
School of Arts and Sciences
126 Park Avenue
Bridgeport, CT 06601
http://www.bridgeport.edu

University of Connecticut
School of Fine Arts
Storrs, CT 06269
http://www.uconn.edu

University of Hartford
Hartford Art School
200 Bloomfield Avenue
West Hartford, CT 06117
http://www.hartfordartschool.org

Western Connecticut State University
School of Arts and Sciences
81 White Street
Danbury, CT 06810
http://www.wcsu.edu/sas

DELAWARE

University of Delaware
College of Arts and Sciences
104 Recitation Hall
Newark, DE 19716
http://www.udel.edu

DISTRICT OF COLUMBIA

Corcoran School of Art
500 17th Street NW
Washington, DC 20006
http://www.corcoran.edu

Gallaudet University
College of Liberal Arts, Sciences, and
    Technologies
800 Florida Avenue NE
Washington, DC 20002
http://www.gallaudet.edu

Georgetown University
Department of Art, Music, and Theater
37th and O Streets NW
Washington, DC 20057
http://www.georgetown.edu

FLORIDA

Art Institute of Fort Lauderdale
1799 SE 17th Street
Fort Lauderdale, FL 33316
http://www.aifl.edu

Florida State University
School of Visual Arts and Dance
Tallahassee, FL 32306
http://www.fsu.edu

**Miami International University of Art
    and Design**
1501 Biscayne Boulevard, #100
Miami, FL 33132
http://www.ifac.edu

New World School of the Arts
25 Northeast 2nd Street
Miami, FL 33132
http://www.mdc.edu

Pensacola Christian College
P.O. Box 18000
Pensacola, FL 32523
http://www.pcci.edu

Ringling School of Art and Design
2700 North Tamiami Trail
Sarasota, FL 34234
http://www.rsad.edu

Stetson University
College of Arts and Sciences
06 Elizabeth Hall, 421 North Woodland
    Boulevard
DeLand, FL 32720
http://www.stetson.edu

University of Florida
College of Fine Arts
Gainesville, FL 32611
http://www.ufl.edu

GEORGIA

Atlanta College of Art
Woodruff Arts Center
1280 Peachtree Street NE
Atlanta, GA 30309
http://www.aca.edu

Augusta State University
College of Arts and Sciences
2500 Walton Way
Augusta, GA 30910
http://www.aug.edu

Savannah College of Art and Design
P.O. Box 3146
Savannah, GA 31401
http://www.scad.edu

University of Georgia
Lamar Dodd School of Art
212 Terrell Hall
Athens, GA 30602
http://art.uga.edu

University of West Georgia
College of Arts and Sciences
1601 Maple Street
Carrollton, GA 30118
http://www.westga.edu

HAWAII

Brigham Young University Hawaii
College of Arts and Sciences
55-220 Kulanui Street
Laie, HI 96762
http://www.byuh.edu

University of Hawaii at Manoa
College of Arts and Humanities
2500 Campus Road, Hawaii Hall 202
Honolulu, HI 96822
http://www.uhm.hawaii.edu

IDAHO

Boise State University
College of Arts and Sciences
1910 University Drive
Boise, ID 83725
http://www.boisestate.edu

Brigham Young University–Idaho
College of Performing and Visual Arts
525 South Center Street
Rexburg, ID 83460
http://www.byui.edu

College of Southern Idaho
Fine Arts Department
315 Falls Avenue
P.O. Box 1238
Twin Falls, ID 83303
http://www.csi.edu

ILLINOIS

American Academy of Art
332 South Michigan
Chicago, IL 60604
http://www.aaart.edu

Northern Illinois University
College of Visual and Performing Arts
Wilson Hall 101
DeKalb, IL 60115
http://www.niu.edu/art

School of the Art Institute of Chicago
37 South Wabash
Chicago, IL 60603
http://www.artic.edu/saic

Southern Illinois University
College of Applied Sciences and Arts
Carbondale, IL 62901
http://www.siuc.edu

Western Illinois University
College of Arts and Sciences
One University Circle, Morgan Hall 118
Macomb, IL 61455
http://www.wiu.edu/CAS

INDIANA

Ball State University
College of Fine Arts
Muncie, IN 47306
http://www.bsu.edu

College of Dupage
Liberal Arts Office
425 Fawell Boulevard
Glen Ellyn, IN 60137
http://www.cod.edu

Indiana University–Purdue University Indianapolis
Herron School of Art
1701 North Pennsylvania Street
Indianapolis, IN 46202
http://www.herron.iupui.edu

Indiana University–Purdue University Fort Wayne
School of Arts and Sciences

2101 East Coliseum Boulevard
Fort Wayne, IN 46805
http://www.ipfw.edu

Indiana Wesleyan University
Division of Art
4201 South Washington Street
Marion, IN 46953
http://www.indwes.edu

Purdue University
College of Liberal Arts
100 North University Street
West Lafayette, IN 47907
http://www.sla.purdue.edu

IOWA

Iowa State University
College of Design
Ames, IA 50011
http://www.iastate.edu

University of Northern Iowa
1227 West 27th Street
Cedar Falls, IA 50614
http://www.uni.edu

Upper Iowa University
Division of Liberal Arts
P.O. Box 1857
Fayette, IA 52142
http://www.uiu.edu

KANSAS

Kansas State University
College of Arts and Sciences
Art Department
322 Willard Hall
Manhattan, KS 66505
http://www.ksu.edu/art

University of Kansas
School of Fine Arts
466 Murphy Hall
1530 Naismith Drive, Building 76
Lawrence, KS 66045
http://www.ku.edu/~sfa

KENTUCKY

Murray State University
College of Humanities and Fine Arts
P.O. Box 9
Murray, KY 42071
http://www.murraystate.edu

University of Kentucky
College of Arts and Sciences
Lexington, KY 40506
http://www.uky.edu

LOUISIANA

Louisiana State University
Art Department
102 Design Building
Baton Rouge, LA 70803
http://www.lsu.edu

McNeese State University
College of Liberal Arts
4205 Ryan Street
Lake Charles, LA 70609
http://www.mcneese.edu

MAINE

University of Maine
College of Liberal Arts and Sciences
5774 Stevens Hall
Orono, ME 04469
http://www.umaine.edu/las

University of Southern Maine
College of Arts and Sciences
P.O. Box 9300
Portland, ME 04104
http://www.usm.maine.edu

MARYLAND

College of Notre Dame of Maryland
Art Department
4701 North Charles Street
Baltimore, MD 21210
http://www.ndm.edu

Maryland Institute College of Art
1300 Mount Royal Avenue
Baltimore, MD 21217
http://www.mica.edu

Salisbury State University
Fulton School of Liberal Arts
1101 Camden Avenue
Salisbury, MD 21801
http://www.salisbury.edu

Towson State University
College of Fine Arts and Communication
8000 York Road
Towson, MD 21252
http://www.towson.edu

University of Maryland
College of Arts and Humanities
College Park, MD 20742
http://www.umd.edu

MASSACHUSETTS

Art Institute of Boston
700 Beacon Street
Boston, MA 02215
http://www.aiboston.edu

Massachusetts College of Art
621 Huntington Avenue
Boston, MA 02115
http://www.massart.edu

Montserrat College of Art
P.O. Box 26, 23 Essex Street
Beverly, MA 01915
http://www.montserrat.edu

University of Massachusetts Amherst
College of Humanities and Fine Arts
South College UMass
Amherst, MA 01003
http://www.umass.edu/hfa

University of Massachusetts Dartmouth
College of Visual and Performing Art
285 Old Westport Road
North Dartmouth, MA 02747
http://www.umassd.edu/cvpa

University of Massachusetts Lowell
One University Avenue
Lowell, MA 01854
http://www.uml.edu

MICHIGAN

Andrews University
College of Arts and Sciences
Berrien Springs, MI 49104
http://www.andrews.edu

Center for Creative Studies
201 East Kirby
Detroit, MI 48202
http://www.ccsad.edu

Central Michigan University
College of Communication and Fine Arts
Mount Pleasant, MI 48858
http://www.cmich.edu/

Ferris State University
Kendall College of Art and Design

17 Fountain Street
Big Rapids, MI 49503
http://www.kcad.edu

Grand Valley State University
Art and Design Department
Allendale, MI 49401
http://www.gvsu.edu/art

Hillsdale College
33 East College
Hillsdale, MI 49242
http://www.hillsdale.edu/academics/art.asp

Lawrence Technological University
College of Architecture and Design
21000 West Ten Mile Road
Southfield, MI 48075
http://www.ltu.edu

Michigan State University
College of Arts and Letters
320 Linton Hall
East Lansing, MI 48824
http://www.cal.msu.edu

Northern Michigan University
College of Arts and Sciences
1401 Presque Isle Avenue
Marquette, MI 49855
http://www.nmu.edu/departments/colleges/
    artsandsciences

Western Michigan University
College of Fine Arts
1903 West Michigan Avenue
Kalamazoo, MI 49008
http://www.wmich.edu/cfa

MINNESOTA

Art Institutes International Minnesota
15 South Ninth Street
Minneapolis, MN 55402
http://www.allartschools.com/schools/
    ID1034

Bemidji State University
College of Arts and Letters
1500 Birchmont Drive NE
Bemidji, MN 56601
http://www.bemidjistate.edu

Metropolitan State University
College of Arts and Sciences
700 East Seventh Street
St. Paul, MN 55106
http://www.metrostate.edu/cas

Minneapolis College of Art and Design
2501 Stevens Avenue South
Minneapolis, MN 55404
http://www.mcad.edu

Moorhead State University
College of Arts and Humanities
1104 7th Avenue South
Moorhead, MN 56563
http://www.mnstate.edu

University of Minnesota–Duluth
School of Fine Arts
1049 University Drive
Duluth, MN 55812
http://www.d.umn.edu

MISSOURI

Central Missouri State
College of Arts and Sciences
P.O. Box 800
Warrensburg, MO 64093
http://www.cmsu.edu

Culver-Stockton College
Division of Fine Arts
One College Hill
Canton, MO 63435
http://www.culver.edu

Drury College
Division of Fine Art
900 North Benton Avenue
Springfield, MO 65802
http://www.drury.edu

Kansas City Art Institute
4415 Warwick Boulevard
Kansas City, MO 64111
http://www.kcai.edu

Southwest Missouri State
College of Arts and Letters
901 South National Avenue
Springfield, MO 65804
http://www.smsu.edu

Stephens College
1200 East Broadway
Columbia, MO 65212
http://www.stephens.edu

Truman State University
Division of Fine Arts
100 East Normal
Kirksville, MO 63501
http://www.truman.edu

Washington University in St. Louis
School of Art
Campus Box 1143, One Brookings Drive
St. Louis, MO 63130
http://www.wustl.edu

William Jewell College
500 College Hill
Liberty, MO 64068
http://www.jewell.edu

MONTANA

Carroll College
Department of Art
1601 North Benton
Helena, MT 59625
http://www.carroll.edu

NEVADA

University of Nevada, Las Vegas
College of Fine Arts
4505 Maryland Parkway
Las Vegas, NV 89154
http://www.unlv.edu

NEW JERSEY

College of New Jersey
P.O. Box 7718, Pennington Road
Ewing, NJ 08628
http://www.tcnj.edu

Georgian Court University
900 Lakewood Avenue
Lakewood, NJ 08701
http://www.georgian.edu

Kean University
1000 Morris Avenue
Union, NJ 07083
http://www.kean.edu

Montclair State College
School of the Arts
Montclair, NJ 07043
http://www.montclair.edu

**Richard Stockton College
  of New Jersey**
School of Arts and Humanities
P.O. Box 195
Pomona, NJ 08240
http://www2.stockton.edu

Rowan University
College of Fine and Performing Arts
201 Mullica Hill Road
Glassboro, NJ 08028
http://www.rowan.edu

NEW MEXICO

College of Santa Fe
School of Art
1600 St. Michael's Drive
Santa Fe, NM 87501
http://www.csf.edu

NEW YORK

Adelphi University
College of Arts and Sciences
Garden City, NY 11530
http://www.adelphi.edu

Brooklyn College
Art Department
5306 Boylan Hall, 2900 Bedford Avenue
Brooklyn, NY 11210
http://www.brooklyn.cuny.edu

Cooper Union
School of Art
41 Cooper Square
New York, NY 10003
http://www.cooper.edu

Cornell University
College of Architecture, Art, and Planning
Ithaca, NY 14850
http://www.cornell.edu

College of St. Rose
School of Arts and Humanities
432 Western Avenue
Albany, NY 12203
http://www.strose.edu

Fashion Institute of Technology
227 West 27th Street
New York, NY 10001
http://www.fitnyc.suny.edu

**Long Island University C. W. Post
  Campus**
College of Liberal Arts and Sciences
720 Northern Boulevard
Brookville, NY 11961
http://www.cwpost.liu.edu

Marist College
3399 North Road
Poughkeepsie, NY 12601
http://www.marist.edu

Nazareth College of Rochester
Art Department
4245 East Avenue
Rochester, NY 14618-3790
http://www.naz.edu

Parsons School of Design
66 Fifth Avenue
New York, NY 10012
http://www.parsons.edu

Pratt Institute
200 Willoughby Avenue
Brooklyn, NY 11205
http://www.pratt.edu

Pratt Manhattan
144 West 14th Street
New York, NY 10012
http://www.pratt.edu

Rochester Institute of Technology
College of Imaging Arts and Sciences
One Lomb Memorial Drive
Rochester, NY 14623
http://www.rit.edu

Saint John's University
College of Liberal Arts and Sciences
8000 Utopia Parkway
Queens, NY 11439
http://new.stjohns.edu

School of Visual Arts
209 East 23rd Street
New York, NY 10010
http://www.schoolofvisualarts.edu

SUNY Buffalo
Fine Arts Department
202 Center for the Arts/North Campus
Buffalo, NY 14260
http://www.buffalo.edu

SUNY Farmingdale
School of Arts and Sciences
2350 Broadhollow Road
Farmingdale, NY 11735
http://www.farmingdale.edu

SUNY Fredonia
Department of Visual Arts and New
  Media
280 Central Avenue
Fredonia, NY 14063
http://ww1.fredonia.edu

SUNY New Paltz
Art Department

75 South Manheim Boulevard
New Paltz, NY 12561
http://www.newpaltz.edu

SUNY Purchase
School of Art and Design
735 Anderson Hill Road
Purchase, NY 10577-1400
http://www.purchase.edu

Syracuse University
College of Visual and Performing Arts
202 Crouse College
Syracuse, NY 13244
http://vpa.syr.edu

NORTH CAROLINA

Barton College
School of Arts and Sciences
Box 5000
Wilson, NC 27893
http://www.barton.edu

East Carolina University
School of Art
Jenkins Fine Arts Building
Greenville, NC 27858
http://www.ecu.edu/art

North Carolina State University
College of Design
Campus Box 7701
Raleigh, NC 27695-7701
http://ncsudesign.org

**University of North Carolina at Chapel
Hill**
College of Arts and Sciences
Chapel Hill, NC 27599
http://artsandsci.unc.edu

**University of North Carolina at
Charlotte**
College of Arts and Sciences
9201 University City Boulevard
Charlotte, NC 28204
http://www.coas.uncc.edu

Western Carolina University
College of Arts and Sciences
Cullowhee, NC 28723
http://www.wcu.edu

NORTH DAKOTA

North Dakota State University
College of Arts, Humanities, and Social
Sciences

1301 12th Avenue North
Fargo, ND 58105
http://www.ndsu.nodak.edu

OKLAHOMA

Oral Roberts University
School of Arts and Sciences
7777 South Lewis Avenue
Tulsa, OK 74171
http://www.oru.edu

**Southwestern Oklahoma State
University**
College of Arts and Sciences
100 Campus Drive
Weatherford, OK 73096
http://www.swosu.edu

OHIO

Art Academy of Cincinnati
1125 Saint Gregory Street
Cincinnati, OH 45202
http://www.artacademy.edu

Cleveland Institute of Art
11141 East Boulevard
Cleveland, OH 44106
http://www.cia.edu

Columbus College of Art and Design
107 North Ninth Street
Columbus, OH 43215
http://www.ccad.edu

Kent State University
College of Fine and Professional Arts
Taylor Hall
Kent, OH 44242
http://dept.kent.edu/f&pa

Miami University
School of Fine Arts
112 Hiestand Hall
Oxford, OH 45056
http://www.fna.muohio.edu/fnaWeb1

Ohio Northern University
Getty College of Arts and Sciences
Ada, OH 45810
http://www.onu.edu/a+s

Ohio University
School of Art
Athens, OH 45701
http://www.ohiou.edu/art

University of Akron
School of Art
Falk Hall
Akron, OH 44325
http://www.uakron.edu

University of Dayton
300 College Park
Dayton, OH 45469-1690
http://www.udayton.edu

Youngstown State University
One University Plaza
Youngstown, OH 44555
http://www.ysu.edu

OREGON

Pacific Northwest College of Art
1241 NW Johnson Street
Portland, OR 97209
http://www.pnca.edu

Oregon State University
College of Liberal Arts
207 Gilkey Hall
Corvallis, OR 97331
http://oregonstate.edu/cla

PENNSYLVANIA

Art Institute of Philadelphia
1622 Chestnut Street
Philadelphia, PA 19103
http://aiph.aii.edu

Art Institute of Pittsburgh
420 Boulevard of the Allies
Pittsburgh, PA 15219
http://www.aip.aii.edu

Carnegie Mellon University
College of Fine Arts
5000 Forbes Avenue
Pittsburgh, PA 15213
http://www.cmu.edu/cfa

Edinboro University of Pennsylvania
Edinboro, PA 16444
http://webs.edinboro.edu

Kutztown University of Pennsylvania
P.O. Box 730
Kutztown, PA 19530
http://www.kutztown.edu

Marywood University
2300 Adams Avenue
Scranton, PA 18509
http://www.marywood.edu

Moore College of Art and Design
20th & the Parkway
Philadelphia, PA 19103
http://www.moore.edu

Moravian College
1200 Main Street
Bethlehem, PA 18018
http://www.moravian.edu

Pennsylvania College of Art and Design
P.O. Box 59, 204 North Prince Street
Lancaster, PA 17608
http://www.pcad.edu

Philadelphia Academy of the Fine Arts
1301 Cherry Street
Philadelphia, PA 19107
http://www.pafa.org

Point Park University
201 Wood Street
Pittsburgh, PA 15222
http://www.pointpark.edu

Temple University
Tyler School of Art
7725 Penrose Avenue
Elkins Park, PA 19027
http://www.temple.edu/tyler

University of the Arts
320 South Broad Street
Philadelphia, PA 19102
http://www.uarts.edu

RHODE ISLAND

Rhode Island School of Design
2 College Street
Providence, RI 02903
http://www.risd.edu

SOUTH DAKOTA

Black Hills State University
College of Arts and Sciences
1200 University Unit 9003
Spearfish, SD 57799
http://www.bhsu.edu

TENNESSEE

East Tennessee State University
College of Arts and Sciences
Box 70267
Johnson City, TN 37614
http://www.etsu.edu

Memphis College of Art
1930 Poplar Avenue, Overton Park
Memphis, TN 38104
http://www.mca.edu

TEXAS

Art Institute of Houston
1900 Yorktown
Houston, TX 77056
http://www.aih.aii.edu

Lamar University
College of Fine Arts and Communication
P.O. Box 10009
Beaumont, TX 77710
http://www.lamar.edu

Stephen F. Austin State University
Department of Art
1936 North Street
Nacogdoches, TX 75962
http://www.sfasu.edu

Texas State University
College of Fine Arts and Communication
112 Old Main
601 University Drive
San Marcos, TX 78704
http://www.finearts.txstate.edu

University of North Texas
School of Visual Arts
P.O. Box 305100
Denton, TX 76203
http://www.art.unt.edu

University of Texas at Arlington
College of Liberal Arts
701 South Nedderman Drive
Arlington, TX 76019
http://www.uta.edu

UTAH

Brigham Young University
College of Fine Arts and Communication
Provo, UT 84602
http://www.byu.edu

Southern Utah University
College of Performing and Visual Arts
351 West University Boulevard
Cedar City, UT 84720
http://www.suu.edu

University of Utah
College of Fine Arts
201 South Presidents Circle

Salt Lake City, UT 84112
http://www.utah.edu

Utah State University
College of Humanities, Arts and Social
  Sciences
Logan, UT 84321
http://www.usu.edu

VIRGINIA

James Madison University
College of Arts and Letters
800 South Main Street
Harrisonburg, VA 22807
http://www.jmu.edu

Marymount University
2807 North Glebe Road
Arlington, VA 22207
http://www.marymount.edu

Virginia Commonwealth
School of the Arts
Richmond, VA 23284
http://www.pubinfo.vcu.edu/artWeb

WASHINGTON

Art Institute of Seattle
2323 Elliott Avenue
Seattle, WA 98121
http://www.ais.edu

Central Washington University
College of Arts and Humanities
400 East University Way
Ellensburg, WA 98926
http://www.cwu.edu

Cornish College of the Arts
1000 Lenora Street
Seattle, WA 98102
http://www.cornish.edu

Eastern Washington University
College of Arts and Letters
101 Sutton Hall
Cheney, WA 99004
http://www.ewu.edu

WEST VIRGINIA

Shepherd College
School of Arts and Humanities
P.O. Box 3210
Shepherdstown, WV 25443
http://www.shepherd.edu

West Virginia University
College of Creative Arts
P.O. Box 6111
Morgantown, WV 26506
http://www.ccarts.wvu.edu

WISCONSIN

Cardinal Stritch University
College of Art and Sciences
6801 North Yates Road
Milwaukee, WI 53217
http://www.stritch.edu

Milwaukee Institute of Art and Design
273 East Erie Street
Milwaukee, WI 53202
http://www.miad.edu

University of White Water
College of Arts and Communication
800 West Main Street
Whitewater, WI 53190
http://www.uww.edu

University of Wisconsin Eau Claire
College of Arts and Sciences
105 Garfield Avenue, P.O. Box 4004

Eau Claire, WI 54702
http://www.uwec.edu

University of Wisconsin Parkside
Art Department
900 Wood Road, P.O. Box 2000
Kenosha, WI 53141
http://www.uwp.edu

University of Wisconsin Stevens Point
College of Fine Arts and Communication
2100 Main Street
Stevens Point, WI 54481
http://www.uwsp.edu

C. GRADUATE PROGRAMS

While a good number of the schools above also offer graduate degrees, the listings below have particularly excellent postgraduate programs for the study of visual arts.

CONNECTICUT

Yale University
School of Art
1156 Chapel Street
New Haven, CT 06511-8921
http://www.yale.edu/art

GEORGIA

Medical College of Georgia
School of Graduate Studies
Augusta, GA 30912
http://www.mcg.edu

ILLINOIS

University of Illinois at Chicago
College of Applied Health Sciences

1919 West Taylor Street, Room 213,
   M/C 527
Chicago, IL 60612
http://www.uic.edu/ahs

MARYLAND

John's Hopkins School of Medicine
1830 East Monument Street, #7000
Baltimore, MD 21205
http://www.hopkinsmedicine.org

MASSACHUSETTS

Boston University
Graduate School of Arts and Sciences
705 Commonwealth Avenue
Boston, MA 02215
http://www.bu.edu/cas

NEW YORK

Fordham University
Graduate School of Arts and Sciences

Rose Hill Campus
Bronx, NY 10458
http://www.fordham.edu

New York Academy of Art
111 Franklin Street
New York, NY 10013
http://www.nyaa.edu

TEXAS

University of Texas
Department of Biomedical
   Communications
5323 Hines Boulevard
Dallas, TX 75235
http://www.utsouthwestern.edu/medillus

APPENDIX II
PROFESSIONAL ASSOCIATIONS, ORGANIZATIONS, AND TRADE UNIONS

BUSINESS

American Advertising Federation
1101 Vermont Avenue NW, Suite 500
Washington, DC 20005-6306
Phone: (202) 898-0089
Fax: (202) 898-0159
E-mail: aaf@aaf.org
http://www.aaf.org

American Finance Association
Haas School of Business, University of
California
Berkeley, CA 94729-1900
Phone: (800) 835-6770
Fax: (781) 388-8232
http://www.afajof.org

**American Society of Association
Executives**
1575 I Street NW
Washington, DC 20005-1103
Phone: (888) 950-2723, (202) 371-0940
Fax: (202) 371-8315
http://www.asaenet.org

Arts and Business Council, Inc.
520 Eighth Avenue, Suite 319
New York, NY 10018
Phone: (212) 279-5910
Fax: (212) 279-5915
E-mail: info@artsandbusiness.org
http://www.artsandbusiness.org

ArtTable, Inc.
270 Lafayette Street, Suite 608
New York, NY 10002
Phone: (212) 343-1735
E-mail: women@arttable.org
http://www.arttable.org

**Association for Financial
Professionals**
7315 Wisconsin Avenue,
Suite 600 West
Bethesda, MD 20814
Phone: (301) 907-2862
Fax: (301) 907-2864
http://www.afponline.org

Childrenswear Marketing Association
236 Route 38 West, Suite 100
Moorestown, NJ 08057
Phone: (609) 231-8500
Fax: (609) 231-4664

Financial Executives International
200 Campus Drive
Florham Park, NJ 07932-0674
Phone: (973) 765-1000
Fax: (973) 765-1018
http://www.fei.org

**International Association of
Administrative Professionals**
10502 NW Ambassador Drive, P.O. Box
20404
Kansas City, MO 64195-0404
Phone: (816) 891-6600
Fax: (816) 891-9118
E-mail: service@iaap-hq.org
http://www.iaap-hq.org

**National Association of Executive
Secretaries and Administrative
Assistants**
900 South Washington Street, Suite G-13
Falls Church, VA 22046
Phone: (703) 237-8616
Fax: (703) 533-1153
E-mail: Headquarters@naesaa.com
http://www.naesaa.com

Professional Apparel Association
994 Old Eagle School Road, Suite 1019
Wayne, PA 19087-1802
Phone: (610) 971-4850
Fax: (610) 971-4859
E-mail: info@proapparel.com
http://www.proapparel.com

**Professional Picture Framers
Association**
3000 Picture Place
Jackson, MI 49201
Phone: (517) 788-8100
Fax: (517) 788-8371
E-mail: ppfa@ppfa.com
http://www.ppfa.com

**Society of Photographers and Artists
Representatives**
E-mail: info@spar.org
http://www.spar.org

**Sporting Goods Manufacturing
Association**
200 Castlewood Drive
North Palm Beach, FL 33408-5696
Phone: (561) 842-4100
E-mail: info@sgma.com
http://www.sgma.com

**Support Center for Non-Profit
Management**
305 Seventh Avenue
New York, NY 10001
Phone: (212) 924-6744
Fax: (212) 924-9544
http://www.supportctr.org

United States Chamber of Commerce
1615 H Street NW
Washington, DC 20062-2000
Phone: (202) 659-6000
http://www.uschamber.com

EDUCATION

**American Federation of
Teachers–AFL-CIO**
555 New Jersey Avenue NW
Washington, DC 20001
Phone: (202) 879-4400
http://www.aft.org

**National Association of Schools of Art
and Design**
11250 Roger Bacon Drive, Suite 21
Reston, VA 20190
Phone: (703) 437-0700
Fax: (703) 437-6312
E-mail: info@arts-accredit.org
http://nasad.arts-accredit.org

National Education Association
1201 16th Street NW
Washington, DC 20036-3290

Phone: (202) 833-4000
Fax: (202) 822-7974
http://www.nea.org

Public Relations Society of America
33 Maiden Lane, Eleventh Floor
New York, NY 10038-5150
Phone: (212) 460-1400
Fax: (212) 995-0757
http://www.prsa.org

INDEPENDENT ARTISTS

Advertising Photographers of America
28 East Jackson Building, #10-A855
Chicago, IL 60604-2263
Phone: (800) 272-6264
Fax: (888) 889-7190
http://www.apanational.org

Amalgamated Lithographers of America, Local One
113 University Place
New York, NY 10003
Phone: (212) 460-0800
Fax: (212) 460-0859
http://www.litho.org

American Institute of Architects
1735 New York Avenue NW
Washington, DC 20006-5292
Phone: (800) AIA-3837 or (202) 626-7300
Fax: (202) 626-7547
E-mail: infocentral@aia.org
http://www.aia.org

American Institute of Graphic Arts
164 Fifth Avenue
New York, NY 10010
Phone: (212) 807-1990
Fax: (212) 807-1799
E-mail: membership@aiga.org
http://www.aiga.org

American Print Alliance
302 Larkspur Turn
Peachtree City, GA 30269-2210
E-mail: printalliance@mindspring.com
http://www.printalliance.org

American Society of Architectural Illustrators
8437 Jericho Way
Plain City, OH 43064
Phone: (614) 879-4222
Fax: (614) 879-4220
E-mail: hq@asai.org
http://www.asai.org

American Society of Furniture Designers
144 Woodland Drive
New London, NC 28127
Phone: (910) 576-1273
Fax: (910) 576-1573
E-mail: info@asfd.com
http://www.asfd.com

American Society of Interior Designers
608 Massachusetts Avenue NE
Washington, DC 20002-6006
Phone: (202) 546-3480
http://www.asid.org

American Society of Media Photographers
150 North Second Street
Philadelphia, PA 19106
Phone: (215) 451-ASMP
Fax: (215) 451-0880
http://www.asmp.org

American Society of Portrait Artists
P.O. Box 230216
Montgomery, AL 36106
Phone: (800) 62-ASOPA
E-mail: info@asopa.com
http://www.nysopa.org

Art Directors Club
106 West 29th Street
New York, NY 10001
Phone: (212) 643-1440
Fax: (212) 643-4266
E-mail: info@adcglobal.org

Artists Rights Society
536 Broadway, Fifth Floor
New York, NY 10012
Phone: (212) 420-9160
Fax: (212) 420-9286
E-mail: info@arsny.com
http://www.arsny.com

Association of American Editorial Cartoonists
P.O. Box 37669
Raleigh, NC 27627
Phone: (919) 329-8129
Fax: (919) 772-6007
E-mail: AAEC@nc.rr.com
http://info.detnews.com/aaec

Association of Graphic Communications
330 Seventh Avenue, Ninth Floor
New York, NY 10001-5010
Phone: (212) 279-2100

Fax: (212) 279-5381
E-mail: info@agcomm.org
http://www.agcomm.org

Association of Medical Illustrators
245 First Street
Cambridge, MA 02142
Phone: (617) 395-8186
E-mail: hq@ami.org
http://medical-illustrators.org
http://www.ami.org

Association of Science Fiction and Fantasy Artists
P.O. Box 15131
Arlington, TX 76015
http://www.asfa-art.org

Chelsea Ceramic Guild
233 West 19th Street
New York, NY 10011
Phone: (212) 243-2430

Computer Integrated Textile Design Association
P.O. Box 38143
Charlotte, NC 28278
http://www.citda.org

Editorial Photographers
P.O. Box 591811
San Francisco, CA 94159-1811
E-mail: info@editorialphoto.com
http://www.editorialphotographers.com

Fashion Group International
8 West 40th Street, Seventh Floor
New York, NY 10018
Phone: (212) 302-5511
Fax: (212) 302-5533
http://www.fgi.org

Foundation for Interior Design Education Research
146 Monroe Center NW, Suite 1318
Grand Rapids, MI 49503-2822
Phone: (616) 458-0400
Fax: (616) 458-0460
E-mail: fider@fider.org
http://www.fider.org

Garment Industry Development Corporation
275 Seventh Avenue, Ninth Floor
New York, NY 10001
Phone: (212) 366-6160
Fax: (212) 366-6162
E-mail: info@gidc.org
http://www.gidc.org

Gemology Institute of America
Robert Mouawad Campus
5345 Armada Drive
Carlsbad, CA 92008
Phone: (800) 421-7250
http://www.gia.edu

Giclée Printers Association
http://www.gpa.bz

Graphic Artists Guild
90 John Street, Suite 403
New York, NY 10038-3202
Phone: (212) 791-3400
Fax: (212) 791-0770
E-mail: membership@gag.org
http://www.gag.org

Guild of Natural Science Illustrators
P.O. Box 652
Ben Franklin Station
Washington, DC 20044
Phone/Fax: (301) 309-1514
E-mail: gnsihome@his.com
http://www.gnsi.org

Illustrators' Partnership of America
845 Moraine Street
Marshfield, MA 02050
Phone: (781) 837-9152
E-mail: info@illustratorspartnership.org
http://www.illustratorspartnership.org

**Industrial Designers Society of
America**
45195 Business Court, Suite 250
Dulles, VA 20166-6717
Phone: (703) 707-6000
http://www.idsa.org

**International Association of Clothing
Designers and Executives**
34 Thornton Ferry Road #1
Amherst, NH 03031-2601
Phone: (603) 672-4065
Fax: (603) 672-4064
E-mail: dmschmida@aol.com
http://www.iacde.com

**International Interior Design
Association**
13-500 Merchandise Mart
Chicago, IL 60654
Phone: (888) 799-4432
Fax: (312) 467-0779
E-mail: iidahq@iida.org
http://www.iida.org

International Sculpture Center
14 Fairgrounds Road, Suite B
Hamilton, NJ 08619-3447
Phone: (609) 689-1051
Fax: (609) 689-1061
E-mail: isc@sculpture.org
http://www.sculpture.org

Jewelers of America
52 Vanderbilt Avenue, 19th Floor
New York, NY 10017
Phone: (646) 658-0246
E-mail: info@jewelers.org
http://www.jewelers.org

Jewelers Vigilance Committee
25 West 45th Street, Suite 400
New York, NY 10036
Phone: (212) 997-2002
Fax: (212) 997-9148
http://www.jvclegal.org

**National Association for Printing
Leadership**
75 West Century Road
Paramus, NJ 07652-1408
Phone: (201) 634-9600
Fax: (201) 986-2976
E-mail: Information@napl.org
http://public.napl.org

**National Association of Independent
Artists**
http://www.naia-artists.org

National Caricaturist Network
18963 Duquesne Drive
Tampa, FL 33647
E-mail: prez@caricature.org
http://www.caricature.org

National Cartoonists Society
1133 West Morse Boulevard, Suite 201
Winter Park, FL 32789
Phone: (407) 647-8839
Fax: (407) 629-2502
E-mail: crowsegal@crowsegal.com
http://www.reuben.org

**National Council on Education for the
Ceramic Arts**
77 Erie Village Square, Suite 280
Erie, CO 80516-6996
Phone: (866) 266-2322 or (303) 828-2811
Fax: (303) 828-0911
E-mail: office@nceca.net
http://www.nceca.net

**National Press Photographers
Association**
3200 Croasdaile Drive, Suite 306
Durham, NC 27705
Phone: (919) 383-7246
Fax: (919) 383-7261
E-mail: info@nppa.org
http://www.nppa.org

National Sculpture Society
237 Park Avenue
New York, NY 10017
http://www.nationalsculpture.org

New York Society of Renderers
c/o Perspective Arts
181 North 11th Street, Suite 403
Brooklyn, NY 11211
Phone/Fax: (718) 387-1551
http://www.nysr.com

PrintImage International
70 East Lake Street, Suite 333
Chicago, IL 60601
Phone: (800) 234-0040
Fax: (312) 726-8113
E-mail: info@printimage.org
http://www.printimage.org

**Printing Industries of
America/Graphic Arts Technical
Foundation**
200 Deer Run Road
Sewickley, PA 15143
Phone: (412) 741-6860
Fax: (412) 741-2311
E-mail: piagatf@piagatf.org

Sculptors Guild
110 Greene Street, Suite 601
New York, NY 10012
Phone: (212) 431-5669
Fax: (212) 431-5669
http://www.sculptorsguild.org

Society for News Design
1130 Ten Rod Road, Suite F-104
North Kingstown, RI 02852-4177
Phone: (401) 294-5233
Fax: (401) 294-5238
http://www.snd.org

Society for Technical Communication
901 North Stuart Street, Suite 904
Arlington, VA 22203
Phone: (703) 522-4114
Fax: (703) 522-2075
E-mail: stc@stc.org
http://www.stc.org

Society of Arts and Crafts
175 Newbury Street
Boston, MA 02116
Phone: (617) 266-1810
Fax: (617) 266-5654
http://www.societyofarts.org

Society of Children's Book Writers and
Illustrators
8271 Beverly Boulevard
Los Angeles, CA 90048
Phone: (323) 782-1010
Fax: (323) 782-1892
E-mail: scbwi@scbwi.org
http://www.scbwi.org

Society of Illustrators
128 East 63rd Street
New York, NY 10021
Phone: (212) 838-2560
Fax: (212) 838-2561
E-mail: info@societyillustrators.org
http://www.societyillustrators.org

Society of Publication Designers
475 Park Avenue South, Suite 2200
New York, NY 10016
Phone: (212) 532-7527
Fax: (212) 268-1867
E-mail: e-mail@spd.org
http://www.spd.org

Surface Design Association
P.O. Box 360
Sebastopol, CA 95473-0360
Phone: (707) 829-3110
Fax: (707) 829-3285
E-mail: surfacedesign@mail.com
http://www.surfacedesign.org

Surfacing—Textile Artists and
Designers Associations
Box 6828, Station A
Toronto, Ontario
Canada M5W 1X6
http://surfacing-tada.com

Textile Society of America
P.O. Box 70
Earleville, MD 21919-0070
Phone: (410) 275-2329
Fax: (410) 275-8936
E-mail: tsa@dol.net
http://www.textilesociety.org

Type Directors Club
127 West 25th Street, Eighth Floor
New York, NY 10001
Phone: (212) 633-8943

Fax: (212) 633-8944
E-mail: director@tdc.org
http://www.tdc.org

Unite Here!
275 Seventh Avenue
New York, NY 10001-6708
Phone: (212) 265-7000
http://www.unitehere.org

MUSEUMS

American Association of Museums
1575 Eye Street NW, Suite 400
Washington, DC 20005
Phone: (202) 289-1818
Fax: (202) 289-6578
http://www.aam-us.org

American Institute for Conservation of
Historic and Artistic Works
1717 K Street NW, Suite 200
Washington, DC 20006
Phone: (202) 452-9545
Fax: (202) 452-9328
http://www.aic-faic.org

Art Dealers Association of America
575 Madison Avenue
New York, NY 10022
Phone: (212) 940-8590
Fax: (212) 940-6484
http://www.artdealers.org

Association for Preservation
Technology
4513 Lincoln Avenue, Suite 213
Lisle, IL 60532-1290
Phone: (630) 968-6400
Fax: (888) 723-4242
E-mail: information@apti.org
http://www.apti.org

Getty Conservation Institute
1200 Getty Center Drive, Suite 700
Los Angeles, CA 90049-1684
Phone: (310) 440-7325
Fax: (310) 440-7702
E-mail: gciWeb@getty.edu
http://www.getty.edu

International Centre for the Study of
the Preservation and Restoration of
Cultural Property
Via di San Michele 13
I-00153 Rome, Italy
Phone: +39 06 585531
E-mail: iccrom@iccrom.org
http://www.iccrom.org

International Council of Museums
Maison de l'UNESCO
1, rue Miollis
75732 Paris Cedex 15
France
Phone: +33 (0) 1 47.34.05.00
Fax: +33 (0) 1.43.06.78.62
E-mail: secretariat@icom.museum
http://icom.museum

THEATER

Animation Film Association
(Association International du Film
d'Animation)
E-mail: president@asifa.net
http://www.asifa.net

Art Directors Guild, Local 800
11969 Ventura Boulevard, Suite 200
Studio City, CA 91604
Phone: (818) 762-9995
Fax: (818) 762-9997
http://www.artdirectors.org

Association of Stylists and
Coordinators
18 East 18th Street, Apartment 5E
New York, NY 10003
E-mail: info@stylistsasc.com
http://www.stylistsasc.com

Broadcast Designers Association
9000 West Sunset Boulevard, Suite 900
Los Angeles, CA 90069
Phone: (310) 788-7600
Fax: (310) 788-7616
http://www.bda.tv

Costume Designers Guild, Local 892
http://www.costumedesignersguild.com

Independent Film Project
(Note: Chapters also in Chicago, Los
Angeles, Miami, St. Paul, and Seattle)
104 West 29th Street, 12th Floor
New York, NY 10001-5310
Phone: (212) 465-8200
Fax: (212) 465-8525
E-mail: newyorkmembership@ifp.org
http://www.ifp.org

International Alliance of Theatrical
Stage Employees, Moving Picture
Technicians, Artists and Allied
Crafts (I.A.T.S.E.)
1430 Broadway, 20th Floor
New York, NY 10018

Phone: (212) 730-1770
Fax: (212) 730-7809
E-mail: organizing@iatse-intl.org
http://www.iatse-intl.org

**International Game Developers
   Association**
870 Market Street, Suite 1181
San Francisco, California 94102-3002
Phone: (415) 738-2104
Fax: (415) 738-2178

E-mail: info@igda.org
http://www.igda.org

United Scenic Artists Local USA 829
New York:
   29 West 38th Street
   New York, NY 10018
   Phone: (212) 581-0300
   Fax: (212) 977-2011
Chicago:
   203 North Wabash, Suite 1210

Chicago, IL 60601
   Phone: (312) 857-0829
   Fax: (312) 857-0819
Los Angeles:
   5225 Wilshire Boulevard, Suite 506
   Los Angeles, CA 90036
   Phone: (323) 965-0957
   Fax: (323) 965-0958
   E-mail: usamail@usa829.org
   http://www.usa829.org

APPENDIX III
ADDITIONAL RESOURCES

The following organizations offer resources that aren't readily available elsewhere for those interested in a specialized field of the visual arts industry. In many cases, the sites listed offer specialized services, databases of content, opportunities to promote one's work, or educational materials online.

ALL VISUAL ARTISTS

Volunteer Lawyers for the Arts
1 East 53rd Street, Sixth Floor
New York, NY 10022
Phone: (212) 319-2787
Fax: (212) 752-6575
http://www.vlany.org

ANIMATORS

Big Cartoon Database
http://www.bcdb.com

CARTOONISTS

National Cartoonists Society Syndicate Directory
http://www.reuben.org/ncs/syndicates.asp

DESIGNERS/ART DIRECTORS

Type Directors Club
http://www.tdc.org

INDEPENDENT ILLUSTRATORS

The iSpot
http://www.theispot.com

PAINTERS/SCULPTORS

National Endowment for the Arts
http://www.nea.gov

SEQUENTIAL ARTISTS/CARTOONISTS

OSU Cartoon Research Library
http://cartoons.osu.edu

WEB DESIGNERS

Webmaster Organization
http://www.Webmaster.org

GLOSSARY

acrylic   1. polymer vehicle used for painting. 2. solid polymer used in sculpture and display construction

advance   money paid upfront or during execution of commissioned work; usually considered payment against future royalties

analog   recording term being co-opted by visual art industry; indication of nondigital execution

application   1. in computer terms, a software program that performs a specific task (e.g., word processing). 2. in painting terms, method of putting paint onto a ground (e.g., scumbling)

bitmap   a particular type of graphic composed of pixels, or "bits"

bleed   area surrounding printed image intended to be cut off; allows continuous imaging to run edge to edge on final printed piece

blues   photographic prints made from printing films in nonreproductive blue; generated by printers so client has a chance to preview a document prior to platemaking

body copy   the main text of a publication or advertisement

camera-ready   1. final mechanical (or layout) with finished art in place that is prepared prior to photographing for plate production in printing process (somewhat archaic term in contemporary print world). 2. digital file with high-resolution art in place and all document resources placed on removable media (CD, DVD, or Zip Disk)

CGI   computer generated image; also common gateway interface, in the Web development field

chrome   positive transparency film, usually $4'' \times 5''$, used to scan high-resolution images for print

clip art   visual art, typically line art, distributed as royalty-free for use in print or Web design

CMYK   cyan, magenta, yellow, and black; four-color printing process

color separation   also called "separations" or "seps"; photographic process that divides full-color imagery into basic colors (typically the three primary colors plus black), which then correspond to individual plates used in the printing process

copyright   exclusive legal right to publish or reproduce a work, be it written, visual, or recorded

copywriter   author of literary content in advertising or publicity

CSS   cascading style sheets; method for controlling display of text in Web development

digital   relating to calculation done by numbers; has come to mean a work executed through use of computers in the visual art industry

DPI   dots per inch; measure of resolution in an image file; refers to the number of dots—or points—generated per inch on both the horizontal and vertical axes

dummy   preliminary book or pamphlet designed to show final placement of imagery and copy in rough form; executed to reflect proportionate size of final product

emulsion   suspension of light-sensitive materials used to coat paper, plates, or film; photographic and printing term

film   1. thin membrane of cellulose-based substance coated with light-sensitive emulsion used in photography. 2. sheets of exposed film used in etching process for printing plates

font   an assortment of type characters, numerical characters, and special characters all of a single style (e.g., Helvetica)

FTP   file transfer protocol; networking term

ground   sized and primed surface on which paint is applied; painting term

halftone   shades of value between absolute dark (100%) and absolute light (0%) achieved by photographing images through a screen pattern

headline   also called "head"; line of type atop a newspaper story, magazine article, advertisement, or pamphlet that typically runs in large letters; used to introduce or categorize

HTML   hypertext markup language; Internet protocol

kerning   spacing between pairs of letters

kill fee   payment made to professional when job is either cancelled or rejected after it's been commissioned; different tiers exist for kill fees based upon the amount of work completed on a project prior to cancellation

live area   space within a final printed page beyond which no key elements should be placed

logo   a visual identifier of a company or individual; typically consists of styled text and graphic element

mechanical   layout created by professional artist to indicate placement of elements and text for final print; consists of an individual sheet for each color separation being prepared by printer

medium   1. in painting, a type of vehicle (e.g., acrylic). 2. in painting, a thinner or extender made primarily of nonpigmented vehicle to extend paint or dilute it for glazing. 3. in popular culture, a system of communication (e.g., television)

oil   natural oil extracted from seeds (typically linseed) used as a vehicle for painting

pen and ink   use of any various types of pen (most typically a quill pen) with ink (most typically India Ink) for drawing

per diem   literally "for each day"; a daily fee paid a by client for work completed

pixel   "picture element"; smallest element of image projected by a screen (television, CRT monitor, LCD monitor)

RGB   red, green, blue; colors used to project images onto monitors, television screens, etc.

royalty   percentage of profits generated by sale of product (typically books, periodicals, and musical recordings) that are paid to contributing artists

subhead   line of type that runs below the headline in letters larger than body copy but smaller than headline text; typically used to categorize or outline within a larger topic

support   1. in painting, the physical object on which paint is applied. 2. in sculpture, a physical object on which sculptural material is applied; also called "armature"

thumbnail   very rough preliminary sketch done for composition

tracking   adjustment of spacing between groups of letters in an entire word, sentence, or block of text

typography   the appearance of typeset material, including its arrangement, sizing, and juxtaposition of differing styles

vector   also "vector art"; resolution-independent graphic file format composed of objects drawn in computer applications by generating mathematical calculations

vehicle   binder used to encapsulate pigment for application as paint; painting term

watercolor   pigment suspended in a transparent vehicle (typically gum Arabic) for application on paper; painting term

work-for-hire   copyright term; denotes that commissioner of work is owner of all copyrights attributable to the work and is considered the author of the work

BIBLIOGRAPHY

A. PERIODICALS

The following is a collection of periodicals that relate to several different disciplines within the visual art industry. You should be able to find them on newsstands, in libraries, or in schools.

GENERAL ART

ART News
48 West 38th Street
New York, NY 10018
http://www.artnewsonline.com

American Artist
770 Broadway
New York, NY 10003
http://www.myamericanartist.com

INDEPENDENT

Architectural Digest
6300 Wilshire Boulevard, Suite 1100
Los Angeles, CA 90048
http://www.archdigest.com

Architecture
770 Broadway, 4th Floor
New York, NY 10003
http://www.architecturemag.com

Graphis
307 Fifth Avenue, 10th Floor
New York, NY 10016
http://www.graphis.com

How
4700 East Galbraith Road
Cincinnati, OH 45236
http://www.howdesign.com

Popular Photography
1633 Broadway, 43rd Floor
New York, NY 10019
http://www.popularphotography.com

Print
38 East 29th Street, 3rd Floor
New York, NY 10016
http://www.printmag.com

3X3: The Magazine of Contemporary Illustration
244 Fifth Avenue, Suite F269

New York, NY 10001
http://www.3x3mag.com

POPULAR CULTURE

Entertainment Weekly
1675 Broadway, 28th Floor
New York, NY 10019
http://www.ew.com

Paper
365 Broadway, 6th Floor
New York, NY 10013
http://www.papermag.com

Premiere
1633 Broadway, 41st Floor
New York, NY 10019
http://www.premieremag.com

Rolling Stone
1290 Avenue of the Americas, 12th Floor
New York, NY 10104
http://www.rollingstone.com

B. BOOKS

Listed below are books recommended for further reading about visual arts both in general and specific to several of the job titles discussed in this book. Many creative professionals may suggest additional titles to add to this list.

Of particular note: While *On Writing: A Memoir of the Craft* has mostly to do with the nuts and bolts of the literary profession, it's included for two reasons. First, more than a few interviewees polled for this volume made mention of this title and how many of the steps taken by aspiring popular writers are similar to those taken by professional artists, especially when it comes to the work ethic described.

Second, many of the jobs listed herein require at least a familiarity with the written word, and several require a high degree of facility with it. This title offers a great many suggestions about how one can put oneself on that track.

ADVERTISING
Berger, Warren. *Advertising Today.* New York: Phaidon Press, 2004.

ART IN GENERAL
Bakewell, Elizabeth, and Brenda Jo Bright. *Looking High and Low: Art and Cultural Identity.* Tucson: University of Arizona Press, 1995.
Gopnick, Adam, and Kirk Varnedoe. *High and Low: Modern Art and Popular Culture.* New York: Museum of Modern Art, 1990.
King, Stephen. *On Writing: A Memoir of the Craft.* New York: Scribner, 2000.

ART INSTRUCTION BOOKS
Allrich, Steve. *Oil Painting for the Serious Beginner.* New York: Watson-Guptill Publications, 1996.

Bridgeman, George. *Bridgeman's Complete Guide to Drawing from Life.* 1952. Reprint, New York: Sterling Publishing Company, 2001.

Clair, Kate. *A Typographic Workbook.* New York: John Wiley, 1999.

De Reyna, Rudy. *How to Draw What You See.* New York: Watson-Guptill Publications, 1996.

Edwards, Betty. *The New Drawing on the Right Side of the Brain.* New York: Putnam, 1999.

Ryder, Anthony. *The Artist's Complete Guide to Figure Drawing: A Contemporary Perspective on the Classical Tradition.* New York: Watson-Guptill Publications, 1999.

CAREERS

Bureau of Labor Statistics, U.S. Department of Labor. *Career Guide to Industries, 2004–2005 Edition (Bulletin 2571).* Washington, D.C.: Superintendent of Documents, US GPO, 2004.

Bureau of Labor Statistics, U.S. Department of Labor. *Occupational Outlook Handbook, 2004–2005 Edition (Bulletin 2570).* Washington, D.C.: Superintendent of Documents, US GPO, 2004.

INDEPENDENT

American Society of Media Photographers. *ASMP Professional Business Practices in Photography.* New York: Watson-Guptill Publications, 2001.

Cox, Mary, and Lauren Mosko, eds. *2005 Artist's & Graphic Designer's Market.* Cincinnati, Ohio: Writers Digest Books, 2004.

Crawford, Tad. *Legal Guide for the Visual Artist.* New York: Allworth Press, 1999.

Foote, Cameron S. *The Business Side of Creativity: The Complete Guide for Running a Graphic Design or Communications Business.* New York: W. W. Norton, 2002.

Heller, Stephen, and Marshall Arisman. *Inside the Business of Illustration.* New York: Allworth Press, 2004.

Massey, Robert. *Formulas for Painters.* New York: Watson-Guptill Publications, 1967.

Michels, Caroll. *How to Survive and Prosper as an Artist,* 5th ed. New York: Owl Books 2001.

Poehner, Donna, and Erika Kruse, eds. *2005 Photographer's Market.* Cincinnati, Ohio: Writers Digest Books, 2004.

Slade, Catherine. *The Encyclopedia of Illustration Techniques.* Philadelphia: Running Press, 1997.

MUSEUMS/GALLERIES

Anderson, Gail. *Reinventing the Museum, Historical and Contemporary Perspectives on the Paradigm Shift.* Lanham, Md.: AltaMira Press, 2004.

PUBLISHING

Eisner, Will. *Comics & Sequential Art.* Tamarac, Fla.: Poorhouse Press, 1985.

Hart, Christopher. *Drawing Cutting Edge Anatomy: The Ultimate Reference for Comic Book Artists.* New York: Watson-Guptill Publications, 2004.

King, Stacey. *Magazine Design That Works: Secrets for Successful Magazine Design.* Gloucester, Mass.: 2001.

Lee, Stan, and John Buscema. *How to Draw Comics the Marvel Way.* New York: Fireside, 1984.

Leslie, Jeremy. *magCulture: New Magazine Design.* New York: HarperCollins, 2003.

McCloud, Scott. *Understanding Comics.* New York: Perennial Currents, 1994.

Salisbury, Martin. *Illustrating Children's Books: Creating Pictures for Publication.* Hauppauge, N.Y.: Barrons Educational Series, 2004.

Trotman, Felicity, and Treld Pelkey Bicknell, eds. *How to Write & Illustrate Childrens Books and Get Them Published.* Cincinnati, Ohio: Writers Digest Books, 2000.

THEATRICAL

Anderson, Barbara, and Cletus Anderson. *Costume Design,* 2nd ed. Florence, Ky.: Wadsworth Publishing, 1998.

Preston, Ward. *What an Art Director Does: An Introduction to Motion Picture Production Design.* Los Angeles: Silman-James Press, 1994.

INDEX